Signposts in Cyberspace

The Domain Name System and Internet Navigation

Committee on Internet Navigation and the Domain Name System: Technical Alternatives and Policy Implications

Computer Science and Telecommunications Board
Division on Engineering and Physical Sciences

NATIONAL RESEARCH COUNCIL
OF THE NATIONAL ACADEMIES

THE NATIONAL ACADEMIES PRESS
Washington, D.C.
www.nap.edu

THE NATIONAL ACADEMIES PRESS 500 Fifth Street, N.W. Washington, D.C. 20001

NOTICE: The project that is the subject of this report was approved by the Governing Board of the National Research Council, whose members are drawn from the councils of the National Academy of Sciences, the National Academy of Engineering, and the Institute of Medicine. The members of the committee responsible for the report were chosen for their special competences and with regard for appropriate balance.

Support for this project was provided by the U.S. Department of Commerce and the National Science Foundation under Grant No. ANI-9909852 and by the National Research Council. Any opinions, findings, conclusions, or recommendations expressed in this publication are those of the authors and do not necessarily reflect the views of the National Science Foundation or the Commerce Department.

International Standard Book Number 0-309-09640-5 (Book)
International Standard Book Number 0-309-54979-5 (PDF)

Cover designed by Jennifer M. Bishop.

Copies of this report are available from the National Academies Press, 500 Fifth Street, N.W., Lockbox 285, Washington, D.C. 20055, (800) 624-6242 or (202) 334-3313 in the Washington metropolitan area. Internet, http://www.nap.edu

Printed in the United States of America

THE NATIONAL ACADEMIES

Advisers to the Nation on Science, Engineering, and Medicine

The **National Academy of Sciences** is a private, nonprofit, self-perpetuating society of distinguished scholars engaged in scientific and engineering research, dedicated to the furtherance of science and technology and to their use for the general welfare. Upon the authority of the charter granted to it by the Congress in 1863, the Academy has a mandate that requires it to advise the federal government on scientific and technical matters. Dr. Ralph J. Cicerone is president of the National Academy of Sciences.

The **National Academy of Engineering** was established in 1964, under the charter of the National Academy of Sciences, as a parallel organization of outstanding engineers. It is autonomous in its administration and in the selection of its members, sharing with the National Academy of Sciences the responsibility for advising the federal government. The National Academy of Engineering also sponsors engineering programs aimed at meeting national needs, encourages education and research, and recognizes the superior achievements of engineers. Dr. Wm. A. Wulf is president of the National Academy of Engineering.

The **Institute of Medicine** was established in 1970 by the National Academy of Sciences to secure the services of eminent members of appropriate professions in the examination of policy matters pertaining to the health of the public. The Institute acts under the responsibility given to the National Academy of Sciences by its congressional charter to be an adviser to the federal government and, upon its own initiative, to identify issues of medical care, research, and education. Dr. Harvey V. Fineberg is president of the Institute of Medicine.

The **National Research Council** was organized by the National Academy of Sciences in 1916 to associate the broad community of science and technology with the Academy's purposes of furthering knowledge and advising the federal government. Functioning in accordance with general policies determined by the Academy, the Council has become the principal operating agency of both the National Academy of Sciences and the National Academy of Engineering in providing services to the government, the public, and the scientific and engineering communities. The Council is administered jointly by both Academies and the Institute of Medicine. Dr. Ralph J. Cicerone and Dr. Wm. A. Wulf are chair and vice chair, respectively, of the National Research Council.

www.national-academies.org

COMMITTEE ON INTERNET NAVIGATION AND THE DOMAIN NAME SYSTEM: TECHNICAL ALTERNATIVES AND POLICY IMPLICATIONS

ROGER LEVIEN, Strategy & Innovation Consulting, *Chair*
S. ROBERT AUSTEIN, Internet Systems Consortium
STANLEY M. BESEN, Charles River Associates
CHRISTINE L. BORGMAN, University of California, Los Angeles
TIMOTHY CASEY, University of Nevada, Reno
HUGH DUBBERLY, Dubberly Design Office
PATRIK FÄLTSTRÖM, Cisco Systems
PER-KRISTIAN HALVORSEN, Hewlett-Packard Labs
MARYLEE JENKINS, Arent Fox, PLLC
JOHN C. KLENSIN, Independent Consultant
MILTON L. MUELLER, Syracuse University
SHARON L. NELSON, Washington State Attorney General's Office
CRAIG PARTRIDGE, BBN Technologies
WILLIAM J. RADUCHEL, Ruckus Network
HAL R. VARIAN, University of California, Berkeley

Staff

ALAN S. INOUYE, Study Director (through December 2004)
CHARLES N. BROWNSTEIN, Director (from January 2004)
MARGARET MARSH HUYNH, Senior Program Assistant
KRISTEN BATCH, Research Associate

Preface

The Domain Name System (DNS), which was developed in the early 1980s, provides a way of associating alphanumeric names, which are easier for humans to use, with the numerical addresses that designate every location on the Internet. The system of DNS servers distributed across the Internet invisibly converts the names—serving as signposts in cyberspace—into the numerical addresses required by network routers to reach the signposted locations.

The mnemonic quality of domain names became a practical necessity when the rapid increase in the use of e-mail and the World Wide Web caused the number of Internet users and uses to increase tremendously. Web sites often became known to their visitors by their distinctive domain names—for example, pepsi.com or whitehouse.gov. Carefully chosen domain names often enabled a searcher to navigate to a site simply by guessing (e.g., www.un.org). Consequently, those signposts gained economic, social, cultural, and political value and they became the objects of pride, competition, and dispute. It was fitting, therefore, that the DNS also provided the name—the Dot-Com Era—for the period of the 1990s when "gold rush fever" drove frenzied efforts to stake out and exploit virtually every potentially valuable site on the Web. Inevitably, such efforts led to intense conflicts, especially disputes involving trademarks, which provided the impetus for the 1998 congressional mandate to initiate this study (see Box P.1). However, the passage of time, the rapid evolution of the Internet and the DNS, the additional and differing interests of the funding agencies, and the logic of the committee's charter have resulted in a report whose scope differs in some respects from the original

BOX P.1 Excerpt from Public Law 105-305

SEC. 6. STUDY OF EFFECTS ON TRADEMARK RIGHTS OF ADDING GENERIC TOP-LEVEL DOMAINS

(b) Matters To Be Assessed in Study.—The study shall assess and, as appropriate, make recommendations for policy, practice, or legislative changes relating to—
(1) the short-term and long-term effects on the protection of trademark rights and consumer interests of increasing or decreasing the number of generic top-level domains;
(2) trademark rights clearance processes for domain names, including—
(A) whether domain name databases should be readily searchable through a common interface to facilitate the clearing of trademark rights and proposed domain names across a range of generic top-level domains;
(B) the identification of what information from domain name databases should be accessible for the clearing of trademark rights; and
(C) whether generic top-level domain registrants should be required to provide certain information;
(3) domain name trademark rights dispute resolution mechanisms, including how to—
(A) reduce trademark rights conflicts associated with the addition of any new generic top-level domains; and
(B) reduce trademark rights conflicts through new technical approaches to Internet addressing;
(4) choice of law or jurisdiction for resolution of trademark rights disputes relating to domain names, including which jurisdictions should be available for trademark rights owners to file suit to protect such trademark rights;
(5) trademark rights infringement liability for registrars, registries, or technical management bodies;
(6) short-term and long-term technical and policy options for Internet addressing schemes and the impact of such options on current trademark rights issues; and
(7) public comments on the interim report and on any reports that are issued by intergovernmental bodies.

congressional request, but is as a result more responsive to the current interests of the report's sponsors and audience.

CURRENT CONTEXT AND STUDY TASK

Although the initial feverish period of Internet exploitation appears to have passed, in its third decade the DNS faces new challenges arising from continued growth in the size and scope of the Internet and from its increasing integration into almost every aspect of human activity almost everywhere on the globe. The Internet needs more signposts, in more languages, to satisfy more uses and users. And the DNS has to be carefully developed and managed to ensure that it can meet those needs while continuing to provide reliable, efficient, and secure service.

Furthermore, even if the DNS successfully adapts and grows, users of the Internet will confront new challenges in reaching the resources that they are seeking on the Internet, whether they are educational, social, political, cultural, commercial, or recreational. The challenges will arise not from the absence of resources or of signposts for them, but from their presence in such volume and variety that navigating through the maze to find the right ones may become too arduous or too complex for most users. Reciprocally, those who put resources on the Internet will want them to be easily found by their prospective users in the cluttered bazaar of competing or confusing resources and signposts on the Internet. Thus, the larger issue of the third decade of the DNS is that of navigation through the Internet—the need for its users to find their way quickly and confidently to the resources they desire and for its resources to be easily and reliably found by the users they seek.

This study builds on CSTB's prior work related to the Internet, most notably on *The Internet's Coming of Age* and *The Digital Dilemma*.[1] One of the important lessons from this prior work is that contentious issues in information technology policy (e.g., the domain name trademark issues as described in Public Law 105-305) are often much more complex and require analysis in a much larger context than a popular characterization of "us versus them" would suggest. In the interval between the enactment of Public Law 105-305 and the initiation of this study, CSTB was able to conduct preliminary background work to develop a statement of task (see Box P.2) that addresses the congressional mandate but also ensures that the necessary larger context is included explicitly. Moreover, the larger context was necessary to respond appropriately to the interests of the National Science Foundation, which joined with the U.S. Department of Commerce as co-sponsors of this study.

COMMITTEE COMPOSITION AND PROCESS

The CSTB convened a cross-disciplinary study committee comprising computer scientists and engineers, information science/retrieval and

[1]See Computer Science and Telecommunications Board (CSTB), National Research Council (NRC), *The Internet's Coming of Age*, National Academy Press, Washington, D.C., 2001; and CSTB, NRC, *The Digital Dilemma: Intellectual Property in the Information Age*, National Academy Press, Washington, D.C., 2000.

search Council (NRC) staff made several site visits, which included participation in meetings of the Internet Corporation for Assigned Names and Numbers (ICANN), the Internet Engineering Task Force, and the World Summit on the Information Society. Significant input was also derived from committee members during the course of their professional activities outside of the committee's work. During the editorial phase of the study, facts were checked for accuracy with either published sources or subject experts.

At the outset of the study, some conflict and controversy were expected, given the intense debate about the DNS and its associated institutions such as the ICANN and the rapidly growing interest in the use of commercially sponsored navigation services. We were not disappointed. However, the committee was able to achieve consensus in a number of areas as described in the main text. Moreover, the committee believes that this report represents a contribution to future discussions related to the DNS by serving as a reference document containing much of the basic, relevant technical and institutional background material and many of the policy alternatives in as clear and objective a manner as possible.

A number of committee members withdrew from the committee for various reasons. In a few instances, new employment or professional opportunities raised conflict-of-interest concerns. Several committee members were simply unable to participate in the committee's work because of increased professional or personal obligations.

Although the report refers to several companies, products, and services by name, such reference does not constitute an endorsement by the committee or the National Academies.

ACKNOWLEDGMENTS

The committee appreciates the support and guidance of its sponsors. The committee's initial contacts at the U.S. Department of Commerce were J. Beckwith Burr, Amy Page, and Karen Rose, and in the later portion of the study, Cathy Handley and Robin Layton. Aubrey Bush and George Strawn were the committee's initial contacts at the National Science Foundation, with Darleen Fisher assuming this role during the final months of the project. The committee also appreciates the financial support of CSTB's core sponsors: the Air Force Office of Scientific Research, Cisco Systems, the Defense Advanced Research Projects Agency, Department of Energy, Intel Corporation, Microsoft Research, National Aeronautics and Space Administration, National Institute of Standards and Technology, National Library of Medicine, National Science Foundation, Office of Naval Research, and the Vadesz Family Fund. Additional financial support was provided by the National Research Council.

In addition, we would like to thank those individuals who provided valuable inputs into the committee's deliberations. Those who briefed the committee at one of our plenary meetings are listed in Appendix B. Others who provided us with important inputs include Ronald Andruff (RNA Partners, Inc.), Carl Bildt (AG Global Solutions and ICANN At-Large Study Committee), Mason Cole (SnapNames), Shari Garmise (Cleveland State University), Carolyn T. Hoover (dotCoop), Cary Karp (MuseDoma), Kalpana Shankar (University of California, Los Angeles), Paul Twomey (Internet Corporation for Assigned Names and Numbers), Anastasia Zhadina (Robin, Blecker & Daley), and Matthew Zook (University of Kentucky). We would also like to acknowledge those organizations that hosted committee meetings: AOL Time Warner, Inc.; University of California, Berkeley; University of California, Los Angeles; Harvard University; and VeriSign, Inc. Thanks go, too, to Jonathan O. Chan, consultant, for his help with a translation.

The committee appreciates the thoughtful comments received from the reviewers of this report and the efforts of the NRC's report review coordinator and monitor. The review draft stimulated a large volume of comments, each of which was taken into account during revision of the draft. Many of the comments provided additional reference material and observations to bolster or counter the committee's earlier thinking, thus helping the committee to sharpen and improve the report. However, the reviewers are not responsible for the report's conclusions or recommendations, with which some of them may disagree, or for its structure and specific content. Those are solely the committee's responsibility.

Finally, the committee would like to acknowledge the staff of the NRC for their work. Special appreciation is accorded to Alan S. Inouye, who as the study director had overall staff responsibility for the conduct of the study and for the development and completion of this report. Margaret Marsh Huynh handled the administrative aspects of the project, such as organizing meeting logistics. Marjory S. Blumenthal, as director of CSTB through June 2003, and her successor, Charles N. Brownstein, provided the committee with valuable administrative and technical guidance. Cynthia Patterson and Kristen Batch supplied research and writing support at various stages of the report drafting and revising process. The committee would also like to thank Jennifer M. Bishop, Janet Briscoe, and Renee Hawkins of the CSTB staff; Susan Maurizi of the NRC's editorial staff; Liz Panos of the staff of the Division on Engineering and Physical Sciences; and Janice Mehler of the Report Review Committee for their support of the committee's work.

Roger Levien, *Chair*
Committee on Internet Navigation and the Domain Name System

Acknowledgment of Reviewers

This report has been reviewed in draft form by individuals chosen for their diverse perspectives and technical expertise, in accordance with procedures approved by the National Research Council's Report Review Committee. The purpose of this independent review is to provide candid and critical comments that will assist the institution in making its published report as sound as possible and to ensure that the report meets institutional standards for objectivity, evidence, and responsiveness to the study charge. The review comments and draft manuscript remain confidential to protect the integrity of the deliberative process. We wish to thank the following individuals for their review of this report:

Aristotle Balogh, VeriSign, Inc.
Timothy Bray, Textuality
J. Beckwith Burr, Wilmer, Cutler and Pickering
kc claffy, Cooperative Association for Internet Data Analysis
David D. Clark, Massachusetts Institute of Technology
Steve Crocker, Shinkuro, Inc.
Bruce Croft, University of Massachusetts, Amherst
Leslie Daigle, VeriSign, Inc.
Graeme Dinwoodie, Chicago-Kent College of Law
Joseph Farrell, University of California, Berkeley
Michael Froomkin, University of Miami
Hector Garcia-Molina, Stanford University
Marti Hearst, University of California, Berkeley

Randy H. Katz, University of California, Berkeley
Butler W. Lampson, Microsoft Corporation
F. Thomson Leighton, Akamai Technologies and the Massachusetts Institute of Technology
Michael Lesk, Rutgers University
Lars-Johan Liman, Autonomica
Clifford Lynch, Coalition for Networked Information
M. Stuart Lynn, Independent Consultant*
Tom M. Mitchell, Carnegie Mellon University
Ivan Png, National University of Singapore
Fred B. Schneider, Cornell University
Paul Vixie, PAIX.net, Inc.
Tan Tin Wee, National University of Singapore

Although the reviewers listed above have provided many constructive comments and suggestions, they were not asked to endorse the conclusions or recommendations, nor did they see the final draft of the report before its release. The review of this report was overseen by Alexander H. Flax, independent consultant, and Joseph Bannister, University of Southern California. Appointed by the National Research Council, they were responsible for making certain that an independent examination of this report was carried out in accordance with institutional procedures and that all review comments were carefully considered. Responsibility for the final content of this report rests entirely with the authoring committee and the institution.

*Formerly, Internet Corporation for Assigned Names and Numbers.

Executive Summary

Most people who use the Internet rely on the Domain Name System (DNS) and navigation aids and services to find the resources they seek or to attract users to the resources they provide. Yet, although they perform well, both the DNS and Internet navigation services face challenges arising from technological change and from institutions with a wide variety of commercial, cultural, social, and political agendas. Individually, or together, those pressures could force operational changes that would significantly reduce access to Internet-linked resources by segments of the user community, reducing the Internet's value as a global resource.

This document reports the conclusions of an assessment of the current state and the future prospects of the DNS and its interactions with Internet navigation, including its uses as a means of navigation itself and as an infrastructure for navigation by other means. The assessment is the result of the deliberations of a committee that encompasses a wide range of disciplines, experience, and viewpoints. The report is addressed to the technologists, policy makers, and others whose decisions will affect the future of the DNS and Internet navigation aids and services. The specific conclusions and recommendations of the Committee on Internet Navigation and the Domain Name System appear throughout this summary in boldface type.

DOMAIN NAME SYSTEM

Domain names are commonly used to designate services and devices on the Internet, as a more memorable and more permanent alternative to the numerical addresses employed by its routing computers. They are the valued, often valuable, and often user-friendly names on the signposts that designate many things connected to the Internet. Consequently, which names are available, who controls their allocation, what is charged for their use, how their uses are managed, and the answers to many related questions are important to virtually everyone who uses the Internet, whether as information seeker or provider.

Overall, the DNS's technical system and institutional framework have performed reliably and effectively during the two decades of the DNS's existence. The DNS has coped with the extremely rapid expansion of Internet usage driven by the wide deployment of the World Wide Web in the 1990s and the widespread adoption of e-mail. The hierarchical, distributed structure of the DNS technical system, operated collaboratively by a group of mostly autonomous organizations, has proven to be scalable, reliable, secure, and efficient.

The DNS technical system can continue to meet the needs of an expanding Internet. Early in the committee's assessment it became apparent that it would not be fruitful to consider alternate naming systems. As noted, the DNS operates quite well for its intended purpose and has demonstrated its ability to scale with the growth of the Internet and to operate robustly in an open environment. Moreover, significantly increased functionality can be achieved though applications—such as navigation systems—built on the DNS, or offered independently, rather than through changing the DNS directly. Hence, the need did not seem to be to replace the DNS, but rather to maintain and incrementally improve it. Furthermore, given the rapidly increasing installed base and the corresponding heavy investments in the technical system and the institutional framework, the financial cost and operational disruption of replacing the DNS would be extremely high, if even possible at all.

However, the continued successful operation of the DNS is not assured; many forces, driven by a variety of factors, are challenging the DNS's future. Required and desirable technologies to increase security and enable the use of non-Roman scripts for domain names are not being incorporated into the technical system as quickly as many would like. There are persistent and substantial controversies concerning the structure and policies of the DNS's institutional framework. Moreover, there have been many efforts to use the DNS, because it exists and is so widely deployed, for many purposes for which it may not be appropriate. In addition, national legislation and court decisions are addressing Internet and domain name issues with potentially conflicting consequences for the operation of the DNS.

Security Challenges

Like all public networked systems, the system of public domain name servers is threatened by a variety of purposeful attacks, both malicious and mischievous, by individuals or groups that aim to disable or divert their operations. The operators of the DNS are responding to these threats, but not all the desirable steps to ensure security have yet been implemented.

Denial-of-Service Attacks

Denial-of-service attacks attempt to overwhelm key name servers and their links to the Internet with so much traffic that they are incapable of responding to legitimate queries. The root name servers have the capacity and capability to respond to many times the normal number of queries they receive, and have alternate connections to the network if some are blocked. Their ability to respond to attacks has been improved by some operators' recent addition of multiple distributed copies (called "anycast" servers) of the base name servers, increasing both capacity and connectivity. **In anticipation of future denial-of-service attacks and normal growth in demand, and to improve service globally, anycast server deployment should be expanded.**

Physical Vulnerability

Notwithstanding the deployment of anycast servers and installation of backup servers at remote locations, the concentration of root name server facilities and personnel in the Washington, D.C., area and, to a lesser extent, in the Los Angeles area is a potential vulnerability. **The need for further diversification of the location of root name servers and personnel should be carefully analyzed in the light of possible dangers, both natural and human in origin.**

Message Alteration

In response to the threat of alteration of messages being transmitted among name servers, the technical community has developed DNS Security Extensions (DNSSEC), which uses digital signatures to verify that the content of a message to or from a name server arrives unaltered and that its origin is as stated. DNSSEC only gives assurance that what was sent was not changed during transmission; it cannot and is not intended to assert that the message is factually correct. For example, DNSSEC has no capability to guarantee that it is communicating the correct address for a given domain name. **The security of the DNS would be significantly improved if DNSSEC were widely deployed among name servers for the root zone and top-level domains in particular, and throughout the DNS in general.**

Performance Monitoring

Although some steps have been taken, more could be done to continuously monitor the performance and traffic flows of the DNS so as to enable rapid detection of and response to attacks or outages.

Governance Challenges

The DNS works through the voluntary cooperation of its autonomous component entities. That cooperation, in turn, depends on their tacit agreement on two principles that together enable the Internet and the DNS to evolve and remain effective:

- *Universal open standards.* The first principle is that the protocols and standards defining operation of the Internet and the DNS will be open and established by the Internet Engineering Task Force (IETF), an international voluntary organization of technical specialists. This technical framework enables every device on the Internet to connect to and communicate with every other, and it has been critical to the success of the Internet and the DNS. Because changes in Internet and DNS protocols, standards, and practices are matters of consequence beyond specific Internet services, alterations to the functions of or modifications to established standards and practices have traditionally been vetted by the IETF before being implemented.
- *Innovation at the edges.* The second principle is that applications should be offered by devices on the edges of the Internet, rather than at the Internet's internal nodes or on its links. In general, applications located at the edges have little effect on the stability of the Internet, so there is no need to regulate them. The DNS is not, strictly speaking, internal to the Internet (the translation service is performed by computers at the edges), but functions as though it were. It can thus be thought of as a core service, which although not absolutely necessary, is extremely useful in giving a relatively user-friendly face to Internet resources, and for enabling access to those resources even when their Internet addresses change. Moreover, it is a deeply embedded and ubiquitous service that enables other services and functions, including most aids to Internet navigation.

This tacit agreement governs the basic behavior of the many autonomous operators of the DNS, but there is also a need for an authority to make decisions about the allocation of limited resources central to DNS operations. The most critical of these decisions are the determination of which top-level domains (TLDs) shall appear in the root zone file of the DNS, which organizations shall be designated as responsible for their operation, and the terms under which those organizations shall operate.

The principal organizations that constitute this authority are, currently, the U.S. Department of Commerce (DOC) and the Internet Corporation for Assigned Names and Numbers (ICANN), although national bodies have considerable influence over the operations of the associated country-code top-level domains (ccTLDs). Both the DOC and ICANN face significant challenges to their authority and legitimacy in management of the DNS.

Stewardship of the DNS

As the Internet has become an increasingly important component of the international infrastructure, there has been growing pressure to introduce some form of international political control over the DNS. This pressure comes both from existing international organizations seeking authority over the Internet or the DNS, and from individual countries that would like to end the stewardship role of the United States.

Governance of the DNS is part, but not all, of governing the Internet. Efforts to leverage it to influence broader Internet policy are, therefore, likely to be ineffective and could also be detrimental to the DNS. Many of the governance issues that concern governments—control of spam and uses of the Internet for illegal purposes; resolving the disparities between developed and developing countries in Internet usage; protection of privacy, freedom of expression, and intellectual property other than domain names; and the facilitation and regulation of e-commerce—have little or nothing to do with the DNS per se. The DNS would not be an effective vehicle for addressing such issues. Attempts to change the DNS or extend its management and administrative processes to do so could interfere with reaching agreements on the already contentious issues concerning the DNS itself.

Governance of the DNS is not an appropriate venue for the playing out of national political interests. One valued and essential quality of the DNS institutional framework has been its relative freedom from direct pressures arising from conflicts among competing national interests and policy agendas (apart from sovereignty-associated issues such as ccTLD delegations and redelegations). International disputes arising in other contexts have largely been kept away from the DNS—as they should be.

For that reason: **The committee does not support efforts to put the**

DNS directly under the control of governments or intergovernmental agencies. In practical terms, the U.S. government, which must agree, has not supported turning DNS stewardship over to other governments or an international organization, although that could change. Although the 2005 U.N.-sponsored World Summit on the Information Society (WSIS) may produce proposals for a non-governmental agent—an internationally negotiated convention or multi-stakeholder organization—with oversight or other influence over the DNS, no proposal that can be evaluated for either practicality or feasibility has yet (in June 2005) been made.

One way to respond to concerns about the U.S. government's role as steward of the DNS is for it to transfer its stewardship role to a non-governmental body—specifically, ICANN. In the September 2003 revision of its agreement with ICANN, the DOC stated its intent to transfer its stewardship to ICANN if within 3 years ICANN is able to fulfill a mutually agreed set of tasks.

If ICANN does not fulfill the agreed tasks, and a proposal for creation of a non-governmental organization having Internet governance responsibilities results from the WSIS process before the transfer date, the DOC could consider transferring the stewardship role to the proposed organization. That would entail comparing a not-yet-existing organization to one with 8 years of experience and evolution.

Life without the stewardship of the U.S. government will open ICANN to political and commercial pressures. A free-standing ICANN would lack the oversight and, importantly, the protection provided by the U.S. government's stewardship. If ICANN becomes steward of the DNS, legitimacy based on the "consent of the governed" would be the principal basis for its continued authority and its ability to resist inappropriate pressure from governments and other powerful interests. Final responsibility for satisfying the needs of its constituencies in an equitable, open, and efficient manner would lie with its board.

Before completing the transfer of its stewardship to ICANN (or any other organization), the Department of Commerce should seek ways to protect that organization from undue commercial or governmental pressures and to provide some form of oversight of performance.

Legitimacy of ICANN

ICANN is a work in progress; its long-term success is not assured. After a troubled start, it has introduced several innovations to the institutional framework of the DNS, including competition among registrars and an arbitral process for resolving disputes over domain names, the Uniform Domain Name Dispute Resolution Policy. In 2003 it had to undertake a major reform of its own organization, stimulated by dissatisfaction with its operation under its initial structure. It is working on the revision of key decision processes in response to complaints about their lack of transparency and fairness. Furthermore, ICANN has been unable to conclude formal agreements with many of the organizations critical to its responsibilities, notably the root name server operators and the vast majority of the ccTLD registries. Nevertheless, through its responsibility for recommending changes in the root zone file, which defines which TLDs are in the DNS and where their operators are located on the Internet, ICANN has been able to exercise authority over the coherence and stability of the DNS.

Since its beginning, ICANN has been the subject of controversy and contention flowing from the many diverse constituencies that have been attracted to it and their correspondingly diverse views. The critics' concerns have been with ICANN's scope, its organizational structure, and its management processes. The concern about scope has been principally the extent to which ICANN has exceeded its technical-administrative responsibilities, for example, to regulate TLD registry operations; but others have been disappointed by its unwillingness to take on broader issues. The structural concerns have included perceptions of imbalance in the historical composition of ICANN's board, of failings in the board selection processes, and of inadequate representation of certain constituency groups. The process concerns have been the perceived lack of transparency, effectiveness, accountability, and recourse in ICANN's electoral and decision processes.

ICANN is more likely to achieve perceived legitimacy by narrowing its scope and by improving its processes rather than by seeking an ideally representative composition of its board. No composition of its board is likely by itself to confer the perception of legitimacy on ICANN among all its possible constituency groups. A narrowing of scope and improvement of processes are elements of the path that ICANN claims to be following in carrying out its 2003 reform. However successful its reform, ICANN faces the challenge of reaching an effective modus operandi with three critical sets of participants in the DNS's institutional framework: the root name server operators, the generic TLD registries, and the ccTLD registries.

Root Name Server Operators

No greater oversight of the root name server operators will be necessary so long as they continue to operate effectively and reliably and to improve the DNS's security, stability, and capability. The effective daily operation of the root, and therefore the DNS, lies in the hands of the operators of the 13 critical root name servers. They have provided reliable and efficient service as the Internet has undergone rapid growth in the numbers of its users and providers. Although the DOC has assigned ICANN responsibility for the stability and security of the root name server system, ICANN's authority has not been sufficient for it to manage or regulate the root name server operators directly, nor is it clear that doing so is desirable or necessary. The real challenge to ICANN is to identify how it can best ensure the stability and security of the root name server system, given the long-standing autonomy of the operators and the effectiveness of their operations.

More formal coordination of the root name server operators is desirable in the longer term. ICANN is currently the most appropriate organization to assume the coordination role. Although direct management or oversight may be neither necessary nor feasible, with continued growth in the Internet and demands on the DNS, a more formal process of coordination of the root name server operators with ICANN's facilitation will become desirable so as to ensure rapid response to persistent security needs and to other challenges.

The present independent funding arrangements for the root name servers are advantageous and should continue, because the multiplicity of sources contributes to the resilience, autonomy, and diversity of the root name server system. The root name server operators do not receive direct compensation for the services they perform. While running a root server may only add an incremental cost in the range of tens of thousands of dollars for an organization already operating a secure Internet site, fully loaded costs have been estimated at up to $1 million or more depending on numerous factors including the number of locations, bandwidth requirements, and staffing levels. The costs are covered by each organization as part of other operations. Although a central source of funds to compensate all the root name server operators for their services might appear desirable, it is likely to be accompanied by an unacceptable regulatory or control role for the funding organization and would reduce the robustness of the current arrangement.

ICANN should work with the root name server operators to establish a formal process for replacing operators that directly engages the remaining root name server operators. Under the process, ICANN would be responsible for the final decision on the basis of recommendations from the root name server operators. One or more of the current root name server operators may withdraw for organizational or performance reasons, and it would be reasonable to have in place an agreed process to deal with such eventualities.

Generic Top-Level Domain Registries

A major challenge to ICANN since its founding has been deciding whether, when, and how to add generic top-level domains (gTLDs) and, if any are added, how many. It has faced strong pressures both to add gTLDs and to stop, or at least moderate, the pace of such additions. The committee addressed the issue of gTLD addition broadly in terms of both effects and constituencies affected, but for simplicity the multidimensional arguments for and against new gTLDs were clustered into two groups: technical and operational performance, and user needs and economic benefits.

Considering technical and operational performance alone, the addition of tens of gTLDs per year for several years poses minimal risk to the stability of the root. However, an abrupt increase (significantly beyond this rate) in the number of gTLDs could have technical, operational, economic, and service consequences that could affect domain name registrants, registries, registrars, and Internet users.

From the standpoint of user needs and economic benefits, neither the arguments in favor of nor those against additional gTLDs are conclusive. Thus, the decision to add gTLDs is one requiring judgment and cannot be determined by formal analysis alone.

If new gTLDs are added, they should be added on a regular schedule that establishes the maximum number of gTLDs (on the order of tens per year) that could be added each time and the interval between additions. Addition of gTLDs should be carried out cautiously and predictably, so that on the one hand, the stability and reliability of the system can be protected, and on the other hand, those considering acquiring a gTLD can do so with a realistic view of future prospects.

A mechanism to suspend the addition of gTLDs in the event that severe technical or operational problems arise should accompany a schedule of additions. It should explicitly specify who has the authority to suspend additions and under what conditions.

A neutral, disinterested party should conduct an evaluation of new gTLDs approximately 1 or 2 years after each set of new gTLDs is operational to make recommendations for improving the process for selecting and adding gTLDs.

If new gTLDs are to be created, the currently employed comparative hearing or expert evaluation processes should not be assumed to be the *only* processes for selecting their operators. In its addition of gTLDs in 2000, ICANN used a comparative hearing process to select 7 from the 44 applicants. In its 2004 addition of sponsored gTLDs, ICANN used a non-competitive process that replaces subjective judgments by its staff and board with judgments by expert groups that are insulated from lobbying, but whose decision-making processes are not transparent. By doing so, it has reduced a few of the potential sources of dissatisfaction with the resultant selections compared with the process used in 2000. However, the question remains as to whether it is necessary for ICANN to qualify new gTLDs, as this process does, on such matters as sponsorship by a community, business and financial plans, and addition of new value to the name space.

For creation of new gTLDs, ICANN should consider alternate processes that are less reliant on expert, staff, or board judgments. One such approach would be pre-qualification of applicants only on technical capability, basic financial viability, and adherence to registrant protection standards and ICANN policies. (ICANN should establish requirements to minimize the dangers of domain name registrants losing their service—and the value invested in their domains—if a registry fails and should carefully consider possible side effects.) If the number of qualified applicants turns out to be less than the number of available slots, all would be chosen; if not, a market-based selection process—an auction—could be used to select among them. Because of the wide range of intents and corresponding designs of such processes, they must be carefully planned, drawing on the breadth of previous experience in the design of auctions.

Country-Code Top-Level Domain Registries

Resolution of ICANN's role vis-á-vis the ccTLDs is one of the critical challenges to establishing an ICANN that is viewed as a legitimate and appropriate steward for the DNS. Although the ccTLDs represent 243 of the 258 TLDs, ICANN had formal agreements with only a dozen of the ccTLD operators as of June 2005.

The ccTLDs as a group now operate only partially under the oversight of any higher authority, ICANN or government. A number of ccTLDs are overseen by their national governments; some have established non-governmental bodies to represent the local Internet community and exercise varying degrees of oversight; some are completely autonomous non-profit bodies that operate voluntarily to meet local Internet community interests; and some are commercial bodies with some contractual linkage to the national government.

The only body that currently has an opportunity to exercise oversight over all the ccTLDs is ICANN. The principal way in which it exercises that authority is through recommendations to the DOC about which organization should be delegated responsibility for a specific ccTLD. Yet this issue arises only when the present delegatee resigns or is challenged or a new ccTLD is established.

The relationship between ccTLDs and ICANN has been difficult from the beginning of ICANN. First, a large number of the ccTLDs felt no need to contribute to ICANN's budget, since they did not think that they received any corresponding benefits. Second, many ccTLDs resented ICANN's major role in deciding on delegations and redelegations—essentially a policy role that they felt would be better performed locally. They also believed that their position as one constituency within ICANN's initial Domain Names Supporting Organization, whose other constituencies primarily addressed gTLD issues, did not adequately reflect their importance.

Under its 2003 reorganization, ICANN attempted to respond to their concerns by replacing the Domain Names Supporting Organization with two organizations, the Generic Names Supporting Organization (GNSO) and the Country-Code Names Supporting Organization (ccNSO). ICANN intends thereby to draw the ccTLDs more actively into its operations and build a stronger basis for their support. Furthermore, in April 2005 ICANN's Governmental Advisory Committee issued a revision of its "Principles for the Delegation and Administration of Country Code Top Level Domains" to address many of the concerns expressed about them.

If the creation of the ccNSO does not result in increased participation by the ccTLDs in ICANN policy making, then ICANN may find itself subject to increasing pressures to constrain its role to that of gTLD management and root zone file record keeping and to turn ccTLD oversight over to some other organization. The success of the ccNSO will depend on its ability to attract an increasing number of members, both from the large ccTLDs that are needed for financial and other support of ICANN and the smaller ccTLDs that can benefit from the support that ICANN could offer them. Even more critical is the refinement of the principles and processes for delegation and redelegation of ccTLD registries and their acceptance by most of the ccTLDs.

Commercial Challenges

Perhaps the most subtle, but still significant, challenge that the DNS faces is that arising from the imperative faced by commercial operators of parts of the DNS—they must strive to increase their revenues and profits in the face of competition. On the Internet, increasing revenues generally means increasing traffic to one's service, sometimes by diverting it from another operator's service. This imperative raises the temptation to seek traffic and revenue by breaking or bending the fabric of tacit agreements that underlies the success of the Internet and the DNS.

ICANN should strengthen its contracts with TLD operators (especially the largest ones) to ensure that it has the authority to review proposed changes in their services that could have a detrimental effect on the DNS or on other services that depend on the DNS. It should establish an open, transparent, and speedy process of review for such changes that solicits contributions from the technical community, other DNS operators, other affected Internet operations, and end users. A recent case in point is the unanticipated and unannounced introduction by VeriSign, a commercial registry, of a service, called Site Finder, that altered the conventional response to erroneous queries to the .com and .net TLDs by returning pointers to its own search page, rather than sending back an error message. After being called on by ICANN to suspend the service, VeriSign did so under protest and is currently seeking relief in the courts.

TLDs and other DNS operators that do not have agreements with ICANN should voluntarily agree to adhere to published technical standards and to consult the technical community and conduct public review processes before introducing new services that could have a detrimental effect on the DNS or on other services that depend on the DNS.

Dispute Resolution Challenges

Arbitral domain name dispute resolution processes, rather than national courts, should continue to be encouraged as the initial and primary vehicle for resolving most disputes associated with the rights to domain names. The Uniform Domain Name Dispute Resolution Policy was implemented by ICANN in December 1999 and has been adopted by all registrars in nine of the generic top-level domains, as well as voluntarily by managers of several ccTLDs. In addition, managers of other ccTLDs have adopted their own policies based on modified versions of the UDRP.

The UDRP has generally satisfied the need for an effective and cost-efficient means of resolving disputes concerning domain names; however, it has weaknesses that should be addressed. The UDRP has both positive and negative aspects, which differ, however, depending on whether they are being considered from the perspective of the complainants or of the respondents. Although many observers believe that the UDRP has enabled speedy and fair resolution of domain disputes, others believe that the current system is biased toward the interests of trademark holders. Notwithstanding its perceived disadvantages, by early 2005 more than 9000 decisions concerning over 15,000 domain names had been rendered under the UDRP.

The feasibility and desirability of five specific UDRP improvements should be further considered by ICANN:

- **Improving consistent use of arbitral precedents** to enable similar issues to be addressed in a more consistent manner that also supports case-by-case knowledge building;
- **Establishing an internal appeals process** that would review the small number of decisions that are clearly faulty or that cover a situation or issue for which competing bodies of precedent exist;
- **Using three-member panels.** Some analyses of UDRP proceedings indicated a significant difference in outcomes depending on whether they were heard by one-member or three-member panels: three-member panels found for the complainant in a smaller percentage of the cases;

• **Improving panelist knowledge** about the technology underlying the DNS, the uses of domain names (beyond Web sites), and the application of the policies and rules applicable to domain name disputes; and

• **Improving the nature and structure of incentives in the process.** Under the current funding structure, the revenue for panelists depends on the volume of cases, creating incentives either for haste or for marketing strategies and tactics to attract cases by defining lucrative niches.

Internationalization Challenges

Continuing and increased attention to internationalized domain names (IDNs) is necessary. Efforts to coordinate work across different countries, regions, and language groups should be undertaken to prevent the balkanization of the Internet. Of particular interest in many countries is access to the Internet and the DNS using home-country languages and scripts. Unfortunately, the design of the DNS, as well as the general nature of multiscript environments, presents formidable technical and linguistic challenges for the accommodation of languages that use non-Roman characters, which require compromises for their solution.

Some experts have argued for a major overhaul of the Internet's infrastructure to incorporate IDNs. However, pressure to act quickly reduced support for solutions that would require extensive changes in architectures or standards; the result was an effort led by the IETF that culminated in the Internationalizing Domain Names in Applications (IDNA) mechanism.[1] The central goal of the IDNA scheme is to enable end-user viewing of IDNs without altering the DNS protocols themselves, using a client-side set of procedures, implemented at the edge of the DNS.

However, the IDNA mechanism solved only part of the internationalization problem. Remaining to be addressed are the questions of potential consumer confusion; conflict avoidance or resolution for similar-appearing names; differences in interpretations for different languages; restrictions on registrations on a per-domain basis; implications for the UDRP and the Whois database (of information about domain name registrants); security issues raised by IDNs; and the implications of (and alternatives to) multilingual top-level domains.

[1]IDNA is described in Patrik Fältström, Paul Hoffman, and Adam M. Costello, "Internationalizing Domain Names in Applications (IDNA)," RFC 3490, March 2003, available at <http://www.rfc-editor.org/>.

INTERNET NAVIGATION

In contrast to the unique role played by the DNS, navigation through the Internet is not supported by a unique integrated technical system. Among the many ways to navigate the Internet, only two involve dedicated technical systems—search engines and directories. Moreover, the institutional framework of those technical systems is an open market, with many, generally commercial, competitors offering navigation services, and specialized non-commercial services focused on non-profit resource providers and seekers.

Finding and accessing a desired resource via the Internet poses challenges that are substantially different from the challenges in navigating to resources in non-digital, non-networked environments.

A wide range of navigation aids and services now permit large segments of the Internet, particularly the World Wide Web, to be traversed rapidly and efficiently in ways previously unimaginable. They offer users across the globe convenient access to much human knowledge and experience and open an international audience to purveyors of content and services, no matter where they may be located.

Use of Navigation Aids and Services

Surveys indicate a high level of satisfaction with navigation aids and services at present.

An analysis of navigation behavior, based on survey data from March 2003,[2] indicates that Internet users tend to use preferred sites and services consistently, visiting them repeatedly, using their bookmarks or remembered Uniform Resource Locators (URLs). Search engines produced only 13 percent of site referrals, navigation through entry of a known or guessed URL or use of a bookmark produced 66 percent of referrals, and flow along hyperlinks produced 21 percent.

According to a recent survey,[3] residents of the United States con-

[2]The data were collected on March 6, 2003, by WebSideStory's StatMarket from about 12 million visitors to 125,000 sites using its proprietary analytical platform and were compared with figures from the previous year. Reported in Brian Morrissey "Search Guiding More Web Activity," *CyberAtlas*, March 13, 2003, available at <http://cyberatlas.internet.com/big_picture/traffic_patterns/article/0,1323,5931_2109221,00.html>.

[3]See Deborah Fallows, Lee Rainie, and Graham Mudd. "The Popularity and Importance of Search Engines," data memo, Pew Internet & American Life Project, August 2004, available at <http://www.pewinternet.org/pdfs/PIP_Data_Memo_Searchengines.pdf>. The results came both from a telephone survey of 1399 Internet users and from tracking of Internet use by comScore Media Metrix.

ducted 3.9 billion searches in June 2004, an average of 33 searches per user. Search engines have been used by 84 percent of U.S. residents who use the Internet—more than 107 million people; on an average day, about 38 million of the 64 million U.S. residents who are online use a search engine. Using search engines is second only to using e-mail as the most popular Internet activity, except when major news stories are breaking. A vast majority of searchers say that they find the information they want most of the time, and more than two-thirds consider search engines a fair and unbiased source of information. But only a third of searchers say they could not live without search engines; about half say that, although they like using search engines, they could go back to other ways of finding information.

As the material accessible through the Internet continues its rapid increase in volume and variety and as its societal importance grows, Internet navigation aids and services are likely to be challenged to deliver more precise responses, in more convenient forms, to more diverse questions, from more users with widely varying skills. Efforts to improve the basic algorithms and operations of Internet navigation services will continue because of competitive pressures, evolving user requirements, and technological advances. Among the specific areas where improvements are needed are query interfaces and results displays for desktop, portable, and collaborative devices; navigation of audio and visual materials; management of the navigation process; use of contextual information (while protecting privacy); and understanding the wide range of navigation behaviors of the highly diverse users who now seek resources on the Internet.

As the Internet has become the sole or most accessible location of many valuable resources, the importance has grown of ensuring that they will persist indefinitely at the same URL (or in an archive on the same site) or, alternatively, that they will be preserved at another site where they can be readily found. Ensuring persistence is primarily the responsibility of resource providers, while third parties—national libraries or private organizations such as the Internet Archive—are undertaking some preservation efforts.

Although commercial services can be expected to support substantial research and development on these topics, academic research and development activities have provided the innovative basic technologies for many successful navigation aids and services. **Public support of such academic research and development efforts should be continued.**

Commercial Navigation Services

The Internet navigation services industry has financed the development and evolution of services that meet many of the needs of a wide range of searchers at little or no cost to them, especially when they are seeking commercial material. At the same time, it has provided advertisers with an efficient, cost-effective means to gain access to potential customers at the time that they are most interested in the advertiser's product or service. The primary source of income for commercial Internet navigation services is selling advertising linked to search queries. Consequently, as for many broadcast media, it is the content and service providers that are subsidizing users' access to navigation services so that they can present advertisements to them at the time of their expressed interest in a topic.

The major search services currently identify the results whose presentation in response to specified search terms is paid for by advertisers (so-called sponsored links or sponsored search listings) and set them off from the direct results of more neutral search algorithms. As long as the distinction is clear and users are aware of it, sponsored search listings should present few problems while providing the great benefit of free search services to the user.

The potential for abuse exists, however. It would be possible, for example, for a search service to accept payment for assured placement in the "top 10" of what would appear to be a neutral listing. Should abuses grow, search services could find themselves under increased public pressure for government scrutiny or facing more disputes and criticism concerning such activities from other commercial entities. None of the navigation services have been accused of accepting payment for highly ranked inclusion of particular responses to queries, but some have accepted payment to ensure inclusion, but not ranking, in the otherwise neutral listing. Furthermore, the distinct placement and typography of the sponsored listing could be weakened to the point that a casual user would not be aware of its difference from the neutral algorithmic search results. Thus far, competition among services, third-party evaluations, and the perceived value to the user of search transparency have served as important forces constraining misbehavior of these kinds.

Although competition and the desire to be seen as useful by searchers are incentives for fair and open behavior, appropriate regulatory agencies of the U.S. federal government and of other governments should pay careful and continuing attention to the result ranking and display practices of Internet navigation services and their advertisers to ensure that information can flow freely and that those critical practices are fully disclosed. The behavior of commercial navigation services can have a substantial influence on the kind, quality, and appropriateness of the information that Internet users receive. Although there is no evidence that abuse has yet occurred, the potential for abuse is inherent in the navigation services' ability to affect users' access to information for commercial or other reasons.

In the future, competition among general navigation services is more likely to take the form of rivalry among a small number of established large players rather than competition with a large number of small newcomers. Over the past 4 years, there has been considerable consolidation in the general search services market, which reflects the increasing importance of economies of scale—the considerable hardware and software costs of developing and operating a search engine are independent of the number of users, whereas revenues from advertising are directly dependent on them. The result is that the barriers to entry are high, and only a company with substantial financial resources and technical skills, such as Microsoft or IBM, is in a position to introduce its own competitive general navigation service, as Microsoft began to do in 2004.

Innovation, Competition, and Regulation

The importance of the Internet as the infrastructure linking a growing worldwide audience with an expanding array of resources means that improving Internet navigation will remain a profitable goal for commercial developers and a challenging and socially valuable objective for academic researchers. Consolidation of navigation services makes it difficult for innovative services to start small and build volume over time unless they have a very large amount of patient investment capital. But, so long as no single service becomes dominant, each of the major competitors will face continuing pressure to improve its offerings either through internal innovation or through the acquisition of innovative small companies, paths they are currently actively pursuing.

Since competition in the market for Internet navigation services promotes innovation, supports consumer choice, and prevents undue control over the location of and access to the diverse resources available via the Internet, public policies should support the competitive marketplace that has emerged and avoid actions that damage it.

Potential rulings in some jurisdictions could substantially reduce the abilty of search engines to sell keywords using the current automated methods. As with the Domain Name System, the most contentious intellectual property issues affecting navigation services concern trademarks, specifically the sale of trademarked terms to advertisers as keywords whose use will bring up their advertisements. Since there is no arbitral process, such as the UDRP, by which such disputes could be resolved outside the courts and with worldwide effect, it seems likely that conflicting court decisions in different jurisdictions, worldwide, will establish the potentially conflicting rules by which navigation services will have to abide.

THE DNS AND INTERNET NAVIGATION

The preservation of a stable, reliable, and effective Domain Name System will remain crucial both to effective Internet navigation and to the operation of the Internet and most of the applications that it supports.

Despite the differences in the way in which they developed, the relationship between the DNS technical system and Internet navigation aids and services is strong and fundamental—the DNS has served as the stable core on which the incremental evolution of the different navigation aids and services has depended. The development of navigation services is likely to continue to relieve some of the commercial pressures on the DNS as users become increasingly comfortable with using them as their primary means to navigate the Internet, but both the Domain Name System and Internet navigation aids and services will be significant elements of the Internet for the foreseeable future.

The demonstrated success of the DNS and navigation aids and services in meeting the basic needs of all Internet users should not be jeopardized by efforts to constrain or direct their evolution outside the open architecture of the Internet, or to use them to enable control of the free flow of information across the Internet.

The governance and administration of the DNS should not become a vehicle for addressing political, legal, or economic issues beyond those of the DNS itself.

1

Navigating the Internet: Concepts and Context

The Internet is rapidly becoming everybody's neighborhood. Just a few keystrokes take us to an online bookstore; several mouse clicks deliver us to an online newsstand; only a bit more effort connects us with distant friends or family. For many of us, seeking out a Web site or an e-mail address is almost as important as finding the way to the library, a theater, the nearest mall, the bookstore, or the neighborhood playground. And for those who use the Internet to deliver products or services, their clientele's ability to find them is essential to their success. Navigating the virtual neighborhood has become a life skill for those needing something on the Internet and a life-or-death matter for businesses with something to offer on the Internet.

To navigate—to follow a course to a goal—across any space, a method is needed for designating locations in that space. On a topographic map, each location is designated by a combination of a latitude and a longitude. In the telephone system, a telephone number designates each location. On a street map, locations are designated by street addresses. Just like a physical neighborhood, the virtual neighborhood has addresses—32 or 128 bit numbers, called Internet Protocol (IP) addresses—that define the specific location of every device on the Internet. And also like the physical world, the virtual world has names—called domain names, which are generally more easily remembered and informative than the addresses that are attached to most devices—that serve as unchanging identifiers of those devices even when their specific addresses are changed. The use of domain names on the Internet relies on a system of servers—called name servers—that translate the user-friendly domain names into the corresponding IP addresses. This system of addresses and names linked by name servers establishes the signposts in cyberspace and serves as the basic infrastructure supporting navigation across the Internet. It is called the Domain Name System (DNS).

This report is concerned with the Domain Name System and its interactions with Internet navigation, including its uses as a means of navigation itself and as an infrastructure for navigation by other means. Since the World Wide Web is the application running on the Internet that contains the greatest number of locations to which most users want to navigate, this report often draws examples from the Web. However, there are other applications that use the Internet, not least e-mail, and others that are being developed for it. The DNS supports most of them. Unless otherwise specified, the information in this report, its conclusions, and its recommendations apply to the DNS in its role as a basic infrastructure element of the entire Internet, not just of the World Wide Web.

The report's specific objectives and how it is organized to address them are spelled out in this chapter, which begins with an introduction to the Internet, the Domain Name System, and Internet navigation, and with an examination of the forces affecting them. Four basic concepts that are used throughout this report—names, navigation, technical system, and institutional framework—are defined and briefly described in Box 1.1.

1.1 THE INTERNET

The Internet, according to the National Research Council, is "a diverse set of independent networks, interlinked to provide its users with the appearance of a single, uniform network . . . . The networks that compose the Internet share a common architecture (how the components of the networks interrelate) and software protocols (standards governing the interchange of data) that enable communication within and among the constituent networks." [1]

Internally, the Internet comprises two types of elements: communication links, channels over which data travel from point to point; and routers, computers at the network's nodes that direct data arriving along incoming links to outgoing links that will take them toward their destinations. Altogether, the Internet is a complex network of routers and links, the latter varying in transmission medium (telephone lines, cable lines, optical fiber cable, satellite, wireless); servers and other hosts; and access equipment. Links in the network may be characterized by their transmission capacity (low-capacity local lines

---

[1]Computer Science and Telecommunications Board, National Research Council, *The Internet's Coming of Age*, National Academy Press, Washington, D.C., 2001, p. 29.

to very high capacity "backbone" cables) and by their latency (short-latency local fiber links to long-travel-time satellite links). Data travel along the Internet in packets adhering to the standard Transmission Control Protocol/Internet Protocol (TCP/IP) that defines the packets' format and header information.

Each router uses the origin and destination IP addresses in each arriving packet to determine which link to direct it along. A message from a sender to a receiver may be broken into multiple packets, each of which may follow a different path through the Internet. Information in the packets' headers enables the message to be restored to its proper order at its destination.

The origins and destinations of data transiting the Internet are computers (or other digital devices) located at its "edges." They are, typically, connected to the Internet through an Internet service provider (ISP) that handles the necessary technical and administrative arrangements. A distinctive feature of the Internet is that all the user services (such as e-mail or the World Wide Web) accessible through it are provided by applications running on computers located at its edges. The "center" of the Internet—its links and routers—provides the critical connectivity among them. As a consequence of this architecture, most of the service innovation takes place at the edges, completely independently of the network itself. It is an embodiment of the end-to-end argument in systems design[2] that says that "the network should provide a very basic level of service—data transport—and that the intelligence—the information processing needed to provide applications—should be located close in or close to the devices attached to the edge of the network."[3]

A consequence of this architecture is that innovation at the edges is eased and facilitated, requiring no coordination with network architects or operators, as long as the basic protocols are adhered to. Conversely, innovation at the center of the network is difficult and often slow, since it requires the cooperation of many providers and users. Because of the higher potential for inadvertent disruption as a side effect of a change at the center of the system, difficult and time-consuming effort must be devoted to testing and validating each proposed change. All such changes have been subject to cooperative collaboration and agreement by the Internet engineering community since the earliest days of research and implementation. (See "Maintenance of DNS Standards" in Section 3.2.5.) That principle has been a major factor in the successful design, development, and implementation of the technology.

---

[2]See Jerome H. Saltzer, David P. Reed, and David D. Clark, "End-to-End Arguments in System Design," *ACM Transactions on Computer Systems* 2(4):277-288, 1984.

[3]CSTB, NRC, *The Internet's Coming of Age*, 2001, p. 36.

BOX 1.1 Four Basic Concepts

Names and Naming Systems

Names and naming systems are everywhere in society. A license plate on a car, a serial number on a product, and a stock market symbol for a company are a few examples of names that are used within formal naming systems. Each of these examples is a unique identifier, created according to the specifications of a naming system, which is associated through strict naming rules with a single automobile, product, or company. Equally important are a host of informal or less strict naming systems, such as the naming of people by families, the naming of streets or locations, or the naming of files and directories on a personal computer. In these processes, there is no guarantee of unique names for objects.

More generally, naming is used to distinguish individual objects within a broad class, the object space. The set of allowable names for objects in that class is called the name space. A name is then a member of that set used to differentiate one member of the object class from another. A naming system is the combination of an object space, the name space that is applied to it, the rules governing the assignment of names to objects, the files recording the assignments, and the administrative processes (if any) applying the rules and maintaining the files.

Navigation, Navigation Aids, and Navigation Services

Navigation is the process of following a course from one place to another. In the narrow sense, the term is used to refer to a person or entity (e.g., a vehicle) being directed along a course from an origin to a specified destination. In the broader sense, navigation refers to following a course on, across, or through (e.g., navigate a stream) or making one's way somewhere (e.g., Lewis and Clark navigating to the "western passage" or Dr. Livingstone navigating to the source of the Nile). Navigation involves a set of skills (e.g., reading a compass, using a search engine). The place to which one wishes to navigate may be known explicitly (e.g., latitude and longitude, a street address, a Web site address) or only in general terms (e.g., source of the Nile, sites with information about veterans' benefits). In the former case, navigation requires only the two steps of laying out a route to the known location and following it. In the latter case, however, there is a prior step of identifying the desired location (or locations) through a search process of some form.

A navigation aid is anything that assists navigation, such as a map or a compass. In the physical world, navigation aids include a sextant and precision clock, and a compass and topographical map. In document-oriented environments, navigation aids include printed directories for the telephone system and card catalogs for library collections. Human intermediaries also can serve as navigation aids in these environments, such as directory assistance operators in the telephone system and reference librarians for library services. In the Internet, navigation aids include bookmarks and lists of favorites, hyperlinks, and restricted keyword systems, such as AOL keywords.

A navigation service is a navigation aid that is based on a complex technical system (see below). In the physical world, the Global Positioning System is a navigation service, as is an inertial navigation system. Automated directory assistance and online white pages are navigation services for the telephone network, and online card catalogs are navigation services for libraries. In the Internet, directories and search engines are navigation services.

Internet navigation, navigation aids, and navigation services are discussed in greater detail in Chapters 6, 7, and 8.

Technical Systems

A technical system is an integrated set of engineered elements (components and practices) that delivers a specific service to users. Some familiar examples of technical systems are the telephone system, the air transport system, the electric power system, and the Domain Name System. In the case of the telephone system, the engineered elements are organized in a complex network that includes the switching facilities (both hardware and software) that set up the circuits linking telephones for a call, the transmission lines that carry the calls, and the telephone instruments that originate and receive calls; the service it delivers is telephone connectivity; and the users are people who want to communicate with others by voice, data, or facsimile.

The single technical system that is the Domain Name System is described and discussed in detail in Chapters 2, 3, and 4; the technical systems that support Internet navigation services are characterized more broadly in Chapters 6, 7, and 8.

Institutional Framework

An institutional framework is a collection of organizations and policies whose decisions and actions enable a technical system to be constructed, operated, controlled, regulated, and improved. An institutional framework and its technical system are complementary to each other. Each of the examples of technical systems described above has a complementary institutional framework. The telephone system, for example, depends for its effective and efficient development and operation upon a complementary framework comprising equipment suppliers, operating companies, local, state, national, and international regulatory bodies, international standards organizations, and the technical community.

The institutional framework of the DNS is discussed in Chapters 2, 3, and 5; that of Internet navigation services, in Chapters 6, 7, and 8.

The Internet's architecture has enabled it to respond very successfully to the challenges of growth in the number of its users and in the capacity of its links and the complexity of their connectivity, as well as to provide a robust base for the growth of services such as e-mail and the World Wide Web.

1.2 THE DOMAIN NAME SYSTEM

The DNS was put into place by technologists in the early 1980s when the Internet provided basic non-commercial services to a small community of specialists.[4] The World Wide Web had not yet been invented. The DNS's designers intended it to be a simple and stable way for users and applications to identify computers on the Internet. They gave it a hierarchical structure so that the responsibility for maintaining the necessary information tying domain names to IP addresses (and other data) could be distributed to the organizations actually managing the relevant networks and groups of hosts across the edges of the network.[5] They designed it as an inverted tree with the expectation that most domain names would lie several branches down, requiring relatively few names in the upper part of the tree. Figure 1.1 illustrates the Domain Name System's role in support of navigation across the Internet.[6] Complete domain names[7] incorporate the names of the nodes in the tree above them. So in Figure 1.1, the domain name www.cstb.nas.edu designates the www leaf lying on the .cstb branch, which lies on the .nas branch, which lies on the .edu branch.

A number of factors, including the introduction of the World Wide Web in the early 1990s, have transformed the Internet community from a small town into a great and rapidly expanding metropolis with an extremely large, highly diverse body of users, relatively few of whom are computer specialists. These users employ the Internet as the communications backbone for a vast range of commercial and non-commercial purposes. As a result, the Internet has expanded both in scale and in the scope of its applications. Because of the elegance of its technical design, the DNS has, thus far, been able to adjust to the expanded scale of the Internet, evolving to meet the increased operational demand adequately. However, as a consequence of the growth in the scope of the Internet, the DNS is now used in ways that were not anticipated when it was designed. These

---

[4]Chapter 2 describes the development of the Domain Name System.

[5]Chapter 3 describes the design and operation of the Domain Name System.

[6]This depiction of the DNS is highly simplified. More detailed descriptions of the DNS are provided in Chapters 2 and 3.

[7]Formally, these are called "fully qualified domain names" to distinguish them from partial domain names that describe the path only from some node below the root.

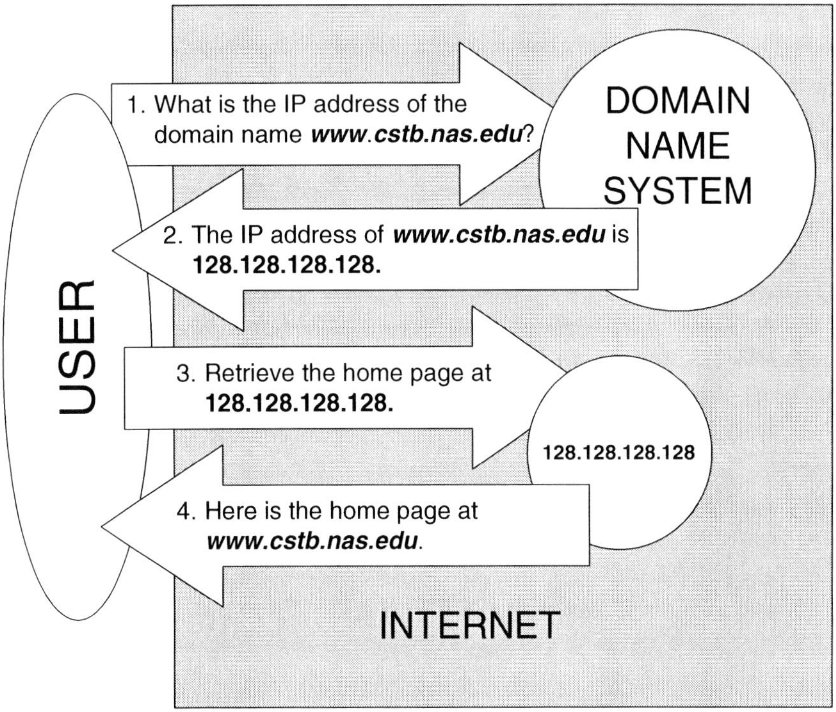

FIGURE 1.1 The Domain Name System and Internet navigation for the Web—navigating to www.cstb.nas.edu. The Web site and IP address used are fictional.

unanticipated uses have led, in turn, to a substantial increase in the number and complexity of the institutions responsible for its operation and management and to less use than was originally expected of deep naming hierarchies and distributed, but localized, management of names. This growth in institutional complexity has been driven primarily by the fact that domain names acquired increased value, which required mechanisms to deal with their allocation and control. Their acquisition of increased value followed from four developments:

• *Preference for short and memorable names.* The first development was a preference among users for short and memorable domain names, which led to an unexpectedly unbalanced distribution of domain names. More devices were named at the second or third level of the inverted tree, thereby widening it, rather than deepening it to the fourth and lower levels as had been anticipated. And although the implementation of the DNS offered a range of generic top-level domains—such as .com, .net, .org,

.gov, and .edu—for a variety of reasons, .com became the preferred choice, further unbalancing the tree. Even with the addition of new generic top-level domains after the year 2000, memorable domain names within the .com domain remain the preferred choice for most businesses, many non-profit organizations, and numerous individuals.[8]

• *Navigation role of* .com. What led most directly to the growth in importance of the .com domain was the second development—its self-fulfilling role in navigation. For example, as commercial uses grew, users seeking IBM's site on the World Wide Web could guess www.ibm.com with an expectation of success. That common behavior naturally led organizations and individuals to seek registration of domain names that users might be able to guess to find their site, which in turn improved the users' chances of navigating by guessing. That users were inclined to use domain names to search for content of interest increased the desirability of domain names corresponding to generic words, such as "business," "jobs," or "sex." And the importance of having those names in the .com domain was increased even more by the design of Web browsers. Recognizing user inclinations, designers made the default behavior of many Web browsers when confronted by an incomplete domain name the automatic addition of .com to the end of it and www as the default prefix.[9] Thus, domain names became not only the way of designating locations on the Internet, but also a principal means of navigating to them.[10]

• *Valuable second-level domain names.* The third development was the recognition that certain domain names within the top-level domains—second-level domain names—are more valuable than most others. The result was an aftermarket for domain names, generally in the .com top-level domain, in which some have been resold for prices far greater than the nominal registration fee paid by the original registrant. Furthermore, in an effort to protect their rights and prevent others from abusing them, trademark holders have sought to acquire many of the domain names incorporating their trademarks and, given the likelihood of entry errors, words that are typographically close to them in all of the relevant top-level domains. This effort has, in turn, led to competition among trademark holders with the same mark (though in different industries or regions) for the small number of memorable domain names incorporating their marks. (Individuals or groups with other legitimate claims to a

---

[8]In mid-2004 there were almost 27 million .com registrations compared with 4.4 million for .net and 2.8 million for .org. See also Table 3.3.

[9]Browsers in 2005 no longer make this assumption. Instead, they commonly assume that the entry is a search term.

[10]The unique role of .com is elaborated on in Chapter 2.

name—such as those with the surname McDonald[11] —have also asserted their rights to domain names incorporating trademarks.) It has also attracted speculators who rush to acquire potentially desirable domain names (both trademarks and generic words) in order to resell them to those for whom the value would be substantially greater than the registration fee.[12]

- *Marketing function.* The value of domain names has been further enhanced by their widespread use in marketing materials as a secondary, or even primary (e.g., amazon.com), identifier of an organization. In that role they appear on stationery, in newspaper ads, on billboards, and on the sides of buses. This marketing function of domain names is the fourth unanticipated development.

Because of these developments, the Domain Name System—originally a modest technical system introduced to provide easy-to-remember and portable names for locations on the Internet—has become a critical tool facilitating global communication by designating sources of information, products, and services as well as the e-mail boxes of people and organizations throughout cyberspace. As a consequence, its simple original institutional framework, managed essentially by one person,[13] has been replaced with a complex network of institutions comprising numerous public and private, commercial and non-commercial organizations that register domain names and operate name servers; and one non-governmental organization with international scope that, with the authority and oversight of the U.S. government, provides technical coordination and establishes some elements of global policy—the Internet Corporation for Assigned Names and Numbers (ICANN).

---

[11]The new top-level domain, .name, for registration by individuals was intended to meet that need, although by mid-2004 the companies involved with registrations in that domain had not found business models capable of supporting those operations.

[12]A case in point is the name business.com, which changed hands for $150,000 in 1997 and was resold for $7.5 million in 1999. See Jennifer Mack, "Business.com: The $7.5 Million Domain," *ZDNet News*, December 1, 1999, available at <http://zdnet.com.com/2100-11-516999.html?legacy=zdnn>. However, in the aftermath of the dot-com bust, the prices realized in the aftermarket for domain names have also subsided substantially, although at the end of 2003 the name men.com was sold for $1.3 million by a person who paid $15,000 for it in 1997. See Anick Jesdanun, "Domain Names Once Again Fetch Top Dollar," Associated Press, December 25, 2003.

[13]Jon Postel held this responsibility for many years. For further information, see <http://www.isoc.org/postel>.

1.3 INTERNET NAVIGATION

With the growth of the size, complexity, and variety of applications using the Internet, and especially the rapid growth of the World Wide Web, a range of aids to the navigation process (especially on the Web) have appeared.[14] The DNS is a single technical system providing a single service, which is operated and controlled in a complex institutional framework. In contrast, among aids to navigation on the Web there are numerous specialized navigation services, each operated by different providers that compete openly without any comprehensive institutional framework for their operation and control. Principal among these navigation services are search engines, which at the possible cost of a few more keystrokes open up a far wider range of possibilities on the Web than simple domain name guessing; and directories, which provide a yellow pages or white pages guide to locations, principally on the Web. As search engines have improved in user-perceived quality and ease of use, they have become a principal means of navigation to new destinations for many users.[15] In place of guessing, intrepid Web travelers enter a descriptive word or phrase in the search engine and use the resultant list to direct their journeys. In June 2004, nearly 4 billion searches were conducted each month by almost 110 million people in the United States, an average of 33 searches per person per month.[16] It appears that a consequence of the growing use of search engines for navigation across the Web may be a reduction, though by no means elimination, of the direct use of the DNS to support navigation by guessing domain names.

Because locations that offer search or directory capabilities are accessed so often, a number have evolved into portals, which are Web sites offering directed links to popular categories of services, such as My Yahoo!. Portals such as MSN and AOL have also evolved from provision of

---

[14]If the location of a desired Web site is known, then navigation can be direct—the DNS determines the IP address of the site. If the location is not known, then some navigation aid must first be used to determine the location. See Section 7.1 for a detailed discussion of direct and indirect navigation.

[15]According to data from WebSideStory, both direct navigation using a known domain name and the use of Web search engines increased substantially from 2002 to 2003. In March 2003, 13.6 percent of Web site accesses were generated by search engine listings, while 66 percent were the result of the use of bookmarks or direct entry of a known address. See <http://www.websidestory.com>, press release, March 12, 2003.

[16]Deborah Fallows, Lee Rainie, and Graham Mudd, "The Popularity and Importance of Search Engines," data memo, Pew Internet & American Life Project, August 2004, available at <http://www.pewinternet.org/pdfs/PIP_Data_Memo_Searchengines.pdf>. The results came both from a telephone survey of 1399 Internet users and from tracking of Internet use by comScore Media Metrix.

Internet service. Some users find the portals more desirable than search engines alone and begin their navigation from them. In doing so, they are relying on the editorial judgment and commercial or other arrangements of the portal to get started. However, once a World Wide Web site is reached—no matter how—subsequent navigation often flows along the network of links from one site to others. And it is likely that most experienced users deploy a combination of navigation services and other aids: employing search engines, portals, and direct entry of destinations into browsers at various times.[17] Other navigation aids are also in use. In some Web portals run by ISPs (such as AOL) or through extensions to browsers, a specified vocabulary of key words can be used to reach specific destinations.

The cumulative effect of these services and other aids to navigation has, thus far, been positive. They enable users to find sources of products, services, information, and contacts that they would not have been able to identify previously. Complementarily, they enable providers to reach audiences that might not otherwise have known of their existence. Unlike the development of the top levels of the DNS, which has been under the technical control of the Internet engineering community and the governance of ICANN, national governments, and the operational organizations, these navigation services have for the most part been provided by private organizations. Despite their benefits, however, navigation services and other aids are also beginning to raise policy concerns. Most search engines and directories now accept payment from advertisers for placement of an ad on the pages of responses to queries with specific search terms. If not clearly identified such ads might give searchers a false sense of an advertiser's importance or relevance and reduce the chances that a non-advertiser will be located. Concerns about the practices of the providers of navigation services are likely to grow as Internet users rely increasingly on these services as a principal means of navigation.

1.4 THE DYNAMICS OF CHANGE

Since the early 1980s, when the DNS was developed, five forces have inexorably driven the transformation of the Internet from its origins as a small, primarily North American research network, which was run by a tight-knit group of specialists for use within their research and industrial communities, into its current state as a diffusely managed and increasingly critical part of the global information and communication infrastruc-

---

[17]These destinations might be derived from guesses about domain names as discussed above or references provided by others (e.g., in an e-mail) that are copied and pasted into browsers, as well as by the use of bookmarks for destinations that are accessed frequently.

ture. These driving forces are increasing scale, technological progress, increasing economic value, increasing social value, and internationalization. In addition to having a profound impact on the Internet (and the World Wide Web) as a whole, these forces have simultaneously transformed the DNS and Internet navigation to subjects of substantial commercial, legal, political, and social importance. The likelihood of the continued influence of these forces raises important questions about the future viability, operability, and governability of the DNS and Internet navigation—the subjects of this study.

1.4.1 Increasing Scale

When the DNS was developed, the Internet comprised on the order of 1000 sites and perhaps 10,000 users. In two decades it has grown to more than 30 million sites and over 600 million users.[18] Though its designers did not fully anticipate the rapid growth in users and uses stimulated by the World Wide Web, the DNS has technically scaled quite well to the current size. In addition, new navigation tools have been deployed to assist users in searching the vastly larger Internet. The Internet continues to grow in number of users, number of addresses, and number and diversity of attached devices. By 2010, at current growth rates, the Internet could have more than 60 million sites and well over a billion users worldwide.[19]

1.4.2 Technological Progress

When the DNS was developed, most of the hosts were workstations, minicomputers, or mainframe computers. Personal computers had just begun their penetration of the business and home markets in North America, Europe, and Japan. Internetworking communication took place over backbones that had 56 kbps (kilobits per second) speeds—about 1/180,000th the speeds of backbones in 2005, which run at 10 Gbps (gigabits per second). As the capacities of computers and communications networks have soared, the DNS and navigation systems have taken advantage of the increased computational capability and bandwidth to meet the

[18]These numbers reflect estimates made in May 2003 by CyberAtlas; see <http://cyberatlas.internet.com>.

[19]To serve them, the basic IP address—currently 32 bits—is being enlarged to 128 bits, enabling addressing of a wide range of devices from computers and cell phones to home digital media centers and home appliances. The current IP address space is called the IPv4 address space; the new version is called the IPv6 address space. IPv6 is slowly being adopted, working in parallel with IPv4.

challenges of scaling. Continuing technological advances in computing and communications offer the possibility of strengthening the DNS and increasing the capacities of navigation services, while at the same time further empowering those who would attack the services or attempt to misdirect them for their own benefit.

1.4.3 Increasing Economic Value

When the DNS was developed, there was probably little or no economic value associated with possession of a particular domain name, which could be obtained at no cost, although having a hierarchical naming system was judged to be valuable. A distinctive Internet culture had developed well before this time, led by the relatively small and homogeneous community of engineers and scientists who were its primary users. It placed high value on voluntary service, free access within the community, and consensus decision making. However, the growth of applications on the Internet for commerce, information, art, and entertainment attracted commercial, legal, governmental, and other communities whose values and processes differ from those of the early Internet culture. Their arrival led to the development of a vigorous market for domain names and of a variety of mechanisms to deal with fair allocation of the now economically valuable domain names. Not surprisingly, throughout these developments there has been a continuing tension between the technical community and the public interest community about the proper goals and mechanisms for the allocation of domain names and the management of the DNS.

As domain names have gained economic value, so, too, has the desire grown for opportunities to publicize those names (as part of Web site and e-mail addresses) to potential users of the corresponding Internet locations. Consequently, many search engines and other navigational services, which originally provided a single listing of search results in the order of estimated relevance to the user's query, now also give prominent placement to those willing to pay for it. As noted above, the search engine industry faces a continuing challenge in finding the proper balance between the interests of the users of search engines and the advertisers on them, against the backdrop of the ever present possibility of government intervention.

1.4.4 Increasing Social Value

When the DNS was developed, there was a modest level of social, political, or cultural value associated with specific domain names. As the Internet grew in size and evolved in use, it became a primary medium for communication, commerce, information, art, and entertainment; accordingly, domain names assumed greater social, political, and cultural significance as the memorable designators of the Internet locations of political groups, cultural resources, and social activities. But as a result, the DNS became entangled in issues of privacy versus accountability, freedom of expression versus national legal restrictions, and the rights of producers of intellectual property versus those of its users.

In the future, the Internet can be expected to be even more widely used for interpersonal communication, for the public expression of ideas, for access to information, for the development of virtual communities around common interests, and for the production and distribution of art and entertainment. It will be a major portion of the global social fabric, facilitating and controlling the flow of information, expression, art, and entertainment. Until or unless the DNS is replaced, the signs designating the location of information, art, entertainment, viewpoints, and services will continue to depend on domain names. For that reason, it will be essential to sustain the DNS as the reliable signposting infrastructure of the Internet, facilitating the Internet's use as a medium of free expression openly communicated to all corners of the globe, while balancing that freedom of expression against privacy rights, property rights, cultural mores, and national laws.

As a result of the Internet's increased social value, the desire to navigate freely across it can also be expected to encounter legal, commercial, cultural, and political challenges.

1.4.5 Internationalization

When the DNS was developed, the Internet's geographic scope was limited primarily to North America, parts of Western Europe, and a few countries on the Pacific Rim. And it was operated by a loose confederation of bodies and individuals, primarily in the United States, most of whom had received substantial support from the U.S. government. As use of the Internet has spread beyond its initial sites to encompass every continent and region and almost all nations, the network has responded successfully. But internationalization has posed two specific challenges for the DNS.

First, until recently domain names have been limited to strings of Roman letters, Arabic numbers, and the hyphen, a subset of the ASCII[20]

[20]The American Standard Code for Information Interchange (ASCII) was originally developed for use with teletype. It was extended by IBM to represent 256 characters and has become a de facto standard.

character set. However, the native languages of an increasing number of Internet users employ different character sets. Recently, following years of work, a means of enabling presentation of internationalized domain names (domain names encoding other character sets into ASCII characters) has been adopted. It should become an important facilitator of Internet access and use for those communities.[21]

And, second, although ICANN has international participation, its authority rests on a contract from the U.S. Department of Commerce, which is perceived by some as undercutting its legitimacy as a representative of the international community. That concern may increase as the economic and social value of the DNS as the critical signposting infrastructure of the Internet continues to grow.[22]

Although the DNS is only now moving toward presentation of non-ASCII scripts in domain names, Internet content in most important applications, including e-mail and the Web, has been internationalized for well over a decade. Most Internet navigation services have incorporated the capability to search in multiple languages. For example, in November 2004 the Google search engine supported searches in over 100 languages and dialects and provided a customized version of the search interface for 103 different nations.[23] At the same time, the Yahoo! directory and search service offered portals customized for 32 national or language groups.[24] Since the navigation services are provided by a variety of organizations in an open forum, they are less subject to concerns about the internationalization of their governance. However, as their importance as the principal means of access to the Internet grows, they may well come under pressure from those who believe that in one aspect of their service or another, they do not adequately take into account the concerns or interests of certain nations, ethnic groups, or linguistic communities.

1.5 INTERNET NAMING AND NAVIGATION

Owing to the five forces outlined above, Internet naming and navigation have become matters of broad concern throughout the world. Those

---

[21]Internationalized domain names (IDNs) have recently been approved by ICANN for use by registries with which it has agreements. See "Standards for ICANN Authorization of Internationalized Domain Name Registrations in Registries with Agreements," posted March 13, 2003, on the ICANN Web site, <http://www.icann.org>. See Section 4.3 for a more complete discussion of this subject and more extensive references.

[22]Changes in ICANN's organizational structure and decision processes responded to this concern, although debate continued into 2004 about the effectiveness of those changes. See Sections 5.1 and 5.2 for an extended discussion of this issue.

[23]For a listing see <http://www.google.com/language_tools?hl=en>.

[24]For a listing see <http://world.yahoo.com/>.

concerns are given voice by the large number of competing interest groups that now take a vigorous interest in the DNS and, to a somewhat lesser degree, Internet navigation.

Product and service providers compete for named locations on the Internet and have a strong interest in the means for setting up new regions and allocating named locations in them. Internet users have a complementary interest in being able to find the information or service they want wherever it may be located, even as the Internet continues to grow in size and in diversity. All cultures have an interest in being able to name locations and access and navigate the Internet in their native languages. Trademark holders have an interest in protecting their rights in names from being infringed. Nations and their citizens want assurance that their interests will be treated fairly and their needs supported by the institutional frameworks that affect the Internet's naming and navigation infrastructures. The Internet technical community wants to ensure that everything is done to improve and nothing is done to compromise the reliability, security, and stability of the Internet itself. Individuals also want to be certain that neither their access nor their rights will be unduly affected by the actions of the other groups. The interaction among these various interests in naming and navigating the Internet—a global infrastructure that is undergoing rapid growth in scale while absorbing continual technological change—raises important issues that lie at the intersection of technology, economics, public policy, law, and user behavior.[25]

This report addresses those issues from a specific perspective, that of the Domain Name System. Navigation across the vast and multifaceted complex of human activity connected through the Internet is a subject that warrants a major report in its own right. It is too large, in its full richness, to fit within a report that was initiated to address significant questions about the future of the DNS. Yet, at the same time, navigation is so intertwined with the present and future of the DNS that it cannot be completely absent. Consequently, this report concentrates on navigation over the Internet primarily in its relationships with the DNS. Even under that constraint, however, it is necessary to introduce fundamental issues of Internet navigation to provide a background for the more circumscribed examination of its interrelationships with the DNS.

The DNS interrelates with navigation across the Internet in five ways.

- First, the DNS plays a direct navigational role by providing the IP address of a World Wide Web site, an e-mail server, or another network host or resource whose domain name is known, or can be guessed.

---

[25]See CSTB, NRC, *The Internet's Coming of Age*, 2001.

• Second, the DNS serves as an enhancer of navigation because many navigation services return locators incorporating the domain names of relevant Web sites. These names usually provide more (although not necessarily reliable) information to the user about the provider whose location has been returned than just the IP address or a blank link would.

• Third, navigation services complement the DNS by, for example, enabling navigation to Web sites whose domain names are not known by the user or by enabling searches within sites that have been reached by use of their domain names.

• Fourth, navigation services relieve some of the pressure on the Domain Name System by reducing the need for a site to have a short memorable name in order to be found. It appears that efforts and funds spent in previous years to obtain desirable domain names are now being diverted to some degree to efforts and expenditures to ensure a presence and high ranking in the results of search engines or directories.

• Fifth, navigation services could, in the extreme, substitute entirely for the Domain Name System on the Web because they could directly return IP addresses. However, as noted above, this approach would deprive the user of any information about the provider contained in the domain name. It would also deprive the provider of the marketing value of the domain name. And it would eliminate the use of domain names as stable identifiers of Internet resources whose IP addresses change, which was one of the original motivations for the creation of the DNS.

Of these five roles, it is the third and fourth—navigation as a complement to and a relief for the DNS—that are the focus of this report's examination of Internet navigation.

1.6 OBJECTIVES OF THIS REPORT

This report is addressed to those who are or will be concerned with policies and practices that affect the operation and evolution of the DNS and Internet navigation. That is a large audience. It includes the technologists who research, design, implement, and operate the DNS and navigation systems; the governmental policy makers and their staffs who establish, oversee, and operate the framework of institutions and laws that govern or regulate those systems; the commercial and non-commercial organizations that operate, manage, and use those systems; and the users and providers who depend on those systems for access to and the accessibility of Internet locations.

During the time that this report has been in preparation, the DNS and Internet navigation have seen many technical and institutional changes, some substantial, others modest; some controversial, others agreeable; some likely to last, others temporary expedients that will eventually be replaced. Some of the changes made have addressed the issues that gave rise to the initial request for this report. Clearly, this study was not the proper vehicle to address those specific issues. However, it is equally clear that many issues of similar character are or soon will arrive on the agendas of the policy, technical, provider, and user communities. Yet those called upon to deal with policy and practices affecting the DNS and Internet navigation often have little or no knowledge of the full complexity of those arenas. Those who are engaged with the technology of these worlds do not always appreciate the nuances of the policy, economic, and legal issues, while those experienced with the legal, economic, and policy aspects often are largely unaware of the intricacies of the technology. This asymmetry of knowledge exacerbates cultural differences between the technology and the policy communities, inhibiting both effective policy making and desirable technological change. Both groups would benefit from having a reliable source of information about the technologies and the institutions that control them, upon which they can base reasonable and effective policies. And, where appropriate, they might also benefit from the conclusions and recommendations of a broadly knowledgeable committee that has spent several years reviewing the two worlds.

Therefore, this report, which is the result of extensive and collaborative work by a committee whose members are drawn from both the technology and the policy communities, is intended to serve five objectives:

1. To provide a thorough and objective description and assessment of the Domain Name System—both its technology and the institutional framework within which that technology operates;
2. To describe and analyze alternative approaches to the principal technology prospects and institutional issues that are likely to affect the future of the DNS;
3. To provide a thorough and objective description and assessment of Internet navigation, with sufficient background information to provide context;
4. To describe and analyze alternative approaches to some of the technology prospects and institutional issues that are likely to affect the future of Internet navigation; and
5. To present conclusions and make recommendations where it was possible for the committee to reach agreement—in any case, to characterize the range of alternative views.

This report has been structured to respond to those objectives.

1.7 ROADMAP FOR THIS REPORT

This report is divided into three parts. The DNS is the subject of the first, consisting of Chapters 2, 3, 4, and 5. Internet navigation in its relationship to the DNS is the subject of the second, consisting of Chapters 6, 7, and 8. Chapter 9 summarizes the interaction between the DNS and Internet navigation.

Because the options for moving forward are partially constrained by the decisions taken along the path to the present, the first part begins with a careful review of the development of the Domain Name System. Chapter 2 examines the evolution of the technical design of the DNS and its associated operational, administrative, and governance mechanisms. It describes the sequence of important technical decisions and innovations, as well as the new governance and administrative mechanisms that have been introduced in response to the Internet's rapid growth. Several of the early technical decisions, taken at the time of restricted use of internetworks by specialized groups, still constrain the DNS.

Chapter 3 describes the current state of the DNS, considering both the technical system, which performs the linkage of domain names with IP addresses and associated data, and the higher-level institutional framework, which carries out operational, administrative, and policy-setting functions essential for the DNS to function. It explains and evaluates the operation of the DNS technical system and identifies and assesses each of the functions carried out by the highest levels of the institutional framework.

Chapter 4 describes the prospective technologies that can respond to the challenges the DNS faces from malicious attacks, the growing intersection of the telephone system and the Internet, the need to internationalize the DNS, and the need to regulate the introduction of potentially disruptive new services. Chapter 5 deals with the key institutional issues facing the DNS: governance of the DNS itself, oversight of root operations, governance of the top-level domains, improvement of the dispute resolution process, and improvement of the DNS's information service (called the Whois service).

The distinctive characteristics and historical development of Internet navigation, as it relates to the DNS, are described in Chapter 6. The current state of navigation aids and services and the framework of commercial institutions within which they operate are presented in Chapter 7. Chapter 8 addresses some prospective technologies whose introduction, and a number of the institutional issues whose resolution, can have a major influence on the future development of Internet navigation and its relationship to the DNS.

Finally, Chapter 9 sums up the interaction between the DNS and Internet navigation.

Throughout the chapters on the DNS and Internet navigation, the committee's conclusions and recommendations are incorporated into the text where appropriate.

The goal of this report is to clarify the sometimes controversial, often arcane, and frequently uncertain issues concerning the signposting and navigational infrastructure of the Internet. The committee hopes that by providing such clarification, this report will itself serve as a navigational aid to the policy and technology communities as they find their way to decisions that will enable the Internet to remain an efficient and reliable channel of global communication and commerce.

2

The Domain Name System: Emergence and Evolution

The Domain Name System (DNS) was designed and deployed in the 1980s to overcome technical and operational constraints of its predecessor, the HOSTS.TXT system. Some of the initial design decisions have proven to be extraordinarily flexible in accommodating major changes in the scale and scope of the DNS. Other initial design decisions constrain technical and policy choices to the present day. Thus, an understanding of the system architecture and the rationale for the design characteristics of the DNS provides the base for understanding how the DNS has evolved to the present and for evaluating possibilities for its future. This chapter outlines the origin and development of the DNS and describes its key design characteristics, which include both technological and organizational aspects.[1]

2.1 ORIGIN OF THE DOMAIN NAME SYSTEM

For the first decade or so of the ARPANET,[2] the host[3] table file (HOSTS.TXT) served as its directory. HOSTS.TXT provided the network

[1]A general presentation of the history of the Internet is beyond the scope of this report. One source of documentation on the Internet's history is available at <http://www.isoc.org/internet/history/>.

[2]The Internet grew out of the ARPANET project (funded by the Defense Advanced Research Projects Agency (DARPA), which was known as ARPA for a period of its history); for many years the ARPANET served as the core of the Internet.

[3]A host is the primary or controlling computer in a network.

address for each host on the ARPANET,[4] which could be looked up by using the host's one-word English language name, acronym, or abbreviation. The Network Information Center (NIC) at the Stanford Research Institute[5] managed the registration of hosts and the distribution of the information needed to keep the HOSTS.TXT file current. The list of host names and their mapping to and from network addresses was maintained in the frequently updated HOSTS.TXT file, which was copied to and stored in each computer connected to the ARPANET. Thus, HOSTS.TXT[6] was introduced to:

- *Simplify the identification of computers on the ARPANET.* Simple and familiar names are much easier for humans to remember than lengthy (12-digit) numeric strings; and
- *Provide stability when addresses changed.* Since addresses in the ARPANET were a function of network topology and routing,[7] they often had to be changed when topology or routing changed. Names in the host table could remain unchanged even as addresses changed.

The HOSTS.TXT file had a very simple format. Each line in HOSTS.TXT included information about a single host, such as the network address, and when provided, system manufacturer and model number, operating system, and a listing of the protocols that were supported.

Because a copy of the host table was stored in every computer on the ARPANET, each time a new computer was added to the network, or an-

[4]These network addresses could be represented using the Internet Protocol (IP) format or in the equivalent (now unused) ARPANET Network Control Protocol (NCP) format. The most widely used version (v4) of IP represents addresses using 32 bits, usually expressed as four integers in the range from 0 to 255, separated by dots. An example of an IP address is 144.171.1.26.

[5]Stanford Research Institute became known as SRI International in 1977.

[6]For further discussion, see L. Peter Deutsch, "Host Names On-line," Request for Comments (RFC) 606, December 1973; Ken Harrenstien, Vic White, and Elizabeth Feinler, "Hostnames Server," RFC 811, March 1982; and Ken Harrenstien, M. Stahl, and Elizabeth Feinler, "DOD Internet Host Table Specification," RFC 952, October 1985, all available at <http://www.rfc-editor.org>. RFCs are created to document technical and organizational aspects of the Internet. The Internet Engineering Task Force (IETF) manages the process for discussing, evaluating, and approving RFCs. See Box 3.3. For a discussion of the role of the DNS more generally, see John C. Klensin, "Role of the Domain Name System," RFC 3467, February 2003.

[7]Routing refers to the way data flowed on the ARPANET. Data transmitted from point A to point B might have traversed many different paths, or routes, on the ARPANET. Note that the ARPANET, as the original network to employ the Internet Protocol (IP), was often referred to as "the Internet," although the term later formally encompassed the aggregate of interconnected IP-based networks.

other update was made, the entire table had to be sent to every computer on the network for the change to be recognized.[8] As increasing numbers of computers joined the ARPANET, the updating task became more and more burdensome and subject to error and failure, and, as a consequence, several major problems developed from the use of the HOSTS.TXT file:

- *Failure to scale.* As the ARPANET started to grow rapidly, it became clear that the centralized HOSTS.TXT file failed to scale in two ways. First, the volume of updates threatened to overwhelm the NIC staff maintaining HOSTS.TXT. Second, because every system needed to have an up-to-date copy of HOSTS.TXT, announcement of a new copy of HOSTS.TXT meant that the NIC server where the current version of HOSTS.TXT was stored was inundated with attempts to download the file. Moreover, the download problem was aggravated because HOSTS.TXT kept getting bigger. In short, more hosts on the network meant more updates, more hosts trying to download, and more data to download.
- *Inadequate timeliness.* It often took several days to get a new host listed in HOSTS.TXT while the NIC staff processed the request to add the host entry. Until it was listed and communicated, the host was effectively invisible to the rest of the ARPANET. In a community already becoming accustomed to getting data instantly over the network, this delay was a source of frustration. Similarly, correcting an error often took a few days, because fixes to any errors were not generally available until the next HOSTS.TXT file was released—which caused further frustration. The maintainers of some hosts also did not update their copies of the table at very frequent intervals, resulting in those hosts having obsolete or incomplete information even when the master copy of the table was up-to-date.
- *Susceptibility to failure.* The system had multiple ways to fail. Probably the most famous outage occurred when the NIC released a version of HOSTS.TXT that omitted the entry for the system where the HOSTS.TXT file was stored. When the subsequent HOSTS.TXT file was released, most systems could not download it, because they could not look up the relevant host name! There were also cases where partial tables were inadvertently released. Furthermore, seemingly innocuous additions to HOSTS.TXT could cause the programs that converted HOSTS.TXT into local formats to fail.
- *Name conflicts.* The HOSTS.TXT name space was flat, which meant that host names had to be unique. Popular host names such as Frodo were selected first, and so some people had to invent alternate names for their systems.

---

[8]It was the obligation of individual network and host operators to download the latest HOSTS.TXT file to their machines.

The emergence of these problems caused technologists to develop a new, distributed, method for managing the mapping of names and addresses.

2.2 DESIGNING THE DOMAIN NAME SYSTEM

In the early 1980s, research on naming systems—systems for associating names with addresses—was underway and a few prototype naming systems had just been developed, most notably the Grapevine and Clearinghouse systems at the Xerox Palo Alto Research Center (PARC).[9] Also in progress at this time was preliminary work on other computer network addressing standards such as X.400.[10] Because of the uncertainty as to whether these research and development efforts would yield in the near term an operational system with the required functionality and needed scale, Internet researchers elected to develop their own protocols.

In August 1982, Zaw-Sing Su and Jon Postel authored "The Domain Naming Convention for Internet User Applications," Request for Comments (RFC) 819, which described how Internet naming should be changed to facilitate a distributed name system. As envisioned in this document, Internet names would be organized into logical hierarchies, represented by text components separated by a period (".") (thus the existing host "ISIF"—host computer "F" at the Information Sciences Institute (ISI)—would become F.ISI), and the various parts of the name as assigned (i.e., the parts delimited with periods) would be managed by different network servers. RFC 819 specified only how names would be represented—the details of how the management of various parts of assigned names would take place operationally by the different network servers remained to be determined.

In November 1983, Paul Mockapetris authored "Domain Names—Concepts and Facilities" (RFC 882) and "Domain Names—Implementation and Specification" (RFC 883), which specified a set of protocols, called the Domain Name System, that implemented the hierarchical name space proposed by Su and Postel. Reflecting the discussions of the previous several months on the electronic mail list Namedroppers, the proposed DNS

---

[9]See Andrew D. Birrell, Roy Levin, Roger M. Needham, and Michael D. Schroeder, "Grapevine: An Exercise in Distributed Computing," *Communications of the ACM* 25(4):260-274, 1982.

[10]The International Organization for Standardization and the International Telecommunication Union endorsed X.400 as a standard that describes a messaging service (e.g., electronic mail). The first version of X.400 was published in 1984 by the Comité Consultatif International Téléphonique et Télégraphique (CCITT), which is now the International Telecommunication Union–Telecommunication Standardization Sector (ITU-T).

supported more sophisticated services and features than simply converting host names to addresses (e.g., the proposed system would provide a way to map a name to different addresses, depending on the purpose for which an inquiry was being made). With some modest changes, the proposed protocols are exactly those in use two decades later.

Conceptually, the DNS is implemented through a distributed and hierarchical series of tables, linked like the branches of an inverted tree springing from a single, common root. When an address is sought, the search proceeds successively from the table at the root (or top) of the tree to successive branches and leaves, or lower tables, until the table that holds the desired address is found. For a particular query, only the last table in the search serves as a white pages directory. All of the other tables serve as directories of directories, each one pointing to lower-level directories on a path to the one holding the desired address. Thus, the entries in a table at any given level of the tree can include pointers to lower-level tables as well as final network addresses. See Figure 2.1.

When a change is made in the network, only the table directly affected by that change must be updated and only the local organization (e.g., the system administration function in a university or corporation) responsible for that table needs to make the update. As a result, the work of registering changes is distributed among many organizations, thus reducing the burden each must carry.

The DNS naming syntax corresponds to the levels in the hierarchical tree. Each node in the tree has a name that identifies it relative to the node

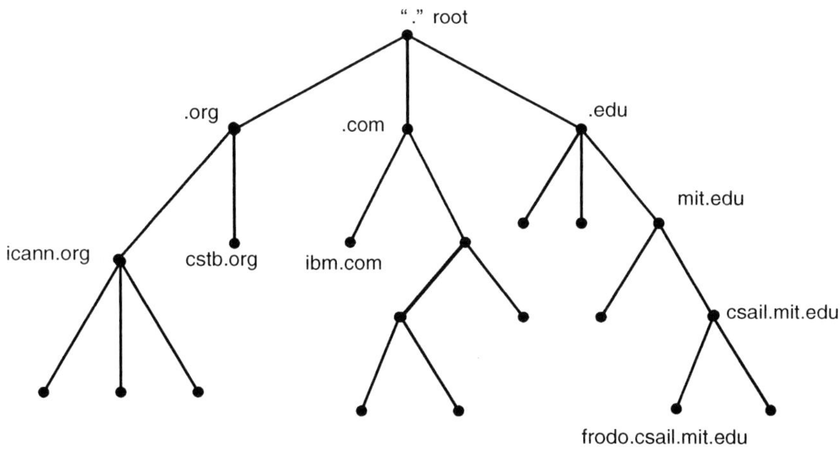

FIGURE 2.1 The hierarchical Domain Name System inverted tree structure.

above it. The highest level, the "root node," has the null name. In text it is written as a single dot (".") or simply implied (and thus not shown at all). Each node below the root is the root of another subtree, a domain, that can in turn be further divided into additional subtrees, called subdomains. Each subdomain is written in text to include its name and the subdomains above it in the applicable hierarchy. In Figure 2.1, .com, .org, and .edu are top-level domains (TLDs) and cstb.org, mit.edu, and ibm.com are subdomains of the TLDs, often called second-level domains. The third-level domain, csail.mit.edu, is a subdomain within the mit.edu second-level domain.

The DNS name of a computer is the name of its node or end point in the Domain Name System. Thus, frodo.csail.mit.edu would be the computer (or device) named "frodo" that is located within the csail.mit.edu subdomain of the mit.edu second-level domain within the .edu TLD. On the other hand, myownpersonalcomputer.com (without any further subdomains) could point directly to a particular computer.

Applications, such as Web browsers and e-mail software, use domain names as part of the Uniform Resource Identifiers (URIs; see Box 6.2) or other references that incorporate information about the protocols required for communication with the desired information source. Examples of URIs are http://www.national-academies.org and mailto:someperson@example.com. In the first example, "http" refers to the Hypertext Transfer Protocol (HTTP) used for communication with sites on the World Wide Web. In the second example, a particular user at the host identified by "example.com" is identified as the addressee for electronic mail.

In terms of information technology, the Domain Name System is implemented through a series of name servers that are located at each of the nodes in the hierarchy. Each name server contains a table that indicates the locations of the name servers immediately below it in the hierarchy and the portion of the hierarchy for which it contains the final (authoritative) network addresses. Thus, the root name servers (at the top of the hierarchy) contain the locations of each of the name servers for the top-level domains.[11] At any given node, such as .com or ibm.com, there are expected to be multiple (physical) name servers at different Internet Protocol (IP) addresses, each with identical information; the purpose of this redundancy is to share the workload to ensure adequate system performance.

When a user wants to reach www.national-academies.org, his or her computer usually sends a message to a nearby name server (usually local or operated by the user's Internet service provider), where software (called

[11]Each of these root name servers contains identical information; the purpose of having multiple root name servers is to distribute the query workload and ensure reliable operation. Specifics concerning the root name servers are discussed in Chapter 3.

a resolver), in conjunction with other name servers and resolvers, performs a series of queries to find the name server that is authoritative for www.national-academies.org. That server is then queried for the corresponding IP address(es) and returns the resulting address(es) to the user's computer.[12]

2.2.1 Simple, Mnemonic, and Deeply Hierarchical Names

As indicated above, domain names were intended to enable a more convenient and efficient way of referring to IP addresses and other information, using a simple taxonomy. The early DNS included eight generic top-level domains (gTLDs): .edu (institutions of higher education—most of which were based in the United States), .gov (U.S. government), .mil (U.S. military), .com (commerce), .net (network resources), .org (other organizations and persons[13]), .int (international treaty organizations), and .arpa (network infrastructure).[14] In addition, country-code top-level domains (ccTLDs) were created based on the two-letter code set (e.g., .gh for Ghana or .au for Australia) in the ISO 3166-1 standard.[15]

Despite the ability of the protocols and data structures themselves to accommodate any binary representation, DNS names were historically restricted to a subset of the ASCII character set.[16] Selection of that subset was driven in part by human factors considerations, including a desire to eliminate possible ambiguities in an international context. Hence, character codes that had international variations in interpretation were excluded; the underscore character (too much like a hyphen) and case distinctions (upper versus lower) were eliminated as being confusing when written or read by people; and so on. These considerations appear to be very similar to those that resulted in similarly restricted character sets being used as protocol elements in many International Telecommunication Union (ITU) and International Organization for Standardization (ISO) protocols.

---

[12]The summary provided in this paragraph is quite simplified; there are many discrete technical processes that are not articulated here. See Chapter 3 for a more detailed explanation.

[13]Initially, the .org TLD was intended as the category for organizations and individuals that did not fall into any of the other categories. Through time, many individuals increasingly viewed .org as representing the domain name space for nonprofit organizations.

[14]These definitions of the gTLDs were generally followed, although a number of exceptions existed.

[15]Thus, the determination of what constitutes a country did not need to be addressed by those who administer the DNS. See <http://www.iso.org/iso/en/prodsservices/iso3166ma/index.html>.

[16]This subset, which derives primarily from the original HOSTS.TXT naming rules, includes the 10 Arabic digits, the 26 letters of the English alphabet, and the hyphen.

Another initial assumption behind the design of the DNS was that there would be relatively many physical hosts for each second-level domain name and, more generally, that the system would be deeply hierarchical, with most systems (and names) at the third level or below. Some domains—those of most universities and some large corporations and the country code for the United States (.us)—follow this model, at least in its original design, but most do not[17] (see Chapter 3 for discussion). However, experience through mid-year 2005 has shown that the DNS is robust enough—given contemporary machines as servers and current bandwidth norms—to operate reasonably well even though the design assumption of a deep hierarchy is not satisfied. Nonetheless, it is still useful to remember that the system could have been designed to work with a flat structure (e.g., the huge, flat structure under .com comprising tens of millions of names) rather than a deeply hierarchical one. For example, based on an assumption of a flat structure at the TLD level, one would probably not wish to assign specific operational responsibility by TLD (as is the case currently). Instead, it might have made more sense to design the system as one database that is replicated on a limited number of servers (to share the workload and coordinate updates in a manageable way).

2.2.2 Experimental Features

The DNS specification included a number of experimental features, intended to enhance the services that the DNS could provide beyond simple name-to-address lookup. Several of these features were intended to facilitate improved support of electronic mail. Several resource records[18] were intended to improve e-mail routing, helping to ensure that e-mail sent to a particular host took a reliable route to that host. The DNS also included features intended to support e-mail lists and aliases. The idea was to make it easier to maintain mailing lists and to forward mail when someone's e-mail address changed. In addition, the DNS contained a feature to track "well-known services." The purpose of this feature was to provide a list of services (e-mail, File Transfer Protocol, Web) that are

[17]The .us country code TLD was designed originally to use geographical and political jurisdictions as subdomains. As one moves to the left, each subdomain represents a subset of the area represented by the immediately preceding name. For example, in the name "www.cnri.reston.va.us," "va" represents the state of Virginia within the United States, "reston" represents a city within Virginia, and "cnri" represents an organization in the city of Reston.

[18]Each table within the domain name tree hierarchy contains resource records, which are composed of fields such as the type (i.e., does this record correspond to a host address, an authoritative name server, or something else) and time to live (i.e., for what period of time may this record be cached before the source of the information should be consulted again?). See Box 3.2 for a detailed discussion of resource records.

available from a host. Most of the experimental features have not been adopted for general use. Indeed, the original set of e-mail-related record types were deprecated in favor of a newer model (see Section 2.3.3) and the "well-known services" record was determined to be unworkable.

2.3 DEPLOYING THE DOMAIN NAME SYSTEM

Whereas the design of the DNS looked reasonable on paper, several limitations of the new system, as with any new system, did not become apparent until initial deployment began. Addressing these limitations caused a delay in the full implementation of the DNS. The plan called for a switchover to the DNS in September 1984, but full conversion did not take place until 1987. Some of the delay was attributable to reconciling naming conflicts.[19] A large part of the delay derived from a far longer than expected period to implement and debug the DNS, of which a significant portion derived from simple procrastination—just not getting around to installing and implementing the DNS. Another delay included the difficulty of retrofitting the DNS into old operating systems that were no longer actively maintained.

2.3.1 Caching

The design of the DNS allows for the existence of caches. These are local data storage or memory that can significantly reduce the amount of network traffic associated with repeated successful queries for the same data by providing access to the data in servers closer to the end user than the authoritative name server.[20] The data in these caches need to be refreshed at regular intervals[21] to ensure that the cached data are valid. In the initial version of the DNS specification, several timing parameters had time-to-live limits of approximately 18 hours. It quickly became apparent, however, that in many cases data changed slowly, and so updating caches every 18 hours or so was unnecessary. As a consequence, the protocol specification was changed to increase the allowed range of these timing parameters; several other protocol parameters were also given expanded ranges, based on the theory that one incompatible protocol change early on would be better than a series of such changes. This happened early

[19]Most or all of these conflicts were internal ones—for example, subunits of a university trying to obtain the same domain name as the university.

[20]An additional potential benefit from the use of caches is an improvement in user response time.

[21]As defined in the time-to-live field in the resource records. See Chapter 3.

enough that there was no serious difficulty in deploying upgraded software.

In its original design, the DNS did not have a corresponding mechanism for reducing the network traffic associated with repeated unsuccessful queries (i.e., queries for which no entry in the relevant authoritative table is found). Within a few years of the initial implementation of the DNS, it became apparent that such a mechanism would be beneficial, given the number of identical queries that are unsuccessful. A proposed mechanism for negative response caching was developed, and the data necessary to support it were added to the protocol in a way that did not affect software based on earlier versions of the protocol, but the full deployment of the new mechanism was slow. The name server side of the new mechanism was very simple and was deployed fairly quickly, but initial support for the client (user) side of the negative caching mechanism was limited to a few implementations and was not adopted more generally until much later. The lack of widespread and correct client-side support for negative caching is a problem that still persists.[22]

2.3.2 Lookup Timeouts

The biggest single difficulty in the transition from HOSTS.TXT to the DNS, however, was not due to any specific shortcoming of the DNS. Rather, it was attributable to the fundamental change in the nature of the lookup mechanism. In the HOSTS.TXT world, any particular host lookup operation would either succeed or fail immediately—the HOSTS.TXT file is located on the user's system; it is not dependent on Internet connectivity at the moment of lookup. The DNS added a third possible outcome to any lookup operation: a timeout attributable to any of a number of possible temporary failure conditions (e.g., the required name server is down, so one does not know whether the particular name is indeed in the table or not). The occurrence of a timeout indicates neither success nor failure; it is the equivalent of asking a yes or no question and being told "ask again later." Many of the network programs that predated the DNS simply could not handle this third possibility and had to be rewritten. While

---

[22]Users derive benefits from the implementation of negative caching, namely faster response times. The larger system also derives benefits through the reduced load of invalid queries. However, there are costs associated with the implementation and maintenance of negative caching. For a given user, if the estimated benefit deriving from faster response times is deemed to be worth less than the costs associated with negative caching, then the user is not likely to implement negative caching, even though the total benefits (which include the reduced load of invalid queries on the larger system) may exceed these costs. This phenomenon is explained under the rubric of what economists refer to as externalities.

this was something of a problem for programs intended to be run directly by a user (e.g., one then-popular e-mail client checked the host name of every recipient during composition), it was a far more serious problem for programs that ran unattended, such as mail transfer agents. These programs had to be rewritten to handle DNS timeout errors in the same way as they would handle any other form of connection failure. Conceptually, this was simple enough, but it took several years to actually track down and fix all the places in all the programs that made implicit assumptions about the host lookup mechanism. Toward the end of this period, the Internet had entered an era of periodic "congestion collapses" that eventually led to a fundamental improvement in certain algorithms used in the Internet infrastructure. During each of these congestion collapses, DNS lookups (along with all other forms of Internet traffic) frequently timed out, which made it much more obvious which applications still needed to be converted to handle timeouts properly. To this day, however, correct handling of the possibility of timeouts during a DNS lookup represents an issue in application design.

2.3.3 Convergence in Electronic Mail Systems

In the mid-1980s, the Internet was one of the major data networks.[23] Although data could not move from one network to the next, e-mail was able to flow—through carefully designed e-mail gateways—between the networks. Some of the busiest computers on each network were the machines whose job it was to relay e-mail from one network to the next.[24] Unfortunately, the system of gateways required users to route their e-mail by explicitly using the e-mail address. For instance, to send e-mail over the Internet to a colleague at Hewlett Packard Laboratories on the Computer Science Network (CSNET), one had to address the e-mail to colleague%hplabs.csnet@relay.cs.net. This complex syntax says that the Internet should deliver the e-mail to relay.cs.net and then send the message on to the appropriate address on cs.net.[25] Thus, some people had

[23]These major data networks included BITNET, Internet, CSNET, UUCP, and Fidonet. See John S. Quarterman, *The Matrix: Computer Networks and Conferencing Systems Worldwide*, Digital Press, Bedford, Mass., 1990; and Donnalyn Frey, Buck Adams, and Rick Adams, *!%@: A Directory of Electronic Mail Addressing and Networks*, O'Reilly and Associates, Sebastopol, Calif., 1991.

[24]For instance, relay.cs.net and seismo.css.gov, the e-mail gateways between the Internet and the Computer Science Network, and an important one of those between the Internet and the Unix-to-Unix network, respectively, were typically the top two hosts (in terms of traffic sent or received) on the ARPANET in the mid-1980s.

[25]In some instances, the messages were even messier; someone on the Unix-to-Unix network (UUCP) might have to write an address such as <ihnp4!seismo!colleague%hplabs.csnet@relay.cs.net> to send an e-mail.

one e-mail box yet had business cards listing three or four different ways to send e-mail to them. There were ample opportunities for confusion and mis-routed e-mail.[26]

The original DNS specification tried to address this problem by making it possible to send e-mail to names that were not connected to the Internet. For instance, if the Example Company was on the UUCP network, but wanted to exchange e-mail over the Internet, it could register Example.com and place an entry in the DNS directing that all e-mail to names ending Example.com should be forwarded to the UUCP e-mail gateway, which would know to forward the e-mail to the Example Company's e-mail hub.

Unfortunately, the original DNS scheme for e-mail routing was not up to the task. It did not handle certain types of e-mail routing well, and, worse, it could cause e-mail errors that resulted in lost e-mail.

The result was a new scheme using Mail eXchangers (MXs) so that, for any domain name, the DNS would store a preferentially ordered list of hosts that would handle e-mail for that name. The rule is to start with the most preferred host in the list and work down the list until a host is found that will accept the e-mail.[27] This simple rule could be combined with the DNS facility for wildcarding (following rules that state that all names ending in a particular domain, or that a particular subset of names ending in a name, should all get the same response)[28] to create e-mail routing for almost any desirable situation. In particular, it was possible to address e-

[26]For instance, at Princeton University there was a weekly tape swap between the operators of princeton.bitnet and princeton.csnet—two machines on different networks that routinely got e-mail accidentally intended for the other.

[27]See Craig Partridge, "Mail Routing and the Domain Name System," RFC 974, January 1986, available at <http://www.rfc-editor.org>.

[28]For example, in the early days of e-mail connectivity to much of Africa, e-mail hubs were set up inside the countries, serving all users there. These hubs did not have direct Internet connectivity to the rest of the world but were typically served through occasional dial-up connections that, in turn, usually used non-TCP/IP connections. To facilitate this arrangement, the DNS was set up so that all traffic for, say, South Africa (the .za ccTLD), regardless of the full domain name, would be routed to a mail-receiving system in the United States. That system would then open an international dial-up connection at regular intervals and transfer the accumulated e-mail over it. The e-mail hub in South Africa would then distribute the e-mail to other hubs within the country, often using the originally specified domain as an indication of the appropriate domestic server. This model had the added advantage that, when permanent connectivity became available, user and institutional e-mail addresses and domain names did not have to change—users just saw a dramatic improvement in service and turnaround time. More information on the history of this strategy may be found at <http://www.nsrc.org/> and in John C. Klensin and Randy Bush, "Expanding International E-mail Connectivity: Another Look," *Connexions—The Interoperability Report* 7(8):25-29, 1993, available at <http://www.nsrc.org/articles/930600.connexions>.

mail to domains that were off the Internet, or domains that were partly on and partly off the Internet.

The development of a dependable and highly flexible mechanism for routing Internet e-mail had two almost immediate consequences. First, all the other major e-mail networks converted to using domain names or names that looked like domain names.[29] These other networks all had non-hierarchical (i.e., flat) name spaces, with many of the same scaling problems that were experienced with HOSTS.TXT, and were looking for a workable hierarchical name space. Once it was shown that the DNS would work for e-mail, it was simpler for companies to adopt domain names and, in some cases, adapt the DNS to run on their networks rather than to devise their own naming scheme. Thus, within a matter of 18 months to 2 years, the Babel of e-mail addresses was simplified almost everywhere in the world to user@domain-name. A second effect was that companies could now change networks without changing their host names and e-mail addresses, providing incentives for some companies to make the switch to the Internet. Indeed, by 1990, almost all the networks that had offered services comparable to the Internet were either gone or going out of business.[30] Around the same time, companies began to encourage their employees to put e-mail addresses on business cards (it had often been discouraged because, as previously noted, e-mail addresses were so complicated). Domain names thereafter became a (small) part of everyday business.

There were also some longer-term effects. First, it was very clear that the DNS could provide names for things that were not hosts. For instance, almost every organization soon made it possible to send e-mail to someperson@example.com, even though there was no actual machine named example.com, but rather a collection of servers (e.g., mailserver1.example.com, mailserver2.example.com, and so on) that handled e-mail for the example.com domain. The DNS began to be viewed as a general naming system. Second, because almost all naming

[29]For convenience and as a transition strategy, many sites chose to treat, for example, "BITNET" and "UUCP" as if they were top-level domain names, mapping those names through the DNS or other facilities into gateway paths. So a generation of users believed that, for example, smith@mitvmb.bitnet was an Internet domain name when, in fact, it was mapped to smith%mitvmb.bitnet@mitvma.mit.edu, where the latter was a gateway between the Internet and BITNET. The full use of MX records, so that the same user could be addressed as smith@mitvmb.mit.edu, came along only somewhat later.

[30]In economics, network effects (or, alternatively, positive network externalities) explain the rationale for the convergence to Internet-based e-mail: The value of a network to a user increases as more users join the same network, or other networks that are compatible with it. See, for example, Jean Tirole, *The Theory of Industrial Organization*, MIT Press, Cambridge, Mass., and London, 1988, pp. 404-409.

systems had been designed primarily to support e-mail, and domain names had won the battle for how e-mail was done, the other naming systems diminished in importance and use, leaving the DNS as the only widely available naming system. The result was that the DNS was viewed as a general service, albeit an imperfect one: but even if imperfect, it was the only naming system that was widely available, and thus it became the one of choice.

2.3.4 The Whois Database

The Whois database was developed in the 1970s to track authorized ARPANET users and, in particular, those users that could request addresses on the network. For each host or domain name, the information in the Whois database was supposed to include the contact information (such as the contact person's name, organization, street address, electronic mail address, and phone number) of those with responsibility for the host or domain name; additional information could also be stored and accessed. From a technical design and operational viewpoint, the Whois database is independent of either the HOSTS.TXT file or the DNS.[31] For a while, the Whois database, maintained by the Network Information Center (NIC), served as a de facto white pages directory of ARPANET users. Beyond the online database, the NIC printed a phone book of everyone listed in the Whois database about once a year until 1982.

Around the time of the last NIC phone book, the Whois database was rapidly losing its value as a white pages directory because many new Internet users were not being included in the database. However, at the same time, the Whois database was becoming increasingly important for network operations because the NIC (which at the time also managed the allocation of IP addresses) would not give out an IP address, a host name, or a domain name to anyone who did not have a Whois entry. Furthermore, the NIC put all address and name registrations into the Whois database. So, given a host name or address, any user on the network could query the database to learn who had control of that host name or address. Thus, if a network operator noticed (or had a user complain) that a domain name suddenly could not be looked up, or that a particular network appeared to be unreachable, the operator could query the Whois database and find out whom to call about the issue.

---

[31]"Whois" represents the name of the implemented system/database as well as the name of the underlying protocol. This caused, and continues to cause, some confusion, since several universities and enterprises maintained local "white pages" and similar services, which had nothing to do with the central databases, that were accessed using the Whois protocol.

By the late 1980s, problems began to develop with the Whois database. The first problem, which proved easy to solve, was that in many cases the formal institutional contact for the name or address was a corporate or university officer or administrator and was not the network operations person who actually managed the network or domain name server. The NIC resolved this problem by updating the database to keep track of both the administrative and operational contact for each address and domain. The second problem, which was not so easy to solve, was trying to keep the Whois data current—a problem that existed even before the explosive growth of the Internet and demands on the DNS in the 1990s.[32]

2.3.5 The DNS as a Production System

By 1990, the DNS was a production system and deeply ingrained in the Internet and its culture.[33] The use of HOSTS.TXT was declining rapidly. But the move to a production system was not easy: Deploying the DNS in the 1980s required several years of debugging and resolving various issues. Timeouts and negative caching remain, to some extent, open issues in 2005.

Several lessons are apparent from the process of developing and deploying the DNS. A good new design that solves important problems can catch on, but it will take time for solid implementations to be developed. And even if a new design offers significant advantages, adoption will take time. Even when the Internet was comparatively small, switches from HOSTS.TXT to DNS or from e-mail Babel to uniform naming took a significant amount of time. Given the decentralized nature of the Internet, network service providers, hardware and software vendors, end users, or others can inhibit worthwhile technical advances from being implemented through mere procrastination or a deliberate decision that the implementation of a particular software upgrade is simply not sufficiently beneficial to them. Given the much larger scale and scope of the DNS and the embedded base of software two decades later, successful implementation of any proposed new system or major changes to the existing DNS may prove difficult.[34]

---

[32]The history of the Whois database through the 1990s can be found in Section 2.5.3.

[33]By the late 1980s, the Internet was in fact an operational network and not only a subject of research and, as such, increasingly fell outside DARPA's research mission. At this time, DARPA was working with other federal agencies, notably the National Science Foundation, to hand off the infrastructure it had created.

[34]See Tirole, *The Theory of Industrial Organization*, 1988, pp. 406-409, for a brief discussion of the kinds of coordination and strategic issues that can arise in a network like the DNS.

2.4 CONTINUING GROWTH AND EVOLUTION OF THE INTERNET AS A TECHNICAL INFRASTRUCTURE

The increasing popularity of personal computers changed the basic model of computing in most organizations from a model based on central computing using mainframes or minicomputers with terminals to one based on personal computers connected in local area networks, which in turn were connected to central resources (i.e., the client/server model of computing). The adoption of the personal computer by consumers (which is correlated with the improving price/performance of computers and, in particular, increasing modem speeds at affordable prices) provided the household infrastructure for supporting widespread dial-in access to the Internet by the mid-1990s in the United States.[35]

To function on the Internet, a computer needs to have some basic information, such as its IP address, the IP address of at least one router,[36] and the IP addresses of a few critical services.[37] In the world of a relatively small number of large mainframes or minicomputers, such information was entered manually on each new computer when installed and, once configured, rarely changed. In such a world, IP addresses functioned as de facto stable identifiers, with the DNS (or its HOSTS.TXT predecessor) representing a convenience, not a necessity.[38]

However, as the number of computers increased sharply, such a custom approach became increasingly impractical. Thus, a mechanism to

---

[35]According to the Current Population Survey (conducted by the U.S. Census Bureau), personal computer adoption in the United States continued to increase throughout the 1990s and demonstrated a 5-fold increase from 1984, the first year data was collected on computer ownership to the year 2000. By the year 2000, 51 percent, or 54 million households, had access to at least one computer at home, up from 36.6 percent in 1997. The percentage of households with Internet access more than doubled between these years, from 18 percent in 1997 to 41.5 percent, or 42 million households, by the year 2000. Computer access and Internet access were becoming synonymous: more than four in five households with computer access also had Internet access. For the full report, see Eric C. Newburger, "Home Computers and Internet Use in the United States: August 2000," *Current Population Reports*, U.S. Department of Commerce, U.S. Census Bureau, Washington, D.C., September 2001, available at <http://www.census.gov/prod/2001pubs/p23-207.pdf>.

[36]A router is a device that determines the next Internet Protocol (IP) network point to which a data packet should be forwarded toward its destination. The router is connected to at least two networks and determines which way to send each packet based on its current understanding of the state of the networks to which it is connected. Routers create or maintain a table of the available routes and use this information to determine the best route for a given data packet.

[37]Examples include the address of an e-mail server (because most computers do not operate their own mail server) and the address of a DNS resolver (explained in Chapter 3).

[38]Indeed, the IP addresses of certain important servers were well known to system administrators.

automate this startup process was developed. One approach is contained within the Bootstrap Protocol (BOOTP), a very simple protocol that enabled a computer to ask a local central server for and receive a number of critical parameters. BOOTP and other protocols of a similar type shared one important characteristic: Each protocol had a mechanism to allocate IP addresses to computers, but did not have any mechanism to reclaim IP addresses when they were no longer needed. In the 1980s, this was not a problem because IP addresses were plentiful. However, by the early 1990s IP addresses, which had once seemed to be a nearly inexhaustible resource, were starting to look like a scarce resource that required conservation, a consequence of the tremendous growth of the Internet. Protocols to support the "leasing" or temporary assignment of IP addresses were developed,[39] such as the Dynamic Host Configuration Protocol (DHCP)—a direct successor of BOOTP—or the Point-to-Point Protocol (PPP).[40] An important reason for the development of these protocols was to support system and local area network (LAN) management and auto-configuration, but the timing was fortuitous inasmuch as these protocols could also help with the conservation of IP addresses.

The spread of network address translators (NATs)—in part, a response to the increased difficulty of obtaining large blocks of IP addresses in the latter half of the 1990s—further degraded the usability of IP addresses as stable identifiers. The basic function of a NAT is to rewrite IP addresses in the data that it forwards. NATs map the set of IP addresses for external traffic (i.e., the IP addresses that are visible to the world) to a set of IP addresses for internal traffic (e.g., an organization's LAN); thus, an organization can have many more internal IP addresses than external ones. The use of NATs distorts the one-to-one mapping between Internet hosts and IP addresses that many applications assumed in their design—thus, any application that depends on IP addresses is at risk when its traffic goes through a NAT.[41]

As a result of these changes, IP addresses have become much less useful as stable identifiers than they once were. In the case of most appli-

---

[39]After the lease expires, ownership of the address reverts back to the server that issued the address. The protocol includes mechanisms for lease renewal, and lease times can be quite long at the discretion of the DHCP server administrator. These "leases" did not include a financial component—"temporary assignment" is perhaps a more accurate characterization.

[40]PPP supports address assignment for dial-up networking by assigning IP addresses to ports on access servers. Users connect to the access server and are allocated to a port, which has an IP address assigned to it. Thus, users "lease" the assigned IP address for the duration of their session.

[41]In particular, peer-to-peer applications and security protocols that require different public addresses for each host become much more difficult to deploy.

cation protocols, the "obvious" answer has been to replace the use of IP addresses with DNS names wherever possible. Thus, over the last decade, applications have come to rely on DNS names very heavily as stable identifiers in place of IP addresses.

Another departure from transparent architecture[42] came with the introduction of packet-filtering routers, one of the simplest kinds of firewalls.[43] A number of organizations introduced such firewalls beginning in the late 1980s with the intent to defend their sites against various real and perceived threats. The much-publicized Morris worm[44] further raised the profile of network security and provided network administrators with an additional motivation to install firewalls (thereby further inhibiting transparency in the network architecture).[45]

As network security attracted increasing attention, some focus was directed to the DNS itself. DNS security emerged as an issue in the form of a proposed addition of a cryptographic signature mechanism to the DNS data.[46] Such a mechanism would help ensure the integrity of the DNS data communicated to the end user. The original DNS design did not include a mechanism to ensure that a name lookup was an accurate representation of the information provided by the entity responsible for the information. DNS information was assumed to be accurate as the result of general notions of network cooperation and interoperation (i.e., based on the presumption that nobody would deliberately attempt to

---

[42]In this context, a transparent network is one that does not interfere with arbitrary communication between end points.

[43]Packet-filtering routers attempt to block certain types of data from entering or leaving a network.

[44]In 1988, a student at Cornell University, Robert T. Morris, wrote a program that would connect to another computer, find and use one of several vulnerabilities to copy itself to that second computer, and begin to run the copy of itself at the new location. Both the original code and the copy would then repeat these actions in a theoretically infinite loop to other computers on the ARPANET. The worm used so many system resources that the attacked computers could no longer function, and, as a result, 10 percent of the U.S. computers connected to the ARPANET effectively stopped at about the same time. From "Security of the Internet," available at <http://www.cert.org/encyc_article/tocencyc.html>. Also published in *The Froehlich/Kent Encyclopedia of Telecommunications*, Vol. 15, Marcel Dekker, New York, 1997, pp. 231-255.

[45]The relative value of firewalls in advancing network security can be debated, and such discussions can be found elsewhere; see, for example, Fred B. Schneider, editor, Computer Science and Telecommunications Board, National Research Council, *Trust in Cyberspace*, National Academy Press, Washington, D.C., 1999.

[46]Digital signatures do not provide foolproof security, but they can demonstrate that the holder of the corresponding private cryptographic key (i.e., a secret password) produced the data of interest. This is more or less like trusting a document that bears a particular seal—one must independently make a determination that an authorized person had possession of the seal when it was used and that the seal is legitimate but, if both of those conditions are met, it provides some assurance of the authenticity of the document.

tamper with DNS information). Work on DNS Security Extensions (DNSSEC) started in the early 1990s and continues more than a decade later.[47] See Chapter 4 for further discussion of DNSSEC and DNS security in general.

2.5 ECONOMIC AND SOCIAL VALUE OF DOMAIN NAMES

The nature of the growth in the Internet during the 1990s was qualitatively different from the growth in the 1980s. Most of the new Internet users in the 1990s were non-technical people who were not associated with academic institutions or the computer and communications industry. Instead, these new users represented a cross section of society that typically accessed the Internet from their places of employment, through dial-up connections from their homes, and by gaining access through libraries, schools, and community organizations.

These new users and the organizations that supported them (such as Internet service providers, electronic commerce companies, non-profit information services, and so on.) were primarily interested in how the Internet in general, and Internet navigation and the Domain Name System in particular (especially using the World Wide Web and e-mail), could advance and support personal and business goals—that is, they were not very interested in the technology per se. Consequently, increasing effort was directed to support these non-technical goals, and thus, it is not surprising that economic value, social value, and globalization emerged as major forces influencing the DNS and Internet navigation in the 1990s.

2.5.1 Demand for Domain Names and Emergence of a Market[48]

The rapid growth of the World Wide Web stimulated interest in and the demand for domain names because Web addresses (Uniform Resource Locators; URLs [see Box 6.2])[49] incorporate domain names at the top of their naming hierarchy. One of the early major uses of the Web that appealed to a wide range of the new users—and helped to continue attracting additional new users to the Web—was electronic commerce. The .com generic top-level domain (gTLD) became a kind of directory service for companies and their products and services. If a consumer wanted to find

---

[47]For further information on the historical progression of DNSSEC, see Miek Gieben, "A Short History of DNSSEC," April 19, 2004, available at <http://www.nlnetlabs.nl/dnssec/history.html>.

[48]A significant portion of this subsection was derived from Milton L. Mueller, *Ruling the Root: Internet Governance and the Taming of Cyberspace*, MIT Press, Cambridge, Mass., and London, 2002.

[49]Examples of URLs include <http://www.whitehouse.gov> or <http://www.un.org>.

the Web site for a company, the consumer would often be able to guess the URL by entering part or all of the company's name followed by .com in the browser command line; often, the desired site would be located. This practice was further encouraged by the use of second-level domain names in advertisements and by the naming of companies by their second-level domain name (e.g., priceline.com). Even if the user's initial guess(es) did not work, users would often then try the company's name followed by .net or .org, or variations of the company's name in combination with one of these gTLDs, such as ibmcomputers.net.[50]

It did not take users long to discover that shorter, shallower, URLs were easier to guess, use, remember, and advertise than longer ones. The shortest URL of all was based solely on a domain name. Thus, if one wanted to post a distinct set of resources on the Web, or create an identity for an organization, product, or idea, it often made sense to register a separate domain name for it rather than create a new directory under a single domain name. Hypothesizing that customers would look for products and services by guessing at a similar domain name, companies like the Procter & Gamble Company, for example, registered pampers.com and used that as a URL (namely, <http://www.pampers.com>), which also had the advantage of being much easier to communicate to users, and for users to remember, than, say, <http://www.pampers.procterandgamble.com>. These different domain names would be used even if all the information resided on a single computer. In short, domain names began to refer to products or services rather than just network resources (e.g., host names).[51]

Before the rise of the Web, the largest concentration of domain name registrations was under the .edu TLD (as of March 1993). The Internet's rapid growth after 1993, however, radically altered the distribution of domain names across TLDs; until at least 1997, .com attracted the large majority of new domain name registrations.[52] Most of the users rushing to take

---

[50]Sometime in 1996 or 1997, browser manufacturers made .com the default value for any names typed directly into the browser command line. That is, whenever a user typed <name> without a top-level domain into the command line, the browser automatically directed the user to www.<name>.com. Making .com the default value for all browser entries reinforced the value of .com registrations relative to other TLDs. In effect, a .com domain name functioned as a global keyword, and the possession of a common, simple word in the .com space was sure to generate significant traffic from Web browsers. This explains, to some degree, why some domain names sold for hundreds of thousands or even millions of dollars. As noted in Section 1.2, footnote 9, browsers no longer operate in this way.

[51]Generic words were also registered (e.g., cough.com was registered by Vicks).

[52]See <http://web.archive.org/web/20020816085435/www.wia.org/pub/timeline.txt>. Initiatives to use the Internet for commercial purposes (including R&D within companies) before the rise of the Web led to an increase in .com registrations. And with wide use of the Web came registrations of multiple domain names to single companies, a practice that had been discouraged in the past.

advantage of the Web were businesses, and .com was the only explicitly commercial top-level domain. Furthermore, the U.S.-based InterNIC operated the only unrestricted, large-scale registry (supporting .com and other gTLDs). Most country-code registries at this time were slow, or expensive, or followed restrictive policies and considered a domain name a privilege rather than a commercial service.[53] Indeed, in some of the countries with restrictive country-code registries, such as Japan and France, more businesses registered in .com than under their own ccTLD. The available statistics provide the basis for estimating that roughly 75 percent of the world's domain name registrations resided in .com at the end of 1996.[54] Thus, the .com TLD became the dominant place for domain name registration worldwide in the mid-1990s, which by the late 1990s became reflected in popular culture through phrases such as a "dot-com company" (or simply a "dot-com") or "dot-com economy."

Interest in domain names extended beyond the for-profit sector. The visibility of governmental entities and non-profit organizations also became increasingly tied to domain names as the Web became a key mechanism for providing information and services to the public and their constituencies. Moreover, individuals also wanted their own domain name as the identifier for their personal information posted on the Web or for a myriad of other purposes (e.g., establishing fan sites[55]). Opportunistic companies capitalized on (and perhaps helped to create) this demand by developing services so that users could register a domain name and obtain support for establishing and maintaining a Web page as an integrated service for a monthly or annual fee.

Domain names also became involved in electoral politics and social commentary. Political campaigns established Web sites with descriptive domain names in the URLs such as <http://www.algore2000.com> or <http://www.georgewbush.com>[56] to provide access to information

---

[53]In February 1996, when the InterNIC had about a quarter of a million second-level registrations, Germany (.de) had only 9000 total registrations, and Great Britain (.uk) had only 4000. Japan, Canada, Australia, and other major leading participants in the Internet had numbers comparable to the United Kingdom's. However, some countries (e.g., the United Kingdom) have restrictive policies with respect to registering in the second-level domain so that most entities actually have to register in the third-level domain (e.g., sothebys.co.uk) that would instead be a second-level domain registration in other TLDs (e.g., sothebys.com).

[54]InterNIC gTLD registrations accounted for an estimated 85 percent of all domain name registrations worldwide, and .com accounted for 88.6 percent of all InterNIC gTLD registrations. (About 62 percent of all registered domains worldwide resided in .com in 2002.)

[55]See, for example, <http://www.juliaroberts.de>, a fan site and tribute to the actress Julia Roberts that is based in Germany; accessed on April 16, 2005.

[56]Note that campaign information was not available at the Al Gore site as of April 16, 2005.

about their respective candidates, to organize volunteers, and to solicit contributions. Web sites were also created to critique or parody virtually anything, from the practices of certain companies or their products or services to various social and political causes. A common practice was to register a domain name that included the name of interest followed by "sucks," or something similar, and to associate that domain name with a Web site that criticized the entity in question. In addition to motivating legal actions to try to prevent the use of domain names in this fashion, this practice caused many companies to pre-emptively register these types of domain names for themselves.[57]

Therefore, for various reasons, the demand for domain names increased tremendously during the 1990s.[58] Further fueling the demand was aggressive marketing by companies that register domain names and provide related services, efforts by IT companies more generally that played up domain names (especially .com names) in their larger marketing campaigns, and the popular and technical press, which devoted a lot of attention to anything related to domain names.

The increasing demand for domain names was attributed to interest in facilitating Internet navigation as well as to the value of domain names irrespective of their functional utility on the Internet (e.g., placing a domain name on posters in a subway station as a part of a marketing campaign). Thus, the real value of certain domain names in the rapidly growing and commercializing Web and Internet was far greater than the price of setting up a domain name (which was on the order of $50 at the retail level).[59] The predictable consequence was the development of an aftermarket for certain domain names. In 1996, tv.com sold for $15,000 and in 1997, business.com changed hands for $150,000.[60] Not surprisingly, speculation in the registration of domain names took place: An individual or firm would register domain names (often very many) with the intent of reselling them to others for a premium. Such speculators would not only register generic or descriptive names (e.g., "business," "fever," and so on) with the hope of appealing to multiple pro-

[57]However, this was a difficult proposition, considering the nearly limitless variations of less-flattering names that can be devised. See further discussion in the next section.

[58]The growth in the registration of domain names was phenomenal. For example, in September 1995, there were approximately 120,000 registered domain names. By May 1998, 2 million domain names were registered. See "Fact Sheet: NSF and Domain Names," National Science Foundation, Arlington, Va.

[59]Domain names are registered through and maintained by registrars; see Chapter 3 for an extended discussion.

[60]Business.com was resold for $7.5 million in 1999. With some irony, the committee observes that www.business.com links to "The Business Search Engine" (as of March 27, 2004), a "comprehensive business directory."

spective purchasers, but would also register domain names incorporating the trademarks of third parties with the hope that the corresponding trademark owner would purchase the domain name from the speculator as well. See Box 2.1 for further discussion on the value of domain names.

An industry emerged to provide services related to the transfer and assignment of domain names and related services.[61] The pressure for new TLDs led to the conversion of some country codes to quasi-generic TLDs. For example, the marketing of .cc (a country-code TLD created to represent the Cocos Islands but later marketed as a de facto gTLD) further increased the variety and value of certain domain names. However, true additional gTLDs did not materialize in the 1990s (despite the intense arguments and efforts made by some individuals and organizations), which helped to solidify the dominance of the then-extant TLDs, especially of .com.[62]

2.5.2 The Rise of Conflicts Over Domain Names

As the number of domain name registrations exploded, conflicts developed over the right to register particular names at the second level of many of the TLDs.[63] The basis for most of these conflicts derived from the unique naming associated with the DNS. The DNS does not have the capability to incorporate context into domain names, so each domain name must be unique worldwide and then in turn, a Web site at that domain name can then be accessed throughout the world.[64] The consequence is that it is significantly harder to pick a domain name that is both unused and memorable.

Claims to rights to domain names can be based on a number of different legal, political, economic, ethical, or cultural criteria. A common prob-

---

[61]Registrars, and the industry surrounding registrars and allied services, are discussed in detail in Chapters 3 and 4.

[62]Discussion of the gTLDs added in the early 2000s (e.g., .info) and general discussion of the issues involved with adding new gTLDs can be found in Chapters 3 and 4.

[63]"Rights to names" refers to claims to exclusive or privileged use of an identifier based on the meaning or economic value of the name.

[64]The mythical (or perhaps real) Joe's Pizza illustrates the point. The DNS can support only one www.joespizza.com worldwide, but in the physical world, people can usually distinguish among the (presumably) multiple Joe's Pizza restaurants around the world. If a person is located in the center of a city and asks a taxi driver to take her to Joe's Pizza, it is presumed that she wishes to travel to a restaurant within a few miles, not a Joe's Pizza located in a city 2000 miles away. Although the requestor does not state this context explicitly, it is assumed in the conversation. As of February 4, 2005, joespizza.com was registered by BuyDomains.com and offered for resale at a minimum price of $1488.

BOX 2.1 The Value of Domain Names

Semantic Value

Economic value often arises when names have some semantic distinction—a meaning—and are visible in a public arena. The value of meaningful names will differ from nil to very high depending on the meaning and the potential application. Examples include sex.com and gardentips.com.

Mnemonic Value

In many contexts, it can be important for a name or identifier to be easily remembered. If users cannot remember the name, or it is too long or complicated to reproduce, the object will not be found. Memorability, and in some cases guessability, facilitates more incoming traffic and more business and, therefore, gives rise to economic value. One example is gm.com (i.e., a second-level domain name for the General Motors Corporation).

Personal Value

Even when there is no apparent commercial consequence, the human desire to make a statement and assert an identity can give economic value to identifiers in a public name. Someone with a high regard for himself might want the domain name i-am-the-best.com.[1]

Stability Value

Users can accumulate equity in a particular identifier, which becomes closely associated with them and expensive to change. Changing a telephone number or e-mail address that has been used for many years can be burdensome because of the large number of personal contacts and records that contain the number. Thus, equity in an identifier raises switching costs for consumers, making them more likely to stay with the provider of that identifier.

Pure Scarcity Value

Meaningless identifiers, such as bank account numbers, function economically as an undifferentiated resource pool. They may possess economic value by virtue of their scarcity, but no one cares which particular identifier he or she gets. In the DNS, there are plenty of possible names (accepting that random strings of letters and digits can produce domain names (e.g., akwoeics8320dsdfa0867sdfad02c.org); there is scarcity of some desired names, with desirability defined by one of the reasons above (e.g., only a small subset of all possible domain names have semantic value).

[1]As of March 27, 2004, this domain name was not registered.

lem raised by all such claims is that any reasonable attempt at resolution must balance the value of avoiding confusion or preventing illegal or otherwise undesired appropriation of identity against the value of free expression, open communication, and fair use. Whenever semantics and economics enter the picture, however, society and all of its conflicts come along with them. The resultant conflicts over who has rights to use particular domain names has enmeshed and continues to enmesh apparently technical naming processes in economic, public policy, and legal issues.[65]

Trademark Conflicts

In the commercial world, trademark law provides one of the oldest, most widely recognized and well-developed regimes for recognizing and protecting exclusivities in the use of source identifiers of goods or services within specific fields and territories. Trademark laws developed, in part, to protect consumers against various forms of fraud, deception, or confusion that might result from the ways in which products and services are identified. By giving producers an exclusive right in an identifier, trademarks reduce consumer search costs and channel the benefits of developing a good reputation to the producer responsible for the reputation. Trademark protection is not, however, intended to give firms ownership of common words alone, to prevent non-commercial or fair use, or to inhibit public discussion of companies, products, and services involving direct references to the mark.

The great emphasis placed on second-level domain names created a problem for some trademark holders, especially for those that held trademarks that were well known in the United States or worldwide. Trademark rights (which are traditionally accorded on a country by country basis) generally arise through use of a trademarkable name, logo, color, sound, or other feature, in association with the marketing and sale of particular types or classes of goods and services in commerce. Some coun-

---

[65] In his paper "External Issues in DNS Scalability," Paul Vixie argues for eliminating the disputes associated with domain names by eliminating all meaningful top-level domains and replacing them with meaningless alphanumeric identifiers. See conference paper, November 11, 1995, available at <http://www.ksg.harvard.edu/iip/GIIconf/vixie.html>. Whereas the number of conflicts would surely decline, so, too, would the benefits to those who prefer specific domain names that have meaning or some other characteristic. As with phone numbers, however, competition for certain numbers will ensue unless they are assigned randomly and a secondary market (in either names or entities that control names) is prohibited.

tries will allow someone to reserve or even register a trademark without using it, but most countries (including the United States) require use to claim protection under trademark law.[66] Similar to trademarks, domain names can act as source-identifiers suggesting the identity, quality, or source of a good or service. Accordingly, domain names may conflict with trademarks because of their similarity in function.

If a trademark holder allows someone else to use the trademark or mark either in the same class of goods/services or in some other way that could create confusion in the marketplace, the other party may begin to acquire rights as a result of that use, and those rights reduce the value of the mark to its original owner. Within the United States, the problem is further complicated by the existence of federal and state antidilution laws that permit owners of famous marks to enjoin others from commercial uses of such marks, even where such commercial uses are in classes of goods or services different from that of the famous mark.[67] Designed to prevent the whittling away of the identification value of the plaintiff's mark, antidilution laws differ from more traditional trademark laws, which are designed to prevent consumer confusion within the same class of goods or services.[68] In order to determine whether a mark is subject to federal antidilution protection (i.e., whether it is considered to be a famous mark), the law provides several non-exclusive factors that may be considered.[69] Some states within the United States have more generous definitions of "famous marks," while other countries have similar or different definitions or do not recognize the concept at all. Another one of the factors to be used in this determination under U.S. law is "the nature and extent of use of the same or similar marks by third parties." This factor demonstrates that a potentially famous mark owner's antidilution rights, like rights against infringement, can be lessened or lost by its failure to police its mark.

---

[66]This also means that the failure to use a registered mark can result in the loss of rights.

[67]See J. Thomas McCarthy, *McCarthy on Trademarks and Unfair Competition*, 4th ed., § 24:88 (2003), Clark Boardman Callaghan/West, Deerfield, Ill., 1992.

[68]See McCarthy, *McCarthy on Trademarks and Unfair Competition*, § 24:88 (2003). An example would be if Mack Trucks, Inc., began using the mark "BIG MAC" in association with a new model of truck. It is unlikely that the McDonald's Corporation would argue that there was a likelihood of consumer confusion between Mack's truck and McDonald's large sandwich of the same name. However, it is possible that the McDonald's Corporation would argue that the truck model was diluting the value of its famous mark, BIG MAC.

[69]These factors include "the degree of inherent or acquired distinctiveness of the mark," "the duration and extent of use of the mark in connection with the goods or services with which the mark is used," and "the duration and extent of advertising and publicity of the mark." See 15 U.S.C. § 1125(c)(1).

Thus, trademark holders became quite concerned about the activities of parties that had registered domain names that either were confusingly similar to their trademarks or diluted their famous marks. Generally, to cause a likelihood of confusion under trademark law,[70] a domain name must be used in connection with an offering of goods and services or it must be used commercially for antidilution laws to apply, but cybersquatters raised a slightly different problem. Cybersquatters are generally defined as domain name speculators who register a domain name that incorporates a trademark owned by another party, not in order to use the domain name, but with the intent of reselling the registered domain name to that party for an amount that far exceeded the cybersquatter's registration cost. The most contentious examples of cybersquatting were those in which domain names incorporating trademarks (or phonetic or typographical variants of them) were associated with Web sites that included pornographic content or other information that would confuse or offend users who reached that Web site by mistake or assumed that the trademark holder had registered the domain name and that the Web site associated with it belonged to the trademark holder. The cybersquatter would then offer to sell the domain name to the trademark owner for a substantial sum, which some companies agreed to pay, if for no other reason than to stop the offending use. Such actions, of course, only fueled more cybersquatting activities. Cybersquatters also figured out that users were trying alternative domain names (e.g., ibm-computers.com instead of ibm.com) and began to register many different combinations, such as ibmcomputers.com and ibmcomputer.com. Partially in response to these actions, many companies began to register various combinations themselves—so-called pre-emptive registrations[71]—and to seek remedies through the courts, various dispute resolution processes, and legislative action.[72]

At least one court has held that a cybersquatter's registration of a domain name that incorporated a plaintiff's famous mark, without the sale of any goods or services via the Web site associated with that domain name, was a violation of the federal antidilution statute because the defendant made "commercial use" of the trademark when he attempted to

---

[70]See McCarthy, *McCarthy on Trademarks and Unfair Competition*, § 25:76.

[71]Such pre-emptive registrations were encouraged by the marketing strategy of many registrars.

[72]In fact, the congressional mandate (P.L. 105-305) for this study came largely as a result of actions by representatives of the trademark community. This community was very active and visible in the domain names arena in the late 1990s.

sell the domain name back to the owner of the famous mark.[73] Another court has found the attempted sale or licensing of domain names containing trademarks to be trademark infringement, similarly concluding that the sale of these domain names was a commercial use of the marks.[74] Additionally, the Anticybersquatting Consumer Protection Act (ACPA), enacted in 1999,[75] provides additional rights to trademark owners against those who register, traffic in, or use, with the bad-faith intent to profit, a domain name that is identical or confusingly similar to a registered or unregistered mark that was distinctive or dilutive of a famous mark when the domain name was registered. Despite the creation of ACPA and other domain name dispute resolution mechanisms,[76] the costs involved with pre-emptive registrations and the enforcement of trademarks ultimately led many representatives of trademark holder interests to resist efforts to create new TLDs, fearing that these costs would continue to increase substantially if new additional TLDs were created.

In contrast, the protective efforts by trademark holders in some instances have also raised conflicts with other legally equivalent rights held by the individuals using the domain names. For example, suppose a group critical of a corporation wants to create a public space for discussion and register a domain name associated with that corporation (e.g., companyname.org). Does such a registration constitute an infringement of the corporation's trademark because it creates consumer confusion or is it dilutive because it tarnishes the reputation of the corporation, or rather is it an exercise of a protected right, such as freedom of speech under the First Amendment of the U.S. Constitution? Discussions related to domain names, trademark concerns, and public policy issues will continue into the 21st century.[77]

Other conflicts involving trademarks arose for reasons that had nothing to do with the above-described conflicts between trademark holders and their cybersquatting antagonists. For example, Chris Van Allen, then 12 years old, registered the second-level domain name pokey.org because Pokey was his nickname, and was subsequently ensnarled in a trademark dispute with Prema Toy Company, owner of the trademarks on the claymation character Gumby and his horse Pokey, which wanted control

[73]See *Intermatic, Inc. v. Toeppen*, 947 F. Supp. 1227 (N.D. Ill. 1996).

[74]See *Toys "R" Us, Inc. v. Abir*, 45 U.S.P.Q.2d 1944 (S.D.N.Y. 1997).

[75]See 15 U.S.C. § 1125(d).

[76]See Section 3.5 for an extended treatment.

[77]The state of understanding continues to evolve. See, for example, *The Taubman Company v. Webfeats, et al.*, Nos. 01-2648/2725 (6th Circuit, February 7, 2003).

over the domain name.[78] Ultimately, Prema Toy Company withdrew its complaint.[79] In other cases, disputes arose between different entities with equally valid rights to the same second-level domain name, such as "bob.com," which might have been coveted by many men named Robert, and "avon.com," which might have been coveted by a variety of different companies around the world that have legitimate rights to the trademark Avon for different products or services in different countries.

This latter example presents a particularly difficult point that cannot be easily resolved by simply granting the second-level domain name to the entity with the legal right to use it as a trademark, since multiple entities can have such legitimate rights. Under most countries' trademark laws, multiple entities can use the same trademark in the same country, provided each entity uses the trademark for different categories (called classes) of goods or services, as long as there is no possibility of confusing consumers as a result, and each trademark has to be registered within each country in which it is used in order to be fully protected. Hence it is entirely possible to have one company legitimately use the trademark "avon" for automotive tires in the United States, and a second company to use the same trademark for cosmetics. Unfortunately, however, there can be only one avon.com, and so the first entity to register that domain name has often been able to use it to the exclusion of all other legitimate users worldwide.[80]

Beyond Trademark Conflicts

Trademark issues dominated domain name conflicts in the late 1990s and into the beginning of the 21st century, but other conflicts also demanded attention. For example, some governments asserted rights to control the assignment of country-code TLDs and country names and the registration of those names, even beyond the second level.[81] Some governments assert that this is an extension of national sovereignty. Similar claims may be asserted by ethnic groups and indigenous tribes that have

---

[78]See Courtney Macavinta, "Short Take: Pokey Causes Net Trademark Uproar," *News.com*, March 23, 1998, available at <http://news.com.com/2110-1023-209417.html?legacy=cnet>. The dispute also involved Pokey's Network Consulting, which registered pokey.com.

[79]See Heather McCabe, "Pokey Wins His Domain Name," *Wired* News, April 22, 1998, available at <http://www.wired.com/news/business/0,1367,11846,00.html>.

[80]See Chapters 3 and 5 for a discussion of how trademark conflicts over domain names can be (and should be) managed.

[81]See the principles for delegation and administration of ccTLDs presented by the ICANN Government Advisory Committee, February 23, 2000, available at <http://www.icann.org/committees/gac/gac-cctldprinciples-23feb00.htm>.

not achieved the political status of sovereigns, but that nevertheless wish to protect or control the use of their collective name. In some jurisdictions, the subunits of national governments, such as city administrations or port authorities, have claimed exclusive rights to the use of their name in the DNS.[82] In a similar vein, some international organizations have asserted a right to prevent others from registering domain names identical to their acronyms or names.[83] These claims have more to do with the imputed legitimacy of the association than with commercial confusion. Here, too, issues arise regarding the balance struck between the use of the name as an identifier and its legitimate use as a reference to the identified entity. These claims also raise questions about who in the affected society has the right to control the name. Also, some legal regimes, which are analogous to trademark law because they are related to reputation in commerce, attempt to vest regions or localities, rather than specific firms or products, with exclusive rights to a name for a certain use. These regimes of "controlled appellations of origin" might be applied, for example, to wines or other agricultural products.[84]

In addition to nations, regions, and international organizations, many people feel that they have some ownership right over their personal name and other aspects of their persona. National systems of law often recognize "rights of personality" when defined as the ability of a person "to control the commercial use of his or her identity."[85] In the United States, there currently is no federal right of publicity or privacy; rather, the promulgation of such laws has been left to the states. About half of the states have recognized the right of publicity, either through common law or statute.[86] Other states provide similar protections as a part of the right of

[82]See, for example, *Excelentisimo Ayuntamiento de Barcelona v. Barcelona.com Inc.*, WIPO Case No. D2000-0505, available at <http://arbiter.wipo.int/domains/decisions/html/2000/d2000-0505.html>; and Salinas, California, *National Arbitration Forum, City of Salinas v. Brian Baughn*, WIPO Case No. FA0104000097076, available at <http://www.arbitrationforum.com/domains/decisions/97076.htm>.

[83]For example, international organizations such as the International Monetary Fund (IMF) or the World Health Organization (WHO). See *The Recognition of Rights and the Use of Names in the Internet Domain Name System*, Report of the Second WIPO Internet Domain Name Process, September 3, 2001, available at <http://wipo2.wipo.int/process2/report/pdf/report.pdf>.

[84]For further discussion see, "Geographic Identifiers," in *The Recognition of Rights and the Use of Names in the Internet Domain Name System*, 2001.

[85]See McCarthy, *McCarthy on Trademarks and Unfair Competition*, 4th ed., 1992.

[86]See, for example, *Carson v. Nat'l Bank of Commerce*, 501 F.2d 1082, 1084 (8th Cir. 1974) (recognizing a common-law right of publicity in Nebraska); and FLA. STAT. ANN. §540.08 (West 2002) (providing for a statutory right of publicity in Florida).

privacy.[87] Under the Restatement (Second) of Torts §§ 652A - 652C (1979), invading an individual's right of publicity is similar to invading her privacy through unauthorized appropriation of her name or likeness.[88]

One of the primary motives behind passage of the Anticybersquatting Consumer Protection Act in the United States, for example, was the widespread registration of the names of U.S. politicians as domain names and their linkage to Web sites that were satirical or critical.[89]

Communications technology can create new arenas for disputes over rights to names. In particular, the process of entering an identifier into a network creates numerous opportunities for conflicts over the boundary of a name right. Of course, many of the underlying issues—confusion, fraud, competition, fair use, freedom of expression—are familiar from other contexts.

A good part of the advertising economy of the Internet is based on paying for "hits" (i.e., the exposure of the content of a Web site to a distinct user).[90] Thus, the practice of "typosquatting" developed, wherein entrepreneurs registered domain names that were only a keystroke or two

---

[87]See, for example, *Allison v. Vintage Sports Plaques*, 136 F.3d 1443 (11th Cir. 1998) (describing the appropriation of plaintiff's personality for a commercial use as an invasion of privacy tort in Alabama).

[88]In 1953 in the case of *Haelan Labs. v. Topps Chewing Gum*, the right of publicity was first explicitly recognized as a right independent of the right of privacy and as an individual's right to the publicity value of his photograph. The court distinguished the right of publicity from the right of privacy because "many prominent persons . . . far from having their feelings bruised through public exposure of their likeness, would feel sorely deprived if they no longer received money for authorizing advertisements [or] popularizing their countenances." See *Haelan Labs. v. Topps Chewing Gum*, 202 F.2d 866, 868 (2d Cir. 1953). Thus, the right of publicity has developed into a body of law distinct from, but related to, copyright law, privacy rights, and the law of unfair competition. While certain states encode publicity rights within their right of privacy statutes, prominent case law and jurisprudence acknowledge the development of the right of publicity as an independent body of law. See, for example, *Carson v. Here's Johnny Portable Toilets*, 698 F.2d 831, 834 (6th Cir. 1983) (stating, "[T]he right of privacy and the right of publicity protect fundamentally different interests and must be analyzed separately."). When commercial exploitation of names is involved, personality rights often overlap with, or are informed by a logic that parallels, trademark rights. Indeed, a person's name is often registered as a trademark or used to brand products or services (e.g., Michael Jordan). But rights of personality are often asserted even when commerce is not directly involved.

[89]U.S. Patent and Trademark Office, "Report to Congress: the Anticybersquatting Consumer Protection Act of 1999," January 2000. A law passed by the state of California makes it illegal to register someone else's name as a domain name "without regard to the goods and services of the parties." See Section 17525 of the California Business and Professions Code, at <http://www.leginfo.ca.gov/cgi-bin/displaycode?section=bpc&group=17001-18000&file=17525-17528.5>.

[90]See Section 7.2.2 for an extended discussion.

apart from popular domains. These "typo" domains would then be linked to advertisements in order to collect pay-per-hit revenue from people who mistyped the locator into the browser. The cybersquatter John Zuccarini refined the practice of "typosquatting" to an art, registering hundreds of close misspellings of popular domain names and trapping users into a parade of cascading Web pages, some of them pornographic.[91]

There are even fuzzier boundaries to consider. There are businesses that register large collections of expired domain names in order to collect advertising hits from people who are looking for the old Web site.[92] Is this an abusive practice or one as innocent as putting up a billboard on a choice spot on a busy highway?

Beyond Second-Level Domain Names

Thus far, the discussion has focused on second-level domain names. Although less common, there are disputes involving third-, fourth- and higher-level domain names, as well as involving directory and file descriptors. For example, in *Bally Total Fitness Holding Corp. v. Faber*, 29 F. Supp. 2d 1161 (C.D. Cal. 1998), an infringement suit was brought against a defendant who used the URL <http://www.compupix.com/ballysucks> to post critical comments regarding the plaintiff. The court held that "no reasonable consumer" was likely to confuse the defendant's domain name with the plaintiff's marks BALLY, BALLY TOTAL FITNESS, and BALLY'S TOTAL FITNESS, because, among other things, the defen-

---

[91]See, for example, Joanna Glasner, "Typo-Loving Squatter Squashed," *Wired*, October 31, 2000, available at <http://www.wired.com/news/business/0,1367,39888,00.html>. In 2004, Zuccarini was sentenced to 30 months in prison for using misleading domain names to trick children into visiting pornographic Web sites in violation of the federal Truth in Domain Names Act. See "U.S. Man Jailed for Luring Children to Porn Sites," *Reuters*, February 26, 2004.

[92]Other cases include attempts to protect the "nonproprietary" status of a name by excluding it from a name space. The World Health Organization and the World Intellectual Property Organization (WIPO) proposed to do this with respect to International Nonproprietary Names (INNs), a list of over 3000 names of pharmaceutical substances. See "International Nonproprietary Names (INNs) for Pharmaceutical Substances," in *The Recognition of Rights and the Use of Names in the Internet Domain Name System*, Report of the Second WIPO Internet Domain Name Process, September 3, 2001, available at <http://wipo2.wipo.int/process2/report/pdf/report.pdf>. This proposal is particularly problematic because the list of INNs not only is long, but also expands over time.

Religion is another potential source of rights claims. Certain religions recognize words as sacred and attempt to protect or restrict their use.

dant did not use the plaintiff's mark in his domain name.[93] Based on the facts of the case, the court stated that the result would have been the same even if the defendant's domain name was ballysucks.com.[94] The court also contrasted the defendant's domain name and the hypothetical second-level ballysucks.com domain name with other cases where likelihood of confusion was found when the plaintiff's mark was the only mark (e.g., panaflex.com) used in the defendant's second-level domain.[95]

In another example, the Usenet newsgroup name space contains numerous descriptors that use a variety of names to describe the space, including, for instance, the name Disney (e.g., alt.disney.disneyland or rec.arts.disney.parks). These newsgroups (which are visible to most Internet users) are not run by the Disney Corporation, and the content and administration of the group may or may not have the corporation's approval. In the even more freewheeling world of AOL screen names, any user can appropriate the name of his or her favorite Disney character (even in less than flattering variations) and use it as his or her screen name and e-mail address. While it is clear that no exemption exists for Usenet groups and AOL screen-name aliases, it does appear that trademark holders have chosen not to pursue many of these uses in these naming spaces.[96]

Yet current law and policy regarding domain names erect major distinctions between the various parts of the domain name used in a URL. Within the generic and most country-code top-level domains, all (or at least most) of the political and legal conflict over rights to names takes place over the second-level domain name. The third-level domain and all identifiers to the right of the domain name are generally outside the scope of challenge through dispute resolution processes.[97] Current law and policy therefore regard the top-level domain as a fixed set of generic cat-

[93]See *The Recognition of Rights and the Use of Names in the Internet Domain Name System*, 2001, pp. 1163-1165.

[94]See *The Recognition of Rights and the Use of Names in the Internet Domain Name System*, 2001, p. 1165.

[95]See *The Recognition of Rights and the Use of Names in the Internet Domain Name System*, 2001, p. 1165.

[96]Many trademark holders have not done anything regarding many newsgroup names, in part because it is difficult to police such activities as well as prove that trademark infringement or dilution has occurred. Indeed, as soon as a name was removed or changed in this space, another of the millions of users could create a new one.

[97]There are some important exceptions, such as the case of .uk, for which most entities register at the third level (e.g., Disney.co.uk) rather than at the second level. For these exceptions, it is the fourth level and beyond that are outside the purview of dispute resolution processes. Dispute resolution processes are further described in Chapters 3 and 5.

egories or country codes, the second-level domain as the identifier of an organization, product, or Web site, and the third-level domain as part of a "private" naming system, wherein assignments can generally be left to the discretion of whoever holds the second-level name.

To further illustrate this point, Yahoo! Inc. has been an active defender of its brand name in cyberspace. It has challenged the registration of hundreds of second-level domains, including some rather remote misspellings, such as "jahu" or "yhuu," whenever they appear in the second level of a domain name. But under current legal precedent, it would likely take no action against a name such as yahoo.blatant.cybersquatter.com. In all likelihood, however, Yahoo's decision not to pursue claims for trademark infringement or dilution for alternative uses of its brand name and mark is less influenced by current precedent than it is by Yahoo's likelihood of success on the merits, especially in view of decisions such as that in the above noted *Bally Total Fitness Holding Corp. v. Faber* case.

By contrast, second-level domain names are ripe for generating conflicts over rights to names. They are meaningful, they are perceived as being economically valuable, and they are part of a global, public naming system administered via collective action. And perhaps most importantly, they are susceptible to centralized control because of the existence of a single, central point of coordination, the relevant registry. See Box 2.2.

2.5.3 Whois

In concert with the rise in the interest in and demand for domain names was a corresponding increase in the value of contact information associated with domain names. Hence, interest in the Whois database continued to rise in the 1990s.

Some of the targeted uses of the Whois data were for old-fashioned marketing purposes—for example, to send sales brochures and to make telephone solicitations to network operators and domain name registrants. As domain names became economically valuable after 1995, accessing Whois data also became a popular way to find out which domain names were taken, who had registered them, and the creation and expiration date of the registration. The Whois database also became an investigation and monitoring tool for intellectual property rights holders. When a trademark holder discovered a potentially infringing domain name, the trademark holder could use the Whois database to identify, investigate, and contact the registrant of the domain name. At that time, the Whois database could also be used to determine if the same registrant had registered any similar domain names that the trademark holder did not know about or to search for further evidence of cybersquatting by the registrant. Trademark holders also discovered that they could use the database proactively

BOX 2.2 The Institutionalization of .com

For the most part, the initial dominance of .com among the TLDs was a historical accident, a product of the chance conjunction of the commercialization of the Internet, the rise of the Web, the openness of the InterNIC registry relative to the ccTLD registries, and the lack of any other commercially oriented TLD in the original set of gTLDs. Once .com became established as the most desired TLD for many registrants, other forces contributed to the solidification of .com's increasing dominance. As discussed elsewhere in this section, "Beyond Second-Level Domain Names," the rise in value of .com names (whether for navigation or marketing functions) led to the registration of some domain names for speculative, abusive, or preemptive purposes. Based on a desire to avoid further registration of domain names for these same purposes in new TLDs, some resistance developed to the creation of new TLDs, thereby reinforcing the focus on extant TLDs (with disproportionate advantage to .com , given its dominant market position). Whether the historical dominance of .com from the mid-1990s will continue in the future of the DNS is discussed in Section 5.4.

to perform searches for character strings that matched trademarks, and retrieve many of the domain name registrations in the generic top-level domains that matched or contained a trademark. This automated searching function proved to be so valuable that trademark interests began to demand that the Whois functions be institutionalized, expanded, and subsidized, including the right to purchase the complete list and contact data for all of a registrar's customers. The first World Intellectual Property Organization (WIPO) domain name process, initiated in 1998 in response to a U.S. government request, as detailed by a U.S. Commerce Department white paper,[98] recommended that the contact details in a Whois record be contractually required to be complete, accurate, and up to date, on penalty of forfeiture of the domain name.[99]

2.6 GLOBALIZATION

Worldwide interest in the DNS developed during the 1990s along with increasing concern about U.S. dominance of a critical element of global communication and a commercial resource on which other nations fore-

---

[98]For the text of the white paper, see <http://www.ntia.doc.gov/ntiahome/domainname/6_5_98dns.htm>.

[99]See paragraph 73 of *The Management of Internet Names and Addresses: Intellectual Property Issues. Final Report of the WIPO Internet Domain Process*, April 30, 1999, available at <http://wipo2.wipo.int/process1/report/finalreport.html#49>.

saw their economies and societies becoming ever more dependent. With increasing recognition of this value came a growing desire to participate in the management and policy decision making with respect to domain names.

An issue of particular interest in many countries is access to the Internet and the DNS using home-country languages other than English. As the number of users whose first language is not based on Roman characters grew dramatically during the 1990s, interest developed in domain names based on non-Roman scripts (e.g., Chinese, Hebrew, Arabic, and so on). Several major efforts have been undertaken to accommodate internationalized domain names (IDNs) within the Internet infrastructure.[100]

The design of the DNS, however, presents formidable technical challenges for the accommodation of languages that use non-Roman characters. As a lookup system, the DNS must be able to determine unambiguously whether or not there is a match with a query. Comparing strings is much more difficult than most people realize, because the definition of what is "equal" is often not deterministic. For the French language in Canada and in France, for example, there are different rules as to whether an accent stays over a character when it is converted from lower to upper case. And some languages (e.g., Chinese) cannot be reduced to a relatively small number of standardized characters (e.g., the character set for English). See Section 4.3 for further discussion of the IDN issue and the increasing interest and involvement by parties outside the United States in matters related to the DNS.

2.7 ADMINISTRATION OF DOMAIN NAMES

In the 1980s, the Network Information Center managed the registration of domain names, operating under the auspices of SRI International and funded by the Department of Defense (DOD), by DARPA and the Defense Information Systems Agency (DISA).[101] Jon Postel and other researchers at the Information Sciences Institute at the University of Southern California had been given the authority to establish procedures for assigning and keeping track of protocol and network numbers and controlled the definition of TLDs.[102] Overall, the administration and policy oversight for domain names was relatively straightforward.

---

[100]See discussion in Section 4.3.

[101]Formally, the NIC was the Defense Data Network-Network Information Center (DDN-NIC).

[102]Jon Postel had a central role in the DNS from the beginning as co-author of "The Domain Naming Convention for Internet User Applications," RFC 819. Postel "held leadership positions in several Internet infrastructure activities. He was founder and head of the Internet Assigned Numbers Authority, RFC editor, and chief administrator

In the mid-1980s, the National Science Foundation (NSF) created NSFNet to provide data communication services to researchers and educators. It selected the Transmission Control Protocol/Internet Protocol (TCP/IP) as its transport protocol and worked closely with the Department of Energy, the National Aeronautics and Space Administration, and DARPA to share facilities to extend this infrastructure in the United States and worldwide. NSF encouraged campus network investment by focusing its efforts on high-speed and high-capacity long-haul "backbone"[103] and regional networks to connect the campuses. Thus, the responsibility for the civilian network gradually shifted from the DOD to NSF. (See Box 2.3 for a timeline of the shifting administration of domain names.) In the early 1990s, NSF made another important decision—to withdraw as the primary financial benefactor for the backbone of the Internet and to encourage a commercial market for support of transport facilities.

Continuing on this path, in 1993 NSF replaced DOD as the funding agency for domain name management. As the workload increased, NSF contracted with Network Solutions, Inc. (NSI) to manage the registration for most of the gTLDs (.com, .net, .org, .edu, and .gov), through InterNIC. At this time, NSF, preserving the practice that the registration of domain names would be free to registrants, subsidized the costs associated with domain name registration. See Box 2.3.

Increasing scale was not the only impetus for administrative evolution. The increasing economic and social value of domain names caused new players to become interested in the realm of domain names. As discussed earlier, holders of highly visible and valuable trademarks developed an active interest in domain names. Many other entities, from national governments and public interest groups to the firms in the emerging domain name industry, also developed a keen interest in all things related to domain names. Thus, the 1990s saw the domain name community expand radically, both in scale and, especially important to understand, in the scope of the interests and backgrounds of participants.[104]

---

of the .us domain. He was expected to play a crucial role in the future of Internet administration, which [was] in the process of being transferred to the private sector [the Internet Corporation for Assigned Names and Numbers (ICANN)]." See "In Memoriam, Dr. Jonathan B. Postel, August 3, 1943 – October 16, 1998," *The Domain Name Handbook*, available at <http://www.domainhandbook.com/postel.html>, accessed March 31, 2004.

[103]A backbone is a network that interconnects other networks. Backbone networks often operate over relatively longer distances than do typical networks.

[104]This diversity in the range of participants creates challenges in achieving consensus in the decisions needed to make progress on various problems. Among other things, conflicting goals and varying communication styles and vocabulary contribute to these challenges. Even agreeing on something as basic as defining "DNS" can lead to disputes.

BOX 2.3 Administration of the Domain Name System in the 1990s: The Road to ICANN

1991

Responsibility for much of the Network Information Center (NIC) was transferred from SRI International (operating on the behalf of the Department of Defense; DOD) to Government Systems, Inc., which then subcontracted the entire operation to Network Solutions, Inc. (NSI). NSI started operating the NIC in 1992.

1993

The National Science Foundation (NSF) replaced DOD as the funding source for the NIC. NSF completed a service contract with InterNIC, the umbrella organization for the participating contractors AT&T (directory and database services), NSI (registration services), and General Atomics/CERFnet (information services). Thus, NSF engaged NSI to take over domain name registration services for most of the generic top-level domains (gTLDs) through a 5-year cooperative agreement.

1994

"Domain Name System Structure and Delegation" (RFC 1591), written by Jon Postel, was published and gained general acceptance.[1]

1995

NSF and NSI amended their cooperative agreement, imposing a $100 fee for 2 years of domain name registration.

1997

The International Ad Hoc Committee (IAHC), a coalition of individuals representing various constituencies established in 1996, released a proposal for the administration and management of gTLDs that included a framework for a governance structure, captured in a document known as the Generic Top Level Domain Memorandum of Understanding (gTLD-MoU).[2]

The U.S. government created an interagency group to address the domain name issue and assigned lead responsibility to the National Telecommunications and Information Administration (NTIA), Department of Commerce. This interagency group reviewed the IAHC proposal and solicited public comment.

As a part of the Clinton Administration's "Framework for Global Electronic Commerce,"[3] the Department of Commerce was directed to privatize the

Domain Name System in a manner that would increase competition and facilitate international participation in its management. The department issued a call for public input relating to the overall framework of the DNS.

1998

The NTIA released "A Proposal to Improve Technical Management of Internet Names and Addresses," also known as the Green Paper. This proposal called for a private, non-profit corporation, headquartered in the United States, to manage domain names and IP addresses, and for "the addition of up to five new registries."[4]

A final statement of policy, the "Management of Internet Names and Addresses," also known as the White Paper, was issued by NTIA. The White Paper reaffirmed the goals of the Green Paper, while having the U.S. government take a more hands-off approach, and urged the creation of a new not-for-profit corporation to oversee the management and assignment of domain names and IP addresses. Goals for the new corporation included ensuring stability, competition, private and bottom-up coordination, and fair representation of the Internet community.[5]

NSF transferred authority to the U.S. Department of Commerce to administer the cooperative agreement under which domain name registration services are provided.[6]

Internet constituencies (e.g., those that attended the workshops held under the auspices of the International Forum on the White Paper) discussed how the new entity (the New Corporation, or "NewCo") might be constituted and structured. A group led by Jon Postel (and under his name) proposed a set of bylaws and articles for the incorporation of NewCo. The final version of NewCo's (then named as the Internet Corporation for Assigned Names and Numbers; ICANN) bylaws and articles of incorporation were submitted to NTIA in October. On November 25, NTIA and ICANN signed an official memorandum of understanding (MoU), with an initial termination date of September 30, 2000.

In October, NTIA and NSI extended their cooperative agreement through September 2000. NSI committed to a timetable for the development of a shared registration system (SRS) that permitted multiple registrars to provide registration services within the .com, .net, and .org gTLDs. Also, NSI agreed to separate its registrar and registry operations into separate divisions, to recognize NewCo, and to make no changes to the root without written approval from the U.S. government.

[1]Available at <http://www.rfc-editor.org>.

[2]For further information, see <http://www.gtld-mou.org/draft-iahc-recommend-00.html>.

[3]See <http://www.ta.doc.gov/digeconomy/framewrk.htm>.

[4]See <http://www.ntia.doc.gov/ntiahome/domainname/dnsdrft.htm>.

[5]For the text of the white paper, see <http://www.ntia.doc.gov/ntiahome/domainname/6_5_98dns.htm>.

[6]See <http://www.nsf.gov/od/lpa/news/media/ma9822.htm>.

By 1996, the belief by some (e.g., Jon Postel) that additional TLDs were needed led to the establishment of the International Ad Hoc Committee (IAHC) to develop a framework for the administration of domain names, which became known as the Generic Top Level Domain Memorandum of Understanding (gTLD-MoU). The IAHC's proposal for an institutional framework prompted a strong reaction from a few key constituencies and "sent ripples through the international system," as characterized by Milton Mueller.[105] Although the gTLD-MoU was not implemented, its creation did motivate the discussions leading to the development of the Green and White Papers (see Box 2.3) and the eventual creation of the Internet Corporation for Assigned Names and Numbers (ICANN) in late 1998.

NSI exclusively operated the .com, .net, and .org TLDs through 1998. The registry operations (associated with the management of the TLD databases themselves) and registrar operations (associated with the retail functions of dealing with customers) were integrated. NTIA's agreement with NSI in late 1998 required NSI to separate its registry and registrar functions so that other registrars could enter the market. To facilitate the entry of other firms, NSI also agreed to establish a shared registration system to enable all registrars (including NSI's registrar unit) to interact with the registry database. The vibrant market for domain name registration services in the .com TLD that developed in the late 1990s also spurred interest in the creation of new TLDs.

Thus, the DNS has experienced an extraordinary evolution since its birth in the early 1980s. Initially intended to address specific technical and operational problems of concern to a small, relatively homogeneous group of computer scientists and engineers, the DNS came to involve individuals from many different sectors such as law, business, government, and the public interest. The issues surrounding the DNS became increasingly non-technical in nature and increasingly complex and controversial, and so the founding of ICANN did not end the conflict among constituents, but rather provided the forum for their often intense discussion. Chapters 3 and 5 further explore these conflicts and the alternatives for their possible resolution.

---

[105]From Milton Mueller, "Internet Domain Names: Property Rights and Institutional Innovation," in Gary Libecap, editor, *Entrepreneurship and Growth in the American Economy* 12:93-131, Elsevier, Amsterdam, 2000, p. 111.

3

The Domain Name System: Current State

The Domain Name System (DNS) in 2005 serves a global Internet far larger and more diverse, in users and in uses, than the relatively small homogeneous network for which it was first deployed in the early 1980s. To meet the needs of this expanded and enhanced Internet, the DNS has developed into a complex socio-technical-economic system comprising distributed name servers embedded in a multilayered institutional framework. This chapter describes the DNS as it exists in 2005 to establish a base for consideration of the future of the DNS and of navigation on the Internet.

The chapter begins with an explanation of how the DNS responds to queries, illustrating the process with a query about the Internet Protocol (IP) address that corresponds to a particular domain name. It then describes the basic architecture of the DNS: its domain name space, its hierarchical structure, its basic programs, and its key standards and protocols. The core of the chapter is a description of the implementation of this architecture at three levels of the DNS hierarchy: the root, the top-level domains, and the second- and third-level domains. The distinctive characteristics of each level are examined first, followed by descriptions of the technical system and its institutional framework. The committee's conclusions about the current performance of the DNS architecture and the implementation of each level are presented at the end of each section. Open issues affecting the future of the DNS are collected and analyzed in Chapters 4 and 5.

Many of the contentious issues that arise in the context of the DNS concern domain names themselves—in particular, the definition of permissible names and the rights to their use. Some of those issues are introduced and discussed in Chapter 2.

3.1 OPERATION OF THE DOMAIN NAME SYSTEM1

Many things happen when a query to the DNS is initiated. If the DNS were a centralized database, such as HOSTS.TXT,[2] every query would go directly to a central file where the answer would be found (or its absence noted). However, because the DNS is a hierarchical, distributed database, a search in response to a query generally requires several steps. If necessary, it can begin at the root and traverse a course through the tree of files to the one in which the sought-for answer resides. However, frequently the search can begin further down the tree because previous answers are stored and reused by the querying client. The design of the DNS ensures that the path down the tree will be followed without detours or false starts, leading directly to the desired file because the structure of the domain name spells out the route. This process may best be understood through an example, shown in Figure 3.1, which illustrates the use of the DNS to find the IP address corresponding to the hypothetical domain name indns.cstb.nas.edu.[3]

This is what would happen if, for example, the user wanted to access a Web site at that name, in which case the requesting application would be a browser. However, the same process would be followed for, say, an e-mail application or any other application supported by a host[4] on the Internet.

Two versions of the process are described below: first, the version shown in Figure 3.1, which would be followed if this were a new query from a computer that was not on the same DNS subtree as the cstb.nas.edu server; and then a version shortened by taking advantage of additional information from shared servers or previous queries.

---

[1]This section elaborates on the high-level explanation in Chapter 2. It draws extensively on material in Paul Albitz and Cricket Liu, *DNS and BIND*, O'Reilly & Associates, Sebastopol, Calif., 2001.

[2]HOSTS.TXT is the predecessor of the DNS and is described in Section 2.1.

[3]The process shown in Figure 3.1 assumes that the querying client has stored no relevant previous answers.

[4]A "host" is a network computer on which applications run providing services, such as computation or database access, to end users on the network.

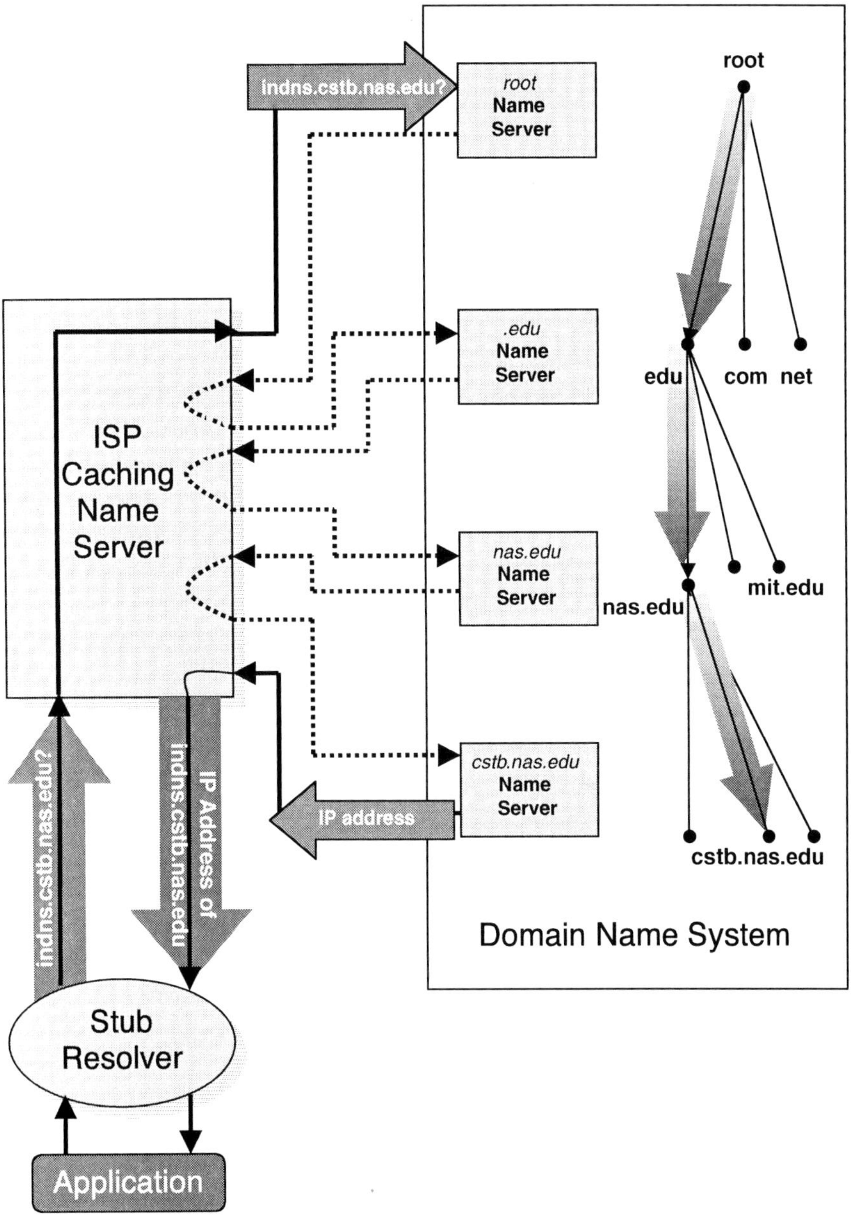

FIGURE 3.1 Operation of the Domain Name System without a local name server.

3.1.1 A New, Remote Query

When a domain name is used in a Web browser, e-mail program, or otherwise, the applications program forms a request—a query. The example query, "What is the IP address corresponding to the domain name indns.cstb.nas.edu?," goes first to a piece of software called a resolver. Resolver software is ordinarily incorporated as part of other software resident on the user's computer[5] or in a host to which it is linked. There are two kinds of resolvers: stub resolvers and iterative resolvers. Both types of resolver send queries to name servers (see below), but they differ in how the resolver selects the name servers to which it sends the query and how much of the work of answering the query is performed by the resolver. A name server is a computer running one of a small number of name-serving programs, the most common of which is the Berkeley Internet Name Domain (BIND) software.[6] A stub resolver simply forwards the query to a local name server and awaits a reply. It places on the name server the burden of searching the DNS for the answer. An iterative resolver, in contrast, retains control of the search by using the answer from each successive name server to guide its search. This example assumes that the query comes from a stub resolver.

Name servers are located throughout the Internet: at the root and the top-level domain registries, in organizations' intranet infrastructures, and at Internet service providers (ISPs). Name servers can perform two important functions:

- First, they are designed to reply directly to queries concerning the portion of the domain name space for which they have complete information, which is called their zone and for which they are said to be authoritative (see Section 3.1.2).
- Second, they can, by incorporating an iterative resolver, reply to queries concerning zones for which they are not authoritative, obtaining information from other name servers in the DNS (described in this section). The incorporated iterative resolver will in almost all cases also contain a file or cache of answers obtained as a result of processing previous queries (see Section 3.1.3). In this case, the combination of name server and iterative resolver is said to be a caching or recursive name server.

---

[5]For example, this is part of the Transmission Control Protocol/Internet Protocol (TCP/IP) stack in Microsoft Windows software, but some applications incorporate their own resolvers. Consequently, a computer may contain more than one resolver.

[6]This name server program was originally written in 1983-1984 by a group of graduate students at the University of California, Berkeley, with funding from the Defense Advanced Research Projects Agency. Name servers are discussed further in Section 3.2.3.

In practice, name servers with a heavy query demand or at the top levels of the DNS hierarchy are often configured to be authoritative only and not to offer caching/recursive services, except through a separate server. The name servers at ISPs, however, will offer caching/recursive services to their customers' stub resolvers, but may not be authoritative for any domain.

In Figure 3.1, the query is shown as going first to a name server offering recursive services located at the user's ISP.[7] Since in this example the iterative resolver incorporated into the ISP's name server has not recently seen this query or any portion of it and the name server is not authoritative for any portion of the query, it sends the query on to the DNS root. It is able to find the root because the IP addresses of the name servers for the root, called the root hints data, were manually entered into a file on the computer, the hints file. Some systems automatically detect changes to the list of root name servers and make use of them, but the software never changes the file because to do so might eliminate the fallback in case of an attack that maliciously delivered an incorrect list.

There are 13 root name servers (and many satellite copies of them)[8] distributed around the world, and the querying name server will go to one chosen by an algorithm that, although differing among name server implementations, usually takes the shortest response time into account. The multiple computer copies of some of the 13 name servers employ a technology called "anycast" addressing (see Box 3.1). Although geographically distributed, each satellite is capable of responding to queries to the same IP address.

If, for some reason, one root name server (or its closest satellite) does not respond, the iterative resolver will continue to try other servers according to its selection algorithm, and so on, until it receives a response. Similar behavior is common to all iterative resolvers at whatever level in the DNS hierarchy they are searching.

The response of a root name server, which is configured to be authoritative only, takes the form: "The address of indns.cstb.nas.edu is not in my zone's name file, but here are the names or addresses of name servers that are authoritative for .edu." The ISP's iterative resolver then sends the same query to one of the .edu name servers, which responds: "The address of indns.cstb.nas.edu is not in my zone's name file, but here are the names or addresses of the name servers that are authoritative for nas.edu."

---

[7]Where a query goes first is a consequence of an explicit configuration choice made by the user, an ISP, an enterprise IT department, or by a dynamic configuration protocol whose values are supplied by one of those sources.

[8]See Table 3.1 for a listing of the 13 root name servers and their base and satellite locations. See Box 3.1 for a description of satellite servers.

BOX 3.1 Anycast Addressing

Anycast addresses, a special type of Internet Protocol (IP) address, were invented in the early 1990s to simplify the process of finding replicated services (i.e., services that are provided by multiple and identical servers).[1] Some of the operators of root name servers have implemented anycast addressing as a way to facilitate load sharing, to improve service, and to reduce vulnerability to attacks.

The use of anycast addresses allows a root name server operator to install copies of the root zone file at different servers (in this report, those servers that replicate the root zone file are called satellites). Properly configured and located, each of the satellites will get a share of the traffic for the root name server. Although the shares will, in most cases, not be equal, the load of queries will be distributed and thus relieve the load burden on the root name server. Satellites that are located at the same physical site are using local anycast addressing, also known as load balancing, which is widely deployed among the root name server operators.

From the user's perspective, the great advantage derived from the adoption of anycast addressing is improved service. The satellites are typically placed at topologically diverse locations in the Internet. Queries can therefore be answered more swiftly. An additional benefit is that the DNS queries use, in the aggregate, fewer network resources, because servers will tend to be "closer" on the network to the sources of the queries.

The use of anycast addressing can sharply reduce the impact of an attack on a root name server: In the short run, physically disabling a root name server does not affect the operation of its satellites, and physically disabling a satellite disables only that satellite. In the long run, there is the question of how satellites would obtain updated root zone information. It is also much harder to mount an effective electronic attack—because queries are routed to the closest satellite (or the root name server itself, if it is the closest). An attacker would need to place (or acquire) machines close to

The ISP's resolver then queries one of the nas.edu name servers, which refers it to a cstb.nas.edu name server, which is authoritative for the requested domain name and replies with the corresponding IP address.

3.1.2 Local Query

A name server can answer many queries quickly when these queries request the address of a domain name for which the name server is authoritative. This is often the case, for example, for name servers on organizational intranets, where most of the requests are for IP addresses of other computers on the intranet. In such a case, the name server can respond to the query without going to the larger DNS, simply by looking up the an-each of the satellites and the root name server if the attacker wished to disable all access to the service.[2] A single attacking machine might disable the closest server—whether a satellite or the root name server itself. The other servers would be affected only in a minimal way, through a slightly increased load if one server were rendered inoperative.

Therefore, the adoption of anycast addressing by the root name server operators is a positive development. However, more general use of anycast addressing is problematic because current methods for deploying these addresses waste a number of IP addresses.[3] Given the importance of a robust DNS, this wastage is acceptable for the operation of the root name servers, but not necessarily for other domain name servers.

Monitoring the performance of satellites presents root name server operators with a difficult problem. Such monitoring involves the placement of monitoring devices within the part of the Internet that each satellite serves and can represent a significant logistical challenge because the satellites may be widely dispersed.

---

[1]The initial motivation for the creation of anycast addressing was to reduce the need manually to configure information about basic services such as DNS resolvers. The basic idea is that a "host transmits a datagram [a data packet carrying its own address information so it can be independently routed from its source to the destination computer] to an anycast address and the internetwork [Internet] is responsible for providing best effort delivery of the datagram to at least one, and preferably only one, of the servers that accept datagrams for the anycast address." See Craig Partridge, Trevor Mendez, and Walter Milliken, "Host Anycasting Service," Request for Comments (RFC) 1546, November 1993, available at <http://www.rfc-editor.org>. See Box 3.3 for an explanation of RFCs. All RFCs are available at <http://www.rfc-editor.org>.

[2]And even then other root name servers and their satellites would be accessible.

[3]As of April 2004, anycast addresses were not fully supported in the current version of IP (version 4). In particular, the Border Gateway Protocol (BGP; the cross-provider routing protocol) was not designed to accommodate anycast addresses and, therefore, a workaround is used that wastes about 256 IP addresses for each root name server that employs anycast addressing.

swer in its local database. For example, if the local name server in the previous example was authoritative for cstb.nas.edu, it could provide the response directly.

3.1.3 Repeat Query

A caching name server can answer many other queries quickly when it has responded previously to queries that were identical or matched at a higher level of the tree. (For example, in 2005 virtually every caching name server is highly likely to have cached the IP address for www.google.com.) It maintains those answers in a cache of information containing the addresses of name servers (and other data) it has previously obtained. Before going to the root, it searches its cache to find the known name servers closest (in the DNS hierarchy) to the domain being sought.

For example, if the ISP's caching name server in the previous example were to receive a query for the address of tdd.cstb.nas.edu, it would check to see if it already knew the address of the name server authoritative for cstb.nas.edu. If it did, its iterative resolver would send the query directly to that server, shortening the path that must be taken to obtain an authoritative response. If it did not, it would then check to see if it had the address of the name server authoritative for nas.edu, and finally .edu. Only if it had none of those addresses would it go to the root.

This property of caching—that it limits the number of queries that are sent to the root name server—has been crucial to the manageability of the growth in the query load on the root system. If all DNS queries were to start at a root name server, the capacity of the root system (as a whole) would have to be of an entirely different magnitude, posing more formidable technical and economic challenges as a consequence.

The Internet and the many services on it are subject to constant, sometimes rapid change. As a result, cached information can become outdated. To reduce that problem, the administrator of each zone assigns a time to live (TTL) to each datum that it sends out in reply to a query. After the corresponding amount of time has passed, the name server is expected to eliminate the datum from its cache.

Often a name server will receive information that a domain name being sought does not exist. That can happen because the query is ill formed, contains a typographical error, is based on a user's incorrect guess about a desired domain name, refers to a name that does not exist or no longer exists, or refers to a domain name on a private network that is not on the public DNS.[9] Since such inquiries do not correspond to a cached address, even the caching name server system will not normally relieve the load on the root name servers related to such requests. To minimize the load on the network and improve response time, however, it is desirable that name servers store information about such non-existent domains. That practice is referred to as negative caching (as introduced in Section 2.3.1). The need to assign a TTL also applies to negative caching, since a previously non-existent domain may come into existence and would be missed if the negative cache did not eliminate responses regularly.

---

[9]A significant portion of queries to the root name servers are ill formed or in error according to studies by researchers. See, for example, Duane Wessels and Marina Fomenkov, "Wow, That's a Lot of Packets," *Proceedings of Passive and Active Measurement Workshop*, 2003, available at <http://www.caida.org/outreach/papers/2003/dnspackets/>.

3.2 ARCHITECTURE OF THE DOMAIN NAME SYSTEM

The architecture of the DNS—its conceptual design—comprises its name space, its hierarchical structure, and the software that specifies operations within that name space and structure.[10] The software comprises two components: programs, which implement the resolver and name server functions on various computers; and technical standards, which define the formats of the communication between the programs, as well as the logical structure[11] of the files in a name server.

3.2.1 Name Space

The name space for domain names is the set of all symbol strings that adhere to the rules for forming domain names specified in the design of the DNS. Those rules define a standard format that imposes a tree structure on the name space. Each node on the tree has a label, which consists of 1 to 63 characters drawn from a restricted subset of ASCII[12] comprising the 26 letters of the Roman alphabet, the 10 numerals from 0 to 9, and the hyphen. Labels may not begin or end with a hyphen.[13] The fully qualified domain name of a node is the list of the labels on the path from the node to the root of the tree written with the deepest node on the left and with those to the right getting successively closer to the root. In external presentation form, the labels are separated by dots (.). By convention, the root label has null length and is written as a dot (.), but its presence is optional. Thus, "www.nas.edu." (with a trailing dot) and "www.nas.edu" (without a trailing a dot) are equivalent domain names. The total length of a domain name must be less than 256 characters. Each node on the tree (including the leaves) corresponds to a collection of data, which may be empty at the internal nodes, unless they constitute a delegation point. The data are represented by resource records, which are described in Box 3.2 in Section 3.2.4.

3.2.2 Hierarchical Structure

The hierarchical, tree structure of the DNS facilitates both an efficient response to queries and the effective decentralization of responsibility for

---

[10]The evolution of the DNS is described in Chapter 2.

[11]They will be stored in whatever data structures the local database software requires.

[12]American National Standards Institute, "USA Code for Information Interchange," X3.4, 1968.

[13]The limitation to the 37 ASCII characters is not a strict requirement of domain names but results from the constraints placed on domain names by other protocols.

its maintenance and operation. That is accomplished through the division of a domain into subdomains, which taken together need not directly include all of the hosts in the domain. The responsibilities for maintaining the name files for some or all of the subdomains can then be delegated to different organizations. They, in turn, can further divide and delegate, a process that can be repeated as often as necessary. The parent domain need only retain pointers to the subdomains so that it can refer queries appropriately.

The hierarchical delegation of responsibility is one of the great strengths of the DNS architecture. It is up to the organization responsible for a zone to maintain the corresponding zone file (thus, the organization has considerable motivation to provide satisfactory maintenance)—the data file in the zone's name servers that contains pointers to hosts in the zone and to the name servers for delegated zones (see "DNS Zone Data File" in Section 3.2.4). The work of keeping the DNS current is, thereby, distributed to organizations throughout the entire DNS tree, down to the lowest leaves. Instead of a central organization being responsible for keeping the DNS data current and accurate, which would have been an impossible task, there are millions of organizations and individuals across the globe doing the work.

Figure 3.2 illustrates the delegation of responsibility from the root to the .edu domain, whose name servers are said to be authoritative for the .edu zone. The .edu domain in turn delegates responsibility, in this limited illustration, for the subdomains to three universities—the University of California at Los Angeles (UCLA), Southern Methodist University (SMU), and the Massachusetts Institute of Technology (MIT), whose name servers are authoritative for their corresponding zones—ucla.edu, smu.edu, and mit.edu. In Figure 3.2 the MIT subdomain is further delegated to two departments for illustrative purposes—Sloan School and Electrical Engineering and Computer Science, whose name servers are authoritative for their zones—sloancf.mit.edu and eecs.mit.edu. Note that in the example, the mit.edu zone includes a pointer directly to a host—web.mit.edu—in addition to pointers to the delegated zones.

This distribution of responsibility, combined with the distributed handling of tasks by the technology, is why the DNS scales, or handles growth so well.

3.2.3 Programs: BIND and Others

The DNS requires only two types of programs to operate within the context of the existing Internet.

First, there must be resolver software. The resolver, recall from Section 3.1, is a client that accepts a query, passes the query to a name server, interprets the response, and returns the response to the source of the query. Generally, resolvers are just a set of library routines within a name server, a browser, or an operating system.

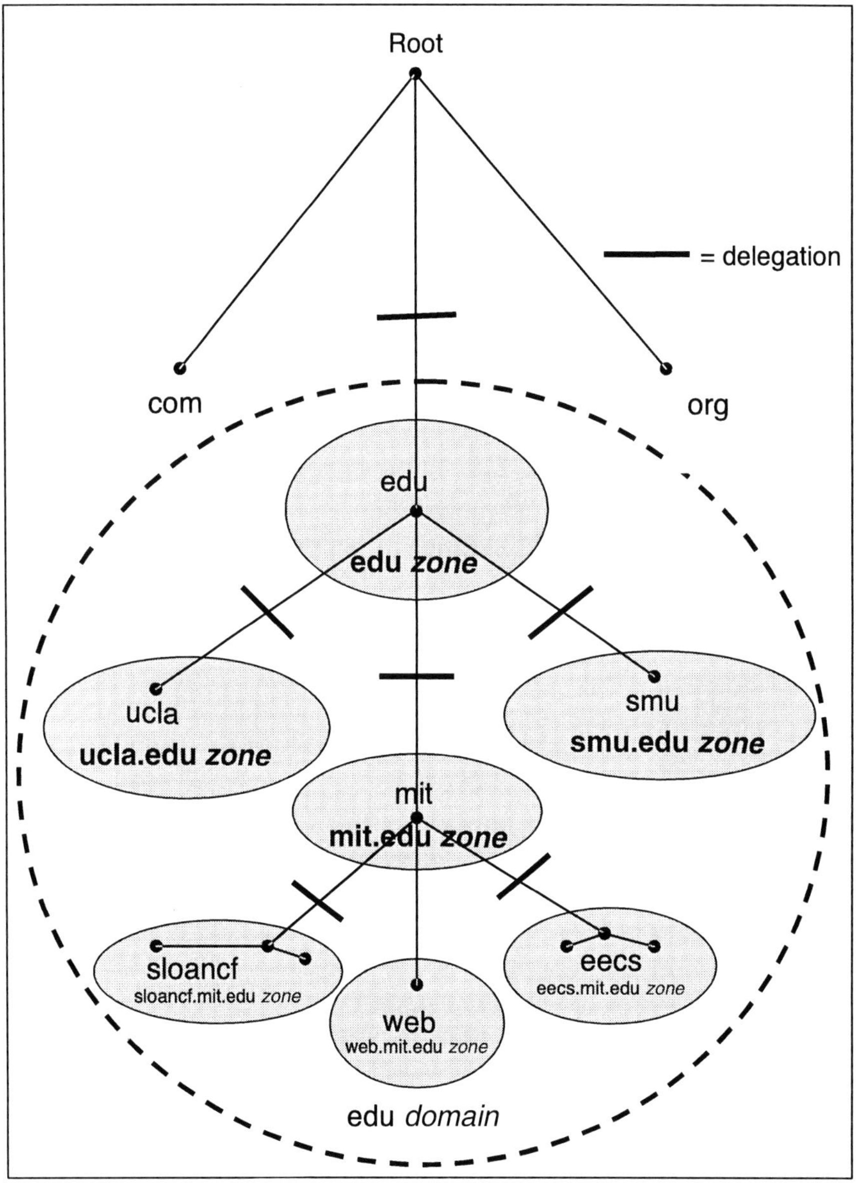

FIGURE 3.2 The .edu domain divided into zones. SOURCE: Based on Figures 2-8 and 2-9 of Paul Albitz and Cricket Liu, *DNS and BIND*, 4th edition, O'Reilly Media, Sebastopol, Calif., 2001.

Second, there must be name server software that performs the functions described in Section 3.1. As noted above, the most common name server software is BIND,[14] which is used on the majority of name servers on the Internet.[15] There have been many versions of BIND produced since it was originally written in the early 1980s. The most recent releases (as of March 2005) are BIND 8.4.6, which extends and enhances prior versions, and BIND 9.3.1 and 9.2.5, which are the latest releases of a major rewrite of the underlying architecture undertaken in response to anticipated demands resulting from the rapid growth of the Internet. Although originally written for Unix operating systems, BIND has been programmed for other operating systems, including Windows NT and Windows 2000.[16] It has also been used as the basis for many vendor name servers.[17]

The rest of this section uses BIND as an example because it is widely deployed. However, other name server software may behave differently in some respects and still conform to the domain name server standards.

A name server running BIND, or a comparable program, has complete information and authority over the zones for which it is authoritative. It contains all domain names from the top of its zone down to its leaves, except for those that are delegated to zones within it. See Figure 3.2.

Each zone must have a primary master (or primary) server that receives the contents of the zone data file from some manually prepared local file. The primary server is the ultimate source of information about the corresponding domain. Generally, there is at least 1 and possibly as many as 12 secondary servers, which obtain copies of the zone data file from the primary or another secondary.

BIND has not traditionally made severe computational or storage demands on the computers that run it. It has often been implemented on old machines that have been taken out of front-line service. However, BIND 9 incorporates security and other features that impose more severe computational loads. In general, the computational requirements on a name server depend on the number of queries per second and the relative distribution of the types of queries (because some types of queries impose greater computational demands than others), as well as the extent of change of the zone files. The memory requirements are determined by the

---

[14]BIND also contains a resolver library.

[15]According to a survey by Internet Systems Consortium, Inc., in January 2004 it was used by almost 75,000 servers; the second most popular name server software was provided by Microsoft for almost 15,000 servers. For more information about the survey and BIND, see "ISC Internet Domain Survey," March 10, 2004, available at <http://www.isc.org>.

[16]See "DNS Server Software" at <http://www.dns.net/dnsrd/servers/> for a survey of DNS servers available on various operating systems.

[17]A current list is posted at <http://www.isc.org/>.

size of its cache and zone files. In the latest versions of BIND, the cache size can be controlled. In general, the cache size for a new name server is determined by observation of the name server's operation over a few weeks to determine how much memory is required to respond to the query demand at its installation.

3.2.4 Standards

The queries and responses that flow between name servers must be in a protocol that is readily interpretable by any name server, no matter which software and hardware it uses. To that end, the data in the queries and responses are, like the zone data, represented as resource records (Box 3.2).

BOX 3.2 Resource Records

Resource records are used in every DNS zone data file and every DNS message.[1] Resource records begin with a domain name (NAME), which is followed by the type (TYPE) and class (CLASS) fields. Those fields are followed by the time to live (TTL) and a data field (RDATA), appropriate to the type and class. Domain names and IP addresses make up a large portion of the data in a typical zone data file.

NAME: The domain to which the record refers.

TYPE: The type of data in the resource record. The list of possible types is open-ended; each is associated with a type code. There were more than 50 in June 2005, of which no more than 20 are used to any extent.

Examples: A = host IP address; NS = an authoritative name server; MX = mail exchange.[2]

CLASS: Only one class, IN for Internet, is widely used. Four classes have been defined to date, one of which is obsolete.

TTL: Specifies the time interval (in seconds) that the resource record may be cached before the source of the information should again be consulted.

Example: 86400 (equivalent to one day).

RDATA: Describes the resource in question.

Example: If the class = IN and the type = A, this field is an IP address.[3]

If the class = IN and the type = NS, this field is a domain name.

---

[1]See P.V. Mockapetris, "Domain Names—Implementation and Specification," RFC 1035, November 1987, available at <http://www.rfc-editor.org>.

[2]For an explanation of "mail exchange," see Section 2.3.3.

[3]Since each Type-A resource record in Class IN can include only one IP address, a domain name that maps to multiple IP addresses will have multiple resource records—one for each IP address.

DNS Zone Data File

Each DNS zone has a zone data file (also called the master file) that contains both resource records describing the zone and actual data records for the zone. The former group specifies:

- The domain name of the primary name server and the e-mail address of the responsible person, as well as times associated with updating the secondary name servers;
- All the name servers that are authoritative for the zone; and
- The IP addresses of the name servers (name-to-address mappings) that are in the zone.

There can also be data files that contain reverse mappings (i.e., tables for conversion from IP addresses back to computer names). The domain names in these files look like IP addresses turned back to front, and they all end in in-addr.arpa.[18]

The zone data file may contain some additional types of resource records. The specification of resource records allows additional types of data to be added in the future, as required.

DNS Message Format

The DNS message format comprises five sections, some of which may be empty:

- Header,
- Question: the question for the name server (includes domain name),
- Answer: resource records answering the question,
- Authority: resource records pointing toward an authority, and
- Additional: resource records holding additional information.

The lengths of the four sections that follow it are specified in the header section.

The practical limitation on the number of root name servers to 13 is a consequence of the DNS message format and the design decision to use datagrams employing a minimal protocol—the User Datagram Protocol (UDP)[19]—to send DNS queries and responses so as to achieve high per-

[18]Addresses are converted to names in the .arpa domain for DNS lookup. The in-addr.arpa zone contains the hosts associated with all registered IPv4 addresses.

[19]For more information on the User Datagram Protocol, see Jon Postel, "User Datagram Protocol," RFC 768, August 28, 1980, available at <http://www.rfc-editor.org>.

formance. Because in current practice there must be room within the datagram answer section for a list of all root servers—in order to update the list of root servers[20] in every iterative resolver—the number of root servers is constrained by the maximum length of that section.[21] To maximize the number of root servers, their names were shortened and standardized for more efficient compression, increasing to 13 the maximum number that could fit in the space available.

3.2.5 Functions and Institutions

There are two critical functions that the DNS institutional framework performs in support of the standards and the programs that define the DNS. The first is maintenance of the DNS standards, and the second is ensuring the availability of DNS name server software. DNS client software, primarily stub resolvers, is widely available in standard software—operating systems, Web browsers—and the specifics of their provision are not further considered here.

Maintenance of the DNS Standards—The Internet Engineering Task Force

The definition and maintenance of the basic standards for the DNS are the responsibility of one informal organization—the Internet Engineering Task Force (IETF) (see Box 3.3). The IETF has attracted experienced and knowledgeable technical talent, who volunteer considerable time to its activities. The requests for comments (RFCs) process has provided a means for this diffuse technical community to build a freely available, peer-reviewed store of knowledge and the successful standards and protocols that enable the Internet and the DNS to function reliably and to adapt smoothly to the additional requirements imposed by increased scale, new applications, and new classes of users. Although the IETF's standards and protocols underpin the worldwide Internet and the DNS, it does not have the authority, the political or economic power, or the interest to force their adoption or validate their implementation. Rather, their universal use has been the result of the practical benefit of having freely

[20]As noted above, every iterative resolver needs to know where the name servers for the root zone are in order to have a starting point for a non-local, non-repeat query.

[21]In theory, the response could be a list of name servers that contain the names and locations of root name servers. Also, the hints file, which is local, could contain information about more than 13 name servers. However, the limitation to 13 has not yet been judged to be a large enough issue to change current practice in either respect.

BOX 3.3 The Internet Engineering Task Force and Requests for Comments

The Internet Engineering Task Force (IETF)[1] is a voluntary, non-commercial organization comprising individuals concerned with the evolution of the architecture and operation of the Internet. It is open to anyone who wishes to participate and draws from a large international community. However, almost all its participants are technologists from universities, network infrastructure operators, and firms in related industries. Although the IETF holds three meetings each year at locations around the world, much of its work is conducted through the circulation of e-mail to electronic mailing lists. The IETF divides its activities among working groups, organized into areas that are managed by area directors (ADs). The ADs, in turn, are members of the Internet Engineering Steering Group (IESG). The Internet Architecture Board (IAB) provides general oversight on Internet architecture issues and adjudicates appeals that are unresolved by the IESG, but it is not actively involved in standards development or implementation. The Internet Society (ISOC) charters the IAB and IESG.[2]

Requests for comments (RFCs) were established in 1969 to document technical and organizational aspects of the Internet (originally the ARPANET). RFC memos discuss protocols, procedures, programs, concepts, and various other aspects of the Internet. The IETF defines the official specification documents of the Internet Protocol suite that are published as "standards-track" RFCs. RFCs must first be published as Internet-Drafts—a mechanism to provide authors with the ability to distribute and solicit comments on documents that may ultimately become RFCs. An Internet-Draft, which can be published by anyone, has a maximum life of 6 months, unless updated and assigned a new version number. The Internet-Drafts that are intended for progression onto the standards track, and some other documents at IESG discretion, are "last called," which involves an announcement being sent out to the Internet community that the IESG wants input on the document. The Last Call is usually of a few weeks' duration. Using input from it, the IESG makes a decision on further processing of the Internet-Draft. Such decisions might include rejection of the draft, publishing it as a standards-track document, or handling it in some other way. Documents that are considered valuable and permanent, including all standards-track documents, are then submitted to the RFC editor for publication as RFCs.[3]

---

[1]For a full description, see Susan Harris, "The Tao of IETF—A Novice's Guide to the Internet Engineering Task Force," RFC 2160, August 2001, available at <http://www.rfc-editor.org>.

[2]For more information on the evolving relationship between ISOC and IESG, see <http://www.isoc.org/isoc/related/ietf/>.

[3]For details on this process, see Scott O. Bradner, "The Internet Standards Process, Revision 3," RFC 2026, October 1996, available at <http://www.rfc-editor.org>. For background on RFCs and a searchable repository of RFCs, see <http://www.rfc-editor.org>.

available high-quality standards that all can share, and that give no organization proprietary advantage. As a volunteer collaborating body, the IETF periodically restructures its processes. In 2003, the IETF identified a number of problems, both routine and structural, in its operations and initiated a process of problem resolution.[22] As is typical, it did so publicly via the RFC process.

Providing Root Name Server Software—Internet Software Consortium, Inc., and Other Software Providers

Internet Systems Consortium, Inc. (ISC), a not-for-profit organization formerly called the Internet Software Consortium, has assumed responsibility for continuing maintenance and development of BIND.[23] Although ISC's scope is considerably more focused than the IETF's, it, too, has played a key role in the smooth development and operation of the Internet and the DNS. By continuing to evolve BIND and making it readily available worldwide, free of charge, ISC has provided a widely adopted implementation of the DNS standards promulgated by the IETF.

Implementations of BIND and other DNS server software are also available from Microsoft and other software companies as well as from various providers in the form of freeware and shareware.

3.2.6 Assessment

Conclusion: The architecture of the Domain Name System has demonstrated the ability to scale to support the Internet's rapid growth, never holding up its development because of an inability to meet the challenges of vast increases in the number of domain names, users, and queries. Furthermore, it has demonstrated robustness, operating reliably despite malicious attacks and a very high volume of erroneous requests. What failures there have been have occurred in subzones of the system and have been insulated from the rest of the DNS by its hierarchical, distributed structure.

The hierarchical architecture and caching have been critical to the ability of the DNS to scale smoothly. First, they ensure that many queries are

---

[22]The problem statement and the history of the response are described in E. Davies, ed., "IETF Problem Statement," RFC 3774, May 2004, available at <http://www.rfc-editor.org>; and E. Davies and J. Hoffman, eds., "IETF Problem Resolution Process," RFC 3844, August 2004, available at <http://www.rfc-editor.org>.

[23]Information about ISC is available at <http://www.isc.org>.

resolved locally, never reaching the higher levels of the DNS. Second, even queries that do reach higher levels of the DNS do so only the first time they are made by a specific name server in a given period (the TTL), with all subsequent queries from the same name server during that period being answered locally.

These benefits are amplified by the ability of large ISPs, such as MCI and Verio, to maintain very large caches and, thereby, to handle a substantial portion of the queries originating from their customers without ever passing them along to the DNS.

Conclusion: Through its RFC process, the IETF has created a store of knowledge and a body of standards and protocols that have, thus far, enabled the Internet and the DNS to function reliably and to adapt smoothly to the additional requirements imposed by increased scale, new applications, and new classes of users. Though ISC's scope is much more focused than the IETF's and its participation and decision-making processes are far less open and public, by continuing the evolution of BIND and making it readily available ISC has brought most of the IETF DNS standards[24] into practical effect.

However, the continued growth of the Internet is posing new challenges and placing new demands on the DNS architecture. The issues of future security and robustness, internationalized domain names, and the intersection of the DNS with the telephone system are addressed in Chapter 4.

3.3 IMPLEMENTATION—THE DOMAIN NAME SYSTEM ROOT ZONE

The top of the DNS inverted tree is its root, or more properly, the root zone (see Section 3.1.1). The root zone name file (or, simply, root zone file) is stored in 13 root name servers, which use it to respond to queries to the root. As shown in Section 3.1, while queries can enter lower on the tree if their resolvers have current cached information, or if the query lies within the zone of the local name server, the root serves as the assured point of entry to the DNS for any other query.

---

[24]This issue is complex since not all of IETF's standards are mandatory or even recommended, and some are experimental or turn out to be bad ideas. The situation also differs between BIND 8, which is on end-of-life maintenance, and BIND 9, which is an entirely new code base. BIND 9 is believed to adhere to all the mandatory specifications, while ISC has eliminated non-compliant code from BIND 8 whenever it has been identified.

3.3.1 Characteristics of the Root Zone

Defining Characteristics

The root zone file defines the DNS. For all practical purposes, a top-level domain (and, therefore, all of its lower-level domains) is in the DNS if and only if it is listed in the root zone file. Therefore, presence in the root determines which DNS domains are available on the Internet.[25] As Internet use has grown, especially with the explosive growth of the Web and its reliance on domain names as key parts of Web site addresses, entry of a top-level domain into the root zone file has become a subject of substantial economic and social importance. Consequently, who controls entry into the root, and by what means, have become controversial subjects. The current process for resolving these issues is described in Section 3.3.3.

Critical Characteristics

The root zone and the root name servers are critical to the operation of the DNS. The effective and reliable operation of the DNS, and of the Internet, is entirely dependent on the accuracy and integrity of the root zone file (and its copies) and the security, reliability, and efficiency of the root name servers. Fortunately, the root zone has proven highly resilient and resistant to errors or disruptions.

One possible source of error is an incorrect entry—a mistyped domain name or an erroneous IP address—in the root zone file. A consequence could be misdirection of queries seeking a particular top-level domain (TLD) name server, say .net. That could prevent users searching for the address of any domain name within that name server's TLD, say any address in .net, from reaching it through the specific root name server containing the incorrect entry. If the error were updated in all copies of the root zone file, access would effectively be denied to all domain names in that TLD, except from name servers that had previously cached the correct address.[26] However, relatively simple error detection and correction procedures can quickly prevent such errors. (For example, most large top-level domains are programmed to regularly query the root to ensure that it is properly routing queries seeking that TLD.)

---

[25]The IP addresses for the servers of well-known TLDs are widely available, and so to them presence in the root may be less important. For less well known and new TLDs, however, presence in the root is the critical question.

[26]This exception would hold true only until the TTLs of the cached addresses expired.

A possibly disruptive event would involve one or more of the root name servers being non-operational for hours or more. This might happen because of the unexpected failure of a computer or communication link (accidental or purposeful) or because of regular maintenance. However, since the capacity of each name server is many times greater than its average load, and iterative resolvers can use any of the root name servers, other name servers can take up the load without degradation in the system's performance that is perceptible to users. Moreover, in recent years such outages have been very rare.[27]

Although, as noted, there have been instances in the past of errors in the root zone file that have had significant effects on the reliable operation of the DNS, there have been none in recent times. At least for the current rates of queries and of changes in the root zone file, the systems of error checking and correction and of capacity sharing appear to be working successfully.

Unique Characteristics

The design of the DNS is predicated on the existence of a single authoritative root that ensures that there is one and only one set of top-level domains. However, some of those who object to the pace at which new generic TLDs have been added to the root, or to the process by which they have been selected, have sought a solution through the addition of one or more roots. They have been joined by some who believe in the principle that having competition in the delivery of root services would benefit Internet users.

On the other side are those who argue that additional roots would compromise the reliable operation of the Internet by, among other things, opening the possibility of multiple addresses, associated with different entities, being assigned the same domain name.[28] Most experienced technologists view the idea of introducing multiple roots for the DNS as threatening the stable operation of the DNS.

---

[27]For example, in 2000, 4 of the 13 root servers failed for a brief period because of a technical mistake. In 1997, a more serious problem involving the transfer of an incorrect directory list to seven root servers caused much of the traffic on the Internet to come to a stop. As reported in "ISC Sets Up Crisis Centre to Protect Domain Name System," *Sydney Morning Herald*, October 21, 2003, available at <http://www.smh.com.au/articles/2003/10/21/1066631394527.html>.

[28]See, for example, M. Stuart Lynn, "ICP-3, a Unique, Authoritative Root for the DNS," ICANN, July 2001, available at <http://www.icann.org/icp/icp-3.htm>; also, Internet Architecture Board, "IAB Technical Comment on the Unique DNS Root," RFC 2826, May 2000, available at <http://www.rfc-editor.org>.

Moreover, since which domains are accessible to a user would depend on which of the multiple roots were used, these technologists see a multiple-root DNS as balkanizing the Internet. Although there may be some benefits from having competing roots, the presence of network externalities[29] encourages ISPs and name servers to converge on a single root that provides global compatibility. Consequently, many technologists and economists believe it is unlikely that an alternative root would achieve widespread success.[30] In their view, while competition may serve a valuable purpose in the short term, the task of maintaining the root zone file will equilibrate on a single, dominant root zone file, albeit an equilibrium in which operational control is shared among a number of (non-competing) entities.[31]

There have been several attempts to create alternate roots that have data about the TLDs that are recognized by the current root servers plus some additional TLDs that the operator of the alternate root is trying to promote. However, these attempts have generally been unsuccessful, in large measure because of the lack of global compatibility among the domain names recognized only by alternative roots, which has made users unwilling to use them. However, one company—New.net—claims to have reached financial profitability, to have registered over 100,000 domain names, and to be potentially accessible to 175 million Internet users through allied ISPs and browser plug-in software. It offers 12 additional TLDs in English as well as in each of Spanish, French, Portuguese, Italian, and German.[32] Although the continued existence of New.net can be seen as a challenge to the DNS and ICANN's management of the root zone file, it has not thus far appeared to have had any significant effect on either. Furthermore, in September 2004, New.net was acquired by the Vendare Group, an online media and marketing company, as the basis for a division offering search services, while continuing to offer domain name registration.[33]

---

[29]Network externalities are the increased benefits received by one user of a system as the number of users of the system increases.

[30]Milton L. Mueller, "Competing DNS Roots: Creative Destruction or Just Plain Destruction?" *Journal of Network Industries* 3(3):313-334, 2002.

[31]If an alternate root attracts a sufficient number of registrations, it raises the possibility that TLDs in the alternate root and registrations within these TLDs could be created for speculative purposes. If ICANN creates a TLD that already exists in an alternate root, the organization that controls the corresponding TLD in the alternate root could be willing to transfer the registered names to the ICANN TLD—for a price.

[32]This information was obtained from <http://www.new.net/> in February 2004.

[33]The Vendare Group, "The Vendare Group, Online Media and Marketing Company, Acquires Search-Services Provider New.net," press release, September 17, 2004, available at <http://www.new.net/id_9172004.tp>.

3.3.2 Technical System of the Root Zone

The Root Zone File

The root zone file contains resource records for all the TLDs as well as for the root. In February 2005, there were 258 sets of entries. Of those, 243 were country code TLDs (ccTLDs) and 15 were generic TLDs (gTLDs). (One of the gTLDs was the domain .arpa that is used for infrastructural purposes, which is sometimes considered a separate category.) Because there are multiple records in the root zone file for each of the subdomains, there were a total of 2143 records in the root zone, which translates to about 78 kilobytes of storage. Moreover, although, as noted earlier, all the root name servers together execute, in total, 8 billion searches a day on this file,[34] this is well within their computational capability because of the substantial overprovisioning of the system.

The Root Name Servers

Like other zone files, the root zone initially had a primary or master server accessible from the DNS and several—in this case, 12—secondary or slave servers. That primary zone file was the most current of the files, and all updates and changes were made to it; it served as the reference source for the root zone. The secondary files were updated from it on a regular basis, at least twice daily. Starting in 1996 and achieving adoption by all secondaries by the end of 2001, the role of the primary was transferred to a "hidden primary," which is a server that is used to update the secondaries but is not itself accessible from the DNS. VeriSign operates this hidden primary. All 13 of the public root name servers are now secondaries, including the former primary. Digital signatures, error checking, and correction processes are in place to minimize the chance of introducing errors or being successfully attacked during updates.

The December 2004 status of the group of 13 named root name servers is shown in Table 3.1.[35] They are designated by the letters A through M. The A-root server, a.root-server.net, was until recently the primary but, as noted above, has been replaced by a hidden primary. See Box 3.4.

---

[34]The F-root server (which includes its satellites), one of 13 root servers, answered more than 272 million queries per day according to the Internet Systems Consortium in January 2004. See <http://www.isc.org>.

[35]For the current version of this table, see <http://www.root-servers.org>. That Web site also contains links to the root name server operators and to other relevant information..

Although the home locations of some of the root servers are the result of historical accident, they were originally determined by analysis of network traffic flows and loads, seeking to have at least one server "close" in terms of message communication time to every location on the network. It is important to have root servers distributed so that they provide a uniform level of service across the network.[36] Having a root server in a well-connected area is fairly unimportant to that area, since users there are likely to be able to reach several servers. By contrast, if an area is fairly isolated from most of the network, it is important that the ISPs that serve it acquire sufficient connectivity to enable the area's users to access one or more root servers at all times.

Considerations of this type are both complex and important but were not sufficient to determine a unique set of locations for the home sites of the 13 root servers. However, as the Internet has evolved, these original locations became less satisfactory, which has been one of the reasons for the proliferation by some operators—notably C, F, I, J, K, and M in Table 3.1—of satellite sites at different locations. These satellite sites use anycast addressing (see Box 3.1), which enables servers with the same IP address to be located at different points on the Internet. Copies of the F-root server, for example, can be placed at multiple locations around the world. The widespread distribution of anycast satellites of the 13 root servers has improved the level of service provided to many previously less well served locations.

Some have believed that 13 root name servers are too few to meet requirements for reliability and robustness, which requires sufficient capacity distributed widely enough to protect against system or network failures and attacks. Others have believed that more root servers are needed to satisfy institutional requirements. Their concern arose from the belief that to be a full participant in the Internet, a nation or region must have its own root name server. While technical reasons[37] make it difficult to increase the number of root name server IP addresses beyond 13, the rapidly increasing use of anycast addressing has enabled the root name server system to respond to both the technical and institutional requirements through the addition of multiple geographically distributed anycast root server satellites. Even so, since it addresses the distribution only of

---

[36]See Tony Lee, Brad Huffaker, Marina Fomenkov, and kc klaffy, "On the Problem of Optimization of DNS Root Servers Placement," Passive Measurement and Analysis Workshop, 2003, available at <http://www.caida.org/outreach/papers/2003/dnsplacement/>.

[37]See "DNS Message Format" in Section 3.2.4 for an explanation of the technical limitations.

TABLE 3.1 The 13 Root Name Servers and Their Anycast Satellites as of December 2004

Name	Operator
A	VeriSign Naming and Directory Services
B	Information Sciences Institute, University of Southern California
C	Cogent Communications
D	University of Maryland
E	NASA, Ames Research Center
F	Internet Systems Consortium, Inc.
G	U.S. DOD Network Information Center
H	U.S. Army Research Laboratory
I	Autonomica/NordUNet
J	VeriSign Naming and Directory Services
K	Réseaux IP Européens— Network Coordination Centre
L	ICANN
M	WIDE Project

SOURCE: This table derives directly from information provided at <http://www.root-servers.org> as accessed on February 13, 2005.

servers and not of the operating institutions, the location issue is likely to continue to add some political acrimony to any selection process that might follow from the withdrawal of one of the current operators. (See Section 5.3.)

There is no standard hardware and software implementation of the root name servers. Each of the responsible organizations uses its preferred equipment and operating and file systems, although most of them run

Locations	Country
Dulles, VA	USA
Marina del Rey, CA	USA
Herndon, VA; New York City; Chicago; Los Angeles	USA
College Park, MD	USA
Mountain View, CA	USA
Palo Alto, CA; San Jose, CA; New York City; San Francisco; Ottawa; Madrid; Hong Kong; Los Angeles; Rome; Auckland; São Paulo; Beijing; Seoul; Moscow; Taipei; Dubai; Paris; Singapore; Brisbane; Toronto; Monterrey; Lisbon; Johannesburg; Tel Aviv; Jakarta; Munich; Osaka; Prague	USA
Vienna, VA	USA
Aberdeen, MD	USA
Stockholm; Helsinki; Milan; London; Geneva; Amsterdam; Oslo; Bangkok; Hong Kong; Brussels; Frankfurt; Ankara; Bucharest; Chicago; Washington, DC; Tokyo; Kuala Lumpur	Sweden
Dulles, VA (2 locations); Mountain View, CA; Sterling, VA (2 locations); Seattle, WA; Amsterdam; Atlanta, GA; Los Angeles; Miami; Stockholm; London; Tokyo; Seoul; Singapore	USA
London, Amsterdam, Frankfurt, Athens, Doha, Milan, Reykjavik, Helsinki, Geneva, Poznan, Budapest	NL
Los Angeles	USA
Tokyo, Seoul, Paris	Japan

some version of the BIND name server software.[38] Although there might be some operational advantages to having standard implementations,

[38]Since BIND 8 and BIND 9 have different code bases, this is less of a problem than it would be if they were identical. The K root and some instances of other servers run NSD name server software from NLnet labs of Amsterdam. VeriSign runs its own name server software.

BOX 3.4 VeriSign

VeriSign, Inc., founded in 1995, describes itself as providing "intelligent infrastructure services that support the digital economy." Its acquisition in 2000 of Network Solutions, Inc. made it the registry for three gTLDs: .com, .net, and .org and the operator of the A-root and the J-root name servers.

It currently operates the A-root and J-root name servers, the hidden root primary, and the name servers for the .com, and .net TLDs. At the end of 2004, its Naming and Directory Services unit managed a database of over 38 million names in the .com and .net gTLDs; owned and maintained 13 gTLD name server sites around the globe that handled the more than 14 billion transactions per day for those two gTLDs; and provided access to the .com and .net gTLD registries for more than 150 ICANN-accredited registrars that submit over 100 million domain name transactions daily to its Shared Registration System.

As a registrar—through a subsidiary renamed Network Solutions, Inc. in 2003—it registered more than 500,000 new domain names during the second quarter of 2002, and an additional 700,000 names were renewed or extended. More than 8.7 million active domain names in .com and .net were under management by VeriSign's registrar. However, in October 2003, it sold Network Solutions to a private equity firm for $100 million.[1]

[1]This information was obtained from <http://www.verisign.com> on February 13, 2005.

most Internet technologists believe that variation in the underlying hardware and software of the root name server system is highly desirable, since it ensures that an error in a particular piece of hardware or software will not lead to the simultaneous failure of all of the root servers.

As the number and rate of queries to the root name servers have increased, hardware and software upgrades have enabled the servers to keep up.[39] However, the pace of inquiries is likely to continue to grow and it is conceivable that it could, in principle, exceed the capacity of a system comprising even the most powerful single computers. Because of anycasting and multiprocessing, through which a root server can comprise multiple processors, the number of computers at each root-server address is effectively unrestricted. Moreover, it is plausible to expect continued improvements in computing and communications performance. Consequently, it is

[39]This is only a portion of the total potential query load to the root zone file because of caching of queries by many name servers, and especially those of large ISPs, as noted above.

unlikely that the query load will ever be able to outrun the computing capacity of the 13 named root name servers and their satellites.

3.3.3 Institutional Framework of the Root Zone

Because the root is central and critical to the operation of the DNS, decisions about the root zone and the root name servers are of substantial importance, and the institutions that bear responsibility for them take on an important role as stewards of the DNS.

Those institutions carry out four critical functions:

1. Deciding what new or revised entries will be permitted in the root zone file;
2. Creating the root zone file, keeping it current, and distributing it to all the root name servers;
3. Selecting the locations and the operators of the root name servers; and
4. Establishing and continually and reliably operating the root name servers.

The diverse collection of institutions that performs these functions includes a not-for-profit corporation—ICANN; a U.S. government agency—the Department of Commerce; a corporation—VeriSign; and an informal group consisting of the commercial, non-commercial, and governmental root name server operators.

Approving the Root Zone File—U.S. Department of Commerce and ICANN

The fundamental importance of the root zone file to the operation of the DNS and, therefore, of the Internet means that special attention is paid to the process by which new or revised entries to the file are authorized. Some process must be in place to decide whether a change is legitimate; otherwise, persons or organizations with malicious motives or inadequate capabilities could make or revise entries. Currently the authority to make changes lies with the U.S. Department of Commerce (DOC).[40] However, the day-to-day operational responsibility is at VeriSign. As part of the DOC's delegation of responsibility to ICANN (see Box 3.5), the process of authorization for new or modified entries in the root zone was changed.

[40]See Section 2.7 for a history of that authority.

BOX 3.5 The Internet Corporation for Assigned Names and Numbers

As described in Chapter 2, the Internet Corporation for Assigned Names and Numbers (ICANN) is a not-for-profit corporation founded in October 1998 in California by a group of individuals interested in the Internet. It was sponsored by the U.S. Department of Commerce (DOC) to serve as a technical coordination body for the Internet. Consequently, ICANN has assumed responsibility (under a memorandum of understanding—and its six amendments—with the DOC) for a set of technical functions previously performed under U.S. government contract by the Internet Assigned Numbers Authority (IANA) and other groups. However, in practice, many of its most important and controversial activities have been as a policy-setting, rather than as a technical coordination, body.

IANA continues as a function of ICANN with overall administrative responsibility for the assignment of IP addresses, autonomous system numbers, top-level domains, and other unique parameters of the Internet. In addition, ICANN is charged with coordinating the stable operation of the Internet's root server system.

ICANN's primary governing body is its board of directors, which now comprises 15 voting members and the president, ex officio. Dissatisfaction with the composition of the board and with the nature of the selection process inspired a reform effort that resulted in new bylaws that guided the selection of a new board in 2003. (See Section 5.2.4, Alternative F, for a description of this reform.)

ICANN has three supporting organizations: the Address Supporting Organization (ASO), which deals with the system of IP addresses; the Country-Code Names Supporting Organization (ccNSO), which focuses on issues related to the country-code top-level domains; and the Generic Names Supporting Organization (GNSO), which handles issues related to the generic top-level domains. In addition, it has four advisory committees: the At-Large Advisory Committee (ALAC) for the Internet community at-large; the DNS Root Server System Advisory Committee (RSSAC) for root server

All such requests go first to the Internet Assigned Numbers Authority (IANA) (now a function of ICANN) and then to the DOC for final approval. Once the addition or change is approved, the DOC notifies IANA and VeriSign. VeriSign Naming and Directory Services then makes the change in the hidden primary, which distributes the changed root zone file to the other root name servers (see "Operating the Root Name Servers" in Section 3.3.3).

There are three kinds of changes to the root zone file. The first kind of change is a modification of the data associated with an existing resource record. This might entail a change in the IP address of one or more of the operators; the Governmental Advisory Committee (GAC) for governments; and the Security and Stability Advisory Committee (SSAC) for security. There is also the Technical Liaison Group (TLG) for standards-setting organizations and an Internet Engineering Task Force liaison who provides technical advice to ICANN. The supporting organizations and advisory committees together represent a broad cross section of the Internet's commercial, technical, academic, non-commercial, and user communities and advise the board on matters lying within their areas of expertise and interest.

As part of the reform effort, ICANN adopted a new mission statement:

> The mission of ICANN is to coordinate the stable operation of the Internet's unique identifier systems. In particular, ICANN:
>
> 1. Coordinates the allocation and assignment of three sets of unique identifiers of the Internet—domain names, IP addresses and autonomous system (AS) numbers, and protocol ports and parameter numbers.
> 2. Coordinates the operation and evolution of the DNS's root name server system.
> 3. Coordinates policy-development as reasonably and appropriately related to the performance of these functions.

ICANN is open to the participation of any interested Internet user, business, or organization. It holds several meetings a year at locations around the world.[1] ICANN has been the subject of many controversies regarding its governance, its processes, and its decisions since its founding. The primary issues are discussed in Section 5.2. A good sense of the full range of controversies that have surrounded ICANN can be obtained from <http://www.icannwatch.org>, CircleID (<http://circleid.com>), and ICANNFocus (<http://www.icannfocus.org>), through the resources that can be linked to from these sites, and from innumerable articles written about ICANN.

[1]Information about ICANN was derived from <http://www.icann.org> on February 13, 2005.

name servers resulting, for example, from a change in the network service provider. The data entry process is straightforward, and so such changes should be routine and rapid. However, they do require a stage of verification to ensure that the request is legitimate and not, for example, an effort by a third party to capture a top-level domain. Nevertheless, such requests should be processed in a few hours or days.

The second kind of change is a shift in the responsibility for a TLD, typically a ccTLD. In such redelegation cases, the questions that must be resolved may be more difficult and time-consuming. (See "Selecting the Organizations Responsibile for the TLDs" in Section 3.4.3 for a discussion of the issues.) In particular, they may entail judging which organization has the "right" to operate the registry for a ccTLD, which can become embroiled in national politics. These changes will generally take longer but should proceed according to a formal and transparent process.

The third kind of change is the addition of data about a new TLD to the root zone file (see "Selecting the Organizations Responsible for the TLDs" in Section 3.4.3). This is a single process for new gTLDs. An ICANN selection process recommends both the domain name that shall be added and who shall operate it. It is a two-step process for new ccTLDs. Who will be responsible for operations is a separate recommendation from the decision to add a ccTLD name to the list of ccTLDs. Such changes should take place within a few days after the appropriate decisions have been made.

Maintaining the Root Zone File—VeriSign

VeriSign, as the operator of the hidden primary root zone server, is responsible for maintaining the root zone file and for distributing it to the secondary servers. It performs this function under the terms of a memorandum of understanding (MoU) with the DOC.

Since any errors in the root zone file can affect large numbers of sites and users, accurate and error-free preparation and distribution of the file are essential. In the first instance, this is a human function. Someone must enter additions and updates into the database, create a new zone file, and check it for errors. Individuals at the secondary sites must check to ensure that the file has not been corrupted during its distribution. However, computer techniques and aids can be used to support this process and reduce the demands on humans. Furthermore, regular queries of the root by each of the TLD operators can be used to test the entries corresponding to their TLDs and provide further assurance that no undetected errors are present in the file.

Selecting the Root Name Server Operators—Self-Selection

The current root name server operators were not selected through a formal evaluation and qualification process, although they play a fundamental role in ensuring the availability and reliability of the root. Rather, the group is the cumulative result of a sequence of separate decisions taken over the years since the establishment of the DNS. It is a loosely organized collection of autonomous institutions whose names are given in Table 3.1. Ten of them are based in the United States. Of those, three are associated with the U.S. government (National Aeronautics and Space Administration (NASA), Department of Defense (DOD), and the U.S. Army), two are universities (University of Maryland and University of

Southern California), two are corporations (VeriSign and Cogent Communications), and two are not-for-profits (ISC, Inc. and ICANN). Three are based outside the United States: one in Sweden, one in the Netherlands, and one in Japan.

One of the responsibilities that ICANN assumed under its agreement with the DOC is coordinating the stable operation of the root server system. To do so, it established the DNS Root Server System Advisory Committee, whose responsibilities were spelled out in ICANN's bylaws (Article VII, Section 3(b)).

> The responsibility of the Root Server System Advisory Committee shall be to advise the Board (of ICANN) about the operation of the root name servers of the domain name system. The Root Server System Advisory Committee should consider and provide advice on the operational requirements of root name servers, including host hardware capacities, operating systems and name server software versions, network connectivity and physical environment . . . should examine and advise on the security aspects of the root name server system . . . [and] should review the number, location, and distribution of root name servers considering the total system performance, robustness, and reliability.
>
> The parties will collaborate on a study and process for making the management of the Internet (DNS) root server system more robust and secure.

ICANN's intent is to enter into an MoU[41] with each server operator that will spell out the root name server performance requirements, such as service levels, reliability, and security. However, as of February 2005, no MoUs had yet been signed.

In the absence of an agreed oversight role for ICANN, there is, at present, no formal process for selecting a new root name server operator if one of the incumbents should withdraw, although it is clear that the set of remaining operators could, and probably would, work together to make the selection. (See Section 5.3 for a discussion of this issue.)

Operating the Root Name Servers—The Root Name Server Operators

The role of the operators of the 13 root name servers is to maintain reliable, secure, and accurate operation of the servers containing the current root zone on a 24-hour-a-day, 365 days-per-year-basis. Each server is expected to have the capacity to respond to many times the rate of queries it receives and must increase its capacity at least as fast as the query rate

---

[41]The DNS Root Server System Advisory Committee has drafted a model memorandum of understanding, available at <http://www.icann.org/committees/dns-root/model-root-server-mou-21jan02.htm>.

increases. An attempt to define the responsibilities of the root name server operators was made in RFC 2870, issued in June 2000,[42] but the ideal that it describes has not been achieved.

Historically, the operators of the root servers have not charged fees for resolving Internet address queries, instead obtaining support in other ways for the substantial costs they incur in providing the service. These operators choose to do so either because (1) they believe that operating a root server is a public service (and sufficiently inexpensive that they can afford the cost) or (2) they believe that operating a root server conveys a business, or other, advantage to them. Nevertheless, it is a valuable service, whose provision is a little-known and little-appreciated gift in kind to all users of the Internet.

3.3.4 Assessment

Conclusion: The system of DNS root name servers currently responds to more than 8 billion queries per day[43] and does so reliably and accurately as shown by its virtually uninterrupted availability and the very low occurrence of root-caused misdirections. Because the majority of queries are served from cached answers lower in the hierarchy, the entire DNS responds to many times that number each day with correspondingly good results. However, the robust operation of the root name servers is potentially vulnerable to an excessive query load, either inadvertent or malicious, that might slow down their responses or cause them to fail to respond.

Data collected about root name server operation has revealed that a substantial fraction—between 75 percent and 97 percent—of the load on those servers may be the result of erroneous queries.[44] These errors fall into three categories: stupid—for example, asking for the IP address of an IP address; invalid—for example, asking for the IP address of a nonexistent domain; and repetitive—for example, continuing to send an incorrect query even after receiving a negative response. Analysis has revealed that the sources of many of these errors lie in faulty resolver or name server software and faulty system management that misconfigures name servers

---

[42]See Randy Bush, Daniel Karrenberg, Mark Kosters, and Raymond Plzak, "Root Name Server Operational Requirements," RFC 2870, June 2000, available at <http://www.rfc-editor.org>.

[43]The monthly average load on all root name servers in December 2004 was around 90,000 queries per second according to the Internet Society's Member Briefing No. 20, "DNS Root Name Servers—Frequently Asked Questions," January 2005, available at <http://www.isoc.org/briefings/020/>.

[44]The 97 percent figure is from Wessels and Fomenkov, "Wow, That's a Lot of Packets," 2003. However, according to an anonymous reviewer, VeriSign's experience on its two servers is closer to 75 percent.

or resolvers and does not monitor performance closely enough to catch errors. The latter is not purely a technical issue but poses an institutional issue.[45] Software developers, system administrators, and users generally have few incentives to make an effort to prevent the occurrence of this extra load.

In addition, the system of root name servers may be vulnerable to malicious attempts to overload it. In October 2002, the root name server system was subjected to such a denial-of-service attack that sought to swamp the system with queries.[46] Eight of the 13 servers were inaccessible from some places on the Internet for an hour or more, but the remaining 5 served the Internet without observable degradation. Although the system successfully resisted this attack, which lasted only an hour and a half, it should serve as a warning about the potential for longer and more sophisticated attacks in the future.

Conclusion: The root name servers receive far too many incorrect or repetitive queries, increasing the load that they must serve. This unnecessary load arrives at the root name servers because many sites on the Internet employ faulty software, misconfigure their resolvers or name servers, or do not manage their systems adequately. The root name server operators, however, lack the means to discipline the sites at fault.

Conclusion: The root name servers are subject to malicious attack, but through overprovisioning and the addition of anycast satellites have substantially reduced their vulnerability to denial-of-service attacks. Furthermore, the widespread caching of the root zone file and its long time to live mean that the DNS could continue to operate even during a relatively long outage of most or all of the root name servers and their satellites.

Recommendation: To be able to continue to meet the increasing query load, both benign and malign, the root name server operators should continue to implement both local and global load balancing through the deployment of anycast satellites.

---

[45]These analyses have been sponsored by the Cooperative Association for Internet Data Analysis (CAIDA) and have been reported in many publications. In addition to the Wessels and Fomenkov study, see, for example, Nevil Brownlee, kc claffy, and Evi Nemeth, "DNS Measurements at a Root Server," *Proceedings of IEEE Globecom*, CAIDA, San Antonio, Tex., November 2001, pp. 1672-1676. Also see <http://caida.org/outreach/papers/2001/DNSmeasroot/>.

[46]See, for example, David McGuire and Brian Krebs, "Attack on Internet Called Largest Ever," *Washington Post*, October 22, 2002. Three root server operators coauthored an authoritative report about the attack. It can be found at <http://d.root-servers.org/october21.txt>.

Conclusion: Notwithstanding the deployment of anycast servers and installation of backup servers at remote locations, the concentration of root name server facilities and personnel in the Washington, D.C., area and, to a lesser extent, in the Los Angeles area is a potential vulnerability.

Recommendation: The need for further diversification of the location of root name server facilities and personnel should be carefully analyzed in the light of possible dangers, both natural and human in origin.

Conclusion: The system of root name servers lacks formal management oversight, although the operators do communicate and cooperate. Not everyone would agree that formal oversight is desirable. Should one or more of the current root name server operators withdraw from that responsibility, or fail to exercise it reliably, effectively, or securely, there would be no responsible organization or formal process for removing the failed operator or for recruiting and selecting a replacement. In their absence, the informal, collegial processes that led to the current group of operators would likely continue to be used.

Conclusion: The root name server operators have provided effective and reliable service to the community of Internet users without any form of direct compensation for that service from the users. With the growth in the scale and economic importance of the Internet, and with the expense of ensuring secure operation, the root name server operators face increasing costs and potential liabilities that some, at least, may find too great to meet without compensation.[47] Indeed, the current system for maintaining root servers may well face additional economic pressures, as well as technical ones, as the volume of Internet traffic increases, especially if the number of TLDs were to be expanded.

The root zone must be kept secure and robust in the face of possible future threats. Moreover, the continued stable management and financing of root zone operations must be ensured for the DNS to function. These challenges and approaches to meeting them are discussed in Section 5.3.

---

[47]As noted in *President's Report: ICANN—The Case for Reform*, February 24, 2002, ". . . some organizations that sponsor a root name server operator have little motivation to sign formal agreements [with ICANN], even in the form of the MOU that is now contemplated. What do they gain in return, except perhaps unwanted visibility and the attendant possibility of nuisance litigation? They receive no funding for their efforts, so why should they take on any contractual commitments, however loose?" The same logic raises questions about their incentives to continue to operate the root name servers. See <http://www.icann.org/general/lynn-reform-proposal-24feb02.htm>.

3.4 IMPLEMENTATION—THE TOP-LEVEL DOMAINS

The portion of the DNS hierarchy that has captured the most public attention and attracted the greatest controversy is the level just below the root, the top-level domains. As noted above, in February 2005 there were 258 such domains in the two major categories defined in the early days of the DNS (see Section 2.2.1): 243 country code top-level domains (ccTLDs) and 15 generic top-level domains (gTLDs). These TLDs are, in turn, the top of a hierarchy of second-level domain names. Typically, the commercial gTLDs have very flat structures with many second-level names, but the others vary widely, some having very deep structures. The ccTLDs also have a wide range of structures, some having several levels of hierarchy, which may be structured geographically or generically.

3.4.1 Characteristics of the TLDs

ccTLDs

The 243 ccTLDs are each associated with a nation or region or external territory and designated by the two-letter abbreviation for that entity assigned by the International Organization for Standardization in ISO 3166-1.[48] Examples of ccTLDs are .ke for Kenya, .jp for Japan, and .de for Germany.[49] The expectation was that a ccTLD would signify a location and would be supervised and administered by an organization in the corresponding location, and be limited to registrants with a presence there; however, these criteria are not effectively enforced. Moreover, a number of small nations and territories have licensed administration of their domains—for example, .tv for Tuvalu and .cc for the Cocos Islands—to commercial bodies that register anyone who wishes to use that ccTLD's two-letter domain. Such ccTLDs are for all practical purposes equivalent to commercial gTLDs. This equivalence is further explored in "Recharacterizing TLDs" in Section 3.4.1.

The largest ccTLDs are listed in Table 3.2, as are most of those ccTLDs, shown in boldface, that have contracted for commercial use of their domains. The .us domain, which had been limited to third- and fourth-level registrations in a locality-based hierarchy, is shown in italics. In April 2002, registration at the second level in .us was opened with

[48]See <http://www.iso.org/iso/en/prods-services/iso3166ma/index.html> for a list of the abbreviations.

[49]There are a few exceptions to the use of ISO 3166-1 two-letter abbreviations. For example, the United Kingdom is assigned .uk rather than .gb (for Great Britain). ICANN has also assigned ccTLD two-letter codes to each of the Channel Islands and to Ascension Island, which are not in ISO 3166-1, because it was anticipated that they would be added to the list.

the intent that any U.S. citizen or resident and any business or organization with a bona fide presence in the United States could register a domain name in .us.[50]

Table 3.2 shows the number of domains registered at the first available level under each top-level domain in February 2003. The total at that time was just over 19 million. By December 2003, almost 24 million domains had been registered in ccTLDs, and by November 2004 it had reached 25.6 million. As noted above, some country code TLDs have further generic or geographic substructures. In those cases, the count of domains is the sum of those registered under each second- or third-level domain, depending on the highest level at which registration by the general public is permitted.

gTLDs

There are 15 gTLDs, 8 that date from the early years of the DNS—.net, .com, .org, .edu, .gov, .mil, .int, and .arpa—and 7 that were authorized by ICANN in November 2000. As their designations suggest, the expectation was that registration in the original gTLDs would be by types of organizations. Commercial organizations were expected to register in .com, accredited educational organizations in .edu, network infrastructure organizations in .net, U.S. government organizations in .gov and .mil, and international treaty organizations in .int. The .org TLD was created for organizations that did not fit into one of the other gTLDs. The designation .arpa was assigned for network infrastructural use.

In announcing the authorization of the seven new gTLDs—.biz, .info, .name, .aero, .museum, .coop, and .pro, ICANN distinguished between sponsored and unsponsored TLDs. Those that are sponsored have a not-for-profit organization representing the community of potential registrants. The charters of the sponsored TLDs specify that registrants are restricted to those satisfying criteria appropriate to that community. Thus, .aero is restricted to people, entities, and government agencies that (1) provide for and support the efficient, safe, and secure transport of people and cargo by air and (2) facilitate or perform the necessary transactions to transport people and cargo by air. Registrations in .museum are restricted to entities that are recognized by the International Council of Museums as museums, professional associations of museums, or individuals who are professional museum workers. And registrations in .coop are restricted to members of the international cooperative movement, which is further defined by mem-

[50]The locality-based use of .us seems to be declining, which raises questions about the relative merits of registrations at the second level and their associated revenue motivations versus the benefits of the locality-based structure of .us.

TABLE 3.2 Some Large Country-Code Top-Level Domains

ccTLD	Country or Territory	Registered Domain Names[a]
.de	Germany	6,117,000
.uk	United Kingdom	4,168,000
.nl	Netherlands	827,000
.it	Italy	767,000
.ar	Argentina	627,000
.jp	Japan	568,000
.us	*United States*	529,000
.kr	Republic of Korea	507,000
.cc	**Cocos (Keeling) Islands**	**500,000**
.ch	Switzerland	500,000
.dk	Denmark	428,000
.br	Brazil	427,000
.au	Australia	343,000
.ca	Canada	310,000
.at	Austria	272,000
.tv	**Tuvalu**	**262,000**
.be	Belgium	238,000
.ws	**Western Samoa**	**183,000**
.cn	China	179,000
.pl	Poland	175,000
.fr	France	163,000
.ru	Russian Federation	156,000
.za	South Africa	134,000
.tw	Taiwan	123,000
.nu	**Niue**	**112,000**
.to	**Tonga**	**97,000**
Total (including ccTLDs not listed above)		25,637,000

NOTE: Individual domain data is for February 2003; the total is for November 2004.

[a]SOURCE: ICANN's Budget for Fiscal Year 2003-2004. See <http://www.icann.org/financials/revised-proposed-budget-24jun03.htm>. Domain name counts where not available are estimated from the average of all other ccTLDs for which data is available (from Web sites or other direct information). These estimated counts represent about 16 percent of all ccTLD domain names. The total (for November 2004) was provided by Matthew Zook, Department of Geography, University of Kentucky.

bership in one or more of eight specific classes. ICANN allows unsponsored TLDs to be either restricted or unrestricted. Thus, .info is unrestricted—anyone can register a name in .info, whereas .name is restricted to individuals and .biz is restricted to bona fide business or commercial uses. Determination of who is eligible to register is up to the domain operator operating under the terms of its agreement with ICANN.

TABLE 3.3 Generic Top-Level Domains in 2004

gTLD	Type	Current Purpose
.com	Unsponsored	Unrestricted
.net	Unsponsored	Unrestricted
.org	Unsponsored	Unrestricted
.edu	Sponsored	U.S. accredited higher educational institutions
.mil	Sponsored	U.S. military
.gov	Sponsored	U.S. governments
.arpa	Sponsored	Internet infrastructure
.int	Unsponsored	International treaty organizations
.info	Unsponsored	Unrestricted
.biz	Unsponsored	Businesses
.name	Unsponsored	Individuals
.pro	Unsponsored	Professionals
.museum	Sponsored	Museums
.aero	Sponsored	Air-transport industry
.coop	Sponsored	Cooperatives

[a]SOURCE: ICANN's Budget for Fiscal Year 2003-2004. See <http://www.icann.org/financials/revised-proposed-budget-24jun03.htm>. Domain count data provided courtesy of Matthew Zook, Department of Geography, University of Kentucky. Ongoing data series are available at his Web site <http://www.zooknic.com/>.

[b]Neulevel is a joint venture of Neustar, Inc., and Australia-based Melbourne IT, Ltd.

[c]*.pro* started accepting registrations in the United States on June 1, 2004, from licensed MDs, lawyers, and CPAs; added Canadian and U.K. professionals in September 2004; and added engineers in February 2005.

The 15 generic TLDs are shown in Table 3.3 together with, for each, its type and purpose, the organization responsible for its operation, and the number of second-level domains that are registered in it. Note, however, that in many domains there are far more registrants at the third and lower levels.

Recharacterizing TLDs

Although a distinction between generic TLDs and national or country code TLDs is widely accepted and used in policy discussions, the reality of practice is that the distinctions have been significantly eroded.

Organization	Domains[a]
VeriSign GRS	33,352,000
VeriSign GRS	5,324,000
Public Interest Registry (PIR) as of January 1, 2003	3,307,000
Educause	7,400
U.S. DOD Network Information Center	?
U.S. General Services Administration (GSA)	1,100
Internet Architecture Board/Internet Assigned Numbers Authority (IANA)	?
IANA	88
Aflilias, LLC	3,334,000
Neulevel[b]	1,088,000
Global Name Registry	87,000
Registry.pro	—[c]
MuseDoma	658[d]
SITA	4,000+[e]
DotCooperation, LLC	7,992[f]
Total	46,412,000[g]

[d]Data provided by Cary Karp, president and CEO, MuseDoma, personal communication, February 20, 2004.

[e]As listed on the .aero Web site in February 2005. See <http://www.information.aero/users.php>.

[f]As of February 2004. Carolyn Cooper, dot Coop Operations Center, personal communication, March 17, 2004.

[g]Total reported on the Zooknic Web site at <http://www.zooknic.com>, February 2005.

Among the generic gTLDs, three—.edu,[51] .mil, and .gov—are currently restricted to new registrations by U.S. organizations and, in principle, could have been established as second-level domains under the .us ccTLD.

As noted above, among the ccTLDs, a number—including .cc, .tv, .bz, .ws, .nu, and .to—actively seek global registrants and function as though they were gTLDs.

[51]Some non-U.S. educational institutions, such as the University of Toronto and the United Nations University, retain their registrations from an earlier, less restrictive time. Also, registrations from foreign but U.S.-accredited educational institutions are currently being accepted.

Moreover, the registrants in some gTLDs have not been limited to those originally expected. In practice, .com, .net, or .org have all been operating as unrestricted TLDs—any person or organization can register in them.

Since many policy issues concern the desirable number and type of TLDs, it is useful to introduce a characterization of TLDs that better captures the reality of their current state.

In Table 3.4, the TLDs are recharacterized into eight types, designated by the numbers 1 to 8, which are given in the first column. The second column, "TLD," indicates whether the domain is currently considered a gTLD or a ccTLD.

The "Scope" column shows whether the TLD is open to registrants from anywhere on the globe—global—or is primarily for those who are located within the national boundaries of the country—national. (Many ccTLDs that are primarily national will accept some non-national registrants, but usually they must have an association with the country.) In addition, the .arpa TLD is open only to register elements of the infrastructure of the Internet, so its scope is designated as infrastructural.

The "Restriction" column in Table 3.4 indicates whether the generic TLD or, within national boundaries, the ccTLD has second- or third-level domains that are intended to be restricted to members of specific communities (however, the enforcement of these restrictions varies widely). Most ccTLDs have no restrictions on registrations at the second level, but some, such as .ar (Argentina) and .au (Australia), and the .us (United States) until recently, register only at the third level under a limited number of restricted second-level domains, such as com.ar and com.au for commercial organizations. However, Great Britain, .uk, has some second-level domains that are restricted, such as ltd.uk and plc.uk, and others, such as co.uk, that are not. As with other aspects of the DNS, restriction within ccTLDs is not really "yes" or "no," but more accurately "yes," "no," or "some." That situation is reflected in Table 3.4 by treating second-level domains of such ccTLDs as though they were "separate" TLDs—see the examples in 7 and 8.

The "Sponsor" column indicates whether an organization representative of a community has responsibility for managing a gTLD and for enforcing registration restrictions, if any. The concept of sponsor for a ccTLD is less clear. To some degree, for example, the governments of the United States and of France, for example, can be viewed as the sponsors of their ccTLDs. The corresponding entries are left blank.

Thus, among the 15 current gTLDs, 4 are of Type 1—.com, .net, .org, and .info. Type 2 includes three TLDs–.museum, .aero, and .coop. There are four in Type 3: .name, .biz, .pro, and .int. That leaves three in Type

TABLE 3.4 Types of Top-Level Domains

Type	TLD	Scope	Intended Restriction	Sponsor	Examples
1	gTLD	Global	No	No	.com, .net, .info, .org
2	gTLD	Global	Yes	Yes	.aero, .museum, .coop
3	gTLD	Global	Yes	No	.biz, .name, .pro, .int
4	gTLD	National	Yes	Yes	.mil, .gov, .edu
5	ccTLD	Global	No	–	.cc, .tv, .bz
6	ccTLD	National	No	–	.jp, .fr, .us, .co.uk
7	ccTLD	National	Yes	–	com.au, id.au, .ltd.uk
8	gTLD	Infrastructural	Yes	Yes	.arpa

4—.edu, .mil, and .gov, which are discussed below as ccTLDs—and one in Type 8, .arpa.

It has not been possible to assign a type to each of the 243 ccTLDs, but examples of each of the four types have been identified in Table 3.4.

Type 5 comprises many ccTLDs that function as generic TLDs. As noted above, they are generally small countries that have recognized, or been shown, that their two-letter designation can be marketed globally to companies and individuals who would find it commercially or personally valuable. Thus, the lease of the domain name of Tuvalu (population: 11,000) could provide that Pacific Island nation with $50 million in royalties over the next dozen years. The .TV Corporation, a subsidiary of VeriSign, in June 2005 listed on its site such "premium registrations" as business.tv, which is available for $1 million, and weather.tv, which would cost the registrant $250,000. The administrator of this TLD is the Ministry of Finance and Tourism of Tuvalu, although in fact, the ministry appears to have delegated all of its decision-making authority to the .TV Corporation as a part of the lease. Other nations are managing their globally available domains themselves. Western Samoa (population: 178,000), another Pacific island nation, markets .ws directly and handles the registration locally. Western Samoa had two ISPs and 3000 Internet users in 2002.[52]

[52]See CIA, *The World Factbook*, 2004, available at <http://www.odci.gov/cia/publications/factbook/fields/2028.html>.

While some ccTLDs function as gTLDs, Type 4 comprises the three gTLDs that function like ccTLDs—.edu, .gov, .mil. All three are limited to registrants in the United States that are, in turn, restricted to specific communities—primarily accredited higher educational institutions,[53] civilian government[54] agencies, and federal military agencies.

The remaining two types distinguish between restricted and non-restricted ccTLDs. Almost all ccTLDs are unrestricted at the second and third levels and fall into Type 6, but some, such as Australia, Argentina, and Austria, have introduced categories resembling the gTLD categories as their second levels. They belong to Type 7. Thus, Australians cannot register directly in the .au domain but must instead use the category appropriate to their status: com.au for commercial organizations, asn.au for associations, id.au for individuals, and so on.

Thus, the apparently simple distinction between gTLDs and ccTLDs is really more complex. The differences among TLDs lie in the differences in the policies that they operate under, not in whether they were originally associated with a country code or a generic category.

3.4.2 Technical System of the TLDs

Every TLD has an associated zone file, which is stored in name servers whose addresses are recorded in the root zone file. ICANN requires that there be at least two name servers for each ccTLD and at least five for each gTLD with which it has agreements. Some TLDs have as many as 13 name servers, depending on the query load, the need for security against attack, and their desire to improve access by their users. Each name server is implemented on one or more computers, most of which run a version of BIND.[55]

The zone files on all TLDs are larger, generally very much larger, than the root zone file. At the extreme, .com contains more than 33 million second-level domains, but even Greenland has more than 1200 domains registered. Moreover, because of the hierarchical nature of DNS search,

---

[53]As noted previously, some non-U.S. academic institutions have been "grandfathered in" or will be registered if they are accredited in the United States. Also, there are some other exceptions such as the Thomas Jefferson High School for Science and Technology, whose domain name is tjhsst.edu.

[54]Originally it was limited to federal agencies. It is now open to registration by state and local governments and Native Sovereign Nations.

[55]However, the name server for .org (and for some other TLDs) is operated by UltraDNS, which uses its own proprietary name server software; and VeriSign, which runs .com, .net, .bz, and .tv, also uses its own proprietary name server software, Atlas.

the ease of caching the labels and associated resource record sets in the small root zone file, and the long TTLs within that file, the TLD name servers receive a greater number of queries than the root name servers. For example, according to VeriSign .com and .net alone receive over 14 billion queries per day, while the root receives about 8 billion queries per day.

TLD name servers face specific unique technical issues distinct from those that involve the roots. One issue is increased traffic resulting from low TTLs on second-level zone records. A popular second-level zone can increase traffic to its parent TLD name servers by lowering its TTL, effectively defeating the DNS's caching mechanism. (The root name servers do not suffer from this potential problem to the same extent, since TLD name servers give out mostly referrals. As a result, name server caches throughout the Internet retain the copy of the TLD records from the root zone with their 48-hour TTLs.[56])

TLDs probably receive some bogus queries, but perhaps not as many as the root, since at least a portion of the query must be correct—the TLD name. Their name servers face the same vulnerabilities that are faced by the root name servers. However, although the effect would be significant if the operations of large TLDs such as .com or .uk were to be interrupted, the consequence of a short interruption of most TLDs, individually, would not be significant for the overall Internet. An attack that could take out a substantial number of TLD servers would be significant but difficult to sustain because of the number of distinct targets that would be involved.

3.4.3 Institutional Framework of the TLDs

The effective operation of the top-level domains requires that an institutional framework perform four functions:

1. Deciding which new TLDs will enter the root zone file,
2. Determining the organization to be responsible for a TLD,
3. Determining the organization to operate a TLD's name server, and
4. Operating the TLD registry.

Many different organizations, international and national, governmental and private, for-profit and not-for-profit, including ICANN, VeriSign, and the DOC, are engaged in these activities. Their processes and interactions are complex and, often, controversial.

---

[56]Information provided by an anonymous reviewer.

Selecting New TLDs

The original DNS design assumed a single, unified, name space (in which the set of names that one user is able to look up is the same set of names that any other user is able to look up).[57] Unless uncoordinated entry into the root zone file is permitted, which would require that the operators of the root servers recognize any TLD that chooses to operate, some entity must decide how many and which TLDs there will be and who will operate them. "Selecting new TLDs" means deciding which new TLDs will enter the root zone file. As described above, that decision is made by the U.S. Department of Commerce upon the recommendation of ICANN. Therefore, it is in the first instance a decision for ICANN. The decision process that is employed differs between ccTLDs and gTLDs.

ccTLDs

There is generally no need for a complex decision process for entry of ccTLDs since, as noted earlier, they are available to countries and external territories represented by country codes in ISO 3166-1. This list has been used as the authoritative source for country codes because, as was stated in RFC 1591, "the IANA is not in the business of deciding what is and what is not a country."[58] When new entities are assigned a two-letter identifier by the ISO, that entity is automatically entitled to have a ccTLD. However, two situations have arisen that cannot be resolved solely by this rule. The first occurs when a country is removed from the ISO list. The two-letter code for the Soviet Union, SU, was removed from the list in September 1992 and placed in "transitional reserved status," which means that its use should be stopped as soon as possible. But, although this issue is on ICANN's agenda, it has not yet addressed the complicated issues that arise when a country is removed from the ISO 3166-1 list. Indeed, it is still possible to register in the .su domain, and this domain remains in the root.

The second situation occurs when an international entity requests a ccTLD that is not on the ISO 3166-1 list. In July 2000, the European Commission wrote to ICANN requesting the inclusion of the .eu domain in

---

[57]It is this assumption that alternative or multiple roots violate. This discussion assumes a single root.

[58]Jon Postel, "Domain Name System Structure and Delegation," RFC 1591, March 1994, p. 6, available at <http://www.rfc-editor.org>.

the DNS root.[59] Its request noted that the ISO had agreed to use of the two-letter code EU as a TLD. (The code, although not in ISO 3166-1, had "exceptional reserved status" enabling its use for specific ISO-approved purposes.) At its September 25, 2000, meeting, the ICANN board passed a resolution that approved for delegation as ccTLDs those codes from the ISO's exceptional reserved list for which the reservation permits any application requiring a coded representation of the entity.[60] In March 2005, ICANN authorized the creation of the .eu TLD, which is expected to begin operation in early 2006.[61] It will be open to any person living in the EU, as well as businesses with their headquarters, central administration, or main base in the EU.[62] The exceptional reserved list is no longer published, and a policy has been implemented to prohibit the creation or reservation of an unrestricted name that is not on the ISO 3166-1 list.

The process of deciding who will be delegated responsibility for operating a ccTLD upon its first entry into the root, or for redelegating responsibility subsequently, can become very complex. This process is discussed in the next section and in Section 5.5.

gTLDs

The gTLDs are a different matter. They fall into two groups: the first eight, which were selected at the time of initiation of the DNS—the legacy gTLDs; and the seven that were selected by ICANN in 2000 for addition to the root—the new gTLDs. (An additional 4 to 10 are being added during 2005 as the result of an ICANN selection process initiated in 2004. See Alternative A under "What Selection Process Should Be Used" in Section 5.4.2.)

The legacy gTLDs were selected by the developers of the DNS and a group of network and information center operators. Jon Postel, writing

---

[59]Letter from Erkki Liikanen, member of the European Commission, to Mike Roberts, (then) CEO and president of ICANN, dated July 6, 2000, available at <http://europa.eu.int/ISPO/eif/InternetPoliciesSite/DotEU/LetterLiikanenRoberts.html>.

[60]ICANN, "Preliminary Report. Special Meeting of the Board," September 25, 2000, available at <http://www.icann.org/minutes/prelim-report-25sep00.htm#00.74>.

[61]See Ellen Dumout, "ICANN Approves .eu Net Domain," *c/net news.com*, March 24, 2005, available at <http://news.com.com/2100-1038_3-5634121.html>.

[62]See the October 2004 EU Fact Sheet, "Open for Business in 2005: yourname.eu.," available at <http://europa.eu.int/information_society/doc/factsheets/017-doteu-november04.pdf>. There is a more complex story behind the .eu TLD, but it is beyond the scope of this chapter.

almost 10 years later, still maintained a policy that he expressed as: "It is extremely unlikely that any other TLDs will be created."[63] However, by the following year, Postel had changed his mind and recommended the creation of new TLDs to compete with NSI, which had a monopoly in commercial gTLD registrations, and in 1996 he recommended the creation of 150 or 300 new TLDs. At the same time, the rapid growth in size and scope of the Internet, driven by the introduction of the World Wide Web, created a heavy demand for second-level domain names in the gTLDs, especially in .com. (See Section 2.5.1.) That, in turn, led to a public demand for additional gTLDs. In response to that demand (some would argue it was a belated response), ICANN created a process, which it used during the year 2000 to select the new gTLDs. ICANN treated the addition of gTLDs as an experiment in order to seek compromises that would satisfy the contending interest groups, although that did not prevent the additions from becoming controversial. Since that process also entailed selecting the organizations responsible for the TLDs and the TLD name server operators, its description is deferred to "Selecting the TLD Registry Operators" below.

To at least some degree, TLDs compete with one another for the patronage of those entities that wish to register domain names, although the maximum prices that ICANN has negotiated with the gTLDs limit the extent of this competition. This competition might be more intense—both with respect to the prices charged and the services offered—the larger the number of competitors, although beyond some point the effect of additional entry is likely to be small and the costs of switching from one domain to another are likely to give incumbents a strong advantage. In any event, even when firms wish to operate TLDs, either because they observe incumbents earning large profits or because they believe they can offer better or cheaper services, entry is constrained by their need to obtain approval from ICANN for inclusion in the root file.[64]

Over the past few years, the demand for registrations in the TLDs has gone through several changes. While the ccTLD registrations have grown continually throughout the period, those in the previously rapidly growing gTLDs declined in the aftermath of the dot-com bust and only began to grow again in mid-2002. According to ICANN writing in mid-2003: "The domain name counts for ccTLDs have jumped 22% over the numbers used last year [in the budget]. The count for gTLDs, however, has

---

[63]Postel, RFC 1591, 1994, p. 1.

[64]Some limitations on entry may have a legitimate practical basis. Nor is it clear whether a small number of large TLDs are to be preferred to a large number of smaller ones. In any event, incumbents can be expected to wish to limit the competition that they face, whether or not there is a legitimate basis for such limits.

declined 5%, largely due to a drop-off in .com whose statistics dominate the overall gTLD count because of its comparative size."[65] In fact, the name counts in all three of the largest gTLDs—.com, .net, and .org—declined from 2002 to 2003. Both .net and .org declined by 14 percent. However, by August 2003, another source reported that the total number of .com, .net, and .org domain names had returned to the high mark of 30.7 million reached in October 2001.[66] Sustained growth had returned in July 2002, and over the next 13 months the total registrations in those three domains grew an average of 250,000 per month. As further confirmation of the renewed demand for those gTLDs, VeriSign reported[67] that an average of 1.2 million new registrations for domain names ending in .com and .net were added each month in the third quarter of 2004—a 33 percent increase over the third quarter of 2003."[68]

Selecting the Organizations Responsible for the TLDs

ICANN has been delegated authority by the DOC (and subject to the DOC's approval) over entries in the root zone and, consequently, it can determine which organization is delegated responsibility for each ccTLD and gTLD. The delegated responsibility entails arranging for the establishment and operation of (1) name servers for the TLD satisfying Internet technical requirements and (2) a domain name registration process that meets the needs of the local or international Internet communities.

In the case of ccTLDs, the organizations with delegated responsibility are designated managers or sponsors, and they are designated the sponsors for sponsored gTLDs. Sponsors are primarily either government or not-for-profit organizations that provide their own funding, although profit-making organizations run the commercial gTLDs and some ccTLDs. In both groups of TLDs, the responsible organization need not operate the required name server and domain registration functions itself and generally contracts with a specialist organization, which may be a commercial service, to carry out those functions. In the case of the seven unsponsored

---

[65]See ICANN's Budget for Fiscal Year 2003-2004, available at <http:// www.icann.org/financials/revised-proposed-budget-24jun03.htm>.

[66]Zooknic Internet Intelligence, "gTLD Domains Returning to 2001 Levels," press release. August 25, 2003, available at <http://www.zooknic.com/pr_2003_08_25.html>.

[67]VeriSign, "VeriSign Issues Quarterly Domain Name Industry Brief; Overall Domain Name Registration Tops Past Record of 66.3 Million," December 1, 2004, available at <http://www.verisign.com/verisign-inc/news-and-events/news-archive/us-news-2004/page_019484.html>.

[68]See also Linda Rosencrance, "Domain Name Registrations Hit All-Time High," *Computerworld*, June 8, 2004, available at <www.computerworld.com/developmenttopics/websitemgmt/story/0,10801,93716,00.html>.

gTLDs (other than .int), the responsible organization and the operating organization are the same and had until recently all been commercial services. However, ICANN designated Public Interest Registry (PIR), a not-for-profit, to manage .org beginning in 2003. PIR has contracted with a Dublin-based company, Aflilias, to provide the registration services and Afilias has contracted, in turn, with a commercial provider of DNS services, UltraDNS, to run the name servers.

For the ccTLDs and the legacy gTLDs, ICANN must have a process for recognizing the organizations that will be responsible for the TLD when a new ccTLD is added or when a change of responsibility is desired for whatever reason. The processes used for the ccTLDs and the legacy gTLDs are different. They are described below. For the new gTLDs, the processes of selecting a manager and selecting an operator were combined since the prospective manager's choice of operator was one factor in the manager selection decision. That combined process is described below in "Selecting the TLD Registry Operators."

ccTLDs

IANA began delegating responsibility for ccTLDs shortly after the deployment of the DNS and most delegations predate the formation of ICANN. ICANN's policy has been not to challenge these except in cases where a government seeks redelegation.[69] In the early days of the DNS, responsibility for ccTLD management was usually assigned to the Internet pioneers who volunteered for the task. Generally, there was only one interested organization since, at the time, the commercial prospects were thought to be minimal. Even so, there was considerable due diligence on many applications to determine that other possible applicants had been identified and, if there were any, that they supported the active application. There were, however, some cases of multiple applications and post-delegation challenges by those who sought various other benefits such as prestige or the ability to leverage the role into sale of Internet services. The managers agreed to abide by a set of policies for the administration and delegation of ccTLDs that covered technical requirements and the circumstances under which IANA would make or change a delegation of responsibility.[70] Often the corresponding governments did not know or did not care about the Internet or the applicable ccTLD.

---

[69]This section draws extensively on material in ICANN, "Update on ccTLD Agreements." September 20, 2001, available at <http://www.icann.org/montevideo/cctld-update-topic.htm>. See also Jon Postel, RFC 1591, 1994.

With the growth in the size and importance of the Internet and the formation of ICANN, that situation has changed. Governments increasingly want to participate in the selection and oversight of the manager of their ccTLDs.[71] Furthermore, ICANN felt the need for more precisely described agreements spelling out the mutual obligations and responsibilities among governments, ICANN, and the delegated managers of ccTLDs. Consequently, the board of ICANN authorized the development of such agreements with the ccTLDs.

According to ICANN, it was soon realized that no single agreement or, even, structure of agreement would fit every ccTLD. However, after consideration of the wide variety of specific circumstances in the 243 ccTLDs, ICANN found that most would fit into one of two general situations that differ principally in the involvement of the local government or public authority. In the first, legacy situation, the government is not involved. In the second, triangular situation, it is, thus yielding three participants: a ccTLD, ICANN, and a local government. ICANN proposed two types of agreements, corresponding to these two situations.

According to the proposed agreement for the legacy situation, the ccTLD manager would operate under the oversight of ICANN only, subject of course to the laws of the country. ICANN would have the sole responsibility to ensure that the ccTLD manager operates as a trustee for both the local and the international Internet communities.

According to the proposed agreement for the triangular situation, ICANN would retain the responsibility to see that the ccTLD manager meets its responsibilities to the international Internet community and to any non-national registrants, while the local government would assume responsibility for ensuring that the interests of the local Internet community are served.

According to ICANN, the decision as to which arrangement to pursue would be reached by the government and the ccTLD manager (or candidate manager) in consultation with the local Internet community, with ICANN adopting "a neutral stance."

In the legacy situation, ICANN would have the full authority to select and, when necessary, change the ccTLD manager. (Although they are not signatories to the agreements, governments are notified if one is in preparation in case they want to be involved.) In the triangular situation, the

---

[70]The general responsibilities of the ccTLD managers are documented in RFC 1591 and in the ICANN publications *ICP-1, Internet Domain Name System Structure and Delegation (ccTLD Administration and Delegation)*, May 1999, and *ccTLD Constituency Best Practice Guidelines for ccTLD Managers*, 4th Draft, March 10, 2001. However, neither of the ICANN documents appears to have achieved consensus among all the ccTLD managers.

[71]See discussion in Section 5.5.2.

relevant government or public authority would communicate its designation of a ccTLD manager to ICANN, which would then decide whether or not to accept the designee and, assuming a positive decision, seek to negotiate an appropriate agreement with the manager.

The proposed agreements with the ccTLDs are intended to cover the following areas: (1) the delegation of responsibility to the ccTLD and description of the circumstances that would lead to its termination, (2) specification of the local and global policy responsibilities of the ccTLD, (3) characterization of the relationship with ICANN and their respective responsibilities, and (4) funding for ICANN.

Despite ICANN's efforts to get ccTLDs to enter into agreements with it, by June 2005 it had completed only 12 of them. A number of ccTLDs object to accepting ICANN's formal authority over their operations. This issue is discussed in detail in Section 5.5.

gTLDs

ICANN has acted to change the organization responsible for several of the eight legacy gTLDs. The most significant instance was its negotiation with VeriSign Global Registry Services, the legacy manager of .com, .net, and .org. Because those three gTLDs contain the registrations of the vast majority of the Internet's gTLD second-level domains and, in particular, almost all of those on its unsponsored and unrestricted domains, VeriSign's position as the profit-making sole supplier of those three was felt by many in the Internet community to be detrimental to the long-term health of the Internet. In May 2001, VeriSign, Inc., ICANN, and the DOC signed a revised agreement in which VeriSign agreed to give up its operation of .org at the end of 2002 while extending the term of its operation of .net to the beginning of 2006 and of .com to November 2007. Both of the latter agreements are renewable, although under different terms: under existing agreements, .net had to be put out for bid by ICANN by the end of 2005, while VeriSign has presumptive renewal rights for .com, unless it materially breaches the agreement. ICANN initiated an open bidding process for .net in March 2004 and in June 2005 selected VeriSign, Inc., to continue as the operator.[72]

To select a new manager for .org, ICANN issued a request for proposals (RFP) in May 2002. In response, it received 11 proposals from a variety of organizations, both commercial and not-for-profit. According to ICANN, those proposals were reviewed by three independent evaluation

[72]See ICANN, ".NET Request for Proposals," December 10, 2004, available at <http://www.icann.org/tlds/dotnet-reassignment/net-rfp-final-10dec04.pdf>.

teams that were charged with looking at technical issues and at the ability of the proposals to meet the specific needs of .org. Comments were also received from the public and the applicants, which, according to ICANN, were used by the ICANN staff to prepare an evaluation report and recommendation. The ICANN board accepted the staff recommendation and ICANN contracted with the PIR, a wholly-owned subsidiary of the Internet Society, to become the manager of .org, effective January 1, 2003. A similar process was followed for .net.

Selecting the TLD Registry Operators

An organization that is responsible for reliably performing the functions of (1) operating the TLD name servers and (2) registering second-level domains in the TLD is called a registry.[73] It may or may not be the same as the delegated manager for the TLD.

For example, VeriSign is the manager and operates the registry for .com and .net. PIR is the manager of .org, but, as noted above, it has subcontracted with Afilias to operate the TLD registry, which has contracted the name server function to UltraDNS. Afilias also operates the registry for .info, for which it also serves as the manager, and for .vc, the ccTLD for residents of St.Vincent and the Grenadines, which is managed by the Ministry of Communications and Works of St.Vincent and the Grenadines.

There is always one, and only one, registry for a given TLD, but, as noted above, an organization can be the registry operator for more than one TLD. While the majority of TLD managers are non-commercial organizations, some registry operators are commercial organizations that operate for profit; they register the vast majority of domain names.

ccTLDs

The manager of a ccTLD may also be the registry operator, or it may subcontract the registry services in whole or in part to other organizations. The process for selecting the registry services operator is entirely up to the ccTLD manager, subject only to whatever restrictions the national

[73]Registries can exist at any level, except the root, in the DNS (although in some respects ICANN could be viewed as the registry for the root). In this section, only TLD registries are considered. The term "registry" is unfortunately used ambiguously in this context. The database maintained by a registry is also called a registry, as are the organizations that some registries subcontract with for database maintenance and operation, which are here called registry operators.

government may impose. The situations differ widely among the 243 ccTLDs.

Since the growth of the World Wide Web has vastly extended the scope, scale, and importance of the Internet, two phenomena have worked to shape the operational arrangements of ccTLDs in a country. First, there has been a movement from the early informal arrangements, which often involved voluntary efforts by the computer science department of a university in the country, to more formal arrangements that provide legal protection and engage a wider national community in policy-setting roles. Second, there has been a tendency to contract the actual operations to commercial organizations more willing and able to undertake the responsibilities than academic institutions.

For example, in Austria, the current manager and registry is Nic.AT, which is a limited-liability company that since 2000 has been wholly owned by a charitable foundation, the Internet Private Foundation Austria. Nic.AT was established in 1998 by the Austrian ISP Association to take over responsibility for the ccTLD from the University of Vienna, which had managed it from its inception but was faced with an increasing number of registrations, legal questions, and name conflicts beyond its competence. While Nic.AT handles the name registration, it contracts with the University of Vienna computer center to run the .at name servers.

In contrast, the new registry and registry operator for the .us TLD is a commercial company, Neustar, which also is the registry and registry operator for the new gTLD .biz. In the .us case, the manager, the DOC, decided to change the operational model from a deeply hierarchical, mostly geographic, extensively delegated structure to one that would be exploited commercially at the second level. Unlike the Austrian case, there was no pressure for the change in strategy from the previous manager or operator, and no significant pressure from users/registrants in the domain—indeed, many of them argued against it. And the DOC RFP essentially required a commercial operator with commercial intentions.

Legacy gTLDs

The registries for the legacy gTLDs are the consequence of history. NSI had been operating the registries for .com, .org, and .net by agreement with the U.S. government when VeriSign purchased it and assumed the responsibility. As noted above, PIR, upon becoming manager of .org, contracted with Afilias to run the registry. The organizations shown in Table 3.3 for each of the other legacy gTLDs are the associated registries (and also sponsors).

New gTLDs

In July 2000, the ICANN board adopted a policy for the introduction of new gTLDs that called for the solicitation and submission of proposals to sponsor or operate them. In August 2000, the RFP was published. It specified the contents of the detailed multipart proposal, which was to be accompanied by extensive supporting documentation and a non-refundable $50,000 application fee. The deadline for applications was October 2000.

As explained by ICANN, two types of gTLDs were specified: sponsored and unsponsored. In the latter case, the application was to be submitted directly by the organization proposing to serve as the registry. In the former case, the application was to be submitted by the sponsoring organization but would include the proposal of an organization that had agreed to perform the registry functions for the sponsoring organization. Thus, the registries for the new TLDs were selected through the ICANN process whether ICANN made the decision directly or accepted the sponsoring organizations' selections.

ICANN announced that the selection criteria would be the following:

- The need to maintain the Internet's stability;
- The extent to which selection of the proposal would lead to an effective proof of concept concerning the introduction of top-level domains in the future;
- The enhancement of competition for registration services;
- The enhancement of the utility of the DNS;
- The extent to which the proposal would meet previously unmet types of needs;
- The extent to which the proposal would enhance the diversity of the DNS and of registration services generally;
- The evaluation of delegation of policy-formulation functions for special-purpose TLDs to appropriate organizations;
- Appropriate protections of rights of others in connection with the operation of the TLD; and
- The completeness of the proposals submitted and the extent to which they demonstrate realistic business, financial, technical, and operational plans and sound analysis of market needs.

ICANN received 47 applications, of which 2 were returned for nonpayment of the fee and 1 was withdrawn, leaving 44 to be evaluated. The ICANN staff carried out evaluation with the assistance of outside technical, financial/business, and legal advisors. ICANN's goal was to select a "relatively small group of applications" that (1) were functionally diverse and (2) satisfied the selection criteria.

At its November 2000 meeting, the ICANN board acted on the staff evaluation and selected the seven new gTLDs—.biz, .info, .name, .pro, .museum, .aero, and .coop. Four were unsponsored—.biz, .info, .pro, and .name—and, therefore, amounted to the direct selection of a registry as well as the TLD. The other three were sponsored, and each included a designated registry chosen by the sponsor to operate its TLD.

The registries for .com, .net, .org and for the seven new gTLDs have agreed to pay certain fees and adhere to certain requirements as spelled out in ICANN's sponsored and unsponsored TLD agreements. (The registries for .edu, .gov, and .mil operate under separate agreements with agencies of the U.S. government. ICANN is the registry for .int, and the Internet Architecture Board (IAB) manages .arpa. Therefore, they do not have agreements with ICANN.)

ICANN's TLD agreement obligates the sponsor and the registry to (1) satisfy functional and performance specifications set by ICANN; (2) enter into agreements with any ICANN-accredited registrar (see "Selecting the Organizations to Register Domains" in Section 3.5.2) desiring such an agreement and accord the registrar fair treatment; (3) provide query and bulk access to registrant data—Whois information (see Box 3.6); (4) periodically deposit its registrant data into escrow with an ap-

BOX 3.6 Whois Service

Whois services provide contact information about the registries, registrars, or registrants in the DNS. (See Sections 2.3.4 and 2.5.3 for information on the development of the Whois service and background on the issues surrounding it.)

ICANN-accredited registrars are contractually obligated to collect and provide access to information about the name being registered, the names and IP addresses of its name servers, the name of the registrar, the dates of initiation and expiration of the registration, the name and postal address of the registrant, and the name and postal, telephone, and e-mail addresses of the technical and administrative contacts for the registered name. These must be made available either directly by the registrar or, in some cases, by the registry.

There are many separate Whois services on the Internet run by registrars, registries, and other organizations (often, as with universities, of their own second- or third-level domains). In addition, there are numerous Web sites that provide links to many of the Whois sites, such as Allwhois.com and Better-Whois.com.

proved escrow operator; and (5) comply with consensus policies established by ICANN.

The ICANN process for adding gTLDs that was implemented in 2000 was quite controversial. Many participants and observers complained about the design and implementation of the process. The issue of whether and how to add new gTLDs is examined in detail in Section 5.4.

Operating the TLD Registries

Every TLD registry operator must perform two basic functions: register domain names requested by registrants and operate the name servers that will link those domain names with their IP addresses and other critical information. Even these basic responsibilities may be divided between organizations, some commercial and some non-commercial, as noted above in the cases of Austria and of .org. In contrast, a single commercial organization, VeriSign, is the manager, runs the registry, and runs the name servers for .com and .net.

The registration operation produces the entries to the zone file for that domain, the content of the Whois file, and records of billing and payment, where appropriate. When the TLD has restrictions on who may register either in the domain (such as restricting registrations to nationals or residents of a country or to professionals or museums) or in its generic subdomains (such as Australian businesses in com.au or British limited liability corporations in ltd.uk), each application for a domain name must be examined to ensure that those restrictions are satisfied.

The ICANN agreements with 12 gTLDs include functional and operational specifications that the registry operators are responsible for meeting, while the few agreements with ccTLDs specify only general requirements for Internet connectivity, operational capability, and adherence to key RFCs, as well as agreements to make financial contributions to ICANN. Ideally, all operators of TLD name servers should satisfy certain minimal technical conditions to ensure their compatibility with the Internet and that they are configured so as not to pose a danger to the stability of the Internet, although there is no mechanism for enforcing this for the TLDs not covered by ICANN agreements.

3.4.4 Assessment

Conclusion: The level of technical capability and competence varies widely across the 258 TLD registries. The gTLDs and the large ccTLDs generally operate at a high level of availability and responsiveness. Although there are no readily available measures of the performance of the majority of ccTLDs, they appear to provide adequate service.

Recommendation: Regular and systematic testing of the availability and operation of secondary servers should be adopted by top-level domain registry operators. Policies and procedures should be developed to clarify what to do when problems are identified and what measures can be taken when problems are not resolved within a reasonable period of time.

Conclusion: No single organization has the authority and the ability to oversee the operation of all the TLDs. ICANN's formal authority extends only as far as the provisions of its agreements with 10 gTLDs and 12 or so ccTLDs and the authority it has to recommend changes in the root zone to accommodate new or reassigned TLDs.

Even where there is a contract, ICANN's authority has been tested. VeriSign's introduction in October 2003 of its Site Finder service raised fundamental issues of both a technical and an institutional nature and has been challenged in the courts.[74]

3.5 IMPLEMENTATION—THE SECOND- AND THIRD-LEVEL DOMAINS

The domain names in the DNS hierarchy that Internet users interact with most directly are those at the second level (or in those ccTLDs with fixed second-level domains, such as ltd.uk, those at the third level). They are generally the key identifiers in e-mail addresses (such as recipient@mailserver1.**nas.edu**) or a Web address (such as http://www.**nas.edu**). They are the names that businesses, individuals, government agencies, non-profit organizations, and various other groups acquire to identify themselves on the Internet—the names on their signposts in cyberspace. More than 70 million second-level (and, in some instances, third-level) domain names were registered during early 2005, with about two-thirds in the gTLDs (more than half in the two largest gTLDs—.com and .net) and about one-third in the ccTLDs.[75]

3.5.1 Technical System of the Second- and Third-Level Domains

Second- and third-level domains may have their own name servers to respond to queries to their zone files, as most large organizations do, but often the services are provided by ISPs or other Web site hosting organi-

---

[74]See Chapter 4 for a discussion of the Site Finder case.

[75]See Tables 3.2 and 3.3.

zations that store the zone file on their name servers. This is the course taken by most small organizations and individuals, although there are many exceptions.

The zone file of a second- or third-level domain may be very small if it belongs, for example, to an individual, or it may be quite large, if it is owned by a commercial or governmental organization. In the latter case, a great many of the entries may be associated with the e-mail addresses of the thousands of employees of the institution, while several, tens, or hundreds may be associated with the name servers of lower-level zones. Often, institutions will register multiple domain names (e.g., nas.edu and nationalacademies.org) that point to the IP address of the same server, enabling access to it under different domain names.

3.5.2 Institutional Framework of the Second- and Third-Level Domains

The effective operation of the second- and third-level domains requires that three functions be performed:

1. Selecting the organizations to register second-level domains,
2. Registering second-level domains, and
3. Resolving second-level domain name conflicts.

The principal organizations participating in this institutional framework are ICANN, the TLD registries, the registrars, and the organizations that provide dispute resolution services. Although many of the organizations at this level are commercial, numerous not-for-profit and governmental organizations play an active role as well.

Selecting the Organizations to Register Domains

In many cases, especially in the ccTLDs and some of the gTLDs, only the registry carries out the registration of second- or third-level domains. However, in a 1998 white paper[76] the DOC, responding to a policy goal of privatizing and increasing competition in the market for domain name registration, recommended opening the business of registering lower-level names in gTLDs to competition. It subsequently amended its agreement with NSI, then the operator of the .com, .org, and .net registries, to require it to develop a system of multiple registrars and put it into opera-

[76]Department of Commerce, "Management of Internet Names and Addresses," *Federal Register* 63(111):31741, 1998.

tion in 1999. The DOC designated ICANN as the organization that would oversee the establishment of the Shared Registration System (SRS) and would be responsible for establishing and implementing a system for registrar accreditation. The SRS and registrar accreditation began operation in 1999. Before the multiple registrar system, NSI charged $35 per year for registrations in its domains. At the beginning of 2005, registrations in those domains in the United States could be obtained for less than $10 per year.[77]

Under the terms of their agreements with ICANN, gTLD registries are required to permit registrars to provide Internet domain name registration services within their top-level domains. In addition, these agreements regulate the price that registries can charge registrars—the "wholesale price," with the current regulated price being a maximum of $6 per year per registrant. One can think of the regulation of the wholesale price as intended to constrain the exercise of market power by registries and the requirement for competing registrars as intended to constrain the retail "margin."

To the extent that regulation of the wholesale price is intended to limit the exercise of market power in the wholesale market, however, it is not entirely obvious why the wholesale price that can be charged by new gTLDs, especially new gTLDs that are intended to serve diverse users, must be regulated.[78] Indeed, increased future competition, especially as the number of gTLDs is expanded, might reduce or eliminate the need to regulate the wholesale price that VeriSign or other registries can charge. But if regulation of the wholesale price is intended to prevent registries from exploiting existing customers that may be locked in, there may be a continuing need to regulate wholesale rates even if the registry market were to become more competitive. The significance of lock-in will depend on the importance of switching costs, the flow of new registrants relative to the existing stock, and on whether registries can discriminate between new and existing registrants.

There were in February 2005 more than 460 registrars from more than 20 countries accredited to register domain names in 1 or more of the 10 eligible gTLD domains.[79] Many of them have decided to operate, at least in part, as wholesalers and suppliers of registrar services; those operations have enabled many agents to sell domain names without any rela-

[77]For example, in February 2005, godaddy.com was offering .com registrations for $8.95.

[78]Some specialized TLDs might continue to have market power even if the total number of TLDs were very large.

[79]For the current list, see the ICANN site at <http://www.icann.org/registrars/accredited-list.html>.

tionship with, or accreditation by, ICANN. Although most ccTLDs use authorized agents, many ccTLDs have adopted the notion of multiple registrars, and many ICANN-accredited registrars also register ccTLD second-level domain names.

ICANN accredits registrars through an open application process. Any organization wishing to become an ICANN-accredited registrar must complete a detailed application concerning its technical and business qualifications and pay a $2500 application fee. If approved by ICANN, the applicant must execute the standard Registrar Accreditation Agreement[80] and pay a yearly accreditation fee that is $4000 for the first TLD and $500 for each additional TLD for which the registrar is accredited. In addition, the registrar must pay a quarterly accreditation fee to cover a portion of ICANN's operating expenses. The fee is based, in part, on the registrar's share of registrations in the TLDs for which it is accredited. Registrars that are accredited by ICANN must also enter into accreditation agreements with the registries in the TLDs in which they want to register domains. Those agreements specify, among other things, the fees to be paid to the registries for each registration. As noted above, a ceiling is imposed on that fee structure by ICANN for the gTLDs that have signed agreements with ICANN.

The ICANN Registrar Accreditation Agreement imposes certain requirements on registrars. The registrar is obligated to (1) submit specified information[81] for each registrant to the registry; (2) enable public Internet access to a file of information about registrants—the Whois file—both in query and bulk access form; (3) maintain a file of all registrant information submitted to the registry; (4) regularly submit a copy of the file to ICANN or to an escrow agent; (5) comply with consensus policies established by ICANN; and (6) have for the resolution of name disputes a policy and procedures that comply with ICANN's Uniform Dispute Resolution Policy. (See "Resolving Domain Name Conflicts" below.) However, some of the newer gTLD agreements anticipate the possibility of "thick" registries, for example, ones in which Whois and similar data are maintained by the registry, not the registrars. This changes requirement (2) and has some impact on the others.

Registering Domain Names

Registration of second-level (or third-level) domain names occurs according to different processes in the different types of TLDs. For the 10

[80]A copy of the agreement can be found at <http://www.icann.org/registrars/ra-agreement-17may01.htm>.

[81]See Box 3.6.

gTLDs that use accredited registrars and for a number of ccTLDs—for example, Great Britain, Australia, Canada, and Denmark—registrars compete to sell second-level domain names in the TLDs they represent. They are free to set whatever fees they like, subject only to competitive market forces and their obligations to pay registration fees to the registries. For the .edu, .gov, .mil, .int, and .arpa gTLDs, as well as for most ccTLDs, registration by members of the restricted group occurs directly at the registries.

The registrar stage of the DNS process appears to be quite competitive, with entry being relatively easy[82] and competition taking place along a number of dimensions. Registrars for the same registry compete with one another for the patronage of registrants[83]—what is sometimes called intra-brand competition—with competition being based on both the prices and the services offered. These services include the efficiency with which registrations take place as well as value-added services that may be bundled with registration.[84] Switching registrars within a given registry is not particularly difficult, but there have been complaints that registrars have not always responded promptly to requests for switching and that some registrars have aggressively and misleadingly solicited other registrars' customers. In addition, domain name theft has been one of the problems associated with inadequate procedures and security measures put in place by the registrars of domain names. In such cases, a third party fraudulently claims to be the registrant in order to have the domain name transferred to its ownership.[85] There have also been instances of fraud charges against domain name registries and registrars of domain names.

The SnapNames *State of the Domain* report listed 148 registrars in the CNO domains (.com, .net, and .org) in the first quarter of 2003.[86] How-

---

[82]This competition is facilitated by the Shared Registration System protocol, which allows registrars to enter names directly in registries.

[83]This is not to say that registrars for different TLDs do not also compete with one another, a form of interbrand competition. In addition to registering new domain names, registrars also participate in the secondary market for domain names, acting as brokers, as well as in assisting registrants in applying for expired names.

[84]SnapNames reported that GoDaddy, a registrar, gained 70,000 registrants in a month when it launched its free online tax preparation software, presumably available only to its registrants. See the next section for a discussion of value-added services, some of which are provided by firms that are not registrars.

[85]In April 2004, the original operator of sex.com received a $15 million settlement from VeriSign because its registrar service had incorrectly transferred ownership of the name to a fraudulent claimant.

[86]SnapNames.com, Inc., *State of the Domain, First Quarter 2003*, May 13, 2003, available at <http://www.sotd.info/sotd/content/documents/SOTDQ103.pdf>. The SnapNames report showed over 150 ICANN-accredited registrars operational at that time (pp. 31-34).

ever, "market shares" in these domains were skewed, with the VeriSign registrar (now Network Solutions)[87] having more than 25 percent of all registrations in .com—which was, however, a significant decline from its 40 percent share only 15 months earlier;[88] Tucows having about 10 percent; Register.com having approximately 9 percent; and GoDaddy having somewhat over 6 percent. Thus, the share of the "market" controlled by the top four firms in .com—the four-firm concentration ratio—was about 52 percent.[89] Seven other registrars each had more than 1 percent of all .com registrations. (More recent data were not available at the time of this writing.)

The situation was somewhat different in the then newly opened .biz domain according to the SnapNames *State of the Domain*, first quarter 2003 report. Although the VeriSign registrar (Network Solutions) was the market leader, its share was only about 19 percent, 6 percent less than its share in the .com domain. Other registrars with shares in excess of 6 percent were Register.com (10 percent), Tucows (9 percent), and Melbourne IT (6 percent),[90] so that the four-firm concentration ratio here was only about 44 percent. SnapNames reports that there were 127 registrars of .biz names. As a result of the wide disparity in the sizes of the various domains, Network Solution's approximately 25 percent share of .com was about 5.8 million names, while its approximately 19 percent share of .biz was only about 170,000 names.[91]

Finally, although registrars charge the same prices to all registrants, some registrars offer a back-order service under which, for a fee, they will track the expiration of a desired domain name and attempt to register it immediately if the registration lapses. However, multiple registrars may be trying electronically to register the same name at the instant it becomes

---

[87]VeriSign sold its registrar, Network Solutions, to a private investment company for about $100 million in October 2003.

[88]SnapNames.com, Inc., *State of the Domain, January 2002*, February 26, 2002.

[89]The quotation marks around "market" and "market shares" are intended to indicate that no claim is being made that registrar services in the .com domain constitute a relevant antitrust market. SnapNames reported that the top 10 registrars had about 75 percent of the market in the first quarter of 2003, down from about 91 percent at the end of 2001.

[90]Recall that Melbourne IT is part of a joint venture with NeuStar, the operator of the .biz registry.

[91]For further discussion of market issues and presentation of market data, see "Generic Top Level Domain Names: Market Development and Allocation Issues," Organisation for Economic Co-operation and Development, Directorate for Science, Technology and Industry, Committee for Information, Computer and Communications Policy, Working Party on Telecommunication and Information Service Policies, July 13, 2004, available at <http://www.oecd.org/dataoecd/56/34/32996948.pdf>.

available. The one that tries at just the right instant wins the prize. Because of this chance element, consumers often enter back orders with multiple registrars. In March 2002, ICANN asked VeriSign to conduct a 12-month trial of a single wait-listing service, which would take just one order—at a $24 fee directly from the consumer—for an expiring name on a first-come, first-served basis. Thus, from the consumer's side, the need to use multiple registrars would be eliminated, but from the registrar's side, the opportunity to derive additional revenue would be lost. On July 15, 2003, a coalition of name registrars filed a lawsuit against ICANN seeking to block the launch of VeriSign's global waiting list for domain names.[92] At its March 2004 meeting, ICANN's board voted to seek the DOC's agreement to its approval of VeriSign's 1-year trial of the wait-listing service.

Resolving Domain Name Conflicts

One of the most difficult institutional roles that the operation of the DNS requires is the resolution of conflicts among competing claimants for domain names. These conflicts arise for a number of reasons that are discussed in detail in Section 2.5. The one that has attracted the most attention is the use of trademarked words in domain names, which is covered in "Trademark Conflicts" in Section 2.5.2. Although domain names can be used for a number of legitimate purposes other than as an address for a World Wide Web site, such as identifying a host, an e-mail server, an FTP site, and so on, the vast majority of the disputes involving domain names are associated with their very visible use in association with World Wide Web sites. Conflicts can also arise over names in which individuals, organizations, or governments claim a proprietary interest other than a trademark.

Whatever the source, the practical use of the DNS, which assumes that every domain name will be registered to one and only one entity, cannot proceed without some means for resolving conflicting claims for the same name. In the early days of the Internet, before strong financial and political interests were involved, such conflicts were handled informally, usually on a first-come, first-served basis, and they still are in many ccTLDs.[93] However, as domain names appeared on the signposts on the World Wide Web and in e-mail addresses, and some gained visibility and potentially great value, the need to use more formal processes became

---

[92]See Susan Kuchinskas, *Embittered Registrars Sue Embattled ICANN*, July 15, 2003, available at <http://siliconvalley.internet.com/news/print.php/2235661>.

[93]See, for example, the terms and conditions for the .uk registry available at <http://www.nic.uk>.

evident. This was especially true for .com at first, and then for .net and .org as they were more widely marketed to general users. For the reasons described in Section 2.5.1, they were the most visible names on signposts on the Web.

Possible Remedies to Conflicts Over Names

There are basically two approaches to resolving conflicts over rights to names: one approach incorporates policies and regulations into the actual administration of the naming system and its assignment rules. The other approach relies on dispute resolution mechanisms that are external to naming system administration.

Internal Remedies. In a completely internalized naming system administration, a single manager owns the naming system and decides who is entitled to which name. Hence there are no rights conflicts. Public or quasi-public naming systems, such as the DNS, can also attempt to link the assignment of names to strict policies and regulations. The available techniques include imposing policies on the assignment of names at the point of registration, name reservations[94] or exclusion, and so-called sunrise proposals.

Policies Imposed at the Point of Registration. Such policies must rely on rules or procedures to determine eligibility for a name. It is difficult to mechanize such rules. Thus, prior review of registration is likely to be expensive and slow if it is administered manually and prone to be crude and unfair if it is not.

Name Exclusions. Name exclusions withdraw specific names or entire classes of names from the available database. For a time, Network Solutions did not allow registration of six of the Federal Communication Commission's "seven dirty words" in the domain name space.[95] The World Intellectual Property Organization (WIPO) recommended eliminating a list of "famous" trademarks from the DNS database and reserving their use to the trademark holder.[96] ICANN has provided all of its

---

[94]The deployment of internationalized domain names involves new processes and challenges with respect to the reservation of names to prevent some conflicts over domain names. See Section 5.6.3 for discussion.

[95]For example, see "Seven Dirty Words," Wikipedia online encyclopedia, available at <http://en.wikipedia.org/wiki/Seven_dirty_words>.

[96]See "The Problem of Notoriety: Famous and Well-Known Marks," in *The Mangement of Internet Names and Addresses: Intellectual Property Issues,* First Report of WIPO Internet Domain Name Process, April 30, 1999, available at <http://wipo2.wipo.int/process1/rfc/3/interim2_ch4.html>.

newly authorized registries with a list of reserved names that consisted of names and acronyms of organizations related to the IETF and ICANN.[97]

Name exclusion is an effective method of protecting the reserved names from abuse, but it is also a crude instrument, and in a global, public name space its crudeness raises significant public policy concerns. Withdrawing words from circulation is in effect a form of automated censorship. Exclusions do not make any distinction between legitimate and illegitimate users; they simply make it impossible to use the names. A rigid exclusion deprives these organizations of the right to register domain names corresponding to their acronyms or trademarks. Exclusions and other regulations are less significant when they are part of the practice of a private naming system, where the owner can be assumed to have property rights over the naming system as a whole. Such exclusions also ignore the fact that certain words have a particular meaning only in a particular language. A "dirty" word in English may have no such meaning in another language.

Sunrise Proposals. Sunrise proposals, in general, establish a period at the start-up of a new name space within the DNS during which certain entities may register names in which they have established rights (e.g., famous trademarks) before the space is opened for public registration.

External Remedies. External methods of resolving rights conflicts include litigation through the courts or alternative dispute resolution procedures, such as the ICANN Uniform Domain Name Dispute Resolution Policy (UDRP), which is discussed below. The advantage of these methods is that they are based on case-specific analysis. Thus, they are sensitive to the specific facts of the conflict and can employ "soft" interpretive principles to adjudicate a dispute. Their disadvantage, of course, is that they are more time-consuming and expensive, and litigation is subject to jurisdictional limitations that may not match the scope of the affected naming system. Litigation is particularly expensive and cumbersome, although it offers a reliably neutral tribunal in many countries. Alternative dispute resolution techniques such as the UDRP greatly reduce the cost of external dispute resolution but sacrifice thoroughness in compiling and verifying facts, and their rapid procedures can put respondents at a disadvantage.

---

[97]For the list of reserved names, see ICANN, "Appendix K, Schedule of Reserved Names," available at <http://www.icann.org/tlds/agreements/unsponsored/registry-agmt-appk-26apr01.htm>.

Remedies to Conflicts Over Names in the DNS

Since the remedies to domain name conflicts differ somewhat between the gTLDs and the ccTLDs, each is described separately below.

gTLDs. Although there are other uses of trademarks with international spillover effects, second-level domains in gTLDs are unusual in the extent to which they are visible in almost every jurisdiction in the world, with the resulting difficulty in making either geographic or sectoral distinctions. Ordinarily, the same trademarks can be used in a single geographic region so long as they are in different economic sectors where confusion is unlikely. On the Internet such distinctions cannot be made. As a result, the question arises as to the means to be used to make decisions about domain name conflicts and disputes that cross national and business sector boundaries and, since such decisions inevitably involve matters of commercial or political or social importance, to ensure that those decisions are regarded as legitimate and enforced. Normally, trademark and related disputes are resolved by the courts of the nation in which they arise, and those in many nations have shown themselves capable of handling domain name disputes. In addition, the United States has passed specific legislation at both the federal and the state levels addressing the rights of trademark owners to domain names. (These are discussed further below.) As noted above, however, legal proceedings can become expensive and time-consuming. Therefore, many in the Internet community felt the need for a less expensive and quicker means of resolving domain name disputes.

Uniform Domain Name Dispute Resolution Policy. An answer, implemented by ICANN in December 1999, based on a recommendation from WIPO, was the Uniform Domain Name Dispute Resolution Policy. The UDRP has been adopted, as ICANN requires, by all registrars in the .aero, .biz, .com, .coop, .info, .museum, .name, .net, and .org top-level domains, as well as voluntarily by managers of several global ccTLDs, such as .tv, .cc, and .ws. In addition, managers of other ccTLDs, such as .ca, have adopted their own policies based on modified versions of the UDRP.

The policy takes effect through agreements between registrars (or other registration authorities) and their registrants. Each registrant agrees to be bound by the provisions of the policy when it registers its domain name.[98] In agreeing to the registration agreement, the registrant also must

[98]The policy conditions, examples of bad-faith actions, and other provisions listed below are paraphrased from the UDRP text available at <http://www.icann.org/dndr/udrp/policy.htm>.

represent that to its knowledge its registration of the domain name does not infringe any third party's rights, nor is it for an unlawful purpose, nor will it be used in violation of any applicable laws or regulations.

By registering the domain name, the registrant is then bound by the policy to submit to a mandatory administrative proceeding if a complainant asserts that:

1. Registrant's domain name is identical or confusingly similar to a trademark or service mark in which the complainant has rights; and
2. Registrant has no rights or legitimate interests in respect of the domain name; and
3. Registrant's domain name has been registered and is being used in bad faith.

The complainant must demonstrate all three of these conditions for the complainant to prevail.

The policy asserts examples of actions that would demonstrate bad faith that include registering and using the domain name:

1. For the purpose of transferring the registration to the complainant, or to one of its competitors, for more than the documented out-of-pocket costs of the domain name; or
2. To prevent the owner of the trademark or service mark from using the mark in a domain name (provided that registrant engaged in a pattern of such conduct); or
3. Primarily for the purpose of disrupting the business of a competitor; or
4. Intentionally to attract, for commercial gain, Internet users to registrant's Web site or other online location, by creating a likelihood of confusion with the complainant's mark on registrant's Web site or location.

It also describes circumstances that would enable the registrant to demonstrate its rights and legitimate interests in the domain name. These are as follows:

1. Before any notice to registrant of the dispute, its use of, or demonstrable preparations to use, the domain name or a name corresponding to the domain name in connection with a bona fide offering of goods or services; or
2. Registrant has been commonly known by the domain name, even if it has acquired no trademark or service mark rights; or

3. Registrant is making a legitimate noncommercial or fair use of the domain name, without intent for commercial gain, to misleadingly divert consumers, or to tarnish the trademark or service mark.

The mandatory proceeding—which is electronically based—must be held before an accredited and administrative-dispute-resolution provider that has been approved by ICANN.[99] The complainant selects the provider and is required to pay the fees, except in the case when the registrant elects to expand the panel from one to three panelists, in which case the fee is split. The registrar, the registry, and ICANN are not parties to a UDRP proceeding. However, during a UDRP proceeding, the registrar does confirm that the domain name has been registered by the respondent named in the proceeding and is required to execute the outcome of a decision. The only remedy available to the complainant through the proceeding is cancellation or transfer of the domain name.

As of May 10, 2004, 9377 proceedings involving 15,710 domain names had been brought under the UDRP.[100] Two-thirds (6262) of these proceedings had resulted in a transfer of the disputed domain name to the complainant or in a cancellation of the domain name. Approximately one-fifth (1892) had resulted in a decision for the respondent, and approximately one-tenth (971) of the proceedings had been disposed without decision or terminated. There were 931 proceedings pending. The 15,710 domain names that had been disputed in 4 years represent 0.03 percent of the more than 46 million domain names registered in the gTLDs subject to the UDRP.

Approximately 60 percent of these proceedings have been filed with WIPO, approximately 33 percent have been filed with the National Arbitration Forum (NAF), approximately 6 percent were filed with eResolution,[101] and approximately 0.7 percent have been filed with the Center for Public Resources Institute for Dispute Resolution (CPR). The Asian Domain Name Dispute Resolution Centre (ADNDRC) began operation in February 2002.

---

[99]The approved providers are listed at <http://www.icann.org/dndr/udrp/approved-providers.htm>. There were four approved providers in February 2005.

[100]ICANN, "Statistical Summary of Proceedings Under Uniform Domain Name Dispute Resolution Policy," January 30, 2004; latest version available at <http://www.icann.org/udrp/proceedings-stat.htm>.

[101]eResolution ceased operating as a dispute-resolution provider for ICANN in late November 2001.

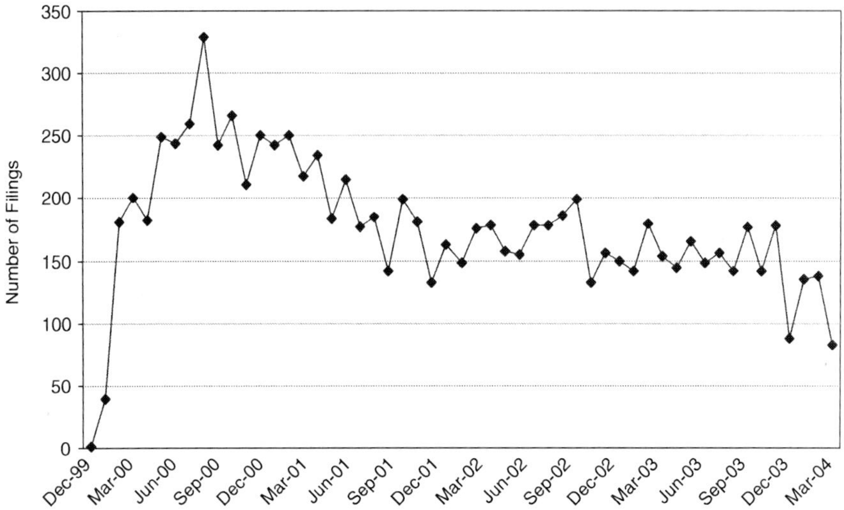

FIGURE 3.3 UDRP filings as of April 30, 2004. NOTE: With respect to gTLD UDRP filings commencing during the period from December 1999 through October 2003, data were obtained from the ICANN Web site at <http://www.icann.org/udrp/proceedings-list.htm>. With respect to such filings commencing during the period from November 2003 through April 2004, data were obtained directly from the Asian Domain Name Dispute Resolution Centre Web sites at <http://www.adndrc.org/adndrc/bj_home.html> and <http://www.adndrc.org/adndrc/hk_home.html>, the Center for Public Resources Institute for Dispute Resolution Web site at <http://www.cpradr.org/ICANN_Cases.htm>, the National Arbitration Forum Web site at <http://www.arb-forum.com/domains/decisions.asp>, and the World Intellectual Property Organization Arbitration and Mediation Center Web site at <http://arbiter.wipo.int/domains/statistics/index.html>. Specialized domain name dispute resolution proceedings (e.g., Start-up Trademark Opposition Policy (STOP) and the usTLD Domain Name Dispute Resolution Policy (USDRP)) have been excluded from these statistics.

Over time, there has been a decline in the number of UDRP proceedings filed. As shown in Figure 3.3, the number of UDRP proceedings filed each month has been steadily decreasing since August 2000.

WIPO explained this decline as suggesting that "an expedited online dispute resolution service has been effective in dissuading Internet pirates from hijacking names."[102] It may also be partly the conse-

[102]WIPO, "WIPO Continues Efforts to Curb Cybersquatting," Press Release PR/2002/303, February 26, 2002, available at <http://www.wipo.org/pressroom/en/releases/2002/p303.htm>.

quence of working through the backlog of cases that UDRP faced upon start-up and entering a more normal steady-state condition. To some extent, as well, it may reflect a change in the attitudes of trademark owners, some of whom may have come to feel that their interests are not jeopardized by every similar domain name, which are not worth the cost and effort to maintain. The decline in cases might also be attributed, in part, to learning by cybersquatters about avoiding a finding of bad faith against them.

As a first step in a policy development process, in 2003, ICANN prepared a report that lists many of the procedural and substantive issues that have been raised about the UDRP.[103]

Start-up Registrations. The UDRP was designed to handle an ongoing rate of domain name conflicts arising in already established gTLDs. However, several of the seven new gTLDs have faced unique issues when they entered the start-up phase. Specifically, under the terms of their contracts with ICANN, they needed a process by which intellectual property rights holders could challenge bad-faith claimants in advance of open registration in order to avoid a rush of cybersquatters followed by a heavy demand on the UDRP process as intellectual property holders asserted their rights. The four most significant—.biz, .info, .name, and .pro—each adopted somewhat different policies, but all are adopting or have a UDRP-like dispute resolution policy.

ccTLDs. Most ccTLD registries, and their agents and registrars when they exist, publish policies about who is eligible to register in the second-level domain, or in its third-level domains when they are open for direct registration. These policies generally also cover the resolution of conflicts over domain names. Where the TLD limits itself to individuals and organizations that have an association with the country, many potential conflicts are readily addressed through national administrative, regulatory, and judicial institutions. For example, matters of trademark priority are handled through the national regulatory and legal systems, and corporations may have defensible rights only in the names that are legally registered.

---

[103]See ICANN, "Staff Manager's Issues Report on UDRP Review," August 1, 2003, available at <http://www.icann.org/gnso/issue-reports/udrp-review-report-01aug03.htm>. ICANN also set up a committee to consider WIPO's proposed amendments to the UDRP. ICANN has not made the committee's report public.

U.S. Legislation. The United States has passed legislation at both the federal and the state levels addressing the rights of trademark owners to domain names.

Federal—The ACPA: On November 29, 1999, President Clinton signed into law the Anti-cybersquatting Consumer Protection Act (ACPA), which provided trademark owners with a further cause of action that was specifically directed to domain names.[104] Under the ACPA, a trademark owner can bring a civil action against a person if that person has a bad-faith intent to profit from a mark and registers, traffics in, or uses a domain name that, in the case of a mark that is distinctive, is identical or confusingly similar to that mark; or in the case of a famous mark, is identical or confusingly similar to or dilutive of that mark; or is a trademark, word, or name protected by law.[105] Mere registration of such a domain in bad faith may be sufficient to violate the trademark owner's rights under the ACPA; there is no further requirement for any use of the domain name in association with any goods or services.

Under the ACPA, factors affecting the judgment of bad faith include, but are not limited to, whether (1) the registrant holds any intellectual property rights in the name; (2) the domain name consists of the registrant's name; (3) the domain name was used in connection with the bona fide offering of any goods or services; (4) the domain name was used in a way that could be viewed as a bona fide noncommercial or fair use; (5) the domain name was intended to divert consumers from the mark owner's online location; (6) the registrant offered to sell the domain name to the mark owner without having used it in a bona fide manner; (7) the registrant provided false contact information in the registration form; (8) the registrant acquired multiple domain names that are identical or similar to the trademarks of others; and (9) the domain name incorporates a mark that is not distinctive and famous.

The ACPA also created a cause of action for individuals with respect to domain names. Specifically, a domain name registrant can be held liable if the domain name consists of, or is substantially and confusingly similar to, the name of another living person and the domain name has been registered without that person's consent with the specific intent to profit from the name by selling it for financial gain. This particular cause of action, however, is not available for domain name registrations that occurred prior to the ACPA's enactment date.

With respect to remedies, the ACPA provided that a court may award injunctive relief, including forfeiture, cancellation, or transfer of the do-

---

[104] 15 U.S.C. § 1125(d).

[105] 18 U.S.C. § 706 ("Red Cross") or 36 U.S.C. § 220506 ("Olympic").

main name. In addition, if the registration, trafficking, or use of the domain name occurred after the ACPA's enactment date, a plaintiff can elect to recover, instead of actual damages and profits, an award of statutory damages in the amount of $1,000 to $100,000 per domain name (as the court considers just).

Furthermore, if personal jurisdiction over the domain name registrant cannot be obtained, the trademark owner could file an *in rem* civil action[106] against the domain name itself in the judicial district of the domain name registrar, domain name registry, or other domain name authority that registered or assigned the domain name. However, the ACPA limits the remedies in an *in rem* action to forfeiture, cancellation, or transfer of the domain name.

States: California, Hawaii, and Louisiana also passed laws that address the registration, sale, and use of domain names within that state and provide for civil remedies in state courts for violations of these laws.

Foreign Legislation. Relatively few countries have chosen to address the rights of trademark holders in domain names in the same legislative manner as the United States. The European Union (EU) has relied largely on new telecommunications laws coordinated at the EU level to provide for the regulation of domain names at the national level. For example, in Spain, the General Telecommunications Act (1998) was modified in July 2001 to impose a number of conditions on the registration of domain names under the ccTLD .es, including a requirement that a domain name to be registered be somehow related to the trademark or name of the company undertaking the registration. In other countries, the judicial process, rather than the legislative process, has been relied on to address conflicts between domain names and trademarks. Since at least 1997, courts within the United Kingdom have been prohibiting the registration of domain names that conflict with trademarks. In 1998, the Delhi High Court in India likewise extended its form of common law trademark protection to domain names, as did the Tribunal de Grande Instance of Draguignan in France. Many ccTLDs, 42 in all, including a number from the EU, have opted to rely on a form of alternative dispute resolution policy.[107] Likewise, the new .eu ccTLD will apply the following rules regarding registrations:

- Governments may reserve geographical and geopolitical names.
- In a 4-month sunrise phase, "prior rights" holders and public bodies can register .eu domain names before the general public can do so.

---

[106] An *in rem* action is taken against property directly, in contrast to an action against people (e.g., the owners of a given piece of property).

[107] See <http://arbiter.wipo.int/domains/cctld/index.html> for an example.

- Two months before the sunrise phase starts, technical and administrative measures will be published in detail.
- In the first 2 months of the sunrise phase, registered national and European Community trademarks and geographical indications as well as names and acronyms of public bodies can be registered as .eu domain names by the holder/public body.
- Two months later, other "prior rights" holders can also register .eu domain names, but only as far as they are protected under national law in the member state where they are held. This provision concerns unregistered trademarks, trade names, business identifiers, company names, family names, and distinctive titles of protected literary and artistic works.
- There will be an alternative dispute resolution procedure in place (similar to ICANN's "Uniform Domain Name Dispute Resolution Policy" UDRP).
- After the sunrise phase, the domain names will be registered according to the first-come, first served-principle.

3.5.3 Assessment

Conclusion: The tens of millions of registered second- and third-level domains are operated by individuals with a broad spectrum of capabilities. It is notable that the DNS has been able to function effectively and reliably despite this range of operator capabilities.

Conclusion: The UDRP is a unique cross-border, electronically based process that has resolved thousands of disputes over domain names without the expense and potential delay of court proceedings.

The issues of dispute resolution and appropriate Whois balance are examined in Chapter 5, where the alternative approaches are described and the committee's recommendations presented.

3.6 SUMMARY

Conclusion: The domain name technical system reliably and effectively handles the billions of queries it receives every day. The institutions that manage it perform the required functions adequately, in many cases without direct compensation.

Conclusion: The DNS technical system can continue to meet the needs of an expanding Internet. Early in the committee's assessment it became apparent that it would not be fruitful to consider alternate naming systems. As noted, the DNS operates quite well for its intended purpose and has demonstrated its ability to scale with the growth of the Internet and to operate robustly in an open environment. Moreover, significantly increased functionality can be achieved though applications—such as navigation systems—built on the DNS, or offered independently, rather than through changing the DNS directly. Hence, the need did not seem to be to replace the DNS but rather to maintain and incrementally improve it. Furthermore, given the rapidly increasing installed base and the corresponding heavy investments in the technical system and the institutional framework, the financial cost and operational disruption of changing to a replacement for the DNS would be extremely high, if even possible at all.

Yet, despite this better than passing grade, the committee's assessments have identified a number of significant technical and institutional issues whose effective resolution is critical to the DNS's successful adaptation to the demands on it. Chapters 4 and 5 address those issues.

4

The Domain Name System: Technology Prospects

The Domain Name System, as described in Chapter 3, has met most of the infrastructural naming needs of the Internet and the applications that rely on it, even as their uses and usage have expanded rapidly. However, the broadening and deepening penetration of the Internet and its applications into global communications, commerce, and culture poses new challenges to the basic technology of the DNS. In anticipation of and in response to those challenges, the technology community has been developing modifications of and extensions to the current technology.

This chapter is a review of the challenges and the prospective or actual technology responses to them. Each challenge and responsive technology is described and evaluated and the implications for the Internet and its applications are explained. Where the committee is in agreement, its conclusions and recommendations are presented. In all cases, the goal is to provide a clear description of the challenges, the technologies, and their prospects in order to inform forthcoming policy deliberations affecting or affected them.

The following challenges and responsive technologies are addressed in this chapter:

1. Improving the security of the DNS,
2. Linking the telephone and Internet naming systems,
3. Internationalizing domain names, and
4. Responding to domain name errors.

Some of these technologies are in or ready for the first stages of implementation, whereas others may never enter into wide-scale usage. Nevertheless, a basic understanding of each of them will enable wiser decisions about them and other innovations in the future.

4.1 IMPROVING THE SECURITY OF THE DOMAIN NAME SYSTEM

Because of its central role in the operation of the Internet, the DNS is a natural target for mischievous and malicious attacks. These can take a wide variety of forms depending on the ingenuity of the attacker and on which of the potential vulnerabilities is attacked.[1] The most severe recent attack was the denial-of-service attack launched in October 2002. It swamped 8 of the 13 root name servers for up to an hour and a half. However, the remaining 5 servers handled the regular requests to the root without difficulty. Since that attack, the root name server operators have taken a number of steps, including the widespread distribution of "anycast" satellites and diversification of network connectivity (see Box 3.1), to reduce their vulnerability to such attacks and to mitigate their effects.

Furthermore, although some steps have been taken,[2] more could be done to continuously monitor the performance and traffic flows of the DNS infrastructure so as to enable rapid detection and response to attacks or outages.

However, another serious vulnerability remains. As described in Section 2.4, "the original DNS design did not include a mechanism to ensure that a name lookup was an accurate representation of the information provided by the entity responsible for the information. DNS information was assumed to be accurate as the result of general notions of network cooperation and interoperation (i.e., based on the presumption that nobody would deliberately attempt to tamper with DNS information)." In more technical terms, the initial design of the DNS did not incorporate data origin authentication and data integrity protection. However, because of increased fear of additional attacks on the DNS, these kinds of security features have now become a major concern.

Data origin authentication is needed to help ensure that the results of DNS lookups come from authoritative sources. A widely publicized case that involved the diversion of Internet users to an undesired Web site drew attention to the lack of such authentication in the DNS.[3]

---

[1]See Derek Atkins and Rob Austein, "Threat Analysis of the Domain Name System," RFC 3833, August 2004, available at <http://www.rfc-editor.org>.

[2]Notably the establishment of the Operations Analysis and Research Center by the Internet Systems Consortium (see https://oarc.isc.org/) and the online performance monitoring by the k-root (see <http://k.root-servers.org/#stats>).

[3]In 1997, Eugene Kashpureff diverted Internet users who were seeking the Network Solutions Web site to his own site, although this was intended as a publicity stunt rather than as a malicious attack. See Rik Farrow, "Locking Up DNS Troubles," *Network Magazine*, August 5, 2000, available at <http://www.networkmagazine.com/showArticle.jhtml?articleID=8702868>.

Data integrity protection is needed because DNS data flows could be compromised at any point between the various name servers, resolvers, or other intermediaries, and the corrupted data can remain in caches for extended periods of time.

To respond to these potential vulnerabilities, the technical community has over a number of years developed DNS Security Extensions (DNSSEC).[4] DNSSEC adds data origin authentication and data integrity protection to the DNS. It aims to ensure that the recipient can validate that the data was sent from an authoritative source and that it arrived at its destination unchanged.

4.1.1 Mechanics of DNSSEC

DNSSEC provides end-to-end protection through the use of cryptographic digital signatures that are created by responding zone administrators and verified by a recipient's resolver software. In particular, DNSSEC avoids the need to trust intermediate name servers and resolvers that cache or route the DNS records originating from the responding zone administrator before they reach the source of the query. DNSSEC also preserves the capacity for localized variations and independence within the DNS hierarchy.[5]

In DNSSEC, resource record sets (RRSets)[6] within a zone are signed based on the model of public-key cryptography.[7] To support each signing operation, two keys are generated: a private key (to sign data) and the corresponding public key that is used to verify that the data were signed by the private key. The process of signing takes data to be signed and a private key as inputs to produce digitally signed data as the output.[8] However, DNSSEC involves signing the hash value of an RRSet, rather

---

[4]Defined in Roy Arends, Rob Austein, Matt Larson, Dan Massey, and Scott Rose, "DNS Security Introduction and Requirement," RFC 4033, March 2005, available at <http://www.rfc-editor.org>.

[5]For example, the control of the private and public keys remains within each respective zone.

[6]Resource records that have the same label, class, and type are categorized as belonging to the same RRSet. See Box 3.2 for a detailed explanation of resource records.

[7]For a review of public key cryptography and digital signatures, see Paul Albitz and Cricket Liu, *DNS and BIND*, 4th edition, Chapter 11, O'Reilly Media, Sebastopol, Calif., 2001; and Fred B. Schneider, editor, Computer Science and Telecommunications Board, National Research Council, *Trust in Cyberspace*, Chapter 4, National Academy Press, Washington, D.C., 1999.

[8]The crucial property of the digital signature is that it could have been produced only by someone with access to the private key.

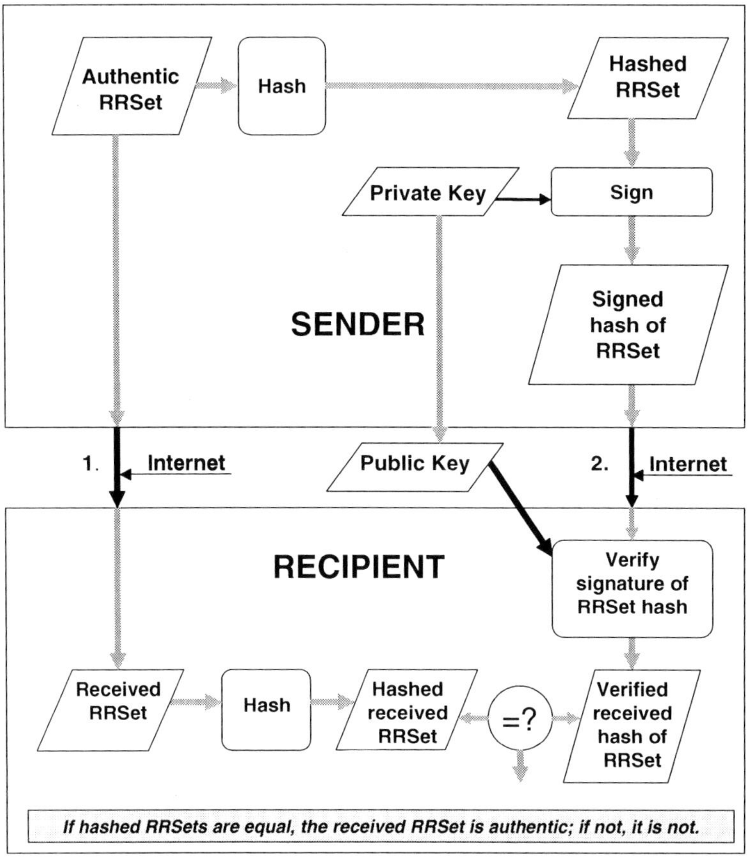

FIGURE 4.1 Use of DNSSEC to authenticate a resource record set (RRSet).

than signing the full RRSet itself.[9] (See Figure 4.1 for an illustration of the DNSSEC signing and verification process.)

Two copies of the RRSet are sent over the Internet to the recipient. One copy is not signed; the other is hashed and then signed as described above. To verify the origin and integrity of the unsigned RRSet, it is hashed using the same algorithm used by the sender. It is then compared with the verified, but still hashed, copy of the RRSet created by the zone

[9]A hash algorithm is a mathematical process that converts a message to a probabilistically-unique fixed-length string of digits that represents the original message. A hash algorithm is essentially unidirectional: given a hash value, it is nearly impossible to reverse the process to derive the original message in order to construct a second message whose hash value matches that of the original message. Since a hash value is typically much less data than contained in an RRSet, it is generally more efficient to sign hash values rather than RRSets.

administrator. Matching hash values provide a high level of assurance that the non-signed RRSet is authoritative and that it has not been altered in transit.

DNSSEC can, when everything works correctly, give the data consumer (validating resolver) some confidence that the received data is what the data producer (signing zone administrator) has sent. It provides a basis for trusting that the data has been received without tampering. It does not, however, assure that the data that the data producer sent is error-free or appropriate for the data consumer's application.

The DNSSEC extensions are based on four new resource record types: the public key (DNSKEY), the resource record digital signature (RRSIG), the delegation signer (DS), and the authenticated denial of existence (NSEC).[10] The public key used to verify the digital signature of an RRSet is stored in the DNSKEY resource record.[11] The digital signature is stored in the RRSIG resource record, and several RRSIG resource records may be associated with an RRSet, if more than one cryptographic algorithm is used for signing the RRSet.

DNSSEC depends on establishing the authenticity of the DNS hierarchy leading to the domain name in question, and thus its operation depends on beginning the use of cryptographic digital signatures in the root zone. The DS resource record facilitates key signing and authentication between DNS zones to create an authentication chain, or trusted sequence of signed data, from the root of the DNS tree down to a specific domain name. To secure all DNS lookups, including those for non-existent domain names and record types, DNSSEC uses the NSEC resource record to authenticate negative responses to queries. NSEC is used to identify the range of DNS names or resource record types that do not exist among the sequence of domain names in a zone.[12]

4.1.2 Deployment of DNSSEC

DNSSEC implementation on a global level faces a number of technical and non-technical challenges. The process of cryptographically sign-

---

[10]For detailed information about these resource records, see Roy Arends, Rob Austein, Matt Larson, Dan Massey, and Scott Rose, "Resource Records for the DNS Security Extensions," RFC 4034, March 2005, available at <http://www.rfc-editor.org>.

[11]The private key must be closely protected from public access, of course, and so it is not stored in a resource record.

[12]The implementation of DNSSEC also necessitates other changes that are too detailed to discuss here. For the specifics on the two "new message header bits" (CD and AD) in DNSSEC, see Roy Arends, Rob Austein, Matt Larson, Dan Massey, and Scott Rose, "Protocol Requirements for the DNS Security Extensions," RFC 4035, March 2005, available at <http://www.rfc-editor.org>.

ing hash values derived from resource records, along with the increase in the DNS packet size to accommodate large key sizes, adds significant operational costs for organizations that manage DNS servers because of the increase in DNS data and the associated increases in server computations and communications traffic.[13] The implementation of DNSSEC also increases the volume of Internet traffic and that, in turn, could increase the vulnerability of the Internet to denial-of-service (DoS) attacks—a threat DNSSEC does not protect against, although DNSSEC may offer more confidence in the responses of anycast satellites, which do provide a measure of defense against DoS attacks. DNSSEC could also cause more timeouts that would degrade the quality of service for end users.[14] DNSSEC also introduces more complexity to the DNS and adds to the administrative requirements for managing the security mechanism.[15] For instance, the administrator of a large zone would probably experience great difficulty in re-signing his or her entire zone daily. This would require dividing the task among many smaller parallel operations that could be managed with software—a solution that is feasible given the DNSSEC design (that makes signatures within a zone remain largely independent), but would not be without additional costs.

Because public keys for the root zone will need to be replaced with new ones on a regular basis, key management for the digital signatures presents another problem for DNSSEC. In particular, the interaction of key revocation with global caching and the distribution of copies of a new public root key remain unresolved,[16] and this adds even more importance to the management of root zone keys. The consequence of a corrupted root zone key is that it would break the chain of trust for source authentication and data integrity that serves as the basis of DNSSEC. A related and more fundamental and thorny problem that technical solutions could only partially resolve is reaching agreement over which organization should have control of the root zone key. Obvious candidates for

---

[13]Estimates for the increased computations and communications traffic associated with the introduction of DNSSEC vary, but range from a 5- to 10-fold increase. See Albitz and Liu, *DNS and Bind*, 2001; Beth Cohen, "DNSSEC: Security for Essential Network Services," May 12, 2003, available at <http://www.rfc-editor.org>; and Diane Davidowicz and Paul Vixie, "Securing the Domain Name System," *Network Magazine*, January 1, 2000.

[14]See David Berlind, "DNS Inventor Says Cure to Net Identity Problems is Right Under Our Nose," August 7, 2003, available at <http://techupdate.zdnet.com/techupdate/stories/main/0,14179,2914447,00.html>.

[15]See Cohen, "DNSSEC: Security for Essential Network Services," 2003.

[16]Distributing new public root keys is difficult as they must be preconfigured in DNS root name servers, but they cannot be delivered via DNSSEC, since they cannot vouch for themselves, and thus they may require an offline distribution mechanism. One proposed solution involves the publication of a public root key in national and international newspapers, which illustrates the magnitude of the problem.

the controlling organization include VeriSign, ICANN, and the Department of Commerce; other entities could also be considered. However, until a controlling organization is identified, the deployment of DNSSEC is likely to be delayed.[17]

While the introduction of DNSSEC imposes significant costs and does not eliminate all Internet security concerns nor address all Internet threats,[18] its implementation would represent considerable progress in improving the security of the DNS. For example, it would raise the level of protection against the falsification of DNS data to help in deterring identity-related theft and SPAM problems.[19] Furthermore, DNSEC provides a basis to build trust on the Internet to support higher-level protocols facilitating Internet Protocol (IP) telephony and other Web services.[20]

Conclusion: The security of the DNS would be significantly improved if DNSSEC were widely deployed among name servers for the root zone and top-level domains (TLDs) in particular, and throughout the DNS in general.

Conclusion: Urgent attention is needed to identify the organization that would maintain control of the root zone key. The deployment of DNSSEC is likely to be delayed until this organization is identified.

Recommendation: DNSSEC should be deployed throughout the DNS as practical, with highest priority given to deployment in the root zone and the TLDs.

4.2 LINKING THE TELEPHONE AND INTERNET NAMING SYSTEMS

The Internet and the traditional telephone network operate differently. When a traditional telephone call is made, switches create a circuit between the caller and the person who is called. That circuit remains in place for the duration of the call. The process is called circuit switching.

---

[17]Several facilities in the Netherlands and Sweden are examining how DNSSEC could operate when it is generally deployed by examining procedures, such as key rollover, determining parameters for DNSSEC mechanisms, such as key length and signature lifetimes, and other issues beyond the scope of this discussion. For more information about current efforts of DNSSEC testing, see <http://www.dnssec.net>.

[18]See Atkins and Austein, "Threat Analysis of the Domain Name System," RFC 3833, 2004.

[19]See Berlind, "DNS Inventor Says Cure to Net Identity Problems Is Right Under Our Nose," 2003.

[20]See John Leyden, "DNS Inventor Calls for Security Overhaul," *The Register*, April 11, 2003, available at <http://www.theregister.co.uk/content/7/30224.html>.

However, when a message is sent from one computer connected to the Internet to another computer, no such circuit is established. Rather, the message is broken into packets and each is routed through the network independently, possibly even following different paths, and reassembled at their destination in the proper order. That process is called packet-switching. For the most part, the circuit-switched world of telephony and the packet-switched world of the Internet have remained distinct. However, in recent years, a convergence between the two has begun to occur, with increasing use of the Internet to transmit telephone calls through a process called Voice over Internet Protocol, or VoIP.[21]

The recognition of the potential convergence of telephony and the Internet was one of the motivations for consideration by the technical community of ways to bring telephone numbers into the Domain Name System. Doing so, it was thought, would facilitate communications between the Internet and the world's telephone networks. The method that was developed is called the Telephone Number Mapping protocol, more commonly known as the ENUM protocol.[22] Under the ENUM scheme, telephone numbers, called E.164 numbers,[23] are mapped (via the ENUM protocol) to domain names. These are then mapped (in the DNS) to various resources by DNS lookups that lead to Uniform Resource Identifiers (URIs).[24] The main premise underlying development of the ENUM protocol is that standard telephone numbers—familiar, globally unique identifiers easily usable on numeric keyboards—are likely to persist. Consequently, making it easy to link the Internet and telephone naming systems may support the development of new and improved services that use a telephony-like model.

Applications that can build on the ENUM protocol include voice communications, fax, e-mail, and messaging. For example, a telephone call

---

[21]See, for example, the explanation of VoIP on the Federal Communications Commission Web site, <http://www.fcc.gov/voip/>.

[22]See Patrik Fältström and Michael Mealling, "The E.164 to Uniform Resource Identifiers (URI) Dynamic Delegation Discovery System (DDDS) Application (ENUM)," RFC 3761, April 2004, available at <http://www.rfc-editor.org>. The mechanism used by ENUM for mapping telephone numbers into the DNS was first specified in late 1992 as part of an Internet "remote printing" model that could substitute for fax and other telephone-enabled transmission mechanisms. That application and the mapping mechanism are described in Carl Malamud and Marshall Rose, "Principles of Operation for the TPC.INT Subdomain: Remote Printing–Technical Procedures," RFC 1528, October 1993, available at <http://www.rfc-editor.org>.

[23]E.164 is the designation for the International Telecommunication Union recommendation that established the global numbering plan. RFC 3761 stipulates that the domain names generated through the ENUM protocol must adhere to the existing E.164 country (or region) delegations.

[24]See Box 6.2 for a definition of URIs.

might originate from a standard desktop telephone set and terminate at a telephone connected to the Internet (after passing through a gateway). The implementation of the ENUM protocol may facilitate the completion of such VoIP telephone calls, although such calls do not require the use of ENUM as an addressing mechanism. The ENUM protocol enables the use of a single E.164 number to access applications based on the telephone network, the Internet network, or both networks. Thus, it may enable increased functionality and/or lower costs for communications in such interconnected networks.[25]

4.2.1 Mechanics and Operations of ENUM

The ENUM protocol specifies how telephone numbers are converted into domain names. The conversion is best explained through an example. Begin with a telephone number such as +46-8-1234567. Then remove all characters except the digits, put dots between the digits, and reverse the order, which yields, in the example above, 7.6.5.4.3.2.1.8.6.4. Then a second-level domain name is appended, which for the implementation of the ENUM protocol is e164.arpa.[26] The resulting ENUM domain name is then 7.6.5.4.3.2.1.8.6.4.e164.arpa.

The deployment of ENUM is typically envisioned in tiers. The highest level within the ENUM hierarchy—tier 0—corresponds with the selected second-level domain e164.arpa.[27] The name server resource records in this second-level domain would point to "national" tier 1 registries, such as 2.6.e164.arpa (for Indonesia—telephone country code 62) or 2.3.e164.arpa (for Belgium—telephone country code 32).[28] The delega-

[25]The resources used to develop this subsection include presentations and discussions at the public forum of the meetings of the Internet Corporation for Assigned Names and Numbers, Rio De Janeiro, Brazil, March 25, 2003, available at <http://www.icann.org/riodejaneiro/captioning-board-meeting-27mar03.htm>; materials from the International Telecommunication Workshop on ENUM, Geneva, Switzerland, February 8, 2002, available at <http://www.itu.int>; the ENUM Web site of the International Telecommunication Union, at <http://www.itu.int/osg/spu/enum/>; "Frequently Asked Questions," available at <http://www.enum.org>; John C. Klensin, editor, "The History and Context of Telephone Number Mapping (ENUM) Operational Decisions: Informational Documents Contributed to ITU-T Study Group 2 (SG2)," RFC 3245, March 2002, available at <http://www.rfc-editor.org>; and "Online Registries: The DNS and Beyond...," Release 1.0, September 16, 2003, EDventure Holdings, Inc., New York.

[26]e164.arpa is the second-level domain name specified by the Internet Architecture Board for ENUM use in RFC 3761. The .arpa TLD is intended to support Internet infrastructure initiatives such as the implementation of the ENUM protocol.

[27]The Réseaux IP Européens (RIPE) Network Coordination Centre (NCC) is the administrator of the e164.arpa domain as determined by the Internet Architecture Board.

[28]Twenty-six codes have been delegated (28 have been approved) as of March 4, 2005, as reported by RIPE NCC at <http://www.ripe.net/enum/request-archives>.

tion beyond tier 1 registries (and the definition of a "tier" itself) may differ among countries. Various trials are underway in a number of countries to identify the most effective models for those countries.[29]

A tier 1 registry could delegate directly to name servers that contain ENUM information. However, in some models for the implementation of the ENUM protocol, a tier 1 registry would delegate to multiple tier 2 operators (e.g., divided in a way that is based on how telephone numbers are partitioned within a country). Tier 2 operators would then operate name servers that contain ENUM information that takes the form of Naming Authority Pointer (NAPTR) resource records.[30] These records include NAPTR records for service-specific addresses (e.g., an e-mail address, cell phone number, fax number, and so on[31]), which would all be returned in the response to any DNS query about a particular ENUM domain name. An important feature of NAPTR records is that they can convey priority ordering (e.g., try this address first—if there is no response, then try this one). The situation described above is referred to by some as the calling-party control model because the DNS query for the NAPTR records retrieves all possible contact modes—that is, access to this information is determined by the requestor.

Tier 3 services could also be offered. Services at this level could support operations after the completion of a lookup of ENUM information (i.e., some of these operations might not depend on the DNS in any way). For example, a lookup from a tier 2 name server could point to a proxy server that contains tailored user information, rather than to service-specific addresses directly. This tailored user information could, in turn, provide office addresses to all queries and, in addition, home addresses only to those requests with particular characteristics. Alternatively, all queries to the NAPTR records could be directed to this tailored user information, thereby providing the called party with control over what contact information is made available (i.e., the called-party control model).[32]

---

[29]For example, see <http://www.itu.int/ITU-T/inr/enum/trials.html>.

[30]NAPTR records are described in Michael Mealling, "Dynamic Delegation Discovery System (DDDS) Part Three: The Domain Name System (DNS) Database," RFC 3403, October 2002, available at <http://www.rfc-editor.org>.

[31]These addresses may be specified using a variety of protocols that include the Session Initiation Protocol (SIP), which supports the negotiation of the parameters between endpoints for a real-time session. See Mark Handley, Henning Schulzrinne, Eve Schooler, and Jonathan Rosenberg, "SIP: Session Initiation Protocol," RFC 2543, March 1999, available at <http://www.rfc-editor.org>.

[32]This discussion was derived, in part, from "Enum: Mapping Telephone Numbers on to the Internet: Potential Benefits with Public Policy Risks," April 2003, Center for Democracy and Technology, Washington, D.C., available at <http://www.cdt.org/standards/enum/>.

4.2.2 Technical and Public Policy Issues

The deployment of the ENUM protocol raises anew most of the challenges associated with the DNS as well as a few new ones. Thus, the technical and policy context for ENUM implementation includes a wide variety of issues that should be resolved prior to the widespread deployment of the ENUM protocol and serves as an illustrative case study for other applications that might be developed on top of the DNS. (It also illustrates another one of the core Internet navigation issues: While ENUM provides mechanisms for mapping from telephone numbers to the DNS and from a domain name to relevant resources, it does not address the problem of determining a telephone number given some (possibly inexact) form of the name of a person or organization (and perhaps some additional qualifying attributes). On a global basis, that navigation problem is far more difficult than the challenges associated with ENUM.)

- *Registrars and consumers.* An important implementation issue is who has control over the information in the name servers. Conflicts over the inclusion or content of NAPTR records need to be resolved in some way. The design of the mechanisms for managing these conflicts can draw from past experience with the DNS and telephone networks, which has included dealing with slamming (the unauthorized change in service providers), number portability, and recourse in the event of fraud.
- *Privacy.* Since the records in the DNS are publicly accessible, there is some concern about the privacy of the personal information stored there. Of specific concern are URIs in the NAPTR records that refer to personal information that an individual would not wish to have linked to a telephone number in a freely accessible way.[33] Alternatives such as the called party control model described above accord individuals the ability to specify what kind of information will be publicly available, and an opt-in strategy provides individuals with the ability to decide whether his or her telephone number will be included in the DNS as an ENUM domain name.
- *Authentication and security.* Under a system in which an individual must make a deliberate opt-in decision, authentication of his or her identity is critical in substantiating that the person who wants a number is really that person and that he or she has the rights to use that number (and to make subsequent modifications to ENUM information). In addition, ensuring that the results from lookups to ENUM information are authentic suggests that the implementation of DNSSEC is as critical for ENUM deployment as it is for other DNS applications, as discussed in Section 4.2.

---

[33]However, note that the storage of E.164 numbers themselves in name servers is not a privacy issue. The issue arises when E.164 numbers are linked to personal information.

• *Institutions.* Because ENUM is also dependent on telephone numbers and the various policies that pertain to telephone numbers, the institutional framework includes the International Telecommunication Union (ITU). Also, as ENUM is based on telephone number country codes, national policies must be considered. A clash of institutional approaches may result, given the strong regulatory tradition associated with telephone numbering that contrasts with the traditionally less regulated management of Internet naming and addressing.

An important design characteristic of the DNS is the existence of a root zone that provides the operational basis for global uniqueness and coherence. By contrast, telephone service providers determine the country codes that they use for routing telephone calls. Each provider might not use the same set of codes. For example, the country code +866 is used from many, but not all, locations in the world to complete telephone calls to Taiwan. The +866 country code is not officially allocated to Taiwan, but it is being reserved by the ITU, which manages the country codes in the world. Because the ENUM model as currently implemented requires ITU and national approval for each ENUM delegation, the use of standard ENUM for communication in and with Taiwan has been prevented by the People's Republic of China.

• *Other.* The deployment of the ENUM protocol raises other issues that are too detailed to be discussed here, such as the disposition of an ENUM domain name when an individual terminates the service for the corresponding telephone number. The references provided in this section provide pointers to documents that explore these issues.

4.2.3 Alternate Models

In principle, ENUM-like domain names could be based on a unique identifier other than a telephone number. For example, consider the use of any random identifier that is globally unique, such as a product bar code. Or one might tie ENUM more closely to the existing country-code TLD model, using ISO 3166 numeric codes rather than E.164 country codes to identify the country-specific part of the number. Another alternative could call for the use (at least in part) of a domain other than e164.arpa. Also, the hierarchy of names need not be based on countries at all. However, it is unclear whether the adoption of an alternate model instead of the ENUM protocol would provide the basis for a superior deployment.

The deployment of the ENUM protocol could support important new applications. However, it is also the case that its deployment would reinforce the utility of telephone numbers. Assuming that it is increasingly desirable to identify an individual or activity rather than a telephone number, the deployment of the ENUM protocol might not be optimal in the long run because its use could forestall efforts to develop systems with greater capabilities.

Conclusion: Overall, the plan to deploy the ENUM protocol could lead to applications that use the DNS without necessitating any changes to DNS protocols or software. However, a number of important technical and public policy issues would need to be resolved in each country that has an interest in deploying ENUM. These issues include establishing the rights and requirements of registrars and consumers, developing practices for the protection of personal privacy, implementing procedures for authentication and security, and developing an effective and efficient institutional framework for operation of ENUM.

4.3 INTERNATIONALIZING DOMAIN NAMES

One of the issues of particular interest in many countries is access to the Internet and the DNS using home-country languages and scripts. As the number of users in countries with first languages that are not based on the Roman characters used in the DNS increased dramatically through the 1990s, interest developed in domain names based on non-Roman scripts (e.g., Chinese, Hebrew, Arabic, and so on). Several major efforts were undertaken in the effort to accommodate internationalized domain names (IDNs) within the Internet infrastructure.

Unfortunately, the design of the DNS presents formidable technical challenges for the accommodation of languages that use non-Roman characters. As a lookup system, the DNS must be able to determine unambiguously whether there is a match with a query or not. Comparing strings is much more difficult than most people realize, because the definition of what is "equal" is often not deterministic. For example, consider the case of the French language in Canada and France, for which there are different rules as to whether an accent stays over the character when it is converted from lower to upper case.[34] And some languages (e.g., Chinese) cannot even be reduced to a relatively small number of standardized characters (e.g., the character set for English). As these challenges were articulated and analyzed by the interested communities, it became clear that the widespread deployment of IDNs would necessitate a number of compro-

[34]Another example is the "a" with diaeresis "¨" ("ä") which in German should be sorted and looked at exactly as an "a" with diacritical character, but in Swedish has nothing to do with the character "a" except the look. In the same way, Å as the abbreviation for the physical unit of length "angstrom" is one character, but the initial character of the word Ångström is another (which in turn is different from an "A"). The other problem with the German "a" with diaresis (umlaut) is that it may be considered to match the string "ae", while not all names containing "ae" match "ä".

mises. Some of these compromises stemmed from intense arguments over the preservation of cultural identities, the use of names that are semantically correct, and other linguistic issues.

Other compromises have their roots in technical issues. Some of those who were very concerned about the integrity of the DNS argued that internationalized domain names should be implemented in applications (e.g., by reworking URL and similar formats to accommodate IDNs directly). Some other technical experts argued that the deployment of IDNs should be executed through a major overhaul of the Internet's infrastructure, rather than as an add-on. However, considerable pressure developed within the interested communities to implement IDNs in the near term and, therefore, solutions that would require extensive changes in architectures or standards did not attract very much support. This pressure provided the impetus for an effort led by the Internet Engineering Task Force (IETF) that culminated in a standard solution, the Internationalizing Domain Names in Applications (IDNA) mechanism.[35]

4.3.1 Internationalizing Domain Names in Applications

The central goal of the IDNA scheme is to enable end-user viewing of IDNs (e.g., 台網中心.cn) without altering the DNS protocols themselves. Hence, even though an end user may see an IDN, the DNS itself sees only the usual LDH-style domain names.[36] IDNA is entirely a client-side set of procedures.

There are a number of encoding systems for representing various language scripts. In the discussions leading to the adoption of IDNA as a standard, it became clear that a constraint would be needed on the number of encoding systems so that the introduction of IDNs would be tractable. Unicode was agreed to be the client-side encoding system for language scripts.[37] Thus, any user application based on other encoding systems would first have to translate its internationalized domain names

---

[35]IDNA is described in Patrik Fältström, Paul Hoffman, and Adam M. Costello, "Internationalizing Domain Names in Applications (IDNA)," RFC 3490, March 2003, available at <http://www.rfc-editor.org>.

[36]These are domain names comprising letters, digits, and the hyphen—a subset of ASCII—as described in Chapter 2.

[37]"Unicode is a coded character set containing tens of thousands of characters. A single Unicode code point is denoted by "U+" followed by four to six hexadecimal digits, while a range of Unicode code points is denoted by two hexadecimal numbers separated by ".." with no prefixes," as described in RFC 3490. Additional information about Unicode may be found at <http://www.unicode.org>.

to a Unicode representation prior to processing by IDNA-compliant procedures.[38]

The algorithms that make up IDNA work on the individual parts of a domain name separated by dots, which are called labels.[39] Translation can occur in two directions: from Unicode to LDH format (ASCII) or the reverse.

The input to the "ToASCII" algorithm is a single label comprising Unicode code points. However, before labels are processed, they must be normalized because different Unicode strings can represent the same domain name.[40] Thus, a profile ("nameprep") is applied—a string preparation and normalization procedure for Unicode that is partially derived from Unicode Technical Consortium (UTC)-specified normalization procedures.[41] An encoding system ("punycode") is then used for mapping "nameprepped" labels into conventional LDH-style labels.[42] These labels are then concatenated (with dots in between the labels) to generate the resulting domain name. In the process of assembling the resulting domain name, "xn—" is added as a prefix to denote that the domain name is an IDN;[43] an example of such a domain name is xn—fiq43lrrlfy5a.tw. At this point, the DNS is used as described in Chapter 3.

The process for going from ASCII to Unicode involves the use of the decoding algorithm in punycode. The details of this process are described in "Internationalizing Domain Names in Applications (IDNA)," RFC 3490.

---

[38]The mappings to and from Unicode may not be obvious (and may become controversial), as the local encodings sometimes make distinctions that Unicode does not, or vice versa.

[39]For instance, in www.example.com, there are three labels: www, example, and com.

[40]For example, upper case characters would be converted to lower case characters. However, this case mapping may be problematic, as in the case for handling diacritical marks where characters are mapped to upper case in modern French as compared to older forms (still used in Québéc and elsewhere). Also, consider the Unicode string www.Exa$(not$)mple.com that would be normalized to www.example.com. Adapted from Eric A. Hall, "The IDNA-to-ASCII Conversion Process," *Network Magazine*, June 1, 2004, p. 60.

[41]See Paul Hoffman and Marc Blanchet, "Nameprep: A Stringprep Profile for Internationalized Domain Names," RFC 3491, March 2003; and Paul Hoffman and Marc Blanchet, "Preparation of Internationalized Strings (Stingprep)," RFC 3454, December 2002, available at <http://www.rfc-editor.org/>. For Unicode normalization, see Mark Davis and Martin Dürst, "Unicode Normalization Forms," Unicode Technical Report #15, available at <http://www.unicode.org/reports/tr15/tr15-23.html>.

[42]See Adam M. Costello, "Punycode: A Bootstring Encoding of Unicode for Internationalized Domain Names in Applications (IDNA)," RFC 3492, March 2003, available at <http://www.rfc-editor.org>.

[43]The description given here is a simplified one. The many details concerning the various algorithms may be found in the RFCs referenced above.

Client-Side Support

There is a gap between "deploying IDNA" (i.e., adding IDNA-format (punycode) domain names in DNS zones) and the actual ability of users to see, or provide as input, domain names expressed in characters that are "native" to their preferred languages. The actual appearance of a domain name in native characters on a screen or printout, or the ability to transcribe such characters from a sign on the side of a bus into a URL to locate a Web page, requires that the relevant applications be upgraded to recognize the IDNA format and to translate to and from local scripts.

Supporting Web Access

Some Web browsers have been upgraded to support IDNA names directly, whereas others, including the most common browser, Internet Explorer, support IDNA through browser plug-ins.[44] These extensions to browser operations and syntax are not standardized and not consistent, leading to different users getting different results depending on which tools they choose to use (or, more commonly, have chosen for them).[45] In the worst case, the consequence is a breakdown of the principle of referential integrity—a putative domain name or URI, when passed from one user to another, acquires a different meaning (or target) depending on the environments of the two users. Even when support for Web browsers is achieved on a consistent and widespread basis, it will take a considerable period of time to replace the millions of copies of Web browsers. Forrester Research predicts that it will take at least 2 to 3 years before IDNs can really be used for Web browsing and up to 5 years until 90 percent of applications are IDN compatible.[46]

Supporting E-mail and Other Access

For applications other than the Web, the situation is yet more problematic. There is, in general, no "patch" option equivalent to the browser plug-ins. While there are only a few heavily used browsers, there are very

---

[44]For an example of a plug-in, see <http://www.idnnow.com>. Internet Explorer does not provide direct support for IDNA as of July 2004.

[45]Improper resolution and browser plug-ins that were not stable enough, complicated, and slow to download were among the reasons why Network Solutions, Inc., pulled out of the IDN business in early 2004. See "NSI Pulls Out of IDN Registration, Citing Technical Problems," *Washington Internet Daily*, January 15, 2004.

[46]See Thomas Mendel, "Internationalized Domain Names: Good Idea; Shame About the Execution," Forrester Research, March 10, 2004, available at <http://www.forrester.com/Research/Document/Excerpt/0,7211,34018,00.html>.

large numbers of client / user interface programs for e-mail, the File Transfer Protocol (FTP), and other protocols. Some of these programs are embedded in firmware on portable devices, which generally cannot be upgraded in a practical way.

Electronic mail poses additional problems. For most users, the Web is largely passive: People find and view Web pages, but relatively few users create their own Web content or need to establish addressing or location information for it. E-mail, by contrast, is not passive. Most e-mail users are actively engaged in the creation and receipt of e-mail. Addresses read over the phone or copied from business cards or notes may well be more common for e-mail than for the Web. Moreover, Internet e-mail operates in a store-and-forward mode: Unlike, for example, the Web, there is normally no reliable mechanism for a sender to determine, or negotiate, the capabilities of the receiver such as whether a receiver can handle internationalized addresses. And, finally, users typically expect the left side or local part (before the "@") of an e-mail address to reflect their names and related conventions (or other personal identifiers such as nicknames) and to do so accurately.[47] People are often extremely sensitive about the spelling of their names (or other personal identifiers), and efforts to replace e-mail addresses based on names with ones that involve semi-random strings have rarely been met with enthusiasm. Even if the domain name part of the address internationalization problem were solved with appropriate user agent software, it may well lead to more demand for properly spelled and formatted local parts in local scripts. Non-English-speaking users who have been using addresses containing Romanized transliterations of their names are not likely to consider a transition to encoded ASCII strings that have no mnemonic value and that generally cannot be pronounced to be a step forward, especially with their expectations for native-script presentation.

Design and standardization efforts for e-mail local parts are in their infancy in 2005. There are two major proposals. One tries to minimize the number of infrastructure changes that are required (just as IDNA avoided requiring, or even permitting, any DNS protocol changes). The other proposal assumes that true internationalization is going to require rethinking e-mail in an internationalized context (and hence requiring those who wish to take advantage of internationalized addresses to implement some upgrades).

---

[47]Although the "local part" of an e-mail address is not within the scope of IDNA standards, it is an important issue concerning the internationalization of the Internet more broadly.

4.3.2 Registries and Registrars

When it approved the initial versions of the IDNA standards, the Internet Engineering Steering Group (IESG) issued a statement that discussed the scope of those documents and areas in which other work was needed by other organizations.[48] Specifically, it pointed out that IDNA addresses characters only and that any relevant language or script issues, including near-equivalencies, must be dealt with on a per-registry basis. It also identified the special problems faced by generic top-level domains (gTLDs), the importance of conservatism in characters that are permitted, and concerns about display issues with converted IDNA strings.

After some discussion, and essentially as part of the process of getting several new country-code TLDs to sign up to a formal ICANN relationship, ICANN issued a set of guidelines for the deployment of IDNs in TLDs.[49] These guidelines build on the IESG statement and the work of the Joint Engineering Team (JET; discussed below) and provide that top-level domain registries must use the IDNA standards and must adopt conservative, language-specific approaches to IDN registration.

To protect their populations from confusion and fraud, and, in at least some cases, to comply with ICANN guidelines, registries have begun to establish language-based policies for registrations. The key to these involves specifying which particular characters can be registered out of the Unicode set or, when language rules are interpreted strictly, which characters are permitted in combination. Of course, there is no standard list of characters for any given language, and the Unicode Technical Consortium has declined to make lists of characters that belong to named (by language or otherwise) scripts, so a "language" for DNS purposes is ultimately a list of characters chosen by registries, with each registry free to make a different choice. For the convenience of registries that are disinclined to reinvent the wheel, the Internet Assigned Numbers Authority (IANA) set up a registry/catalog of these language/script/registry tables.[50] The criterion for registration is that a TLD registry thinks the table is worthwhile; ICANN is not going into the "what is really a language" business.

This leaves the more complex question of what scripts and languages a particular registry should permit. The smaller the number of scripts permitted, the lower the odds of fraud or other undesirable behavior. Prohibition of mixing of scripts (or languages) within a given label is almost implicit in a language-based system and will prevent at least some prob-

[48]See <http://www.ietf.org/IESG/STATEMENTS/IDNstatement.txt>.

[49]See <http://www.icann.org/general/idn-guidelines-20jun03.htm>.

[50]See "IDN Language Table Registry," at <http://www.iana.org/assignments/idn/>.

lems,[51] but it may restrict some registrations that might be considered reasonable.

All of these issues are much more complex for gTLDs, or other TLDs, that are seen as serving the entire world. Within a country, a decision as to which languages or scripts are more important than others is at least tractable. While it may be very difficult, especially in countries that have more than one official language, and where there are constitutional provisions prohibiting treating some of those as more important than others, these are the types of decisions that governments are typically constituted to make. For generic top-level domains, on the other hand, there is an, at least, implied requirement to treat all registration applicants equally, which implies that policies such as "this script is preferred over that one" or "this language is assumed when the choice of language cannot be determined" are much more difficult, if not impossible, to implement.

4.3.3 Chinese, Japanese, and Korean Scripts

The scripts of Chinese, Japanese, and Korean (CJK) present special challenges. These languages are based on Han ideographs, which are derived from pictographs and are constantly evolving. The "simplification" of Chinese writing in the People's Republic of China (PRC) in the early 1950s created a sharp divide in methods of writing Chinese, with the simplified characters being used in the PRC, but not in Taiwan, Hong Kong, Macao, and other Chinese-speaking communities elsewhere in the world. However, the mapping between Simplified and Traditional Chinese forms is not always one-to-one, but sometimes requires knowledge of meaning or context.[52] In addition, Chinese-based characters are used in written Japanese (as Kanji) and in Korean (as Hanji). An algorithm for handling mappings between Traditional and Simplified Chinese characters that was not sensitive to the particular language in use would map, for example,

---

[51] At the time IDNA was adopted, the UTC representatives who were participating in the working group were convinced that a "one label, one script" rule would prevent many, perhaps most, potentially fraudulent cases resulting from confusing one character with another. More examples have been turned up since then, and few, if any, people actively engaged in IDN issues now believe that such a restriction would eliminate even a large fraction of the potential problems.

[52] Increasing communications and commerce among Chinese-speaking groups make it important that simplified and traditional characters be treated as equivalent. The committee that did the writing simplification work, however, followed the historical pattern of language reforms over the centuries: they did more than simply replace one written character or one spelling with another and, instead, made some changes to disambiguate homographs and consolidated other words.

Kanji into Simplified Chinese, resulting in the characters becoming not only incorrect, but also unreadable to a significant fraction of the Japanese population.

To address the CJK script issues, a joint committee known as the Joint Engineering Team (JET) was created among the network information centers and registries for Japan, China, and Korea. That committee created a collection of guidelines for registration of the CJK languages and characters.[53] Those guidelines, in turn, introduced two new concepts into DNS management: "variant characters" and "reserved labels" that could be registered into the DNS only by the registrant of some other, primary, label.

In the JET model, the script associated with a particular language is defined by the entries of a table, with the primary (valid) characters being listed, one per row, in that table. If a label were proposed to be registered that contained any characters that did not appear among these entries, the registration attempt would be rejected as not conforming to the script. Each one of these characters may be associated with zero or more preferred variants—characters that, if they appear, are considered to be fully equivalent to the "valid" character; and character variants—characters that might be confused or substituted for the valid one (see Figure 4.2). That is, many Han ideographs look exactly the same or have a similar appearance but are assigned different code points in Unicode. The variants for the individual characters are then used to generate alternate (variant) versions of the labels. For example, if a label proposed for registration were ABC, and "B" had variants "X" and "Y," a label set (IDN package) would be formed consisting of "ABC," "AXC," and "AYC." All of these labels would be reserved; that is, it would not be possible for anyone but the registrant of "ABC" to actually register them in the DNS.[54] The labels generated from the preferred variants (as well as, of course, the original "ABC") would be automatically registered; those from the character variants would be reserved and could be registered at the option of the package registrant. Of course, if more than one of the characters in a label had a non-zero number of variants, the number of variant labels generated by the combinations, and hence the size of the IDN package, could become quite large—examples have been shown of some Chinese labels that could generate hundreds of variants.[55]

---

[53]See Kazunori Konishi, Kenny Huang, Hualin Qian, and Yanwoo Ko, "Joint Engineering Team (JET) Guidelines for Internationalized Domain Names (IDN) Registration and Administration for Chinese, Japanese, and Korean," RFC 3743, April 2004, available at <http://www.rfc-editor.org>. Also see James Seng, "JET Guidelines for Internationalized Domain Names," *CircleID*, May 8, 2004.

[54]The JET guideline document uses the term "activate."

[55]The JET guidelines view IDN packages as atomic—there should not be a mechanism for moving names in or out of a package once it is created.

Original form: 台網中心.tw (corresponding punycode: xn--fiq43lrrlz83a.tw)

Traditional form: 台網中心.tw (corresponding punycode: xn--fiq43lrrlz83a.tw)

Simplified form: 台网中心.tw (corresponding punycode: xn--fiq43lrrlfy5a.tw)[a]

Relevant domain names: 檯網中心.tw 檯网中心.tw 籉網中心.tw 籉网中心.tw 臺網中心.tw 臺网中心.tw 颱網中心.tw 颱网中心.tw

FIGURE 4.2 Example of multiple forms of an Internationalized Domain Name.

[a]Of course, it is the case that a domain name of the form xn–k0tp21.com, for instance, could have been registered directly, irrespective of any IDN issues (under IDNA processing, it would represent 放弃.com). However, as discussed in Chapter 2, there are strong reasons against the registration of domain names that do not have some kind of semantic or mnemonic significance to someone, and these specially coded labels do not have that property. Indeed, an extensive search was done, and none of these xn–strings actually appeared, at least in the accessible top few levels of the DNS.

SOURCE: Vincent W.S. Chen, "IDN Whois Challenges—TWNIC's Case Study," presentation at the ICANN meeting, October 29, 2003, Carthage, Tunisia, available at <http://www.icann.org/presentations/chen-whois-carthage-29oct03.ppt>.

Introduction of the "package" concept raises varying economic questions that do not arise with LDH-style domain names. How should the pricing of IDNs reflect the reality that each registration may cause other (sometimes many other) domain names to be reserved? Also, given that there is only one possible authorized registrant for a reserved domain name, what options exist for pricing? Many new possibilities arise in the realm of domain name pricing structures for IDNs.

The challenges posed by CJK scripts also exist, though perhaps less severely, in alphabetic languages. Thus, work to generalize the JET guidelines to alphabetic languages is underway. Two attempts have been made so far to make that generalization work, or at least to construct recommendations for considerations as to how to do it for particular alphabetic scripts and languages.[56]

[56]See John C. Klensin, "Suggested Practices for Registration of Internationalized Domain Names," draft, May 17, 2005, available at <http://www.ietf.org/internet-drafts/draft-klensin-reg-guidelines-08.txt>.

4.3.4 Conclusions

It was recognized on its adoption—and it has become much more obvious since—that IDNA solved only part of the internationalization problem. Remaining to be addressed are the questions of consumer confusion—especially those questions that did not involve intellectual property issues; conflict avoidance or resolution for similar-appearing names; differences in interpretations for different languages; restrictions on registrations on a per-domain basis; implications for the Uniform Domain Name Dispute Resolution Process (UDRP) and the Whois database; security issues raised by IDN;[57] the implications of (and alternatives to) "multilingual" top level domains.[58]

Recommendation: Continuing and increased attention to internationalized domain names is necessary. Efforts to coordinate work across different countries, regions, and language groups should be undertaken to prevent the balkanization of the Internet.

Conclusion: The relative merit of an approach for implementing internationalized domain names based on incremental fixes as compared with one that involves an infrastructure overhaul remains uncertain.

Conclusion: Although the ongoing work on internationalized domain names is important, it addresses only a small fraction of the issues associated with internationalization of the Internet in general.

4.4 RESPONDING TO DOMAIN NAME ERRORS

A challenge that has faced the DNS since its inception is that users sometimes make errors when entering domain names as part of Web URIs, e-mail addresses, or other applications on the Internet. The errors may simply be misspellings or they may be the entry of non-existent or inactive domains; often they are the result of a user guessing an address or remembering one incorrectly. When an erroneous domain name arrives at some level in the DNS, the standard response is for a "no such domain" message to be returned to the user. If the application is e-mail, then the

---

[57]The Unicode Consortium has published a draft technical report that addresses Unicode security issues, including IDN issues. See Mark Davis, "Security Considerations for the Implementation of Unicode and Related Technologies," Proposed Draft Unicode Technical Report #36, Unicode Consortium, February 2005, available at <http://www.unicode.org/reports/tr36/>.

[58]The implications of IDN introduction for dispute resolution are discussed in Section 5.6.3 and for Whois data and the Whois protocol in Sections 5.7.2 and 5.7.3.

response may be from a MAILER DAEMON reporting that the mail could not be delivered to the non-existent address. If the application is the Web, then either the Internet service provider (e.g., AOL or Yahoo!) or the browser (e.g., Internet Explorer) may send the erroneous address to a search engine[59] to initiate a search. In any event, the user receives information that the address entered is erroneous.

However, in addition to the return of error information to the originator as specified by the DNS technical standards and conventions, two controversial kinds of response to user errors have appeared recently. Both derive from the fundamental law of Internet commerce: traffic => income. That is, traffic to an Internet location (generally a Web site) can produce income for the owner of the site (through advertising sales); the greater the traffic, the greater the income potential. Consequently, the commercial imperative is to acquire as much traffic as possible. Controversy arises when that imperative leads to actions that confound user expectations or, more fundamentally, challenge the underlying technology standards and conventions on which smooth operation of the Internet has been based.

4.4.1 Traffic Aggregation

The first controversial response is called traffic aggregation.[60] The aggregator sets up a Web site on which multiple advertisers place advertising text that includes links to their marketing sites. The site may or may not have a specific theme, such as travel or electronic products. The advertisers contract to pay for "click-throughs" to their sites, that is, for visits that originate from the links on the aggregator's site. To attract traffic, the aggregator invests in domain names that would result from likely user errors, for example, misspellings or wrong guesses of the domain names of highly trafficked Web sites. It may also buy names that have not been renewed by the original registrant and solicit people who invest in domain names for future re-sale (often called cybersquatters) to link their warehoused domain names to the aggregator's Web site in exchange for a share of the resultant proceeds. The aggregator then awaits the traffic resulting from users who misspell or incorrectly guess a domain name or attempt to visit a domain name that is no longer operative or that has not yet been made operative and collects fees from the advertisers, if any, to which they "click through."

---

[59]For an extended discussion of search engines and various forms of paid advertising on search engines, see Chapter 7.

[60]Two traffic aggregators, for example, are TrafficZ.com and Namerenters.com. Their Web sites are, respectively, <http://www.TrafficZ.com> and <http://www.Namerenters.com>.

Although users finding themselves at entirely different sites from those intended may be annoyed, the operation of a traffic aggregation site is in itself neither illegal nor in contravention of the explicit DNS technical standards. However, by responding to an erroneous query with a Web page that the user was not specifically seeking, it does arguably contravene DNS conventions and reasonable user expectations of the DNS service. Depending on the domain name used to attract the traffic, and the content on the page, it might also result in trademark infringement, unfair competition, or cybersquatting prosecution under the Anticybersquatting Consumer Protection Act or violate a host of consumer and child protection laws. Nevertheless, apparently a sufficient number of users find the advertised sites of enough interest to follow their links and, thereby, provide income to the aggregators. Moreover, there does not seem to be a practical technical or regulatory way to control this practice outside the listed legal realms. Therefore, it not further considered here.

4.4.2 Site Finder by VeriSign

Far more controversial and subject to control was the offering of the Site Finder service by VeriSign, which was launched without notice in mid-September 2003.[61] That service, which was aimed at users of the World Wide Web, re-routed any request concerning an unregistered domain name within the .com and .net zones to a VeriSign-operated Web site featuring paid advertising links and a search engine, rather than returning the usual "no such domain" error message. VeriSign described it as a value-added service for users that could, at the same time, generate significant revenue for VeriSign from the frequent errors in second-level domain names in the .com and .net TLDs.[62] However, the elimination of the "no such domain" error across the .com and .net domains, which numerous applications depend on for their current operation, had a direct and an indirect impact on the performance of applications other than the Web, on the DNS, and on the Internet in general. Many in the Internet technical and operator communities believed that, even though Site Finder was implemented in strict conformance with DNS standards, it was in conflict with their spirit. As a result of their strong complaints and ICANN's written demand that it desist,[63]

---

[61]See VeriSign's Site Finder FAQ at <http://www.verisign.com/products-services/naming-and-directory-services/naming-services/site-finder-services/page_002698.html>.

[62]VeriSign estimated the number of misspellings to be 20 million per day; see *CircleID*, "Facts and Figures," available at <http://www.circleid.com/sitefinder>.

[63]See "Letter from Paul Twomey to Russell Lewis 3 October 2003," available at <http://www.icann.org/correspondence/Twomey-to-lewis-03oct03.htm>.

VeriSign suspended the service (under protest) in early October 2003 and pursued the matter in the courts, as is described below.

The intense reactions from the Internet technical and operator communities[64] that prompted ICANN to demand the suspension of the service[65] until further review raised issues of two types: technical and institutional. The technical issues were, themselves, of two types: first, whether Site Finder would have negative effects on the stability and security of the Domain Name System,[66] and second, whether VeriSign had followed an appropriate process for introducing operational changes that have potential effects on other Internet processes and applications. The unilateral introduction of the Site Finder service by VeriSign also raised fundamental institutional issues about the relationship between ICANN and VeriSign and, by extension, the other gTLD registries.

Technical Issues

The Site Finder service introduced changes to the operation of the .com and .net top-level domains, through the use of the wildcard address (A) record. Wildcards, which can be set up by an authoritative name server to stand in for name and class records (see Box 3.2), are used to synthesize records if no exact match exists in the zone. In the Site Finder case, the wild card entries in .com and .net synthesized a response that sent requests for non-existent second-level domains to the VeriSign service Web site. The use of wildcards is specified within Internet Engineering Task Force (IETF) standards for the DNS protocol,[67] but their use generally has been localized or confined to an organization.[68] In contrast, the

---

[64]Comments expressing concern about the Site Finder service are available at <http://www.icann.org/general/wildcard-history.htm>.

[65]ICANN, "Advisory Concerning Demand to Remove VeriSign's Wildcard," October 3, 2003, available at <http://www.icann.org/announcements/advisory-03oct03.htm>. For a description of ICANN's ability to force VeriSign to suspend the Site Finder service, see Jonathan Weinberg, "Site Finder and Internet Governance," December 28, 2003, available at <http://www.law.wayne.edu/weinberg/sitefinder.new.PDF>.

[66]For a discussion of the broader social, political, and privacy issues raised, see <http://www.circleid.com/article/312_0_1_0_C/>. See also <http://cyber.law.harvard.edu/tlds/sitefinder/concerns.html>.

[67]See Paul Mockapetris, "Domain Names—Concepts and Facilities," RFC 1034, November 1987, available at <http://www.rfc-editor.org> and Paul Mockapetris, "Domain Names — Implementation and Specification," RFC 1035, November 1987, available at <http://www.rfc-editor.org>.

[68]An example of a common use of wildcards is for mail resource records, or MX records, as they allow e-mail server operators to synthesize all records locally that enable immediate notification that a domain name is valid before a message is sent.

introduction of wildcards in the A records of the .com and .net TLDs had an impact across a major portion of the DNS. They produced affirmative responses, instead of the expected "no such domain" response, to every attempt by the numerous applications that use the DNS to find a non-existent domain name within the two TLDs, as noted in the next section.

Security and Stability Issues

Technical Community Views. According to an assessment made by the Internet Architecture Board (IAB) shortly after the introduction of the Site Finder service, VeriSign's unilateral change had direct effects on the many applications that use the Internet.[69] For example, SiteFinder altered the normal operation of e-mail servers, which would be to return to the sender any e-mail addressed to non-existent domains. The result of the consistent affirmative responses for the VeriSign-operated top-level domains was to send e-mail addressed to the non-existent domains to the registry-operated server instead. This change affected users, as the immediate notification of a non-existent domain could be delayed by several days or more. It also affected network administrators that incurred costs to reconfigure servers, if they chose to bypass VeriSign's server.[70]

According to the IAB, these changes also affected the utility of spam filters that rely on identification of invalid domain names to block messages, and limited the operation of sequential lookups that require notice of unsuccessful DNS queries to seek information from other sources.

Other direct effects of these changes, according to the IAB, included the inconvenience to users who were rerouted to an English-language Web site, rather than receiving an error message in their native language; the potential loss of privacy as a result of e-mail and other Internet traffic being rerouted to an unintended destination; and the danger to Internet security and reliability caused by routing all the erroneous traffic to one location, creating a single point of failure and a target for deliberate attacks.[71]

An indirect effect of this change was the development of various technical countermeasures to circumvent the VeriSign Site Finder service. The Internet Systems Consortium (ISC) issued a patch for BIND,[72] the soft-

---

[69]See Internet Architecture Board (IAB), "Commentary: Architectural Concerns on the Use of DNS Wildcards," September 19, 2003, available at <http://www.iab.org/documents/docs/2003-09-20-dns-wildcards.html>.

[70]IAB, "Commentary," September 19, 2003.

[71]As noted in IAB, "Commentary," September 19, 2003. For an additional list of technical problems, see <http://www.packet-pushers.net/tld-wildcards/>.

[72]For more information on BIND, see Section 3.2.3.

ware used on many domain name servers, that disabled the re-direct to the VeriSign Web site and responded with an error message instead.[73] While patches released by ISC and others[74] provided an immediate solution to the re-direct, the ad hoc decision by network administrators or Internet service providers (ISPs) to use a patch or to create another workaround introduced inconsistent changes throughout the Internet,[75] that had the second-order consequence of limiting options for other services that operated within the boundaries of either the protocols or reasonable user expectations.

VeriSign's View. VeriSign responded to the IAB criticism with a point-by-point rebuttal,[76] which asserted that (1) Site Finder did not violate the DNS standards; (2) VeriSign was working to provide other-language responses in the near future; (3) Site Finder, by adding a *wildcard RRSet* to the .com and .net zones and updating its server, can relieve the majority of e-mail problems; (4) applications that rely on error messages can achieve the same effect by querying the DNS for the presence of a *wildcard A record* in the zone; (5) the detection of erroneous domains is not a widely implemented mechanism for spam identification and discovery and, in any event, is easily circumvented; (6) VeriSign has published mitigation strategies for dealing with other protocols; (7) VeriSign's experience in securely and stably operating redundant .com and .net servers enables it to protect the Site Finder service; (8) VeriSign does not collect or retain personal information through Site Finder; and (9) VeriSign is willing to work with ICANN and the technical community to deal with Internationalized Domain Names and domains not in the .com or .net domains. It also said that it shared the IAB's concerns with workarounds to bypass Site Finder and has written a guide for application developers to help them write software consistent with the DNS standards for wildcards.

[73]For a description of the patch, BIND 9.2.3rc2, see <http://www.isc.org/index.pl?/sw/bind/delegation-only.php>.

[74]Such as Imperial Violet; see "VeriSign Countermeasures" at <http://www.imperialviolet.org/dnsfix.html>.

[75]IAB, "Commentary," September 19, 2003. See also Benjamin Edelman, "The Aftermath: How ISPs Responded to Site Finder Around the World," *CircleID*, October 6, 2003, available at <http://www.circleid.com/article/303_0_1_0_C/>.

[76]See VeriSign, "VeriSign's Response to IAB on Site Finder Service," October 3, 2003, available at <http://www.verisign.com/products-services/naming-and-directory-services/naming-services/site-finder-services/page_002695.html>.

Process Issues

Technical Community Views. While the technical communities recognize that the use of the wildcard record does not violate DNS protocol specifications,[77] its implementation in the two largest TLDs did not follow principles that have guided the process for making Internet architecture decisions from the initial development of the Internet to the present, which have sought to minimize the impact of changes on the network.[78] The traditional process of working out proposed changes with the technical communities aims to maintain flexibility for all applications that use the DNS and balance the impact of changes on network operators, users, and the overall stability of the DNS and the Internet in general. Furthermore, as a matter of principle, the technical communities insist that innovation should take place not within the DNS, a core infrastructure of the Internet, but rather on top of the DNS, at the edges—the applications that use the Internet and the DNS.

Examples of innovation at the edges consist of services similar to Site Finder, but which re-route misspelled or non-existent domain names at the Web browser, such as Internet Explorer, or the ISP, such as America Online. Because the service is limited to the Web browser or ISP, other protocols, such as e-mail and FTP, are not affected by the redirect and will still receive a "no such domain" response.

Changes at the core tend to make service offerings at the edges more difficult, as the redirect offered at the DNS level overrides the changes made at the Web browser or ISP level, requiring these services to work around the high-level implementation. While services offered at the edges cause the least harm to the network overall, they are also the most beneficial to users, as they tend to offer more options to elect the service the user wants to receive, to disable it, or to switch to another Web browser or ISP.

Shortly after Site Finder was introduced, ICANN requested that its Security and Stability Advisory Committee (SSAC) undertake a study of Site Finder's implications for the security and stability of the Internet. After public hearings and comments, the SSAC issued its report in July 2004.[79] Its primary focus was not on Site Finder, per se, but rather on the

---

[77]IAB, "Commentary," September 19, 2003.

[78]The two principles include the Robustness Principle, "Be conservative in what you do, be liberal in what you accept from others" (Jon Postel, "Transmission Control Protocol," RFC 793, September 1, 1981), and the Principle of Least Astonishment, "A program should always respond in the way that is least likely to astonish the user" (source unknown; IAB, "Commentary," September 19, 2003).

[79]Security and Stability Advisory Committee (SSAC), "Redirection in the Com and Net Domains," report submitted to the ICANN board, July 9, 2004, available at <http://www.icann.org/committees/security/ssac-report-09jul04.pdf>.

facts that "core registry operations were modified, thereby changing existing services, and the change was introduced abruptly without broad notice, testing, refinement or community agreement."[80] It found that Site Finder (1) "disturbed a set of existing services that had been functioning satisfactorily"; (2) "violated fundamental Internet architectural principles by blurring the well-defined boundary between architectural layers" and moving more control toward the center and away from the periphery; and (3) proposed mechanisms "to ameliorate the undesirable effects of their diversion" that "put VeriSign in the implementation path of every existing and future protocol that uses DNS."

In addition, the SSAC found that "the abruptness of the change violated accepted codes of conduct that called for public review, comment and testing of changes to core systems." That process is intended "to ensure that changes are introduced with minimal disruption to existing services and hence with minimal disruption to the security and stability of the Internet." Moreover, it "precluded the possibility that administrators, IT departments, ISPs and other intermediaries on whom end users rely might be adequately prepared to deal with the consequences." The SSAC also found that "in response, workarounds and patches were introduced quickly, cumulatively reducing the overall coherence of the system and again violating the established practices of public evaluation, testing, discussion and review before core services are implemented and deployed. These workarounds further blurred the functional layers intrinsic to the Internet's robust architecture and in some instances created additional—and unintended—harmful effects."

The SSAC made recommendations to eliminate "synthesized responses" from TLDs that serve the public and that satisfy several technical conditions and to eliminate shortcomings from the specification of DNS wildcards and their use. Most significantly, it recommended that "changes in registry services should take place only after a substantial period of notice, comment and consensus involving both the technical community and the larger user community." It asserted that the process must "(i) consider issues of security and stability, (ii) afford ample time for testing and refinement and (iii) allow for adequate notice and coordination with affected and potentially affected systems managers and end users."

VeriSign's View. As its use of a wildcard A record in the TLDs did not deviate from the IETF standards that describe the DNS protocol specifica-

[80] All quoted material in this paragraph and the next two is from the Executive Summary of the SSAC report "Redirection in the Com and Net Domains," 2004.

tions,[81] VeriSign maintains that this implementation is a legitimate use of the wildcard and a valid service innovation that adds value for user searches that are not well served by the "page not found" error message.[82] Additionally, VeriSign selected its own technical advisory group to test the Site Finder service before it was deployed, arguing that a comparable process within the broader technical community would have taken much longer to complete and was incompatible with the pace and time horizon of business decisions.[83]

In August 2004, VeriSign published a response to the SSAC's report.[84] In VeriSign's view, SSAC's "purported 'findings' and 'recommendations' are inappropriate, unsubstantiated, and themselves contrary to longstanding written standards and specifications for the operation of the DNS and the Internet."[85] According to VeriSign, since the SSAC did not find that "Site Finder, or wildcards generally, pose a threat to the security and stability of the Internet's naming and address allocation system," its "findings" and "recommendations" exceeded the scope of SSAC's charter. VeriSign argued that the SSAC started its analysis with a predetermined conclusion and its report was written by persons who are opponents of Site Finder or competitors of VeriSign. Of greater general significance was its assertion that the report's findings and recommendations "would in effect restrain technical innovation and commercial practices on the Internet on the basis of vague and unwritten 'codes of conduct' and self-styled 'established practices' that, contrary to the Report, do not represent consistent Internet practices and conduct."

VeriSign asserted that the "well-defined boundary between architectural layers" claimed by the SSAC is violated by "multiple technologies widely used on the Internet, such as network translators and firewalls." Furthermore, VeriSign stated that Site Finder did not change the positioning of the DNS in the layering of network services, while the SSAC-en-

---

[81]VeriSign, "Architectural Concerns on the Use of DNS Wildcards" (response to IAB "Commentary" of September 19, 2003), September 23, 2003, available at <http://www.verisign.com/nds/naming/sitefinder/iab_response.html>.

[82]VeriSign's Site Finder Implementation; see <http://www.verisign.com/resources/gd/sitefinder/implementation.pdf>.

[83]See Charles Cooper, "The Cultural Divide and the Internet's Future," *CNET News.com*, October 16, 2003, available at <http://news.com.com/2008-7347_3-5092590.html>.

[84]VeriSign, "VeriSign, Inc.'s Response to Report from the ICANN Security and Stability Committee re 'Redirection in the Com and Net Domains'," August 5, 2004, available at <http://www.verisign.com/static/012393.pdf>.

[85]All quoted material in this paragraph and the next two is from VeriSign, "VeriSign, Inc.'s Response," August 5, 2004.

dorsed processing of IDNs at the DNS level would, by its own analysis, "blur" the boundaries between architectural layers.

In sum, VeriSign charged SSAC with using "a façade of technical orthodoxy to mask rigid adherence to the status quo of the DNS, which is antithetical to the very nature of the Internet and inconsistent with the RFCs, which themselves recognize the importance of innovation to the Internet." VeriSign went on to argue that "contrary to ICANN's clear directive, SSAC has failed to quantify or independently verify any of the purported problems described in the Report, raising serious doubts that they were real, serious, or widespread."

Institutional Issues

While the Site Finder service raised contentious issues of adherence to technical standards and processes, it also brought to the fore a critical and equally contentious issue of authority over and responsibility for the service offerings of TLD registries, especially gTLD registries that have signed agreements with ICANN. (In Section 3.4.3 it is noted that, as of June 2005, ICANN had such agreements with 10 of the 15 established gTLDs.) The issue is of particular significance to the relationship between ICANN and VeriSign, the registry for the two largest TLD domains, which contain over 38 million second-level registrations between them.

Specifically, the issue is this: To what extent and by what processes can ICANN control the offering of new services or the modification of existing services by TLD registries with which it has contracts? (It has no clear authority over most other TLD registries, although it could—in theory—use the threat of exclusion from the root to control the behavior of other registries. In practice, that threat is unlikely to be used or to be effective under current circumstances.)

In his letter to VeriSign[86] demanding the suspension of Site Finder services on .com and .net, the president of ICANN asserted that "our review of the .com and .net registry agreements between ICANN and VeriSign leads us to the conclusion that VeriSign's unilateral and unannounced changes to the .com and .net top level domains are not consistent with material provisions of both agreements." He went on to list six specific provisions of the agreements that VeriSign was, in ICANN's view, violating.

---

[86]See "Letter from Paul Twomey to Russell Lewis 3 October 2003," available at <http://www.icann.org/correspondence/Twomey-to-lewis-03oct03.htm>.

More generally, there is the question of whether the introduction of Site Finder abused the public trust that accompanies the monopoly position granted to VeriSign as the sole operator of the .com and .net TLDs.[87] Did it take advantage of that monopoly position to extract profits from unregistered domain names in unfair competition with ISPs, browsers, and search engines? For example, the second-level domain names directed to the traffic aggregation sites described in Section 4.4.1 must all be specifically registered and a fee must be paid to the registrar, which in turn pays VeriSign for each name. In contrast, Site Finder effectively redirected every unregistered second-level domain in .com and .net to VeriSign's service, generating traffic-based advertising revenue for VeriSign. Because of VeriSign's position as the sole registry for those two TLDs, it did not have to specifically register those names in order to control the response to a request for them.

From VeriSign's perspective, ICANN overstepped its authority as a technical-coordination organization and prevented it from continuing to offer services that benefited Internet users.[88] In pursuit of that argument, in February 2004 it filed a federal lawsuit in the U.S. District Court, Central District of California, charging that ICANN "overstepped its contractual authority and improperly attempted to regulate VeriSign's business in violation of its charter and its agreements with VeriSign."[89] VeriSign asserted that ICANN "stifled the introduction of new services that benefit Internet users and promote the growth of the Internet." It asked the court to assess damages against ICANN and for ICANN to treat VeriSign in a "fair, reasonable, and equitable" fashion in the future.[90]

VeriSign's antitrust claims against ICANN were dismissed in May 2004, but the court initially allowed VeriSign to file an amended com-

---

[87]For more information, see "The Cooperative Agreement Between the Department of Commerce and VeriSign," available at <http://www.ntia.doc.gov/ntiahome/domainname/nsi.htm>, which contains the text of the agreement and the amendments to it from 1998 to the present.

[88]VeriSign reported receiving 5 million unique visitors per day while the service was operating; see John Leyden, "Users 'vote with their mouses' for Site Finder," *The Register*, October 9, 2003, available at <http://www.theregister.co.uk/content/6/32973.html>.

[89]VeriSign, "VeriSign Files Lawsuit Against Site Finder," press release, February 26, 2004, available at <http://www.verisign.com/verisign-inc/news-and-events/news-archive/us-news-2004/page_005186.html>.

[90]Declan McCullagh, "VeriSign Sues ICANN to Restore Site Finder," *CNET. News.com*, February 24, 2004, available at <http://news.com.com/VeriSign+sues+ICANN+to+restore+Site+Finder/2100-1038_3-5165982.html?tag=mainstry>.

plaint to try to strengthen its legal arguments. However, on August 27, 2004, the court dismissed the claims with prejudice; specifically, the court held that VeriSign's claims about competitors controlling ICANN's board could not be supported.

VeriSign's remaining causes of action based upon contractual matters resulting from the registry agreements had to be refiled in California state courts. In August 2004 it made such a filing in the California superior court in Los Angeles County. VeriSign claims that: "Were VeriSign to defer offering such services to the public during the effective period of the 2001 .com Registry Agreement, or to modify such services due to ICANN's conduct and threats, VeriSign will suffer irreparable losses of revenue from third parties, profits, market share, competitive position, reputation and good will. Furthermore, millions of Internet users will be deprived of the improved functionality and quality of VeriSign's services."[91] As of October 2004, the suit remained open.

4.4.3 Conclusions

The Internet and the Domain Name System have operated successfully over two decades, despite manyfold increases in connectivity and connected devices and a great expansion of users and uses. As described in Chapter 3, their successful adaptation to rapid change has been based on a shared commitment among the operators of the Internet and DNS to adhere voluntarily to a set of open standards strictly vetted by the technical community and to a collaborative process of cautious and controlled change. This commitment has held even though the operators are vastly different in nationality and in type—academic, commercial, governmental, not-for-profit—and are not subject to the authority of any overall controlling body. The commitment is threatened, however, by two external forces. One is the desire by some governments and international agencies to introduce stronger international regulation of Internet operations. This force is discussed in Chapter 5. The other is the commercial imperative described earlier.

The commercial organizations that operate key elements of the DNS are appropriately driven by the goal of increasing revenue and profit. As observed earlier, in the Internet that goal is best served by attracting and capturing the attention of user traffic, which can be translated into advertising dollars. Consequently, there is a natural pressure on commercial operators to find ways to do so in competition with other operators. This is what happened in the Site Finder case. VeriSign saw an opportunity to

---

[91] Paul Festa, "VeriSign Sues ICANN in State Court," *CNET News.com*, August 31, 2004, available at <http://news.com.com/2102-1030_3-5331779.html>.

capture substantial traffic from unregistered domain names and, driven by its commercial imperative, took it. In doing so, it made an unanticipated use of a DNS standard for wildcards. Moreover, it launched its new service as a surprise, without vetting it with the technical community or informing other operators. VeriSign has defended its actions as being within its rights to provide innovative new services that offer benefits to users. However, the technical and operator communities have complained vigorously about VeriSign's breaking of the shared commitment to standards and process.

Although Site Finder may adhere strictly to published standards and its introduction might even, in some views, be strictly consonant with VeriSign's rights to innovate, VeriSign's action poses two high-order challenges to the successful operation of the DNS and the Internet.

First, VeriSign is not like any other TLD registry. It contains roughly half of all second-level domain name registrations and almost all the commercial and network infrastructure domains. It was granted the right to operate the registry as a commercial monopoly by the Department of Commerce and ICANN. Therefore, it is effectively an international public utility whose actions have profound and widespread effects across the entire Internet. When it is seen in that light, it becomes clear that it would be reasonable for it to be required to, at the very least, obtain formal approval from its contractual regulator before introducing any new service with wide-ranging consequences.

Second, and more significant, VeriSign's action could set in motion a commercial rush among other operators of the DNS. Suppose VeriSign's actions were copied by other commercial registries. The consequence for the stability and predictability of operations of the DNS could be profound. By ignoring the shared commitment among operators to accept the authority of the technical community on standards and new services and to adhere to a collaborative and cautious process of change, VeriSign tore a hole in the invisible web of implicit understandings that has been critical to the success of the DNS and the Internet. In remains to be seen whether the outcome of its court cases will determine whether that web can be mended.

Recommendation: ICANN should strengthen its contracts with TLD operators (especially the largest ones) to ensure that it has the authority to review proposed changes in their services that could have a detrimental effect on the DNS or on other services that depend on the DNS. It should establish an open, transparent, and speedy process of review for such changes that solicits contributions from the technical community, other DNS operators, other affected Internet operations, and end users.

Recommendation: TLDs and other DNS operators that do not have agreements with ICANN should voluntarily agree to adhere to published technical standards and to consult the technical community and conduct public review processes before introducing new services that could have a detrimental effect on the DNS or on other services that depend on the DNS.

The issues raised by VeriSign's introduction of Site Finder are both technical and institutional. As such they serve as an appropriate bridge to the next chapter, which addresses the issues facing the institutional framework of the Domain Name System.

5

The Domain Name System: Institutional Issues

The institutional framework of the Domain Name System (DNS), as described in Chapter 3, comprises a diverse group of organizations carrying out their various responsibilities with a high degree of autonomy. No single institution—not even the Internet Corporation for Assigned Names and Numbers (ICANN) or the U.S. Department of Commerce—has effective authority over all of the participating organizations. Nevertheless, this group of organizations has successfully managed the DNS through two decades of rapid growth of the Internet, and of the most significant applications on the Internet such as the Web and e-mail, which rely on it. However, as the Internet and its applications have grown in importance, so have the attention and the controversy that the DNS and its institutional framework have attracted. That critical scrutiny has raised a number of issues concerning the structure, governance, management, and operations of the organizations that manage the DNS.

Most of those issues are being actively addressed, but the organizations involved face the reality of multiple, often conflicting interests—both public and private—becoming more actively engaged in their activities. That makes achieving consensus decisions—in the tradition of the early Internet community—increasingly difficult and leaves a residue of dissatisfaction with any decision that is taken. Since attention to the institutional framework of the DNS can be expected to continue to increase with the Internet's growing significance as a critical global communications infrastructure, so too can the critical institutional issues be expected to receive increasing scrutiny and to give rise to increasing controversy.

This chapter is a guide to the principal institutional issues that have already or can soon be expected to come to the fore. For each institutional issue, the principal alternatives that have been publicly identified are summarized, and the alternatives are compared. Where the committee is in agreement, its conclusions and recommendations are presented. In all cases, the intent is to provide a clear description of the alternatives and the arguments for and against them as background for current and future policy deliberations.

Some of the issues, such as ICANN's management structure, may appear to be resolved for the time being. In the committee's view, understanding the conflicting proposals that preceded the present resolution illuminates the pressures that remain in the background and that may, in the future, force the issue once again onto the policy agenda.

The following issues are addressed in this chapter:

1. *Governance of the DNS.* How should the DNS be governed? What should be the role of the U.S. government, international organizations, and ICANN?
2. *Management of the DNS.* What changes in ICANN, if any, are appropriate?
3. *Oversight and operation of root name servers.* Is there a need for greater oversight of the root name server operators? If so, how might it best be conducted?
4. *Regulation of generic top-level domains (gTLDs): number and process.* Can and should new gTLDs be added? If so, how many new gTLDs should be added, and how fast? What types should they be, and how should they and their operators be selected?
5. *Oversight of country code top-level domains (ccTLDs).* Should anything be done to increase ICANN's oversight of and authority over the ccTLDs? If so, what form should its increased authority take, and how can it be implemented?
6. *Resolution of conflicts over domain names.* Does the Uniform Domain Name Dispute Resolution Process (UDRP) need to be improved? If so, how should it be improved?
7. *Provision and protection of Whois data.* What is the appropriate balance among the various interests in Whois data?

In contrast to most of the other chapters in this report, this one deals with issues for which opinion and values play a significant role. Consequently, many of the citations and references are to advocacy documents, not to peer-reviewed scientific or technical papers. These references serve as pointers to places where the proposals being summarized were presented. When there were multiple similar proposals, one or two have been selected as references, either because they appeared to be the most representative or because they were the most readily accessible. The committee's use of these references should in no way be considered an endorsement of the point of view expressed.

5.1 GOVERNANCE OF THE DOMAIN NAME SYSTEM

Issues: How should the DNS be governed? What should be the role of the U.S. government, international organizations, and ICANN?

As explained in Chapter 3, the U.S. government currently possesses the final authority to make key decisions affecting the DNS. Specifically, it must approve all changes in the root zone file and, thereby, controls the designation of top-level domains (TLDs) and the assignment of responsibility for their operation. In this way, it functions as the *steward* of the DNS, exercising its authority and making decisions for the larger Internet community.

Through a memorandum of understanding (MoU) signed in November 1998, the U.S. government delegated day-to-day operational authority to ICANN, which makes recommendations to the U.S. Department of Commerce (DOC) for its decisions affecting the DNS. In this capacity, ICANN recommends the addition of new TLDs and redelegations of existing TLDs. (As noted in Chapter 3, ICANN has additional responsibilities for Internet Protocol (IP) addresses and protocols.) ICANN might be thought of as the registry for the root, sponsored by the U.S. government. ICANN nominally has the same responsibilities as other registries: it registers entries into the zone file and sees to the distribution of that zone file to the name server operators. However, as noted in Chapter 3, unlike the TLD registries, ICANN does not directly contract for operation of the root name servers, nor does it have contracts with all the TLDs. In fact, in June 2005 it had agreements with only 10 of the 15 gTLDs and 12 of the 243 ccTLDs. However, because it recommends any new and revised entries into the root zone, because its agreements with the largest gTLDs set the rules for their operations and those of their accredited registrars, and because those rules strongly influence the operations of the other TLDs, ICANN is generally perceived to be the *manager* of the DNS.

Against this background, the issue of the proper form of DNS governance can be divided into two separate but closely interrelated issues: (1) Where should the stewardship—the final authority for key decisions—of the DNS reside? and (2) How should management authority—the registry function for the root—for the DNS be exercised? Although these roles are distinct at present, one possible answer is that they be combined.

5.1.1 Relationship to Governance of the Internet

Before addressing the questions of stewardship and management authority for the DNS, it is important to emphasize the distinction between governance of the DNS and governance of the Internet. Clarifying this distinction is necessary because the DOC's and ICANN's visible responsibility for a key part of the Internet's infrastructure and the fact that decisions affecting the DNS have economic, social, and political consequences have tended to focus discussions of Internet governance on the DOC/ICANN and the DNS. However, there are many aspects of the Internet that are or might be subject to governance but that lie outside the DNS and the areas of responsibility of its managers.[1] These include, for example, controlling spam; dealing with use of the Internet for illegal purposes; resolving the "digital divide" between developed and developing countries; protecting intellectual property other than domain names; protecting privacy and freedom of expression; and facilitating and regulating e-commerce.[2] Furthermore, there are increasingly important aspects of the Internet that are currently subject to little public governance, such as search engines and directories. Thus, DNS governance is a part of, but does not include many aspects of, Internet governance. Since at the time of this writing in December 2004 there have been no practical proposals for broad governance of the Internet, this chapter focuses solely on governance of the DNS. (The institutional issues associated with Internet navigation are discussed separately in Chapter 8.)

Conclusion: Governance of the DNS is part, but not all, of Internet governance. ICANN and the DNS are not the proper vehicles to address most Internet policy issues.

5.1.2 Where Should Stewardship of the DNS Reside?

The U.S. government acquired responsibility for and authority over the DNS root by virtue of its historical initiative and financial investment

[1]The issue of Internet governance, in general, has become the subject of intense scrutiny in preparation for the second phase of the World Summit on the Information Society (WSIS) in November 2005. The ITU held a workshop on Internet governance in February 2004 at which many views on the subject were presented. For an extensive discussion of Internet governance and the place of DNS governance within it, see, for example, Don McLean, "Herding Schrödinger's Cats: Some Conceptual Tools for Thinking About Internet Governance," ITU Workshop on Internet Governance, February, 2004, available at <http://www.itu.int/osg/spu/forum/intgov04/contributions.html>. In preparation for the WSIS meeting in 2005, the Working Group on Internet Governance (WGIG) was appointed in November 2004.

[2]The ITU invited selected experts to present papers on Internet governance at a workshop. These papers, which present a variety of personal views on this broad range of issues, are available at <http://www.itu.int/osg/spu/forum/intgov04/contributions.html>.

in supporting creation of the Internet and the DNS, as described in Chapter 2. However, as the Internet has become international in extent, support, and operation, the formal legitimacy of the U.S. government's continued authority over the root has come under challenge, such as in the context of the World Summit on the Information Society (WSIS).[3]

Critics, including representatives of the governments of Brazil, South Africa, Russia, and China,[4] have argued that the DNS is so central to the reliable and effective operation of the now fully global Internet that its control by a single nation is no longer justifiable. Some would prefer that the ultimate stewardship reside in an intergovernmental body, such as a U.N.-affiliated agency—for example, the International Telecommunication Union—or a new organization specifically negotiated by treaty, such as a "World Internet Organization"; others prefer an international body that includes governments, the private sector, and civil society. Many of the critics are national governments that have felt left out of the ICANN process, in which their representation is through the Governmental Advisory Committee (GAC),[5] which until 2003 had advisory status only.[6,7] Indeed, Brazil has asserted that "it is a myth that governments have a say in ICANN's activities via the GAC . . . the influence of governments is comparable to the influence of non-shareholders in a private company."[8]

---

[3]For information about the World Summit on the Information Society, see <http://www.itu.int/wsis/>.

[4]See "Global Fight Looms for Net Management," *Reuters*, September 16, 2003, available at <http://news.com.com/2102-1028_3-5077101.html>.

[5]As of March 2005, the Governmental Advisory Committee comprised the representatives of 94 nations, as well as several international and regional organizations with observer status—the African Telecommunications Union (ATU), Agence Inter-Gouvernementale de la Francophonie, Asia Pacific Telecommunity (APT), Commonwealth Telecommunications Organization, Economic Commission for Africa, International Telecommunication Union (ITU), Organization for Economic Cooperation and Development (OECD), Pacific Islands Forum, and the World Intellectual Property Organization (WIPO).

[6]For a history and analysis of the role of the GAC in ICANN, see Wolfgang Kleinwachter, "From Self-governance to Public-private Partnership: The Changing Role of Governments in the Management of the Internet's Core Resources," *Loyola of Los Angeles Law Review* 36(Spring): 1103-1126, 2003.

[7]In September 2004, Norway argued, in a submission to a preparatory meeting for the WSIS, that the GAC needs stronger funding and "cannot continue to have a mere counseling role to the ICANN." Norway called for a stronger and better-funded secretariat that would enable the GAC to focus on more strategic and political issues. See *World Summit on the Information Society, Working Group on Internet Governance, written contribution from Norway*, which is available at <http://www.itu.int/wsis/preparatory2/wgig/norway.pdf>.

[8]As reported by ICANNWatch: "WGIG Will Reassess—or Reassert?—Governments' Role in Internet," which is available at <http://www.icannwatch.com/article.pl?sid=04/09/21/1812238&mode=thread>.

However reasonable the move toward international stewardship might appear in theory, in practice any change can be made only with the acquiescence and active participation of the U.S. government. Not only would the U.S. government have to be an important party to any transfer, but it also holds an effective veto because all of the root name server operators would have to agree to accept the root zone file from a new source, yet 3 of the 12 operators are U.S. government agencies and 6 others are U.S.-based organizations that may well be reluctant to take actions contrary to the wishes of the U.S. government.

5.1.3 Alternatives

In this light, an examination of three alternatives to U.S. government stewardship is instructive: an existing intergovernmental organization, a new international organization formed by treaty, or an international (but non-governmental) organization, such as ICANN or a successor. (Another possibility would be to divide DNS governance responsibilities among several organizations, each of which would have its own steward. Although that may be an outcome of DNS governance decisions, this section addresses the stewardship of the manager or managers of the DNS, whatever form it or they should take.)

Alternative A: Existing Intergovernmental Organization—International Telecommunication Union

Description

Of all the existing intergovernmental organizations, the one that claims the most relevant experience and that has expressed the greatest interest in DNS governance is the Geneva-based International Telecommunication Union (ITU), a treaty organization affiliated with the United Nations.[9] Its membership comprises about 190 nations as well as more than 650 firms and international organizations in the telecommunications and information technology industries. Its Standardization Sector (ITU-T) has long experience with the adoption and implementation of international telecommunications standards, primarily for telephony but also for some computer networking technologies that are now considered histori-

[9]Other U.N. agencies have expressed interest in the broader question of Internet governance, among them the United Nations Educational, Scientific, and Cultural Organization, which prepared a position statement for the U.N. I.C.T. Task Force Global Forum on Internet Governance held in March 2004 in New York. See <http://www.itu.int/wsis/preparatory2/wgig/unesco.pdf>.

cal in much of the world.[10] A separate organization within the ITU, the Radiocommunication Sector (ITU-R), has responsibility for radio frequencies and some regulatory authority under the applicable treaties. Its processes and procedures are mature and, according to the ITU, "there are sufficient checks and balances in place to ensure that vested interests cannot misuse ITU processes for their particular interests."[11] All member governments and any interested private company (including registries, registrars, Internet service providers (ISPs), and equipment suppliers) can participate in ITU-T's work, but unless there is general agreement, only governments can vote and only governments can be represented in ITU's council, which has overall policy and strategy responsibility between ITU plenipotentiary conferences.

Because the ITU is an intergovernmental organization, it has sovereign immunity, which obviates the need for liability insurance or worry about liability affecting its decisions. Since concerns about the legal liability it might be assuming appear to have affected ICANN's willingness to, for example, enter into agreements with some ccTLDs that wanted to hold it to predefined performance standards, and could affect its ability to take on other roles, this advantage of an intergovernmental organization has some weight. Conversely, however, it may make the ITU a less attractive alternative to those ccTLDs and others that want to be able to hold a governing organization liable if it fails to perform its functions satisfactorily.

The ITU members voted at its 2002 Plenipotentiary Conference in Morocco that it should play an active role in "discussions and initiatives" related to the DNS and IP address system with the goal of becoming the forum in which public policy issues of Internet naming and numbering are resolved. In its resolution from the meeting, the ITU identified "stability, security, freedom of use, protection of individual rights, sovereignty, competition rules, and equal access for all" as important public policy issues.[12] Since that meeting, the ITU has campaigned for a more active role in governance of the Internet generally and the DNS specifically. Its

---

[10]"The ITU-T performs world-wide administration, and acts as the forum for policy management, of a number of naming and address allocation systems that are essential for the good functioning of critical infrastructures, including the physical-layer infrastructure of the Internet itself . . . [and] such well-known examples as the E.164 numbering resource and the E.212 mobile numbering resource." See Houlin Zhao, *ITU-T and ICANN Reform*, Telecommunication Standards Bureau, ITU, April 17, 2002, pp. 3-4, available at <http://www.itu.int/ITU-T/tsb-director/itut-icann/ICANNreform.html>.

[11]Zhao, *ITU-T and ICANN Reform*, 2002.

[12]ITU Resolution 102, *Management of Internet Domain Names and Addresses*, Marrakesh, Morocco, 2002, available at <http://www.itu.int/osg/spu/resolutions/2002/res102.html>. Also see Kevin Delaney, "Global Organization Seeks Voice in Internet Addressing System," *Wall Street Journal*, October 21, 2002, p. B4.

sponsorship of the Workshop on Internet Governance in February 2004 and its consultation on forming the Working Group on Internet Governance in September 2004 are indicative of its continuing active interest.[13]

Evaluation

The principal arguments in favor of moving stewardship of the DNS to the ITU are the broad international participation in the ITU, both by governments and industry; its established processes for policy making; its secure funding and sovereign immunity; and its long experience with management of international telecommunications resources. Its international treaty status would, perhaps, also give it greater influence over the ccTLDs and the root name server operators. At the same time, ITU-T cannot make decisions affecting competing parties or take actions without agreement by its membership. If there is a disagreement between governments, aside from attempting to mediate, ITU-T can do nothing until a plenipotentiary conference acts to resolve the matter, since only it has the authority to make recommendations to governments (which, however, can still ignore them). Furthermore, the ITU's charter does not allow intervention in disputes within countries, such as might occur over the delegation or redelegation of a ccTLD registry.

There are, moreover, objections to the ITU's assumption of the DNS stewardship role from the Internet technical and user communities and, significantly, from the U.S. government.

The technical and user communities have a distrust of the ITU for its long record of opposing the Transmission Control Protocol/Internet Protocol (TCP/IP) and for its unwillingness to make its standards publicly available for use on the Internet. Additionally, they fear that the ITU's bureaucracy and its structure and processes, which require that governments sign off on decisions, will lead to extremely slow decision making unable to keep pace with the requirements of managing the DNS. Many also fear that the large telecommunications companies, which have a longstanding interest in and presence at the ITU, will dominate the processes. It has generally been difficult for individuals and public interest groups to participate in the ITU's processes, although the ITU has expressed a commitment to change. Although it engaged individuals and groups in the meeting on Internet governance that it sponsored in association with the WSIS,[14] it excluded non-governmental organizations from the decision-making sessions and it has not moved to change the ITU's charter or ITU-T's internal rules to permit their active participation.

---

[13]See materials at <http://www.itu.int/osg/spu/intgov/index.phtml/>.

[14]See a list of participants at <http://www.itu.int/osg/spu/forum/intgov04/>.

The user communities are also concerned that the ITU would become a vehicle for governments to exercise control over the registration of domain names and would use that control to enforce other policies such as the local taxation of Internet commerce, intellectual property protection, and the restriction of free speech and rights to privacy.

From what is known of current U.S. government attitudes, both in the executive and legislative branches, transfer of DNS stewardship to an intergovernmental organization is not likely to be supported now or in the near future, although such attitudes can change.

Conclusion: Despite the interest of the ITU and some of its national members in its assuming stewardship of the DNS root, that does not appear to be a realistic alternative for the near future.

Alternative B: International Treaty Organization

Description and Evaluation

The negotiation of an international treaty to establish a special agency of the United Nations for Internet governance is also not likely to be supported by the U.S. government. The example of other such negotiations has shown that they take many years to complete, especially if governance or binding regulation are contemplated among its authority, rather than just coordination or standardization, and are unlikely to succeed in the absence of strong and sustained efforts by many nations, which despite the currently expressed concerns does not seem likely. So this alternative does not appear to be realistic in the near term either.

Conclusion: Although it is possible that the U.N.-sponsored 2005 World Summit on the Information Society will lead to proposals for some form of internationally negotiated, quasi-governmental or multi-stakeholder organization with oversight or other influence over DNS governance, specific proposals are not yet (in December 2004) on the table and cannot be evaluated for either their practicality or their feasibility.

This leaves the third alternative, which follows.

Alternative C: Private Organization with International Participation

Description

The only institution to which the U.S. government has expressed its willingness to transfer its stewardship of the DNS is ICANN, or a similar private, non-profit successor. Furthermore, this transfer of stewardship could occur only after ICANN (or a successor) had established its ability to operate effectively, reliably, and with wide international and constituency support for a number of years. Indeed, in its statement regarding the 1-year extension of its MoU with ICANN in September 2002, the DOC said:

> The Department of Commerce (Department) continues to support the goal of a private sector management of the Internet domain name system (DNS). Innovation, expanded services, broader participation, and lower prices will arise most easily in a market-driven arena, not in an environment that operates under substantial regulation. To this end, the Department has long maintained that a private sector organization is best able to respond nimbly to DNS issues in the rapidly evolving Internet space. Further, in order to garner international respect and function stably and soundly in the long-term, such an organization must be globally and functionally representative, operate on the basis of open and transparent processes, and possess robust, professional management.[15]

In September 2003, the DOC granted ICANN a 3-year extension of its MoU and indicated that if the agreement's milestones are met, it is prepared to complete the transition of DNS management to the private sector at the end of that period.[16] More recently, in conjunction with ICANN's July 2004 meeting, the Assistant Secretary of Commerce for Communications and Information issued a statement expressing pleasure that "ICANN has timely met the MoU milestones to date. Clearly more work remains to be done for ICANN to achieve functional, sustainable independence. We look forward to continuing to work collaboratively with ICANN . . . as we complete the transition to independent, private sector management of the Internet Domain Name System."[17]

Evaluation

Although these statements indicate the U.S. government's willingness to give up the ultimate stewardship of the root, they also demonstrate its

[15]Department of Commerce (DOC), "Department of Commerce Statement Regarding Extension of Memorandum of Understanding with ICANN," September 19, 2002, available at <http://www.ntia.doc.gov/ntiahome/domainname/agreements/docstatement_09192002.htm>.

[16]See amendment 6 to ICANN/DOC Memorandum of Understanding, September 16, 2003, available at <http://www.icann.org/general/amend6-jpamou-17sep03.htm>; and DOC, "Department of Commerce Statement Regarding Extension of Memorandum of Understanding with ICANN," September 16, 2003, available at <http://www.ntia.gov/ntiahome/domainname/agreements/sepstatement_09162003.htm>.

[17]Department of Commerce, National Telecommunications and Information Administration, "Statement by Assistant Secretary Michael D. Gallagher on ICANN's July Meeting in Kuala Lumpur," press release, July 19, 2004, DOC, Washington, D.C.

unwillingness to do so until it is assured that ICANN can manage the DNS "in a manner that promotes stability and security, competition, coordination, and representation."[18]

The stewardship role of the DOC, while a matter of political concern to some nations, has not impeded ICANN's governance role, with the important exception of sometimes substantial delays in approvals for routine changes in the root zone file, a situation that improved during 2004.[19] (See "Approving the Root Zone File" in Section 3.3.3). For example, the DOC has not overridden any ICANN recommendations for reasons of U.S. national interest. The issues that have arisen about the governance of the root have, rather, concerned the way in which ICANN operates in preparing its recommendations to the DOC and not in the way that the DOC operates once it receives those recommendations. In that respect, the decision to establish an organization to take on the day-to-day administration of the root has successfully reduced those pressures on the U.S. government while, at the same time, preserving its ultimate stewardship.

The Internet in general and the DNS in particular have been developed and governed with the goal of technically enabling equitable access to all locations on the Internet to users anywhere on the globe. To best serve the worldwide Internet and the DNS, the U.S. government's influence needs to continue to be exercised carefully and, in particular, this influence should not be used as an instrument of U.S. domestic or foreign policy in areas far removed from the Internet.

Conclusion: Governance of the DNS is not an appropriate venue for the playing out of national political interests.

The technical legacy of the DNS's development and initial implementation in the United States, such as the use of the ASCII character set for domain names and the concentration of root servers in the United States, has been a source of concern to some countries. Such concerns have been

---

[18]DOC, "Department of Commerce Statement Regarding Extension of Memorandum of Understanding with ICANN," September 16, 2003, p. 2.

[19]There has been dissatisfaction among the ccTLD managers over the length of time required by ICANN and the DOC to approve routine changes to the root zone file. In response, ICANN prepared a revised process designed to cut the time substantially and to keep requesters informed of progress in the approval process. See Internet Assigned Numbers Authority (IANA), "Procedures for Handling Requests by ccTLD Managers to Change Nameservers," May 13, 2003, available at <http://www.iana.org/cctld/nameserver-change-procedures-13may03.htm>. These revised procedures and other changes have significantly reduced the time taken to make changes in the root zone file as reported by the general manager of ICANN/IANA at the Kuala Lumpur meeting of ICANN. His full report, including specific data, is available at <http://www.icann.org/presentations/barton-forum-kl-22jul04.pdf>.

or are in the process of being addressed and they should, consequently, be substantially reduced or eliminated.

Although there may be continued objection by some nations to the right of the U.S. government to exercise its role,[20] the United States has committed itself to a contractual 3-year transition to ICANN under the conditions laid out in the amended MoU. The real question is whether ICANN will be able to gain full legitimacy in the perception of other national governments and constituencies during this period.

Conclusion: The continued evolution of ICANN to attain legitimacy among its critical constituencies and, consequently, to receive stewardship responsibility from the U.S. government appears to be the most feasible path to governance of the DNS that is broadly accepted as international.

The prospects of ICANN's assuming stewardship of the DNS are addressed in the discussion of ICANN's role that follows.

5.2 MANAGEMENT OF THE DOMAIN NAME SYSTEM

Issue: What changes, if any, are required in ICANN's organization and management for it to achieve greater legitimacy?

When the DOC delegated responsibility for day-to-day management of the root to ICANN in 1998, it was with the expectation that ICANN would soon be perceived as a legitimate steward of the root as well. Yet, although ICANN is not a part of the U.S. government and its board has had an international membership, its legitimacy was not immediately accepted.[21] The critics' concerns have been with (1) ICANN's scope, (2) its organizational structure, (3) or its management processes, or with all three. The concern about scope has been the extent to which ICANN has exceeded its specific technical-administrative responsibilities to, for example, regulate TLD registry operations. The concerns about structure have included a perceived imbalance in the historical composition of ICANN's board, failings in the processes by which the board was selected, and the inadequate representation of certain constituency groups. The concerns about management processes have included the lack of transparency, effectiveness, accountability, and recourse in ICANN's electoral and decision processes.

---

[20]In the recent U.N.-sponsored forums on Internet governance, a few nations have expressed a concern that their ccTLDs could be removed from the root by the U.S. government for political reasons.

[21]See, for example, Jonathan Weinberg, "ICANN and the Problem of Legitimacy," *Duke Law Journal* 50:187-257, 2000.

5.2.1 Scope of ICANN's Authority

The first controversy affecting ICANN's perceived legitimacy is its appropriate scope—the extent of its responsibilities and authority. On the one hand, there are those who believe that ICANN should stick as closely as possible to its technical-administrative charter, eschewing responsibility for seemingly related matters that require it to make value-laden judgments that have political, commercial, or social effects.[22] Such matters include the administrative approval of new gTLDs, regulation of the business practices of gTLD registries, and the delegation or redelegation of ccTLD registries. On the other hand, ICANN currently engages in each of those activities as a result of decisions taken by its staff and board during its early years. ICANN may have assumed those decision responsibilities because there was no other organization able to take them on, because they believed that there was no non-judgmental way of resolving issues that ICANN confronted in connection with its technical-administrative responsibilities, or because of the views and aspirations of the board and staff.

There should be a connection among the breadth of ICANN's activities, the pressure on it to broaden membership on its board and engage more constituencies in its decisions, and the acceptance of its legitimacy by various constituency groups. Were ICANN able, for example, to narrow its scope primarily to the IANA administrative functions, to use economic processes such as auctions or lotteries to allocate TLDs, and to delegate to third parties the politically sensitive decisions such as redelegation of ccTLDs, then the pressures might ease, and acceptance of ICANN's legitimacy as an essentially administrative body might become easier. However, in actual implementation, even economic processes require some potentially sensitive decisions to be taken (see Section 5.4.2); delegation entails the question of delegation to whom; and apparently routine administrative processes, such as contracting with a gTLD registry, entail judgments about what provisions—if any—are necessary to protect the technical integrity of the DNS, safeguard the interests of registrants, and meet the needs of intellectual property owners while preserving freedom of expression.

Conclusion: ICANN is more likely to achieve perceived legitimacy with a narrower scope rather than with a broader one.

---

[22]See, for example, Center for Democracy and Technology, *ICANN and Internet Governance: Getting Back to Basics,* July 2004, available at <http://www.cdt.org/dns/icann/20040713_cdt.pdf>.

However, it may not be possible or desirable to narrow ICANN's scope to a purely technical-administrative one because of the difficulty of performing such functions without making some politically, socially, or economically sensitive judgments. Moreover, ICANN might very well attract controversy simply because it would be the most visible organization with some, however limited, authority over the DNS.

5.2.2 Composition of the ICANN Board

The second controversy concerns ICANN's organizational structure. If it is to be widely perceived as legitimate, what should the composition of the ICANN board be and how should its members be selected? Those questions have been the subject of dispute since ICANN was formed. To a large extent, the dispute stems from different views of ICANN's proper scope.

Those who believe that ICANN is principally a technical-administrative body may favor selection of the board by members of the technical-administrative community from among the members of that community on the basis of expertise and experience—a traditional process in that community. In contrast, those who see ICANN as a major element of Internet governance may favor a board comprising representatives of the broad Internet user community chosen, so as to achieve legitimacy, through an open electoral process—Internet democracy. Those who see ICANN's scope as lying between these two views might favor a board representative of various constituencies selected through some combination of constituency elections and peer selections. Finally, some governments feel that because the Internet (and the DNS) has become a central element of the global communications infrastructure, it requires governmental oversight and regulation and, therefore, ICANN's board should consist only or principally of governmental representatives.[23]

Much of the debate about ICANN's board stems from the differences among these perspectives.

In its first days, the 18-member ICANN board was selected without participation by many Internet constituencies, despite a DOC-imposed requirement in its bylaws that half the board be elected by a membership. The board's composition quickly became a source of controversy as ICANN addressed issues of broad significance and social-economic-political consequence, such as the addition of new gTLDs and the

---

[23]Since those countries have principally been calling for the ITU or another U.N. agency to assume DOC/ICANN functions, they have not at the time of this writing made this suggestion. However, should they determine that those options are not feasible, they might turn to this view.

development of the UDRP. This put ICANN under pressure to implement the requirement for democratically chosen representation of the broad Internet community on the board. That pressure led it to experiment with a process of open Internet voting for five (the DOC-required one-half would have been nine) regionally representative members of the board. That experiment, in turn, raised questions among some ICANN participants about the legitimacy of an open Internet vote, which they charged was vulnerable to capture by intensely interested, but not necessarily representative, groups and open to possible fraud. Others felt that it brought onto the board new members whose views were more representative of those of the broader Internet community than were the views of the previously appointed members.[24] Recently, ICANN has moved away from that model of a partially elected board to one that more closely follows the in-between case described above. The 15-member board in 2004 comprises six representatives selected by the three major constituency groups (the Generic Names Supporting Organization—GNSO; the Country Code Names Supporting Organization—ccNSO; and the Address Supporting Organization—ASO); eight others chosen by a board-selected nominating committee, which includes representatives of ICANN stakeholders, from nominations made by constituency groups and the public; and the ICANN president, serving ex officio.

The legitimacy of the ICANN board has also been undercut by the perception by some that the selection of its initial members was severely flawed. Critics charge that it was done top-down by ICANN's managers and did not represent a diversity of views. In their judgment, board members lacked political experience and ties to constituencies and were, therefore, ill-prepared to supervise the managers who selected them. Most of the members of that initial board remained in place longer than anticipated, during which time many of the key policies and processes of ICANN were put in place. These critics see the selection, composition, and actions of the initial board as having weakened ICANN's claims to legitimacy.

Since disagreements about ICANN's board composition and selection appear to arise in some measure from different views of ICANN's scope, they are likely to be difficult to resolve unless and until there is broader agreement on that scope. In the more likely situation, where there is not agreement among all parties on its scope, ICANN will probably

---

[24]A recent academic study of ICANN's experiment in "running a representative and open corporate decision-making process" judged it to have "largely failed." See John G. Palfrey, Jr., "The End of the Experiment: How ICANN's Foray into Global Internet Democracy Failed," Research Publication No.2004-2, Beckman Center for Internet & Society, Harvard University, 2004, available at <http://cyber.law.harvard.edu/publications>.

continue to be subject to some criticisms of its legitimacy. As in all political processes, ICANN's goal will be to ensure that the most important constituencies are not among the critics. In particular, it will have to convince the Department of Commerce that it has achieved legitimacy among the most important constituencies in order to fulfill the terms of its most recent MoU with the DOC.

It should also be noted that even if there were agreement on ICANN's proper scope, ICANN would still face numerous practical problems of representation. What would it take, for example, for it to be seen as truly international? Does it suffice, for example, simply to have one board member from each region? Or should the distribution of board membership better reflect Internet usage in each country or region? Or should it, perhaps, reflect the geographic distribution of registered domain names? This appears to be an inherently difficult problem to which any proposed solution may incur objections from some of those nations that are not directly represented. (Even direct representation may not suffice. Two of the countries that have been most critical of ICANN in international forums are Brazil and China, both of which have nationals on the ICANN board.)

In a similar way, the broadest view of ICANN's appropriate scope implies that the board reflects the many Internet constituencies having an interest in its decisions. But there is no agreed list of those constituencies, nor would the list be likely to remain unchanged. Even assuming that a list could be agreed upon, should one board member be selected from each constituency despite the fact that constituencies are of different size and degrees of importance? And how should each constituency make its selection? In the event that elections are used: Who is the electorate? How are they to be reached? How can the validity of their votes be assured?

These difficulties are not matters of ICANN's making. They arise from the unique situation in which it finds itself and would confront any other non-governmental organization attempting to manage an economically, socially, and politically significant component of the global infrastructure.

Conclusion: No composition of the ICANN board, no matter how arrived at, is likely by itself to confer the perception of legitimacy on ICANN among all its possible constituency groups.

5.2.3 Nature of ICANN's Management Processes

The third controversy concerns ICANN's management processes. Perhaps the goal of perceived legitimacy could be achieved through refining the processes by which ICANN carries out its work and makes its decisions. From its inception, ICANN has indicated that it would use bottom-up, consensus-based, and transparent decision processes. The aspiration for such processes largely reflected the culture of the early Internet community, especially the Internet Engineering Task Force (IETF). It fit well with that small, relatively homogeneous group in which technical expertise and experimental results drove most decisions. However, it has not turned out to be as effective a tool for making the value-laden decisions that have faced ICANN in an environment with a very large number of users, many of whom are not technical experts, holding highly diverse and often fundamentally different goals and values that are often not susceptible to resolution through consensus.

Although ICANN put in place a formal structure of constituency groups with apparent input into the board's decision processes, prior to the recent reform, at least, it had not succeeded in employing them in such a way that they were perceived to identify consensus views, or even to ensure that all constituency opinions were heard during the process. In part, this was the result of failure of the constituency groups to participate, but there were also questions about the weight given to some constituency groups and the absence of others.

Thus, although ICANN has made efforts to fulfill its promises using the current processes, it appears doubtful that—as long as ICANN is more than a purely technical-administrative body—any set of processes that was both efficient and effective could be restricted to bottom-up, consensus decision making among imperfectly defined constituency groups.

ICANN's existing processes have also been heavily criticized for their lack of transparency, for the failure to document the logic of decisions, for the absence of a process of appeal, and for the heavy reliance on non-accountable staff and consultants. Many ICANN observers view accountability as an "essential component of legitimacy for ICANN."[25]

Conclusion: Improvement of ICANN's processes appears to be a necessary step toward strengthening its perceived legitimacy.

For the reasons noted above, it would be difficult to strengthen ICANN's perceived legitimacy if the focus on bottom-up, consensus decision making were retained. It would be more practical to concentrate on

---

[25]Center for Democracy and Technology, "Comments of the Center for Democracy and Technology to the Committee on ICANN Evolution and Reform," May 3, 2002, available at <http://www.cdt.org/dns/icann/020503ceir.shtml>. See also Tamar Frankel, "Accountability and Oversight of the Internet Corporation for Assigned Names and Numbers (ICANN)," Report to the Markle Foundation, July 12, 2002, available at <http://www.markle.org/news/ICANN_fin1_9.pdf>; and Center for Global Studies, "Enhancing Legitimacy in the Internet Corporation for Assigned Names and Numbers: Accountable and Transparent Governance Structures," final report to the Markle Foundation, September 18, 2002, available at <http://www.markle.org/news/ICANN_Final_Sept18.pdf>.

making conventional majority-vote decisions through processes that are accepted by its constituencies as being open to input from all those having a legitimate interest, transparent and observable in all their stages, and fair to all participants.

5.2.4 Alternatives

In response to the criticisms of its structure and management practices, ICANN began implementing a significant reform in early 2003. During 2002, while it was examining what specific steps to take, a number of external groups put forward specific proposals of their own. Those proposals demonstrate the diversity of the interests that attempt to influence ICANN and that remain active or potential critics of its efforts. Furthermore, should the current ICANN reform not prove successful, those proposals are likely to reappear in their original or a modified form. Thus, both to show the forces that ICANN faces and to characterize the alternatives to its current reform, this section summarizes and evaluates some of the major alternative paths that have been proposed for ICANN to achieve legitimacy in the eyes of its critical constituencies.

Two distinctly different groups of approaches to ICANN's structure were proposed: broadening and narrowing. The broadening approaches would keep or extend ICANN's scope and keep or broaden the number of groups that participate in its processes on the board and through other means. In contrast, the narrowing approaches would narrow both ICANN's scope and the diversity of stakeholders directly involved. Each approach would also have consequences for the nature of the processes ICANN employed.

The alternatives described and evaluated below include two broadening proposals—one by the Markle Foundation and the other by the Non-governmental Organization and Academic ICANN Study group—and two narrowing proposals, one that ICANN serve solely as the registry for the root and another that it be a private trade association. The discussion concludes with two proposals that combine a narrowing of scope with a broadening of participation—a proposal by the Center for Democracy and Technology, and the actual reform that ICANN adopted in 2003.

Alternative A: Markle Foundation Proposal (2002)

Description

The president of the Markle Foundation, Zoë Baird, presented recommendations for improving ICANN's credibility and legitimacy in a 2002

Foreign Affairs article.[26] These recommendations entailed changes to broaden participation in the board and to improve its processes.

With respect to the board, Baird said:

> ICANN's credibility as a global manager of critical parts of the Internet's infrastructure depends on the board's ability to ensure that *all the various private and public interests are represented* [emphasis added]. Government involvement is one step toward providing public-interest representation but is insufficient on its own. Only with truly broad representation on its board—including non-profit organizations—can ICANN adequately address the *crisis of legitimacy* that plagues it [emphasis added].[27]

Baird also recommended changes in ICANN's processes:

> ICANN must take steps to bolster transparency and accountability. These steps should include some kind of public oversight by politically accountable officials; development of due-process principles and clear, publicly available procedures for the resolution of complaints; public disclosure of its funding sources and budgets; staff and board members who are held accountable to a clear set of professional norms and standards; open meetings; and documentation of the rationale for ICANN's policy decisions and actions.[28]

Evaluation

Although pointing in attractive directions, the Markle proposal's recommendations about ICANN board composition are, unfortunately, too general to confront and resolve the practical difficulties of their implementation. For example: What are the groups that constitute "all" public and private interests that should be represented on the board? How many different governments need to be on the board to represent all public interests? How many non-profits need to be represented to cover all other public interests? In sum, how many board members would be required to provide representation of all public and private interests? How can the number be kept from becoming unwieldy?

The Markle proposal's recommendation on process, although still general, appear to lead more directly to practical implementation. In the specific case of "public oversight by politically accountable officials" it should be observed that, in fact, that is the role that the DOC currently plays and effects through its MoU with ICANN. For reasons adduced before, it is not clear that the U.S. government would be agreeable to shar-

---

[26]See Zoë Baird, "Governing the Internet: Engaging Government, Business, and Nonprofits," *Foreign Affairs*, November/December 2002, pp. 15-20.

[27]Baird, "Governing the Internet," 2002.

[28]Baird, "Governing the Internet," 2002.

ing that oversight with officials of other governments. Even if it were, there is the question, once again, of which governments and which public officials should play that role.

Alternative B: Non-governmental Organization and Academic ICANN Study Proposal (2001)

Description

The Non-governmental Organization and Academic ICANN Study (NAIS) group described itself as "a collaboration of experts from around the world, formed to explore public participation in ICANN and the selection of At-Large Directors on ICANN's governing board."[29] The NAIS group was self-selected and directed but was funded by a grant from the Markle Foundation, whose president is Zoë Baird, author of the *Foreign Affairs* article in which alternative A appeared. In its report, published in August 2001, the NAIS group summarized its arguments for broad public participation in ICANN's board:

- "The mission, character, and history of ICANN requires [sic] global public participation and representation for its long-term legitimacy and stability."
- "To the extent possible, the entire affected Internet community—from companies in the business of providing DNS services, to domain name holders impacted by ICANN's rules, to individual Internet users and consumers whose activities online could be shaped by ICANN's rules—should be considered stakeholders in ICANN's activities."
- "ICANN's existing supporting organization structures [in 2001], or representation by governments, do not alone provide appropriate public participation."
- "'At-Large' Participatory Structures and Representation on the Board are therefore essential channels for broader stakeholder involvement and ICANN's legitimacy."

On the basis of these arguments, the NAIS group's report asserted two "overarching principles: The public membership [of ICANN] should be given structure and the public membership should be given representation." To fulfill those principles, it made six recommendations:

[29]Non-governmental Organization and Academic ICANN Study Group, "ICANN, Legitimacy, and the Public Voice: Making Global Participation and Representation Work," August, 2001, available at <http://www.naisproject.org>.

- "ICANN should constitute a broad membership open to all who complete a relatively simple registration process."
- ". . . the At-Large Membership should have internal structures that promote policy deliberation, coalition building and information sharing among Members."
- "The public voice in ICANN should be represented at the Board level through a number of At-Large Directors equal to the number of Directors chosen by the Supporting Organizations."
- "At-Large Directors should be chosen through direct election by the At-Large Membership. Direct elections, while imperfect, are more likely to provide ICANN with global legitimacy than other proposed options."
- Specific processes should be followed to authenticate voters, to achieve both geographic and global representation, and to refine election policies.
- To ensure the public's voice in ICANN, it should develop structural constraints on Board authority, create additional accountability mechanisms, and should pursue Supporting Organization reform—structure, processes, and Board representation.

"Thus," the NAIS group's report concluded, "it is essential for ICANN to establish an inclusive, open At-Large Membership, with a clear means to participate in the decision-making process and substantial direct representation on the Board."

Evaluation

This is a clear and full expression of the view that ICANN's influence on the Internet is so broad and important that the Internet's end users must have a strong role (equal to that of the supporting organizations) in its governance. It avoids the question of determining which constituencies should be represented by merging them all into a common "public" constituency comprising all who sign up and are authenticated through the best available method. Representation would be by region, with some global representatives as well. Voting would be done online, which has the advantages of speed, global availability, and economy but has been criticized because of the potential for fraud, for capture or disruption by a determined group, and for possibly wide national differences in participation. In addition, the populations and Internet participation rates differ greatly among regions, suggesting that equal representation may not be the best approach.

While opening participation to such a broad potential membership would undoubtedly increase the perception of ICANN's legitimacy among a number of its constituencies, open participation might have the opposite effect on those constituencies that take a narrower view of ICANN's role and stakeholders. This illustrates the point made in Section 5.2.2 that differing, perhaps irreconcilable, views of ICANN's role lead to different views about the proper composition and selection of its board. (The ICANN reform (alternative F) that is being implemented did create the At-Large Advisory Committee (ALAC) with a non-voting liaison member on the board.)

Alternative C: ICANN as Registry for the Root (2004)[30]

Description

The opposite approach (to alternative B) to enhancing ICANN's perceived legitimacy would be to focus ICANN on its primary role as registry for the root,[31] with responsibility for reliability, security, accuracy, and availability, and to design its governance and operations accordingly.

Under this approach, ICANN's governance would be simplified by narrowing its controlling constituencies to four groups of primary stakeholders:

- The gTLD and ccTLD registries that depend on the root to direct potential users to them,
- The root name server operators that provide access to the root zone file,
- The Internet service providers (ISPs) and intranets that rely on the root to enable them to do lookups on the TLDs, and
- The technical community that defines protocols and standards affecting the root and its operation.

Only these groups would participate directly in ICANN's governance. Since all of them are directly affected by or directly affect the operation of the root, they would, in effect, constitute a self-governing body. Following the tradition established by ICANN, these stakeholder groups could

[30]This proposal has been constructed for discussion purposes only. It is not a recommendation by the committee. It was created to illustrate how a narrowly focused ICANN might operate and be governed. It bears some resemblance to, but differs in important ways from, the perspective presented in Elliot Noss, Timothy M. Denton, and Ross Wm. Rader, "A New Approach to ICANN Reform: The Heathrow Declaration," March 25, 2002, available at <http://www.byte.org/heathrow/heathrow-declaration-v0r0d5-032502.html>.

[31]ICANN's other roles concerning the IP address space and protocols could be retained or turned over to a strictly technical body.

organize themselves into supporting organizations or forums to consider issues of special interest to their respective groups and to forward proposals to the ICANN board.

(The group of domain name registrants and the registrars that serve them are not directly included in this alternative, although they have a more direct interest in the operation of the DNS than, say, the much larger group of all Internet users. A variant of this alternative could include them, but it would make voting and funding much more complex and difficult to balance. This alternative assumes that their views will be heard either through the registries and ISPs or through direct presentation to the board.)

All other interested parties—international agencies, governments,[32] private commercial and non-commercial users and suppliers, registrars, domain name registrants, individual Internet users, and public interest groups—would be considered secondary stakeholders that could influence ICANN through one of the primary stakeholders, by testifying at hearings and board meetings, and by lobbying individually or through private and public interest organizations.

Although ICANN would remain a not-for-profit organization, the TLDs, ISPs, and intranets would be required to pay a fee for listing in the root (if a TLD) or for access to the root zone file (if an ISP, intranet, or other large user[33]). A portion of the funds collected would compensate the root name service providers[34] for their service and would subsidize the technical community to conduct testing and validation activities. The funds would also cover the costs of the IANA function of ICANN and its other registry activities.

The board's members would be elected for fixed terms by the four or five stakeholder groups. The number of votes cast by each TLD or ISP would be proportional to its annual fee to ICANN, which would be in some relationship to its demand for root service, for example, as measured by the number of registrations for TLDs and the number of IP addresses for ISPs. The number of votes cast by each of the root service providers and by each technical organization would be proportional to the annual payments it received, which would be based on its

---

[32]National governments' interests in their ccTLDs would not be subject to this body, except when a conflict over the operator of the ccTLD registry occurred.

[33]Small, non-commercial users would be exempt unless they wanted to participate in ICANN governance.

[34]Full implementation of this alternative would probably require replacement of the U.S. government-operated root name servers so that they could receive payments.

requirements. (Note that the sum of the payment-based votes would equal the sum of the fee-based votes less a number of votes proportional to the operating expenses of ICANN itself. These could form a third category of votes that would be cast by the ICANN president.) Tying board voting power to payments would provide an incentive both for payment and for participation, particularly by the ccTLDs and root name server operators.

The board would operate like the board of a public agency, taking decisions based on its collective judgment as informed by public hearings. On special issues, stakeholders could petition for a stakeholder vote, similar to a shareholder vote in a commercial corporation.

Evaluation

The approach described in alternative C for narrowing ICANN's scope is in strong contrast to the proposals for a broadly representative board that relies on bottom-up consensus-based processes. It substitutes a board that is intended to reflect the interests and experience of the immediate providers and users of root name service only. In doing so, it reconceives ICANN as a narrower, more technically focused body whose decisions would be limited to those that affect the ability of the root to meet the needs of those who have direct recourse to it. It would have the means to exercise authority over the root service providers through its payments to them, while they would gain influence on its decisions through their consequent voting power. Each TLD would pay a fee to be listed in the root, but the amount would depend on the number of its direct registrants (not including registrants in the subdomains of its registrants) and would be proportional to its voting power. Very large TLDs, such as .com, would have a substantial number of votes, but not enough to overcome the sum of the votes of other TLDs, the root name service providers, and the technical community. The most difficult issue would be imposing a fee on the ISPs for access to the root zone file since there is no practical way to prevent access to those that have not paid. The threat of exclusion from ICANN activities and decisions would be the primary incentive for payment.

Because it runs counter to the design intent of ICANN, to the cultural traditions of the Internet, and to ICANN's own recent reforms, the approach of focusing ICANN on its role as registry for the root is unlikely to be adopted in the near future. However, it illustrates one possible model of a narrowly focused ICANN and stands, therefore, as a clear contrast to the more expansive models described in alternatives A, B, E, and F.

Alternative D: New.net Proposal—ICANN as a Private Trade Association (2002)

Description

Another narrowly focused model for ICANN was proposed in 2002 by New.net. [35] Under this proposal, ICANN would gain legitimacy by reconstituting itself as an international consensus-based trade association for "parties interested in issues related to domain names, IP addresses and Internet protocols."[36] The association would be the vehicle for developing and promulgating industry-wide practices and policies. Because policies would be developed through industry consensus, its proponents believe that these policies and practices would be more likely to be adopted voluntarily by the association members. They point to the consensus process, for example, that led to film producers' widespread adoption of the Motion Picture Association of America's film rating practices.

ICANN as a trade association would also be characterized by a reliance on market forces as the "dominant factor in regulating conduct of persons buying, selling and using Internet-related products and services."[37] The forces of the market would be expected to induce entrepreneurs and companies to introduce a wide range of innovative services that would succeed or fail based on users' experience with them, crucially including their interoperability with other services. In other words, the proponents of this alternative expect that many of the concerns that have driven ICANN to a regulatory model and, in particular, the protection of a single authoritative root and the controlled pace of new gTLD entries would be better handled by letting the market decide. These proponents believe that the market would reject any innovation that harms the functioning of the DNS and the Internet.

Where regulation would be required to supplement industry agreements and market forces, this alternative would rely on existing practices, using national, regional, and local governments or formal intergovernmental treaties. In the proponents' view: "It is hubris to assume that there is something so special about Internet naming issues that the domain name industry requires a unique form of government that is different from all other industries."[38]

One consequence of adopting this alternative would be the possible proliferation of DNS root zones, which might be created by countries un-

---

[35]New.net (see Section 3.3.1) is a commercial organization that offers an alternative root and related search service. It has an obvious self-interest in a proposal that calls for establishment of alternative roots.

[36]New.net, "A Proposal for More Realistic Domain Name Governance," March 2002, p. 13, available at <http://www.new.net/WhitePaper_v2.pdf>.

[37]New.net, "A Proposal for More Realistic Domain Name Governance," 2002, p. 15.

[38]New.net, "A Proposal for More Realistic Domain Name Governance," 2002, p. 16.

happy with U.S. control of the "legacy root" or desirous of one in their national language, or by corporations, like New.net, that see business opportunities in offering roots containing additional TLDs and operating under different policies. To alleviate the concerns of key players, the proposal suggests that the United States retain policy control of the legacy root; that other nations form a ccTLD association that would agree on the contents of the ccTLD component of the root; and that the United States contract with that association to ensure inclusion of those entries in the legacy root. Other root zone providers would decide whether to include the legacy root or the ccTLD entries in their root. Finally, the workings of the market would determine whether any root zone, other than the legacy root, would survive.

Evaluation

As with alternative C, the approach of ICANN as trade association moves away from the notion of a broadly representative board for ICANN and replaces it with a smaller set of stakeholders that have a direct interest in operating the root. However, it retains the basic consensus decision-making process and, while not specifically limiting the range of ICANN's action, does indicate a strong preference for leaving decisions to the operation of market forces. Because of that preference, it loosens restrictions on the technical system of the DNS (such as maintenance of a unique root, regulation of TLD registry services, and a relatively slow, controlled addition of new TLDs) that many in the technical community have said are required to retain the Internet's stability, openness, and uniform accessibility.

While obviously serving the interests of its principal proponent in allowing alternative roots and, thereby, opening the market for gTLDs, alternative D does suggest how a market-based, free-entry management of the root might be designed. Like the preceding alternative, new.net's proposal challenges existing views, in this case those of the Internet technical community, about what constraints are required to protect the DNS technical system. Although it is unlikely to be put into practice in the near future, it is another model available for consideration should other reform efforts fail.

Alternative E: Center for Democracy and Technology Proposal—Narrowed Scope with Broad Participation (2004)

Description

In July 2004, the Center for Democracy and Technology published a report[39] that called for both narrowing the scope of ICANN's mission and

---

[39]See Center for Democracy and Technology, *ICANN and Internet Governance*, 2004. All quoted material in this section, "Description," is from that report.

broadening participation in its activities. At the same time, it supported the consensus-based approach to decision making.

With regard to mission, it urged ICANN to:

- "Reaffirm the extremely limited mission that [it] was created to accomplish . . . the technical function of coordinating the assigning of names and numbers . . . and a few inextricably related policy questions";
- "Refrain from using [its] coordination role as leverage to engage in policymaking in broader areas";
- "Reassess and ensure its contracts with registries provide both the reality and appearance of a limited approach to coordination of registry activities"; and
- "Adopt an approach to coordination that seeks to minimize policy impacts."

With respect to participation in decision making, it urged ICANN to:

- "Strengthen activities to engage diverse constituencies around the world in [its] decision-making."

With reference to decision processes, it urged ICANN to:

- "Support the consensus-based approach to decision-making that was core to the original concept under which [it] was created";
- Make its decision making "transparent, predictable and open to broad global participation by stakeholders, including users"; and
- Make its "future policies binding only if they are supported by a demonstrable bottom-up consensus among affected parties."

It also asserted that ICANN's "only real and legitimate power comes from *voluntary* [emphasis in the original] contracts and certain other mutually acceptable relationships and agreements."

Evaluation

Alternative E was published as a proposal in the context of the World Summit on the Information Society to refute the arguments and correct the misperceptions of those who see ICANN as a "precedent or justification" for international centralization of Internet governance. It does so by emphasizing the limited scope of ICANN's original mission and its charter obligation to apply only policies arrived at by "bottom-up consensus among affected parties."

Because it focuses on narrowing ICANN's scope and at the same time encourages ICANN to broaden participation by diverse constituencies around the world and rely on consensus decision-making policies, alternative E appears somewhat inconsistent. For it would seem that restraining ICANN's role to the technical-administrative function (and a few tightly linked policy matters) would, at the same time, reduce the number of interested constituencies and the range of policy issues requiring consensus decision making, though it would make the latter more feasible. It is primarily a call for ICANN to "get back to basics" and reverse the steps taken to set and apply non-consensus policies beyond ICANN's original narrow scope.

Alternative F: Reformed ICANN—Narrowed Scope with Broad Participation (2003)

Description

The issues facing ICANN in 2002 of board composition, constituency participation, funding, and decision processes were brought into the open and given formal recognition when the then-president, M. Stuart Lynn, published a critique of ICANN's operations.[40] This led to the creation of a committee to study and make recommendations on ICANN's governance. The committee's report was published in October 2002[41] and its recommendations, after board consideration in November 2002,[42] have been implemented.

The new ICANN bylaws, which took effect in 2003, have remade the governing structure of ICANN, especially the board and the supporting organizations that represent its constituencies. They are derived from a mission statement revised and sharpened in response to the widely held perception that ICANN had suffered from a vague and undefined concept of its mission. The new mission statement is as follows:

> The Internet Corporation for Assigned Names and Numbers (ICANN) is the private-sector body responsible for coordinating the global Internet's systems of unique identifiers.
>
> The mission of ICANN is to coordinate the stable operation of the Internet's unique identifier systems. In particular, ICANN:

[40]M. Stuart Lynn, "President's Report: ICANN—the Case for Reform," February 24, 2002, available at <http://www.icann.org/general/lynn-reform-proposal-24feb02.htm>.

[41]Committee on ICANN Evolution and Reform, "Final Implementation Report and Recommendations," October 2, 2002, available at <http://www.icann.org/committees/evol-reform/final-implementation-report-02oct02.htm>.

[42]ICANN Board of Directors Meeting in Shanghai, "Preliminary Report," November 1, 2002, available at <http://www.icann.org/minutes/prelim-report-31oct02.htm>.

1. Coordinates the allocation and assignment of three sets of unique identifiers of the Internet—domain names, IP addresses and autonomous system (AS) numbers, and protocol ports and parameter numbers.
2. Coordinates the operation and evolution of the DNS's root name server system.
3. Coordinates policy-development as reasonably and appropriately related to the performance of these functions.[43]

In conjunction with the mission statement, ICANN adopted 11 core values that ICANN will adhere to, including preservation of Internet stability, reliability, security, and interoperability; limiting activities to those benefiting from global scope; delegation where feasible; broad, informed participation; dependence on market mechanisms where feasible; promotion of domain name registry competition; open and transparent policy development; application of documented policies; speedy action; accountability; and sensitivity to the public interest and related governmental concerns.

Under the new bylaws, the governing structure consists of a board of directors with 15 voting members: 8 selected by a nominating committee; 6 selected by three supporting organizations[44] (2 from each); and the president of ICANN, ex officio. In addition, there are 6 non-voting liaisons to the board: 1 each from five advisory organizations,[45] and 1 from the Internet Architecture Board (IAB)/IETF. The nominating committee is charged to select directors to ensure that in aggregate the board has functional, geographic, and cultural diversity; the capacity to understand the global effects of ICANN's mission and decisions; and credibility.

Each of the supporting organizations has its own internal structure, allowing for the representation of multiple constituencies. Each is responsible for the development of policy recommendations to the ICANN board

---

[43] ICANN Evolution and Reform Committee (ERC), "ICANN: A Blueprint for Reform," June 20, 2002, available at <http://www.icann.org/committees/evol-reform/blueprint-20jun02.htm>, with revisions from ICANN ERC, "Final Implementation Report and Recommendations," October 2, 2002, available at <http://www.icann.org/committees/evol-reform/final-implementation-report-02oct02.htm>.

[44] The three supporting organizations are the Address Supporting Organization (ASO), which deals with the system of IP addresses; the Country-Code Names Supporting Organization (ccNSO), which focuses on issues related to the letter country-code top-level domains; and the Generic Names Supporting Organization (GNSO), which handles issues related to the DNS and the generic top-level domains.

[45] The four advisory committees are the At-Large Advisory Committee (ALAC) for the Internet community at-large; the DNS Root Server System Advisory Committee (RSSAC) for root server operators; the Governmental Advisory Committee (GAC) for governments; and the Security and Stability Advisory Committee (SSAC) for security. The fifth organization is the Technical Liaison Group (TLG) for standards groups.

and developing internal consensus. The Nominating Committee comprises 11 members appointed by constituencies, 3 appointed by advisory committees, and 5 unaffiliated public interest persons appointed by the At-Large Advisory Committee. In addition, there are 2 non-voting liaisons from the other advisory committees and the Technical Liaison Group. The board appoints its chair.

In a move away from the consensus-based, bottom-up process that guided ICANN initially, the policy responsibility of the ICANN board has been strengthened:

> The ICANN Board of Directors is ICANN's ultimate decision-making body. . . . It is ultimately responsible for the management of the policy development process. Therefore, while it is highly desirable to seek and wherever possible find consensus, it does not follow that even proposals that enjoy consensus support should receive uncritical Board approval. The Board has a fiduciary responsibility to make decisions on the basis of good faith judgment in furthering the public interest.[46]

In response to concerns about transparency and accountability, the new bylaws call for the creation of an office of ombudsman, a manager of public participation to encourage full public participation in ICANN, and a strengthening of the reconsideration process applicable to both the staff and board and requiring prompt consideration. It also establishes an independent review process to review whether the board has acted consistently with the bylaws.

To strengthen government participation without directly including government representatives on the board, the bylaws call for the Governmental Advisory Committee to appoint a non-voting liaison to the board, a delegate to the nominating committee, and non-voting liaisons to each of the supporting organizations and to the other advisory committees.

In place of having five at-large board members elected by Internet users, that community is expected to be represented through the At-Large Advisory Committee, which will seek to engage individual Internet users through regional at-large organizations in five geographic regions.

Evaluation

The restated ICANN mission is to focus on its original mission—coordinating the stable operation of the Internet's unique identifier systems. If the board adheres to that mission statement, the effect could be to narrow ICANN's scope from that which has evolved since 1998. The reform, at

[46]ICANN ERC, "ICANN: A Blueprint for Reform," 2002, and "Final Implementation Report and Recommendations," 2002.

TABLE 5.1 Alternatives for Organization of ICANN to Achieve Legitimacy

	ICANN's Role	
Constituency	Broad	Focused
Broad	A. Markle (2002) B. NAIS (2001) *Pre-reform ICANN*	E. CDT (2004) F. ICANN reform (2003)
Narrow		C. Registry for the root (2004) D. Private trade association (2002)

the same time, takes a broad view of ICANN's constituencies. The new bylaws define selection and representation mechanisms that could widen the range and raise the quality of members on the board and, thereby, strengthen ICANN's perceived legitimacy. However, some critics argue that the board member selection mechanisms are vulnerable to capture by the board itself, leading to a narrowing of representation. The structure attempts to respond to concerns about ICANN's processes by defining steps to increase the specificity, transparency, and accountability of ICANN's processes.

Whether this new structure and these new processes will enable ICANN to achieve the perceived legitimacy that it has so far failed to attain can be determined only through the practical experience of the coming years.

Summary of the Alternatives

The six alternative approaches to achieving an ICANN that is perceived as the legitimate steward of the root are summarized in Table 5.1. They are characterized along two dimensions. The first is the breadth of ICANN's role—broad or focused. The second is the breadth of its community of stakeholders—broad or narrow.

5.2.5 Conclusions and Recommendation

The discussion of alternatives in Sections 5.1 and 5.2 leads to four observations. First, the Department of Commerce has expressed the U.S. government's intention to complete privatization of DNS governance by transferring its stewardship role to ICANN by 2006, conditional upon ICANN's satisfying certain pre-conditions. Second, the 2005 WSIS meeting might produce a proposal for a private, non-governmental organization designed to assume certain Internet governance responsibilities. However, as of March 2005, whether such a proposal would in fact be presented and what form it would take were not known. Third, evaluation of any organization proposed by WSIS in late 2005 as a DNS steward would face practical difficulties: It could be done only on the basis of the proposed organization's design, whereas ICANN will be evaluated on the basis of its record. And it might not be possible to complete an evaluation before the intended transfer of stewardship to ICANN in 2006. Fourth, the outcome of implementing ICANN's 2003 reform and other ICANN changes may or may not result in the fulfillment of the DOC's requirements.

These observations suggest three conclusions.

Conclusion: If ICANN satisfies the Department of Commerce's requirements and is generally perceived to be a legitimate manager of the DNS in the view of a substantial majority of its constituencies, and if no preferable alternative results from the 2005 WSIS meeting, the U.S. government is highly likely to transfer its role as steward of the DNS to ICANN during 2006.

Conclusion: Any private, non-governmental organization proposed as a result of the 2005 WSIS meeting is likely to be considered by the Department of Commerce for DNS stewardship only if ICANN fails to satisfy the DOC's requirements.

Conclusion: If ICANN's reforms are not successful and if the 2005 WSIS meeting does not propose an organization to assume DNS stewardship that is acceptable to the U.S. government, the likely outcomes will be a continuation of the Department of Commerce's stewardship role and a basic reconsideration of how DNS governance should be organized.

A transfer of stewardship from the DOC will leave ICANN (and another organization if stewardship is kept separate) without the benefits and controls that the DOC has provided. It independently reviewed ICANN's recommended decisions, regularly oversaw ICANN's performance subject to the sanction of non-renewal of its MoU, and implicitly protected it from attempts by other governments and organizations to gain control of or strongly influence ICANN's decisions. If the DOC does transfer its stewardship either to ICANN or to another private body, how will these benefits and controls be provided?

Conclusion: Without additional protection, legitimacy based on the "consent of the governed" would be the only basis for ICANN's continued authority and its ability to resist inappropriate pressure from governments and other powerful interests. Without additional oversight, final responsibility for satisfying the needs of its constituencies in an equitable, open, and efficient manner would lie solely with its board.

Recommendation: Before completing the transfer of its stewardship to ICANN (or any other organization), the Department of Commerce should seek ways to protect that organization from undue commercial or governmental pressures and to provide some form of oversight of performance.

5.3 OVERSIGHT AND OPERATION OF ROOT NAME SERVERS

Issues: Is there a need for greater oversight of the root name server operators? If so, how might it best be conducted? Should there be a formal process for replacing root name server operators? Should the root name server operators be compensated for their service, and if so, how?

The root has functioned well as the shared responsibility of a group of 12 diverse, autonomous, informally coordinated, and independently funded operators (see Table 3.1). Many observers believe that the diversity and autonomy have been strengths, reducing vulnerability to single point failures. Yet, other observers feel that the DNS and the Internet have become too important to the global society and economy to permit such a crucial system to continue to operate without the oversight of an organization responsible for its continued health—technical, operational, and financial.

The tension between these two views—diverse autonomy versus central oversight—leads to several different potential approaches to the issues identified above. In this section, the current situation is first reviewed and evaluated and then four alternatives are similarly described and reviewed. The committee's conclusions and recommendations follow a comparison of the four alternatives.

5.3.1 Current Situation: Diverse Autonomy

Description

The effective daily operation of the root name servers, described in "The Root Name Servers" in Section 3.3.2, lies squarely in the hands of the root name server operators. The operating organizations have taken on the responsibility voluntarily, are not compensated by users for their base operations (although all are subsidized by their home institutions or outside contributors, and some receive payments from operators of their anycast satellites[47]), and are self-regulating through extensive and continuous intragroup coordination.

Although ICANN's MoU with the DOC[48] assigns it the responsibility to manage the root name server system, its authority, as noted in "Selecting the Root Name Server Operators" in Section 3.3.3, has not been sufficient to enable it to manage or even regulate the root name server operators directly. The recent extension of the MoU places emphasis on ICANN collaborating with the DOC on "operational procedures for the root name server system, including formalization of relationships under which root name servers throughout the world are operated and continuing to promote best practices used by the root system operators." [49] To increase its authority, ICANN has established the DNS Root Server System Advisory Committee,[50] has sought to enter into formal agreements with each of the 11 other root name server operators,[51] and has prepared a draft "Memorandum of Understanding Concerning Root Nameserver Operation."[52] However, it has thus far been unable to complete an agreement with any of the operators. This is not surprising since it is likely that the operators do not expect to receive benefits that would compensate for the additional obligations they would be expected to assume to ICANN or, through it, to the DOC. In addition, many operators are subsidiary organizations within larger U.S. and foreign academic, commercial, or governmental entities, which themselves may not wish to incur the obligations and assume the liabilities that would come with such an agreement.[53] Indeed, it is diffi-

[47]See Box 3.1 for a discussion of anycast satellites of root name servers.

[48]"Memorandum of Understanding (MOU) Between ICANN and U.S. Department of Commerce," November 12, 1998, available at <http://www.icann.org/general/icann-mou-25nov98.htm>.

[49]"Amendment 6 to MoU Between ICANN and U.S. Department of Commerce," September 16, 2003, available at <http://www.icann.org/general/amend6-jpamou-17sep03.htm>. See also DOC, "Department of Commerce Statement Regarding Extension of Memorandum of Understanding with ICANN," September 16, 2003, available at <http://www.ntia.doc.gov/ntiahome/domainname/agreements/sepstatement_09162003.htm>.

[50]For a description of its responsibilities and activities, see <http://www.icann.org/committees/dns-root/>.

[51]ICANN operates the L root name server itself.

[52]The draft memorandum of understanding is available at <http://www.icann.org/committees/dns-root/model-root-server-mou-21jan02.htm>.

[53]As the then-president of ICANN, Stuart Lynn, noted "... some organizations that sponsor a root name server operator have little motivation to sign formal agreements [with ICANN], even in the form of the MoU that is now contemplated. What do they gain in return, except perhaps unwanted visibility and the attendant possibility of nuisance litigation? They receive no funding for their efforts, so why should they take on any contractual commitments, however loose?" "President's Report: ICANN—the Case for Reform," February 24, 2002, available at <http://www.icann.org/general/lynn-reform-proposal-24feb02.htm>.

cult to see how ICANN could induce the operators to sign the "Memorandum of Understanding Concerning Root Nameserver Operation" in the absence of a very attractive quid pro quo. Thus, although ICANN has been assigned the responsibility for "formalization of relationships" among the autonomous root name server operators, it currently has little ability to convince the operators to agree to a stronger ICANN role.

Evaluation

Fortunately, the current operators have operated the system successfully and without major incident up to now, despite the enormous and somewhat unanticipated rate of growth in demand for root name service since the mid-1990s when usage of the Web took off, and despite at least one malicious attack[54] on the system. Recently, through the voluntary adoption of anycast technology (see Box 3.1), the operators have effectively multiplied the number of root name servers severalfold, reducing the vulnerability of the system to denial-of-service attacks, improving the global accessibility of the root, and moderating the political pressure for relocation of the core 13 root name servers.

The root name server operators assumed their responsibilities and, with a modest number of changes, have successfully operated within the context of Internet culture that favors informal, voluntary, and non-bureaucratic institutions run by technical specialists with primarily altruistic motives. In addition, advances in computer technology and the ready availability of free name server software have kept the cost of operating root name servers relatively low,[55] especially when run as an adjunct to other, larger computer operations, as most of them are.

Nor would it be easy to change this situation without the agreement of the operators. Their incumbency and financial independence protect their responsibility and authority, and their informal, collegial relationships serve to strengthen their power as a group. Furthermore, although they do not receive direct financial compensation for their service, they all receive intangible benefits that, together with their fear of potentially destabilizing change in a system that is working well, are evidently suffi-

---

[54]On October 21, 2002, a distributed denial-of-service attack was launched against the 13 DNS root name servers. For more information on the impact of the attack, see <http://www.caida.org/projects/dns-analysis/oct02dos.xml>.

[55]According to discussions in June 2004 with Kurt Erik Lindqvist, managing director of Autonomica AB, which operates i.root-servers.net, the average annual cost of operating an independent root server, including the costs of multiple anycast satellite servers, is about $1 million. However, other root servers are operated as adjuncts to already well-provisioned secure Internet sites, requiring a minimal incremental expenditure on the order of tens of thousands of dollars annually.

cient to support their continued activity. In the absence of strong justification, it appears that they are not inclined to favor a change in the current state.

But despite that fact that the current arrangement is functioning well, it might run into difficulties if for some reason the root name servers' performance deteriorated or some of the operators resigned. Moreover, ICANN is obliged under the MoU to try to take a more formal role in root name server operations. Consequently, it is useful to consider the range of alternatives there might be for operating the root name server system and to see if they might offer advantages over the current arrangement, as well as in meeting ICANN's MoU obligation.

5.3.2 Alternatives

Two alternative models for structuring management of the operations of the root are (1) funding and regulation and (2) a competitive market. They are described and evaluated below. A third, hypothetical possibility—distributing the root zone file—is here raised by the committee as a means of opening a different kind of approach for consideration. A fourth alternative would be for the DOC to release ICANN from its MoU requirement that it formalize relationships with the root name server operators.

Alternative A: Funding and Regulation

Description

Under alternative A, ICANN (or a successor organization) would acquire the means to assume responsibilities for the root name server system. As noted above, the most likely source of authority for ICANN—as a non-governmental body—would be financial. If funds were available to cover all or a significant portion of the operating costs of the root name server operators, ICANN might be in a position to use its financial authority to do some or all of the following regulatory tasks:

- Establish minimal performance standards for the root name server operators.
- Support the implementation of a real-time performance monitoring system for each operator and the system as a whole, perhaps based on the system under development by the Reséaux IP Européens Network Coordination Centre (RIPE NCC).[56]
- Monitor the performance of the root name server system.

[56]See <http://dnsmon.ripe.net/>.

- Enforce performance standards by adjusting compensation to the operators according to the level at which they performed.
- Require performance improvement of operators that do not achieve minimum levels of root name server performance that would be enforced through cut off or reduction of compensation.
- Remove operators whose performance does not meet minimum required levels despite requests and reduced or eliminated payments.
- Identify and qualify new operators to replace removed or resigned operators.
- Use the contingent provision of additional funding to provide incentives for the operators to achieve higher performance levels and introduce new services.

Evaluation

If it performed most or all of those tasks, ICANN would be the central overseer of the root name server system with full responsibility and authority for its reliable and effective operation. It could establish a performance-monitoring system and use financial rewards and punishments to maintain and improve performance. Should change in an operator or in operations be required, ICANN would be in a position to bring it about. ICANN would, in fact, be carrying out natural responsibilities of the registry for the root (see alternative C in Section 5.2.4).

ICANN's capabilities as a monitor and decision maker would strongly influence the performance of the root name server system. If it had capable staff, excellent system understanding, and a knowledgeable board, it could make timely and effective decisions. However, should any of those conditions not apply, its influence could in fact be detrimental to the performance of the root name server system.

Moreover, this alternative depends on the operators responding to financial incentives. Many might, but it is clear that not all of them would. There is some possibility of a significant number of them dropping out if the alternative were additional controls from ICANN (or anyone else), and a change in a number of root server operators at the same time might be destabilizing. In addition, the dropouts could form an alternative root, which could be further destabilizing.

The three U.S. government agencies that run root name servers, for example, would probably not legally be able to give up their autonomy in exchange for a financial inducement, especially from a private organization. They would have to be replaced by non-governmental organizations, and that would probably require the agreement of the U.S. government. The relevant elements of the U.S. government might, in turn, be reluctant to agree for fear of thereby reducing overall stability.

Nor are the funds necessary for this approach available within ICANN's current budget. They would have to be incorporated into a future budget and could require a corresponding increase in ICANN's funding from registries and registrars. (This would be available under "Alternative C, ICANN as Registry for the Root," in Section 5.2.4.) Another option would be to allocate to this purpose a portion of any funds received from the procedure for selecting new TLDs through auction or other processes, as described in "What Selection Process Should Be Used?" in Section 5.4.2. below.

An alternative proposal would be to charge ISPs and other users an annual fee for access to the root, which is similar to what is done today by the root server operators when the cost of an anycast satellite is shared by the ISPs and users that will benefit from it. (However, there is no practical way that such a fee could be enforced, except through the voluntary agreement of the ISPs and other users.)

Alternative B: Competitive Market

The second alternative would be to create a competitive market for root service. To the committee's knowledge, competitive service of the same root has not been formally proposed elsewhere. However, since increasing competition in the provision of DNS services is one of the stated goals of the DOC, the committee has created an example of what a straightforward approach to such competition might mean for root name services.[57] A less straightforward example, which is actually being implemented, is also described.

B1: Competing Root Name Server Systems

In the most straightforward form of market for root name service, competition would entail having two or more distinct groups offering access to the authoritative root zone file. To avoid the confusion that could arise with multiple root zones, each of the operator groups would have to agree to offer access to the same root zone file, which would be provided to each of them at the same time by the authoritative source, say, VeriSign for ICANN.[58] Every ISP, intranet, or other organization running a full-

[57]The recent sixth amendment to the memorandum of understanding includes the statement, "The Department reaffirms its policy goal of privatizing the technical management of the DNS in a manner that promotes stability and security, *competition* [emphasis added], coordination, and representation." See "Amendment 6 to MoU Between ICANN and U.S. Department of Commerce," September 16, 2003, p. 2.

[58]The authoritative root zone file is currently distributed by VeriSign, which operates the hidden primary. However, at some future time, ICANN may take over this function itself.

service resolver on the Internet would have to contract with one (or more) of the competing root server operators, which would charge them a monthly or yearly subscription fee that could be based on volume of queries or, more practically, on how many IP addresses the organization had assigned to it. A technical means of ensuring that only subscribers could gain access to an operator's root name servers would be required.

Evaluation. The committee was unable to conceive a version of this full competitive market for root name service that would be both technically and operationally feasible and beneficial enough to displace the current system.

There are two major technical difficulties. First, the communication and computation overhead of ensuring that only subscribers could gain access to the operators' servers could be a substantial and undesirable load on the root name server system, with the servers spending significantly more effort checking permissions rather than answering queries. Second, there is the difficulty that arises because the content of the root zone file includes the IP addresses of the root name servers. If there is one authoritative root zone file, then there is only one set of IP addresses that it can contain and, therefore, only one set of root name servers. Even if these technical problems could be overcome, two major operational problems would remain.

The first operational problem is that every system that contains a full-service resolver would need access to the root zone. Thus, every laptop and home system so equipped (and there are many) would require a contract with one of the competing root name server systems or would have to change to a stub resolver and contract with an ISP for that service. This, in turn, would cause problems for traveling users who typically encounter and would have to contract for root service from multiple different ISPs in the course of their travels.

The second operational problem is that the switchover to operation of a competitive system would have to take place in a short time, unless the current set of operators were the default choice, to which competitors would likely object. That means that every ISP, organizational intranet, and owner of a full-service resolver would have to sign up for service with one of the competitors. Technically, the root name server Hints File in every resolver/name server on the Internet would have to be changed over in a short time to list the IP addresses of the root name servers of one of the providers.

Even if these technical and operational difficulties could be overcome, there are two pragmatic difficulties that the changeover to a full competitive market for root name service would have to overcome.

First, a fee would be introduced for what is currently a free good. That is only likely to be accepted if it is accompanied by significantly improved performance on dimensions that its customers care about and if the root zone file can be kept secure from all but subscribers. But there has been no suggestion that dissatisfaction with current service is such that any level of "improved performance" would be willingly paid for.

Second, the incumbent operators would have a great advantage, since they have the facilities, the skilled staff, and the operational experience that newcomers would have to develop. However, that might not be a problem for companies that already run large DNS name servers, such as Neulevel or UltraDNS, or for national governments that wanted to establish their own system of local name servers.

These potential difficulties, which mean that the probable costs would significantly outweigh the prospective benefits, effectively eliminate the approach of a full competitive market for root name service. However, there is another approach that is already developing.

B2: Competing Providers of Anycast Servers

The current market for anycast satellite servers is a less direct form of competition for root name service. The competitive providers are a number of the root name server operators who compete on price, service level, and other features to attract customers, which are ISPs or others that want to have an anycast satellite server nearby. The result of the development of this market has been a rapid multiplication and broadened distribution of the number of servers of the root zone file.

Evaluation. Model B2 has shown itself to be a demonstrably feasible path to reducing the geographically uneven distribution of response times and to increasing the reliability of the root name server system without incurring the technical, operational, or practical problems of the model first described. Thus, it provides most of the benefits of model B1, "Competing Root Name Server Systems," without its difficulties.

Alternative C: Distributed Root Zone File

Description

A third alternative, which might avoid the difficulties of regulation or competing root name servers, would be for ISPs and organizational intranets to obtain copies of the root zone file from ICANN (through VeriSign's distribution server) and make local name servers authoritative for the root zone. Something like this is, in fact, done today through the caching of queries by ISPs and through the possibility of an ISP obtaining an anycast satellite of one of the root name servers.[59] However, in this alternative, the intention would be to formalize this practice and have ICANN require every ISP or intranet to subscribe to the authoritative root zone file. The current public root name servers could be retained for use by small and less technically skilled ISPs and intranets, but would be scaled down to serve the smaller load.

Evaluation

The wide distribution of the root zone file and root name servers would significantly enhance the security of the root and the reliability of its operation, in much the same way that anycast satellite sites already have done, but to an even greater extent. Furthermore, the effects of erroneous or malicious queries would be limited to the ISP or intranet from which they originated, and the ISP would have a strong incentive to find and eliminate their sources.

Some fear that widespread distribution of the root zone file and the probable large numbers of poor local configurations and irregular updating of the local name servers would cause havoc at worst, and poor local service at best. The concern is that widespread availability of the root zone file would encourage the offering of alternative roots, from which some TLDs had been removed or to which additional TLDs had been added. The latter problem can, however, be partially addressed through DNS Security Extensions (DNSSEC; see Section 4.2), which would detect, although not prevent, unauthorized changes to the root zone file. What actions would be taken if a change is detected would have to be agreed in advance and enforced through an agreement with the ISPs. The irregular updating problem might be resolved through the use of a distributor-driven process like that currently used to update the secondary root name servers.

If it could not be ensured that organizations (especially ISPs, which in turn have customers) would keep their copies of the root zone file up-to-date and uniform, the approach of having a distributed root zone file could cause a decrease in the integrity of the DNS, which relies on the root zone file being consistent across the Internet.

---

[59]In fact, the root zone file is available for download at <ftp://ftp.internic.net/domain/root.zone.gz>, but there is no encouragement to use it.

Alternative D: DOC Relaxes MoU Requirement

Description

The DOC could relax its requirements for ICANN if it accepted the success of the current diverse, autonomous, self-regulating root name server system instead of viewing it as unsatisfactory because it is subject to neither formal regulation nor the discipline of the market. In place of its cooperation with the DOC on "operational procedures for the root name server system, including formalization of relationships under which root name servers throughout the world are operated," ICANN could be tasked simply to serve as a facilitator, if asked, of the voluntary cooperation among the root name server operators.

Evaluation

The DOC's relaxation of its requirements for ICANN would, in effect, legitimate the current de facto relationship between ICANN and the operators and relieve the pressure on ICANN to take on authority and responsibility that the operators have not yet shown themselves willing to cede.

Summary of the Alternatives

The current state and the four alternatives for oversight of the root name servers are summarized in Table 5.2. It compares them on two dimensions: first, whether the root name server operators are under formal or informal oversight by ICANN, and second, whether there is one set of root name server operators or multiple sets.

TABLE 5.2 Alternatives for Root Name Server Oversight and Operation

	Oversight	
Root Name Servers	Formal	Informal
One set of operators	A. Funding and regulation	(Current situation—diverse autonomy) B2. Competing providers of anycast servers D. DOC relaxes MoU requirement
Multiple operators	C. Distributed root zone file	B1. Competing root name servers systems

5.3.3 Conclusions and Recommendations

Conclusion: The effective daily operation of the root, and therefore of the DNS and the Internet, lies squarely in the hands of the root name server operators. Although ICANN has been assigned responsibility for the stability and security of the root name server system by the Department of Commerce, its authority has not been sufficient for it to manage or even regulate the root name server operators directly.

Conclusion: The committee commends the operators of the 13 root name servers for their reliable and efficient provision of critical root name service as the Internet has undergone rapid growth in the numbers of its users and providers.

Conclusion: The committee believes that greater oversight of the operators will not be necessary so long as they operate effectively and reliably and continue to improve the root name system's reliability and capability.

Conclusion: The committee believes that in the longer term it is desirable for there to be more formal coordination of the operators and that ICANN would be the most appropriate organization to assume the coordination role.

Recommendation: ICANN should work with the root name server operators to establish a formal process for replacing operators that directly engages the remaining root name server operators.

For example, should one of the current operators withdraw, ICANN could convene the remaining root name server operators as a selection committee to recommend a replacement operator to ICANN's board. The board could after appropriate consideration (and after approval by the DOC or a future stewardship organization, if any) then direct IANA to enter the address of the new operator in the root zone file.

Conclusion: Any central source of funds to compensate all the root name server operators for their services is likely to carry an unacceptable regulatory or control role for the funding organization and reduce the diversity of support that is one of the strengths of the current arrangement.

Recommendation: The present independent funding arrangements for the root name servers are advantageous and should continue, because the multiplicity of sources contributes to the resilience, autonomy, and diversity of the root name server system.

5.4 REGULATION OF GENERIC TOP-LEVEL DOMAINS

Issues: Can and should new gTLDs be added? If so, how many new gTLDs should be added, and how fast? What types should they be, and how should they and their operators be selected?

ICANN has faced a demand for the addition of gTLDs since its establishment (see Section 2.7). At that time, the demand for .com addresses was growing very rapidly. Some applicants that were unable to obtain their preferred domain names within .com or .net called for the creation of new TLDs in which they might register. Potential registry operators, seeing an opportunity for profit in the rapidly growing market for domain names, added their strong voices to the cry for more TLDs.

Although the demand for domain names is not growing as rapidly as it did in those very early days, there remains a strong interest in adding gTLDs to the root as well as a strong counterbalancing interest in moderating such additions.

In response to the pressure to add new gTLDs and to a requirement in its 2003 MoU with the DOC, ICANN agreed[60] to deliver by September 2004 a comprehensive evaluation of:

- "The potential impact of new gTLDs on the Internet root server system and Internet stability" and
- "Potential consumer benefits/costs associated with establishing a competitive environment for TLD registries."

It also committed to:

- "Creation and implementation of selection criteria for new and existing TLD registries, including public explanation of the process, selection criteria, and the rationale for selection decisions," and
- "Recommendations from expert advisory panels, bodies, agencies or organizations regarding economic, competition, trademark, and intellectual property issues."

To fulfill this commitment, ICANN at its October 2003 meeting launched a strategic initiative to allow new generic top-level domains.[61] The initiative comprises two stages intended "to move to the full global-

[60]Reported in ICANN board resolutions at the ICANN meeting in Carthage, Tunisia, October 31, 2003, available at <http://www.icann.org/announcements/advisory-31oct03.htm>.

[61]ICANN, "ICANN Launches Broad Strategic Initiative for New Generic Top-Level Domains," announcement, October 31, 2003, available at <http://www.icann.org/announcements/announcement-31oct03.htm>.

ization of the market for top-level domains." One stage is a comprehensive evaluation that includes:

- An assessment of technical standards to support multilingual TLDs,
- An assessment of the introduction of competition into the TLD market and of possible business models for the TLD manager–ICANN relationship,
- A study of intellectual property issues involved in the introduction of new TLDs,
- Reports on technical stability issues related to the introduction of new TLDs, and
- A review of consumer protection issues.

These studies were carried out by independent outside organizations[62] as well as by ICANN's Security and Stability Advisory Committee.

The second stage was an expedited process that was intended to add a new group of gTLDs before the end of 2004. In this process, each of these gTLDs would be sponsored by a non-profit organization representing a specific community, whose members would be the only ones eligible to register domain names in it.

Thus, the question of adding gTLDs is timely and open to careful examination. Although ICANN has accepted the view that new gTLDs should be added and is employing one specific means for doing so, it is useful for a full understanding of the issues involved to take one step back and consider first the fundamental questions: Should new gTLDs be added to the root zone and, if so, how many and how fast? If new gTLDs are to be added, what types should they be, and how should they and their operators be selected?

5.4.1 Should New gTLDs Be Added? If So, How Many New gTLDs, and How Fast?

An increase in the number of gTLDs would have technical, operational, economic, and service consequences that would affect domain name registrants, registries, registrars, and Internet users generally. Thus, responsible decisions about gTLD additions should take into account the different potential effects on the several constituencies. In contrast, the public discourse and controversy have often been framed narrowly—

[62]On August 31, 2004, ICANN published a report, prepared for it by Summit Strategies International, entitled "Evaluation of the New gTLDs: Policy and Legal Issues." The report touches on the second and third topics in the list of studies for a comprehensive evaluation. It is available at <http://www.icann.org/tlds/new-gtld-eval-31aug04.pdf>.

sometimes considering only one type of effect on one constituency. Furthermore, the arguments are often based on assumptions, rather than evidence, and the assertions of one side are often vigorously disputed by the other side.

The issue is addressed here broadly in terms of effects as well as constituencies affected, but for simplicity, the multidimensional arguments for and against new gTLDs are clustered into two groups: (1) technical and operational performance issues and (2) user needs and economic issues. Where relevant evidence is available to support or contradict an argument, it is reported.

(Note: The amount of space devoted to each argument does not reflect the committee's judgment either of its importance or of its credibility. Rather, it is a consequence of the material available and the space required to explain it.)

Technical and Operational Performance Issues

Arguments in Favor

As noted in Chapter 3, the root zone file is very small, comprising data for 258 TLDs and the 13 root name servers—just over 78 kilobytes in total. It is searched on the root name servers about 8 billion times per day. The committee did not find any purely technical reasons that the root name servers could not provide the same level of response with a much larger root zone file. Indeed, the ability of the .com name servers to respond to billions of queries a day against the .com zone file, with more than 30 million entries, is a demonstration of the technical capacity that could be applied to the root zone, if necessary.

Nor are there any fixed limits in the design of the DNS on the size or the rate of addition of domains at any level in the DNS hierarchy. Any such limits would arise from practical matters of implementation and operation.

Moreover, additions have already been made to the root zone—both the seven gTLDs added in 2000 and the numerous ccTLDs added during the mid-1990s, with no noticeable degradation of root name server performance.

Arguments Against

However, there are operational and administrative issues that suggest practical constraints on, at least, the *rate* of addition of new TLDs to the root zone file, and potentially as well, on its total size. Of concern to some members of the technical community are the number and the rate of changes to the root zone file—both at the time of creation of a TLD (as a new entry into the root zone file) and in support of subsequent changes (as a modification of an existing entry to accommodate a changed IP address, for example). Errors or corrupted entries in the root zone file pose a greater risk of harmful consequences for the DNS and Internet than do analogous mistakes made elsewhere in the DNS hierarchy. An increase in the number of root zone file updates increases the probability of inadvertent errors and makes it more difficult to detect them in a timely manner.

Yet, as discussed in Chapter 3, the design of the DNS makes heavy use of address caching. This means that errors at the root will not affect a significant number of users immediately, but rather will gradually be disseminated as the caches time out. Errors at the root zone, while certainly undesirable, should not have catastrophic consequences and should be able to be caught before they do much significant damage.

The administrative procedures for approving additions of new gTLDs (see "Selecting New TLDs" in Section 3.4.3) have been much more intensive and extended than those, for example, for adding a new second-level domain to one of the gTLDs. This has been for technical reasons—to ensure that the gTLD's name server operations will meet Internet standards; for consumer protection reasons—to ensure that registrants in the new gTLD will have reasonable assurance of a competent, reliable, and continuing service; and because of the need to deal with a variety of contending legal and commercial interests. Should a high level of scrutiny be required for approving additions of all new gTLDs and the ongoing workload increase as a consequence of the additional gTLDs, then the rate of buildup of an adequate administrative staff would also set a bound on the rate of addition of new gTLDs.

Committee View

In light of these considerations, several members of the committee hold the view that an extremely cautious approach should be taken toward additions to the root zone file. Their preference would be for no additions at all. And they would certainly limit new gTLDs to those that can be shown to meet an important, unsatisfied need. Furthermore, they think that a process for monitoring root zone operations capable of detecting signs of degradation or instability and of acting to correct their causes must accompany any process for regular addition of new gTLDs.

Taking into account those views, the committee agreed that if additions are to be made to the root zone, it would be prudent to limit their rate. After balancing the various considerations and the differing views of its members, the committee concluded that the addition of tens of new gTLDs per year for several years would be unlikely to jeopardize the technical or operational stability of the DNS. The committee accepted that additions at a faster rate would unacceptably increase the risk at present.

However, further refinement of the practices for making and distributing root zone file changes (as discussed in "Maintaining the Root Zone File—VeriSign" in Section 3.3.3), the addition of administrative capacity to ICANN, and further closely monitored experience with gTLD additions could provide the basis for larger-scale annual increases in the future, should the demand be shown to exist.

Conclusion: Considering technical and operational performance alone, the addition of tens of gTLDs per year for several years would pose minimal risk to the stability of the root.

User Needs and Economic Issues

Arguments in Favor

A principal argument for adding new gTLDs is that only by opening the market for gTLD registry services would a true identification of domain name registrant (user) needs be possible, because only then would entrepreneurs and other innovators have the opportunity to offer a range of gTLDs to potential registrants. Two indicators of the potential demand for new gTLDs are the more than 3 million registrants in .info, the million or so registrants in .biz, and the more than 100,000 registrants in alternate TLDs offered by new.net, which are readily accessible from only 25 percent of the Internet (see "Unique Characteristics" in Section 3.3.1).

While the advocates of adding gTLDs do not claim to know when or if the user demand for new domains would be completely filled, they accept the inevitability of some new gTLDs failing. In their view, such failures would be a reasonable price to pay for clarifying and meeting user needs, many of which may be latent—unrecognized even by the potential beneficiaries. Advocates of this position, however, generally acknowledge that to protect domain name registrants in new gTLDs, registry contracts should require zone file escrow and agreements with other registries to assume responsibility in case a gTLD were to fail.

One question that arises in this context is whether new gTLDs will provide new users opportunities to register their desired (second-level) domain names or whether gTLD proliferation will simply result in existing users registering similar domain names in all gTLDs for which they are eligible. In the latter case, for example, .biz would simply replicate .com, duplicating registration and administrative costs without any associated benefits.[63]

---

[63]Indeed, there may be significant costs in addition to those associated with registering in multiple domains as cybersquatters expend resources in order to acquire names that they may later sell for prices that substantially exceed the costs of registration.

At least as judged by the experience of the operation of the .biz domain, there is only a small amount of duplication. To begin with, no more than a very small fraction of .com registrants have chosen to register the same domain name in .biz, since in February 2005 there were more than 33 million names registered in .com but just over 1 million names registered in .biz.[64] Moreover, even when the same name has been registered, the identity of the .biz and .com registrants is the same in only 25 percent of those cases, according to an earlier study.[65] Thus, the .biz gTLD has, in fact, offered a substantial number of new registrants opportunities to register their desired domain names, with proportionately little duplication of .com domain names.

A demand for additional gTLDs could arise from the implementation of internationalized domain names that use non-Roman scripts (see Section 4.3). Although much of the early activity has been in registering second-level domain names in non-Roman scripts in existing TLDs, that usage could develop into a demand for gTLDs in non-Roman scripts. This demand could be quite large, given that the number of non-English-speaking users of the Internet is already very large and is growing rapidly.

A new gTLD (e.g., .health) might induce additional value-added services at the second level (e.g., example.health) that would be more accessible than the currently possible third-level services (e.g., example.health.com) or second-level services (e.g., examplehealth.com).

Another reason for favoring the addition of gTLDs is economic. First, it would open the opportunity for new participants to enter the registry services market, promoting both price and non-price competition (which includes diversity in naming methods) among registries. The August 2004 ICANN report on the policy and legal issues of new gTLDs noted that "the ICANN community now has several registry operators, as opposed to just one provider, which is [sic] able to operate a global registry of significant scale. . . . Today the three companies [VeriSign, Afilias, and NeuLevel] compete for the ability to provide registry services to new and existing TLDs, both in the gTLD and ccTLD markets."[66] Second, it would encourage innovation. According to the report, "the new gTLDs have had an impact beyond their size or market share . . . in terms of innovation."[67]

Furthermore, a steady and foreseeable supply of new gTLDs could reduce the incentive to cybersquat by lowering the scarcity value of spe-

[64]See <http://www.zooknic.com/Domains/counts.html>, accessed on June 18, 2005.

[65]See Jonathan Zittrain and Benjamin Edelman, "Survey of Usage of the .BIZ TLD," available at <http://cyber.law.harvard.edu/tlds/001/>, accessed July 22, 2002. This estimate is based on a random sample of 823 .biz domain names, where the identities of registrants were matched using zip codes, name server second-level domains, e-mail addresses, or some combination thereof.

[66]Summit Strategies International, "Evaluation of New gTLDs," 2004, p. 111.

[67]Summit Strategies International, "Evaluation of New gTLDs," 2004, p. 111.

cific names and making it more costly to hoard names. Thus, the potential victims of cybersquatters may save money should new gTLDs be added.

New gTLDs would also enable the establishment of additional restricted name spaces, whose registrants would be authenticated by the registry to be members of a specific class and who might also have to accept specified rules of conduct. These would be like the existing sites .edu (primarily for accredited institutions of higher education), .pro (for professionals), and .museum (for the museum community). Possibilities include .kids (for kid-safe sites) and .health (for qualified health care providers). In addition, many organizations, especially medium and large ones, may want their own gTLDs, enabling their computer services to assume responsibility directly for functions they currently must acquire and pay for from TLD registries. For example, IBM might prefer to own and operate the .ibm TLD, rather than rely on the .com registry for service for ibm.com.

Arguments Against

There are strongly held opinions against opening the market in gTLDs as well.[68]

On the question of user needs, opponents of gTLD addition contend that the existing selection of gTLDs (and ccTLDs that act like them—see "Recharacterizing TLDs" in Section 3.4.1) have met registrant needs quite well and are capable of continuing to do so. They perceive few signs that many prospective domain name registrants have an unmet need for new gTLDs that could not be satisfied in one of the available second-level domains. Whatever truly unmet needs there might be are not sufficient, in their view, to justify even a small threat to the reliable operation of the DNS. The August 2004 ICANN report on the policy and legal issues of new gTLDs notes that, despite the entry of the new gTLDs, .com, .net, and .org still have more than 93 percent of the registrations in all gTLDs.[69] It concludes that ".com remains the TLD of first choice for a majority of gTLD registrants, including new registrants"[70] and that a "choice of TLDs has thus far been unable to overcome the advantages the .com TLD enjoys."[71] Nonetheless, the report concludes that "the new gTLDs presented

---

[68]See, for example, Tim Berners-Lee, "New Top Level Domains Considered Harmful," April 30, 2004, World Wide Web Consortium, Design Issues, available at: <http://www.w3.org/DesignIssues/TLD>.

[69]Summit Strategies International, "Evaluation of New gTLDs," 2004, p. 96.

[70]Summit Strategies International, "Evaluation of New gTLDs," 2004, p. 109.

[71]Summit Strategies International, "Evaluation of New gTLDs," 2004, p. 110. Nonetheless, the report notes the views of some members of the "non-commercial community" who believe that, although overcoming the advantages of .com would be difficult, it would not be impossible.

registrants with significantly greater choice, at least in terms of initial registration."[72] Further, the report concludes that "there are indications that a respectable number of the new gTLD registrations have attracted new users to the DNS, and that these new registrations are being actively used."[73]

From the perspective of the user seeking a site through guessing or relying on a possibly faulty memory, the addition of gTLDs increases the number of possible domain names to try. For example, is it "example.com" or "example.biz" or "example.info"? This is already a problem, but it could be exacerbated by the addition of new gTLDs.

There are economic counterarguments as well. Trademark holders, for example, fear that they would face the possible need to defensively register (to preclude cybersquatting) in all unrestricted gTLDs, incurring an expense that could be substantial, particularly for small organizations and individuals. However, the August 2004 ICANN report concludes that "the start-up mechanisms proved generally effective in protecting legitimate trademark owners against cybersquatting."[74] At the same time, the report notes "a contradiction between . . . trying to attract new users and uses to the DNS, and allowing trademark holders to claim priority registration of the same names in new TLDs."[75] And it observes that the number of sunrise registrations[76] in the new gTLDs that used such a process "has turned out to be much smaller than anticipated."[77]

More generally, holders of existing domain names that have built a reputation could find the value of that reputation reduced as similar sites proliferate. For example, the owner of a discount ticket Web site might fear that some of his customers would become confused and unable to remember whether it is "cheaptickets.com" or "cheaptickets.biz" or "cheaptickets.travel" that is known for offering the cheapest tickets.

Furthermore, current registry services stand to lose some of their economic (scarcity) value as a result of the entry of new TLD registry service providers. So trademark holders, the owners of existing sites, and current registry services all fear possible additional costs or losses of value if new gTLDs are added.

Opponents are also concerned that each increment of new gTLDs could be followed by a period of administrative instability, set off by a

---

[72]Summit Strategies International, "Evaluation of New gTLDs," 2004, p. 97.
[73]Summit Strategies International, "Evaluation of New gTLDs," 2004, p. 99.
[74]Summit Strategies International, "Evaluation of New gTLDs," 2004, p. 79.
[75]Summit Strategies International, "Evaluation of New gTLDs," 2004, p. 80.
[76]See "Possible Remedies to Conflicts Over Names" in Section 3.5.2.
[77]Summit Strategies International, "Evaluation of New gTLDs," 2004, p. 81.

race to register potentially valuable domain names and the flurry of administrative and dispute resolution activity that it induces.

In the extreme, if unlimited additions were permitted (say, for example, .ibm, .ge, .sony, .siemens, and so on), the root zone could become comparable to the .com gTLD, which would seem to have uncertain benefits, while threatening considerable upheaval in the technical operations of the DNS and administrative processes of ICANN. However, the imposition of a restriction on the allowable number and rate of additions, as suggested by technical and operational considerations, would alleviate this risk.

Committee View

After taking into account the user needs and economic benefits arguments for and against potential gTLD additions, the committee remained divided on the addition of new gTLDs. Some members felt strongly that on balance those needs and benefits were not great enough to risk the technical and operational stability and reliability of the DNS. Other members believed that within the limits of tens of new gTLDs per year it was worthwhile to enable some form of market process to be used (with proper safeguards, discussed below) to determine how extensive the need might be.

Conclusion: Neither the user needs and economic benefits arguments in favor of nor those against additional gTLDs are conclusive.

In addition to the question of whether and how many gTLDs should be added is the question of how often. Thus far, additions have occurred at an irregular and unpredictable pace: the initial group of 8, 7 more in 2000, and up to 10 more in 2004-2005. That uncertainty makes it difficult for current and potential gTLD registries to develop and operate according to reasonable business plans and has the effect of overvaluing new gTLDs (because of the uncertainty of whether and when there will be any further additions). A regular schedule would enable those who lose out one year to anticipate additional chances in the next year, reducing the price they would be willing to pay (in a gTLD auction, for example) were there no certainty about the addition of gTLDs in the near future.

Recommendations

Recommendation: If new gTLDs are added, they should be added on a regular schedule that establishes the maximum number of gTLDs (on the order of tens per year) that could be added each time and the interval between additions.

Recommendation: Since the effect of continuing increments of new gTLDs on the performance and stability of the root zone is not known, and the consequences of reduced performance and instability can be great, it would be prudent to accompany any process of addition with a process for monitoring and identifying any technical or operational problems the new gTLDs may cause.

Recommendation: A mechanism to suspend the addition of gTLDs in the event that severe technical or operational problems arise should accompany a schedule of additions. It should explicitly specify who has the authority to suspend additions and under what conditions.

Recommendation: A neutral, disinterested party should conduct an evaluation of new gTLDs approximately 1 or 2 years after each set of new gTLDs is operational to make recommendations for improving the process for selecting and adding gTLDs.

As noted in the introduction to Section 5.4, ICANN has included as part of its strategic initiative the need for an evaluation of the additions made in 2000. The committee believes that ICANN should contract with neutral, disinterested parties to conduct such evaluations for every subsequent addition of gTLDs.

5.4.2 If New gTLDs Are to Be Added, What Types Should They Be, and How Should They and Their Operators Be Selected?

If new gTLDs are to be added to the root zone, there remain the questions of deciding which types of gTLDs should be added and which entities should be selected to operate the associated registries.

In some selection processes used in comparable circumstances, what should be added and who should be their operators are considered completely separately.[78] In other cases, what should be allocated and to whom it should be assigned have been determined in the same proceeding. In the case of the DNS, both types of approach have been used. When seven new gTLDs were authorized in 2000, ICANN's selection process combined the choices of the types and the identities of the registries, so that a particular entity was selected as a registry because ICANN favored the type

[78]In radio frequency management, this is referred to as the distinction between "allocation," which denotes setting aside blocks of frequencies in specific geographic areas for a particular use, and "assignment," which denotes the award of these frequencies to particular users. Of course, it may be possible to dispense with the determination of the type of new entrant and to limit the process to determining which entrants to allow.

of service it promised to provide. In contrast, the decision as to which organization would operate .org upon its transfer from VeriSign was independent of the legacy decision to have such a gTLD.

Whatever process is used to make such decisions, it should at a minimum satisfy four fundamental criteria:

1. *Fairness.* The process should not favor an applicant or class of applicants over others.
2. *Transparency.* The reasons for the outcomes should be clear to all involved.
3. *Efficiency.* The process should not place a heavy burden on the applicants or the selection group.
4. *Economy.* The process should not impose undue costs on the applicants or the administrator of the selection process.

The discussion that follows provides a context against which to evaluate ICANN's current round of selections and the process that it is following.

Which Types of gTLDs Should Be Added?

There are three approaches to determining the types of gTLDs. They derive from different views about the desirable structure of the gTLD name space.

Taxonomic/Restricted

The first approach holds that the gTLDs should adhere, as much as possible, to a taxonomic structure. Its adherents believe that such a structure can assist Internet navigation by serving as a high-order directory and that it can channel and bound the addition of gTLDs. In an ideal taxonomic structure, each gTLD would be restricted to members of a specific class, there would be a gTLD for each appropriate class of members, and each possible member would fit into one and only one class.

The current structure of gTLDs is already far from an ideal taxonomy. Although the names of the three largest gTLDs, .com, .net, and .org, imply a restriction to commercial, networking, and non-commercial registrants, respectively, in practice the registries have not enforced such restrictions. Moreover, there is nothing to exclude a Web site having, say, both .org and .edu domain names, even if both were strictly restricted to appropriate registrants. So the best that an adherent to this view could hope for would be that each new gTLD would be restricted to a specific class whose membership could be inferred from the domain name (e.g., names such as .travel, .xxx, .library, and .health).

The "taxonomists" favor an extension of the gTLDs only in the restricted form.[79] In this case, each new gTLD would need a registry willing and able to enforce the specific restrictions, which can be arduous and severely limit the rate of registration. For example, the .pro registry, which was formed in 2000, began registration only in the spring of 2004. It is limiting its rollout to the rate at which it can gain access to records of registered professionals so that it can identify those that it will permit to have a .pro domain.

Although it is no longer feasible to impose a full taxonomy on the DNS, this approach can strengthen its implicit directory function by ensuring that all new gTLD names clearly identify a restricted class of second-level domains. This is the approach taken by ICANN in adding new gTLDs in 2004-2005 as described below.

If there are benefits to using a tightly controlled taxonomy, there is nothing to stop this from occurring at the second level. For example, there could be a gTLD called .industry, with second-level domains describing various instances of industries: travel.industry, health.industry, automobile.industry, and so on.

Market-determined

The second approach favors allowing the processes of supply and demand to determine how many and which domains are offered, first by the willingness of an operator to offer it (supply) and second by the willingness of those desiring domain names to register in it (demand). Under this approach, it would be up to the gTLD registry to decide whether or not it would restrict registrations to members of a certain group.

To the advocates of this approach, opening a new gTLD and then closing it down because of an insufficient number of registrations would be an acceptable outcome, assuming (as noted above) that zone file escrow and alternate registry provisions could be made to protect domain name holders for some period of time after the closure.

In contrast to the taxonomic/restricted view, the market-determined approach holds that attempting to structure or control the gTLD name space provides little navigational value in a world of search engines and other navigational aids. Many also doubt the taxonomic/restricted approach's practicality. They believe that a market-driven name space is more flexible and reflective of users' desires than is adherence to a limiting structure imposed by some authority.

---

[79]See, for example, Business Constituency, "A Differentiated Expansion of the Names Space," ICANN position paper, December 2002, available at <http://www.bizconst.org/positions/BCpositionpaperNewGTLDsV2.doc>.

Regulated

The third approach takes a position intermediate between the first two. It would add new gTLDs, both restricted and not, based on the qualifications and justifications presented by those who propose to run them, on a case-by-case basis. An administrative body, presumably ICANN, would exercise judgment to select which new gTLDs were added and who would operate them. This is effectively the approach taken by ICANN in 2000 when it added seven new gTLDs, selected from the more than 40 applicants because ICANN favored the TLD name and the type of service proposed, as described in "New gTLDs" in Section 3.4.3.

How Should the Operators of gTLDs Be Selected?

The necessity for selection arises when the number of candidates for a resource exceeds the quantity of the resource that is available, when candidates' qualifications to receive the resource must be validated, or both. Three common forms for the selection process in situations comparable to selection of new gTLDs and their operators are comparative hearings, auctions, and lotteries.

Comparative Hearing

A comparative hearing is an administrative process in which would-be entrants attempt to convince the decision body that they, and their proposed service, are qualified for selection in competition with other candidates. It is the form that has been and is being used by ICANN. Comparative hearings typically feature discretionary entry, merit assignment, and heavy regulation. Such hearings can take into account a large number of factors, draw on a wide range of expertise, offer opportunities to learn from experience, and enable judgment to be employed. Through use of a non-refundable application fee, such as ICANN has required, they can reduce speculative applications and be self-funding.

There are downsides to comparative hearings, however, as they can be subject to capture by interest groups. Furthermore, the real decision process may not be transparent, and thus may be perceived as arbitrary and unfair, especially by the losers. Also, decision quality is highly dependent on staff and decision maker competence, while the negotiation and oversight of contracts can be time-consuming and expensive. In addition, depending on the nature of the process and the stakes involved, application costs can be very high.

Auction

In the basic auction model, the highest bidder wins, although participation in the auction might be limited to those meeting a minimum set of qualifications. The advantages of auctions are that they are fair and transparent processes that reflect the economic value perceived by applicants, they may be designed to self-fund the process, and they discourage an excessive number of speculative applications. However, the tradeoffs with the auction model are that it tends to favor well-funded applicants (which could be corporations or non-profits) and thus does not necessarily reflect societal value, only economic value.

In principle, auctions could be designed to choose winners on the basis of who can best minimize prices (say, for example, the price of a domain name registration). However, in such cases, it may be impossible to prevent the winning bidder from later claiming (successfully) that changing conditions justify a higher price.

To the extent that in a specific situation social welfare extends beyond economic considerations, auctions, at least in their pure form, become less appealing.

Lottery

Winners in the lottery selection model are determined through a random choice from all entrants, each of which may be required to meet some minimum qualifications in order to participate and would (in contrast to a fund-raising lottery) be restricted to one entry per entity. The biggest advantage of lotteries is their transparency: they are fair and transparent, giving all entrants an equal chance regardless of means. Lotteries can also be self-funding if a charge is made for each "ticket." Although the cost to a given entrant may be quite small, lotteries can be expensive to society in the aggregate because they can attract a very large number of participants.

Because it can be difficult to determine whether an entry to the lottery is from a distinct qualified entity, a lottery can be gamed by one participant obtaining multiple entries under different "legitimate" guises. Moreover, unless the qualification criteria are very restrictive and carefully vetted, participants may not even have the financial or technical capacity to operate a service if they win, and the winners may simply sell the service to another entity for a significantly greater price. In the latter case, the lottery is turned into an auction, with the proceeds going to the lottery winner rather than the organization holding the lottery.

Combination Methods

It is also possible to integrate two or three of the basic methods into a variety of combination methods, some of which are described below.

What Selection Process Should Be Used?

There is a widely held view that the process employed by ICANN in 2000 to add new gTLDs was faulty. There is much less agreement about how to improve it, although the elements from which an alternative can be developed are described above. In July 2004, the Organization for Economic Cooperation and Development (OECD) issued a report that describes and compares two of those elements, comparative selection (hearing) and auctions, as means for allocation of gTLDs.[80] What follows is a description of several of the alternatives that have been specifically suggested, beginning with the process used in 2004-2005 by ICANN for the next round of additions.

Alternative A: Sponsored gTLDs Selected by Modified Comparative Hearing (2004-2005)

Description. ICANN is using a modified comparative hearing approach to select new sponsored gTLDs. Each new gTLD will be restricted to registrants from a well-defined and limited community and managed by a sponsoring organization with ongoing policy-formulation responsibility for the gTLD. The sponsoring organization will select the registry operator and, to some degree, establish the roles played by the registrars and their relationships to the registry operator.[81]

The request for proposal, evaluation, and selection processes are modifications of those used in 2000 to select seven new gTLDs. Non-refundable application fees of $45,000 have been charged to cover the costs of the selection process.

The eventual registry agreement will be similar to those entered into by the .museum, .coop, and .aero registries. However, the August 2004 report published by ICANN that evaluated the policy and legal issues of

---

[80]Working Party on Telecommunication and Information Services Policies, "Generic Top Level Domain Names: Market Development and Allocation Issues" July 13, 2004, OECD Directorate for Science, Technology and Industry, available at <http://www.oecd.org/dataoecd/56/34/996948.pdf>.

[81]For full details, see ICANN, "New sTLD Application. Part A. Explanatory Notes," December 15, 2003, available at <http://www.icann.org/tlds/new-stld-rfp/new-stld-application-parta-15dec03.htm>.

new gTLDs concluded that "while it is understandable for ICANN to have wished to err on the side of caution as it undertook gTLD expansion . . . the resulting legal framework is cumbersome."[82] It concludes that "the number and length of appendices [in agreements between gTLDs and ICANN] could be reduced in a future round. A streamlined base agreement with perhaps a few appendices could provide a more workable format that also preserves the critical elements of registry performance and mandates compliance with ICANN policies."[83]

Selection is to be determined by the degree to which independent evaluators judge the applicant to have met ICANN's requirements in four major categories, which are divided into 15 subsidiary categories:

1. Sponsorship
   a. Definition of sponsored TLD community
   b. Evidence of support from the sponsoring organization
   c. Appropriateness of the sponsoring organization and the policy formulation environment
   d. Level of support from the community
2. Business Plan Information
   a. Business plan
   b. Financial model
3. Technical Standards
   a. Evidence of ability to ensure stable registry operation
   b. Evidence of ability to ensure that the registry conforms with best-practices technical standards for registry operations
   c. Evidence of a full range of registry services
   d. Assurance of continuity of registry operation in the event of business failure of the proposed registry
4. Community Value
   a. Addition of new value to the Internet name space
   b. Protection of the rights of others
   c. Assurance of charter-compliant registrations and avoidance of abusive registration practices
   d. Assurance of adequate dispute-resolution mechanisms
   e. Provision of ICANN-policy-compliant Whois service

In light of the prior discussions of the types of gTLDs to be added and their potential value, it is useful to examine the specifics under topic 4a, addition of new value to the Internet name space. The subtopics are:

---

[82]Summit Strategies International, "Evaluation of New gTLDs," 2004, pp. 130-131.

[83]Summit Strategies International, "Evaluation of New gTLDs," 2004, p. 131.

1. *Name value.* The proposed name must be of broad significance and establish clear and lasting value. It should categorize a broad and lasting field of human, institutional, or social endeavor or activity. It should represent an endeavor or activity that has importance across multiple geographic regions.

2. *Enhanced diversity of the Internet name space.* The TLD must create a new and clearly differentiated space and satisfy needs that cannot be readily met through existing TLDs. The proposed TLD should enhance competition in registry services and should attract new suppliers and user communities to the Internet.

3. *Enrichment of broad global communities.* The TLD should have broad geographic and demographic impact. "Significant consideration" will be given to those gTLDs that serve larger user communities and attract greater numbers of registrants. "Consideration" will be given to those gTLDs whose charters have relatively broader functional scope.

These specifics, together with the sponsorship requirement, indicate that ICANN is adhering to a taxonomic/restricted approach in this selection, not allowing the TLD applicant to simply let the market decide which TLD names will succeed, but requiring that a gTLD name should categorize a "broad and lasting field of human, institutional, or social endeavor or activity . . . that has importance across multiple geographic regions."

Ten proposals[84] were submitted by the March 2004 deadline. Evaluation of the proposals was carried out by teams external to ICANN and, therefore, not involved in ICANN activities or subject to ICANN political pressures. Each evaluation team comprised three members: a technical, a financial, and a sponsorship-and-other-issues evaluator. The evaluators, whose identities were kept secret during the process, were selected and managed by an outside firm.[85] The evaluation teams made recommendations about the preferred applications from among those that were successful in meeting the selection criteria. Some proposed domains met all of the criteria and entered a contract negotiation with ICANN staff. Other proposals did not meet all the criteria, were sent back to the sponsors with suggestions for improvement, and were resubmitted. The result is that new gTLDs will be announced one at a time and not all at once as in 2000. In October 2004, ICANN announced that it was negotiating with two prospective new gTLDs: .post and .travel; in December 2004, it began negotiations with .mobi and .jobs. In March 2005, ICANN announced the

[84]The list is available at <http://www.icann.org/tlds/stld-apps-19mar04/stld-public-comments.htm>.

[85]Summit Strategies International in Washington, D.C. See Sarah Lai Stirland, "Domain-Name Registry Expansion Process Underway," *National Journal Tech Daily*, May 26, 2004.

completion of negotiations with .jobs and .travel, and in April 2005 the board announced their designation.

Evaluation. Although ICANN adhered to the comparative hearing approach in this selection process, it significantly reduced the use of staff and board judgment and relied instead on the judgment of independent outside evaluators using an explicitly defined set of criteria. By doing so and by giving applicants the opportunity to revise and resubmit their applications, ICANN increased the apparent transparency (although keeping evaluators anonymous) and apparent objectivity of the process (although using criteria subject to a wide range of discretion), and reduced the potential for disappointed applicants to challenge the scores awarded by the evaluators.

Alternative B: Unlimited gTLDs Awarded First-come, First-served to Qualified Sponsors (2003)

Description. Almost at the opposite extreme from the preceding approach lies a proposal by Ross Wm. Rader in which an undetermined number of new gTLDs would be awarded on a first-come, first-served basis to approved "delegants" that would in turn contract with ICANN-accredited "operators" for the day-to-day operation of the gTLD.[86]

The delegant would be the "policy coordinator for the gTLD that ensures that the registry operates in a manner that benefits its target community." A delegant would be approved by ICANN on the basis of four criteria: (1) the requested gTLD name is not confusingly similar to an existing gTLD name; (2) the delegant has a satisfactory plan specifying all significant operational policies; (3) an accredited operator is willing to manage the gTLD; and (4) the delegant yields rights in the gTLD name so that it can be transferred by ICANN to a new sponsor if required.

The operator would perform the registry functions. To be accredited by ICANN, the operator would have to satisfy the minimum standards for technically operating a registry. There would be no limitation on the number of gTLD registries an accredited operator could contract to run.

Evaluation. Alternative B lies squarely in the market determination camp, both with respect to determining how many gTLDs there should be and who should operate them and with respect to the organization of

---

[86]Ross Wm. Rader, "A Sustainable Framework for the Deployment of New gTLDs Part I," *CircleID*, February 26, 2003, available at <http://www.circleid.com/article/100_0_1_0_C/>; and Part II, March 26, available at <http://www.circleid.com/article/108_0_1_0_C/>.

gTLD names. In fact, it essentially allows there to be an unlimited number of gTLDs, simply determined by the number of delegants who qualify. It does not even specify a limit to the rate of addition of new gTLDs.

This process could be combined with—for example—a policy of adding *X* new gTLDs per year by proceeding down the list of first-come, first-served requests and filling them as slots become available. But that raises the question of how to actually implement a first-come, first-served process. How would all the essentially simultaneous electronic entries submitted at the opening instant be prioritized? If a random selection were to be used, for example, then this process would become—at least initially—a lottery.

Nor does the proposal specify a process for resolving conflicts that might arise with trademark holders if, for example, someone other than Sony wished to register .sony as a gTLD. Presumably, however, some variant of the sunrise procedures used to protect trademark holders when the .biz and .info domains were introduced could be used in this instance.

Alternative C: Fixed Number of gTLDs Annually Awarded by Auction and Lottery (2003)

Description. Mueller and McKnight[87] have proposed an auction/lottery process to award a limited number of new gTLDs each year.[88] No structure would be imposed on the specific gTLDs awarded, resulting in a supply-and-demand-driven approach to the types of gTLD names accepted.

Forty new gTLDs would be made available for award each year. That number was chosen based on advice from members of the technical community with the goals of retaining the hierarchical structure of the DNS and avoiding the introduction of errors into the root zone through too many changes, made too fast. Although 40 was the number chosen for the proposal, any number up to about 80 would be compatible with the authors' understanding of the advice they received.

The 40 new gTLDs would be divided into two tranches: 30 would be targeted for commercial applicants (but open to non-commercial as well), which could apply for any number of TLD names but be awarded no

---

[87]Milton L. Mueller and Lee W. McKnight, "The Post-.com Internet: Toward Regular and Objective Procedures for Internet Governance," Syracuse University, Syracuse, New York, August 2003, available at <http://dcc.syr.edu/miscarticles/NewTLDs2-MM-LM.pdf>.

[88]A similar auction model has been proposed in Karl Manheim and Lawrence Solum, "The Case for gTLD Auctions: A Framework for Evaluating Domain Name Policy," Research Paper No. 2003-11, Loyola Law School, Los Angeles, Calif., March 2003, available at <http://papers.ssrn.com/sol3/papers.cfm?abstract_id=388780>.

more than 2; 10 would be reserved for non-commercial and lesser developed country (LDC) applicants, which could apply for and be awarded only 1 name. Each applicant would pay a modest application fee, estimated by Mueller and McKnight at $1000, to cover ICANN's costs of the selection process. The authors leave open the question of whether applications should include a fitness disclosure and statement of financial capability to operate a registry or association with an already accredited registry.

The 10 noncommercial gTLDs would be allocated first, if necessary, by a random selection process, such as a lottery. To avoid possible abuse, the resultant TLD allocations could not be sold or transferred to commercial entities.

The selection of commercial gTLDs would follow. If there were more than 30 commercial (and other) applicants, the selection would be made by a simultaneous multiple-round Web-based auction, with each bidder knowing whether it is in the top 30 or not at every time, just as with e-Bay. When the auction period ended, the winning bidders would pay the amount of the lowest successful bid in order to keep auction prices at a reasonable level. However, should there be multiple bidders for the same gTLD, such as .sex, the high bidder would receive the gTLD and pay the amount bid by the second-highest bidder. Having a predictable annual increment in gTLDs would also be expected to relieve some of the pressure on the auction prices.

If there were 30 or fewer eligible commercial applicants, each would pay ICANN's reserve price, which would be fixed to cover the costs of the auction and of adding new names to the root. (Note that if, as some claim, there is only a limited demand for new gTLDs, this would be the outcome in the first, and possibly only, auction.)

Mueller and McKnight suggest that the proceeds of the auction (or the reserve price) go to maintaining and managing the root, with a portion reserved for the root name server operators. (See Section 5.3.2.)

After the award of the gTLDs, there would be a period during which the gTLD names could be challenged on intellectual property grounds or because of possible confusion with another gTLD. The UDRP-like process would be used to resolve such challenges.

The winning gTLD applicants would enter into standardized and uniform registry agreements with ICANN that would require adherence to a minimal set of ICANN-defined technical specifications and conformity to existing ICANN policies. They would be required to meet standards for transferring a zone file that would allow the domain to be maintained if the registry failed.

Evaluation. The result of the Mueller and McKnight proposal would be a market-determined structure of the DNS name space, presumably responding—at least for commercial TLDs—directly to the supplier-perceived demand for new TLDs. And except for the limitation on the rate of additions and the division between commercial and non-commercial/LDC awards, this is also a clear expression of the market-based approach to gTLD operator selection.

Those who favor a purer market-based approach could argue against the commercial/non-commercial/LDC division on the grounds that LDCs already have country-code TLDs and that just as with the allocation of other goods (e.g., office space, equipment, personnel) there is no need to favor non-commercial organizations, which should be capable of raising funds to acquire a gTLD if they need one.

Consistent with its "let the market decide" approach, this proposal does not specify any restrictions on the registration practices of the awarded TLDs except that non-commercial/LDC TLDs cannot become commercial.

Alternative D: Differentiated Expansion of gTLDs with Selection by Comparative Hearing (2002)

Description. In 2002, the Business Constituency (BC) of ICANN proposed that all future expansion of gTLDs should occur within the framework of a previously agreed set of principles.[89] In its view:

> Given that there is pressure on ICANN to introduce additional names, the BC supports the development of a logical expansion, which will result in a name space with added value, rather than the cloning of the existing space. Such a value-added space will create differentiation and reduce the need for entities to defensively register.
>
> Users—regardless whether they are businesses, non-profit organizations or individuals—want certainty. Spending time searching is not cost-effective. The user community needs a certain process for identifying prospective names and a certain process for selecting sponsors/registries to operate those names.[90]

Under this approach all new domain names would have to satisfy six principles:

1. *Differentiation:* be clearly differentiated from other gTLDs,
2. *Certainty:* give the user confidence that the name stands for what it purports to stand for,

[89]Business Constituency, "A Differentiated Expansion of the Name Space," 2002, p. 1.
[90]Business Constituency, "A Differentiated Expansion of the Name Space," 2002, p. 1.

3. *Honesty:* avoid increasing opportunities for bad faith entities that wish to defraud users,
4. *Competition:* create value-added competition,
5. *Diversity:* serve commercial or non-commercial users, and
6. *Meaning:* have meaning to its relevant population of users.[91]

In the view of the BC, "the principles . . . determine a taxonomized or directory-style domain name structure. . . . The structure does not imply a rapid expansion. The choice of one name will preclude future non-differentiated choices."[92] The BC also argues that all new gTLDs should be both sponsored and restricted. Only bona fide members of the target group would be able to register in a gTLD. The sponsor would be responsible for ensuring that the registered names are appropriate for the registrants and do not infringe on others' intellectual property. The BC believes that this approach "simultaneously solves three intellectual property issues. Cyber-pirates will not be able to obtain the names of others. There will therefore typically be no need for costly defensive registration. New Whois databases will be verified and therefore accurate."[93]

The BC proposal recommends separation of the functions of sponsor and registry, similar to but less specific than the Rader proposal (alternative B) described above. The goal is to create a set of qualified registries that can operate any number of gTLDs under contract with the gTLD sponsor. Should a registry fail, it could readily be replaced by another qualified registry.

Evaluation. One goal of the BC proposal is to enhance the role of the DNS as a directory service for the Internet. (See Chapters 6 and 7 for a discussion of the role of the DNS as an Internet navigation aid.) Its principle of differentiation is intended to avoid the Internet users' navigation confusion that might result from overlap among gTLDs. But it would have precluded the creation of .biz as a way of giving Internet providers another chance at a preferred second-level domain name that had been registered by someone else in .com. Moreover, by emphasizing differentiation, it would limit price competition in favor of non-price competition between gTLDs.

The BC proposal is not specific on the rate of addition of new names, other than that it is not necessarily a rapid expansion. Nor is it specific on the process by which sponsors and registries for the new names would be

---

[91]Business Constituency, "A Differentiated Expansion of the Name Space," 2002, p. 1.
[92]Business Constituency, "A Differentiated Expansion of the Name Space," 2002, p. 2.
[93]Business Constituency, "A Differentiated Expansion of the Name Space," 2002, p. 2.

TABLE 5.3 Alternatives for Adding Generic Top-Level Domains

	Means of Selecting gTLD Operators		
Desirable Structure of Name Space	First-come, First-served	Comparative Hearing	Auction (and Lottery)
Taxonomic/restricted		D. Business constituency A. ICANN 2004 addition	
Regulated		ICANN 2000 Addition	
Market-determined	B. Rader		C. Mueller and McKnight

selected. It is silent on the fact that, as noted above, many of the existing names would not belong in a strictly taxonomic structure.

By requiring that all TLDs be sponsored and restricted, this alternative places on the sponsors and registries the responsibility of enforcing intellectual property rights and qualifying an organization's or individual's right to use a specific domain name. By doing so, it moves from ex post to ex ante enforcement of those rights and from consideration of name assignments when an issue arises to examination of every assignment in advance. This approach can be expected to raise the costs of running a registry and, consequently, to increase the likely registration fees.

Comparison of the Four Alternatives

The four alternatives presented above for adding new gTLDs are compared in Table 5.3 on two dimensions: desirable structure of the name space and the means of selecting gTLD operators. Both the BC and the ICANN alternatives anticipate only sponsored and restricted gTLDs, whereas the Mueller and McKnight and the Rader proposals allow, but do not require, them.

5.4.3 Recommendations

ICANN's 2004 modification of its comparative hearing process so as to eliminate (or at least significantly reduce) subjective judgments by its staff and board and increase the process's transparency and objectivity has reduced the potential sources of dissatisfaction with the resultant selections. However, the question still remains open as to whether it is really necessary for ICANN to qualify new gTLDs on such matters as sponsorship by a community, business and financial plans, and addition of new value to the name space.

An alternative approach would be qualification of applicants only on technical capability, basic financial viability, and adherence to registrant protection standards and ICANN policies. Then a market-based selection process—essentially an auction—could be used to select among qualified applicants when their number exceeds the number of available slots.

Recommendation: If new gTLDs are to be created, the currently employed comparative hearing or expert evaluation processes should not be assumed to be the *only* processes for selecting their operators. ICANN should consider alternate processes that are less reliant on expert, staff, or board judgments.

Recommendation: Any gTLD auction selection process should be designed with reference to the substantial literature on auction design.[94] The following principal matters will have to be decided:

- *What is being auctioned.* Is it a "slot" that the winner can use for a TLD with its choice of name and operating policy, or the "right to operate" one of a prespecified list of TLD names and policies, each of which is subject to a separate auction? Is it an outright sale or the license to operate for a fixed, potentially renewable term?
- *How the winner is chosen.* Does the high bid win, or the low bid? In the latter case the bid would be the maximum amount the winner would charge for a basic registration in the TLD. (This latter case raises the issue of tightly specifying levels of service so that the bids can be comparable.)
- *What is done with the proceeds of a "high bid wins" auction.* Would the proceeds go to cover ICANN operating costs or be allocated to other organizations, such as the root name server operators or the IAB/IETF in support of technical activities related to ICANN responsibilities?
- *How commercial and non-commercial bidders are treated.* Would they participate equally in the same auctions, or would there be separate selection processes for each?
- *What the auction mechanism is.* Would it be open or closed; single or multiple iterations; with a reserve price or not; English or Dutch;[95] and so on?

---

[94]See, for example, Paul Klemperer, *Auctions: Theory and Practice*, Princeton University Press, Princeton, N.J., 2004.

[95]In an English auction, participants bid openly against one another, with each bid higher than the previous one. By contrast, in a Dutch auction, the auctioneer begins with a high asking price that is lowered until someone accepts the auctioneer's price.

• *How the bidders are qualified.* Would it be "no restrictions" or through some combination of technical capability, financial strength, continuity provisions, and so on?

• *How many "slots" or "rights" a bidder could win.* Would it be just one or two or as many as desired?

• *How post-auction actions by winners are restricted.* Would it be at all; no resale for X years; no change in policies; and so on?

• *How various failure modes are dealt with.* What happens if the winner doesn't pay, or doesn't proceed in a timely manner to set up the domain? What if the winner operates the domain poorly from a technical or ethical point of view?

Because of the many choices for each of these matters and their many possible combinations, there can be many different kinds of TLD auctions with different goals and quite different processes. Furthermore, as the previously cited OECD report[96] suggests, there can be various combinations of comparative hearings (say, for qualification of prospective registries) and auctions (where demand for gTLDs exceeds the number made available). The exploration of one or more such designs should be included in ICANN's evaluation of alternative gTLD selection processes.

5.5 OVERSIGHT OF COUNTRY-CODE TOP-LEVEL DOMAINS

Issues: Does ICANN's responsibility for the root require that it work to increase its oversight of and authority over the ccTLDs? If so, what form should its increased authority take, and how can it be implemented? And to what degree should the ccTLDs accept ICANN's authority and participate in its activities?

Although it does not have much visibility in the United States, the issue of who controls the delegation and redelegation of ccTLDs is highly sensitive in many parts of the world. On the one hand, some nations[97] have expressed concern that the U.S. government, acting through ICANN, could unilaterally remove their ccTLDs from the root zone file and, therefore, cut them off from the Internet. On the other hand, some non-governmental ccTLD registries fear that their governments could take over control of the ccTLDs through the use of ICANN's redelegation responsibility. In some sense, these fears are anomalous since although ICANN has been

---

[96]Working Party on Telecommunication and Information Services Policies, "Generic Top Level Domain Names," 2004, p. 51

[97]For example, a Brazilian government representative at the February 2004 U.N. meeting on Internet governance expressed this concern.

given responsibility for management of the root, the vast majority of the TLDs in the root—the ccTLDs—have, for the most part, eluded its direct authority. Fewer than half of them (though they include some of the larger ones) contribute to ICANN's budget. Although many participate in the ICANN meetings (and the special ccTLD meetings that have occurred at the same time), they have not fully participated in ICANN's decisions. And few have signed agreements with ICANN. Yet, through its control of the root zone file, ICANN does have the sole responsibility for recommending delegations and redelegations of ccTLDs to the DOC. So the policy issues that face ICANN are whether its responsibility for the root requires that it work to increase its oversight and authority over the ccTLDs and, if so, what form such oversight should take and how it can be implemented. And the complementary issue for the ccTLDs is the degree to which they should accept ICANN's authority and participate in its activities. This latter issue is, of course, complicated by the fact that the 243 ccTLDs do not act in concert[98] and, as described in "ccTLDs" in Section 3.4.1, represent a very wide range of relationships between government and registry and a very wide range of registry policies.

5.5.1 Current Situation

As the Internet has grown and matured, the role and importance of ccTLDs has grown and changed as well, as have their relationships with their governments, with their local communities, and with ICANN.

A study in 2002 of the ccTLDs of 45 countries revealed a wide diversity of relationships between ccTLDs and the countries' governments.[99] The ccTLDs of 10 of the 45 countries surveyed were operated by government agencies or departments, 9 by private commercial enterprises, 20 by non-profit organizations, 5 by academic institutions, and 1 by an individual. Of the 35 non-governmental sponsoring organizations, only 9 had a formal contractual relationship with their governments and 13 had informal relationships, of which 3 were awaiting formalization. Three of the ccTLDs operators were battling government attempts to take over management of the ccTLD. Altogether, only half of the studied ccTLDs had formal or soon-to-be formal relationships with their governments. Their

[98]There are, however, a number of regional ccTLD associations such as CENTR, the Council of European National Top-Level Domain Registries, which has 39 member registries, not all of which are European. See <www.centr.org>. CENTR has expressed strong positions on ICANN matters, especially its relationships with the ccTLDs.

[99]Michael A. Geist, *ccTLD Governance Project*, 2003, available at <http://www.cctldinfo.com/home.php>. Data for this project was obtained from ccTLD Web sites, ccTLD contacts, and GAC representatives between June and September 2002. It was not claimed to be a representative sample.

formal relationships with ICANN were also weak. By early 2005, only 12 of the 243 ccTLDs had entered into formal agreements with ICANN.

The consequence of this evolution is that the ccTLDs operate in a space that is only in part under the oversight of any higher authority. A few ccTLDs are overseen by their national governments; some have established representative non-governmental bodies to represent the local Internet community and exercise varying degrees of oversight; some are completely autonomous non-profit bodies that operate voluntarily to meet local Internet community interests; and some are commercial bodies with some linkage to the national government.

The only body that currently has an opportunity to exercise oversight over all the ccTLDs is ICANN. According to ICANN, it does so on the basis of RFC 1591 in conjunction with "ICP-1: Internet Domain Name System Structure and Delegation (ccTLD Administration and Delegation)"[100] and the "Principles and Guidelines for the Delegation and Administration of Country Code Top Level Domains," a revision of principles first published in 2000, which was presented by the Governmental Advisory Committee at the ICANN meeting in April 2005.[101]

The delegations in the early days of the DNS placed highest priority on the responsibility of the manager and less on notions of ownership. However, with the current economic, political, and social importance of the Internet to all nations, matters of accountability to the local government, local Internet community, and the global Internet community have assumed much greater significance. Thus, matters of delegation for new ccTLDs and redelegations of responsibility for existing ccTLDs have become much more important and, when combined with the many different ccTLD-government relationships, have also become much more complex.

The relationship between ccTLDs and ICANN has been difficult from the beginning of ICANN. First, a large number of the ccTLDs felt no need to contribute to ICANN's budget, since they did not think they received any corresponding benefits. Whether or not true,[102] many ccTLDs believed that 90 percent of ICANN's resources were devoted to gTLD issues, while they were asked to provide 35 percent of its budget.[103] Sec-

[100]Available at <www.icann.org/icp/icp-1.htm>.

[101]See <http://gac.icann.org/web/docs/cctld/ccTLD_Principles_MDP_ Final.rtf>. This new, revised statement of principles was published in April 2005.

[102]However, according to a reviewer with knowledge of ICANN's activities: "Close to 50 percent of ICANN time/resources has been devoted to ccTLD and international issues. . . . much of that time is spent on small ccTLDs (with) complex redelegation issues. A considerable amount of time is also spent liaising with regional organizations and governments . . . participating in international fora."

[103]Peter de Blanc, "ccTLD Briefing Document," February 19, 2001, available at <http://www.wwtld.org/meetings/cctld/ccTLD-Briefing-document.htm>.

ond, many of them resented ICANN's major role in deciding on delegations and redelegations—essentially a policy role—that they felt would be better performed locally. They also believed that their position as one constituency within ICANN's Names Supporting Organization, whose other constituencies primarily addressed gTLD issues, did not adequately reflect their importance as 243 of the 258 TLDs.

Under its 2003 reorganization (see Section 5.2.4, alternative F), ICANN has responded to that concern by replacing the Names Supporting Organization with two supporting organizations, the Generic Names Supporting Organization (GNSO) and the Country-Code Names Supporting Organization (ccNSO), which formally came into being in March 2004. ICANN hopes, thereby, to draw the ccTLDs more actively into its operations and build a stronger basis for their support. Furthermore, the revised "Principles for the Delegation and Administration of Country Code Top Level Domains" issued in April 2005 by the Governmental Advisory Committee addresses many of the concerns of the ccTLDs and governments.[104]

Although ICANN's actions may have the desired effect, it is useful to lay out the alternative approaches to providing reasonable oversight of the ccTLDs that have been suggested.

5.5.2 Alternatives

ICANN appears to have four goals for the ccTLDs. First, that they operate according to standards, protocols, and practices that are consistent with the reliable and stable operation of the DNS and that allow open connectivity to and from their registrants and the rest of the Internet. Second, that they contribute proportionately[105] to the overall costs of maintaining the DNS root zone file and ccTLD database in which they are listed. Third, that they accept ICANN's authority to decide on delegations and redelegations when controversies arise. And fourth, that they formalize these expectations by means of an agreement with ICANN. However, not all of the ccTLDs accept these as appropriate goals for ICANN's relationship with them. What is the current situation?

The absence of significant and sustained operational problems sug-

[104]See <http://gac.icann.org/web/docs/cctld/ccTLD_Principles_MDP_ Final.rtf>. This new, revised statement of principles was published in April 2005.

[105]In 1999, the Task Force on Funding recommended that the ccTLDs contribute a 35 percent share of ICANN's continuing revenue requirements. See <http://www.icann.org/committees/tff/final-report-draft-30oct99.htm#4>.

gests that the ccTLDs generally meet the first of ICANN's goals, supporting reliable, stable, and open operation of the DNS and Internet.[106]

However, there is only a modest contribution, at present, from a minority of the ccTLDs to ICANN's budget. (In 2004-2005, the 243 ccTLDs' fixed contributions are budgeted at $1.02 million, whereas 10 gTLDs are expected to provide $1.45 million. An additional $14 million is expected from the accredited registrars and gTLD registries in proportion to actual registrations.) So they do not appear to satisfy its second goal.

The ccTLDs represented by the European association of ccTLD registries, the Council of European National Top-level Domain Registries (CENTR), favor a much more limited role for ICANN. In their view, ICANN should restrict its operational responsibilities to maintaining the ccTLD database (containing Whois information about the ccTLDs) and the corresponding root zone file entries and ensuring that the ccTLDs satisfy minimal technical requirements to function within the global DNS. In their view, delegations and redelegations should be made only by ICANN upon verified instruction from the current manager of the ccTLD. Where there is controversy, it should be referred to a third party for resolution. (This approach would be consistent with the proposals noted earlier to increase ICANN's legitimacy by narrowing its range of authority and by delegating sensitive decisions to appropriate third parties wherever possible.)

An even stronger view, held by a number of ccTLD managers, is that the maintenance of the ccTLD database should be the responsibility of a ccTLD-sponsored organization independent of ICANN. This organization would receive entries from the ccTLDs and have full responsibility for updating the database to reflect the latest information. Through a contract with ICANN, it would provide the relevant ccTLD entries for inclusion in the root zone file, but ICANN would play no part in deciding what the entries would be. Participation in the independent database would be voluntary for each ccTLD. If a ccTLD desired, it could continue to submit information directly to ICANN. As a result, each ccTLD would have a "vote" on whose management of the ccTLD database it favored.

Thus, although ICANN's delegation and redelegation authority is accepted de facto—because it currently has sole authority to recommend changes in the root zone file to the DOC—there are many ccTLDs that dispute either the way that authority is exercised or that it should be an ICANN function at all. Consequently, its third goal has not been satisfied.

---

[106]On rare occasions, a ccTLD may temporarily disappear from the Internet as the Libyan ccTLD did in April 2004. This is often the result of political or institutional disputes within a nation over responsibility for the ccTLD, with which ICANN has to deal. See "Who Runs the Dot LY?," Libyan Jamahiriya Broadcasting Corporation, 2004, available at <http://en.ljbc.net/online/subject_details.php?sub_id=26&cat_id=1>.

Finally, as noted above, only 12 agreements have been signed between ICANN and ccTLDs. So ICANN's fourth goal has not been satisfied.

It should be observed that a comparable list of the goals of the 243 ccTLDs cannot be provided, since they are consistent neither with each other nor, necessarily, with ICANN. As efforts are made to increase the ccTLDs' role in ICANN and ICANN's influence over them, many independent ccTLDs will straddle the fence, playing the various forces off against each other until the ambiguities and uncertain power relationships among the U.S. government, their own national governments, ICANN, and the international community are worked out. Because of the diversity of ccTLD models, histories, and relationships to national governments, it is unlikely that any proposal will satisfy everyone; but some aggressive or lopsided proposals are likely to antagonize all of them.

How then can ICANN best interact with the ccTLDs? The differing goals of ICANN and of some of the ccTLDs have led to four proposed models for ICANN's "oversight" of the ccTLDs.

Alternative A: "Thick" ICANN

Description

The model initially implemented by ICANN has had ICANN attempting to achieve its goals by playing a strong role in the oversight of the ccTLDs: maintaining the ccTLD database and ccTLD entries in the root zone file, making recommendations to the DOC concerning delegations and redelegations, establishing standards for ccTLD performance, and inducing compliance through MoUs with the ccTLD managers or the relevant governments. Currently, it is seeking through the newly established ccNSO to engage the more active participation of the ccTLDs in ICANN activities.

Evaluation

By elevating the ccTLDs to the status of a supporting organization, similar to the GNSO, ICANN has both raised their profile in the organization and given them influence over board membership and ICANN policy. By engaging them more directly in its governance, it evidently hopes to gain their support for its role in ccTLD oversight. At the same time, the revised ICANN bylaws[107] give the ccNSO the principal role in establish-

[107]The changes in ICANN bylaws that establish the ccNSO and define its roles are in ICANN, "Appendix A to Minutes of Regular Meeting of ICANN Board," June 26, 2003, available at <http://www.icann.org/minutes/minutes-appa-26jun03.htm>.

ing policy for entry of data concerning ccTLDs into the root zone file. Over time, this may lead to a ccNSO-led redefinition of the delegation/redelegation policies and practices of ICANN.

However, some of the most important ccTLDs were not participants in the ccNSO upon its formation. Most notably, only four of the European ccTLDs (from the Netherlands, the Czech Republic, Gibraltar, and the Cayman Islands) were among the 38 founding members. In April 2004, the European Community (EC) member responsible for the Internet said that the EC will stand by ICANN as long as it continues to make changes and that unless the EC ccTLDs come to agreement with ICANN, the EC will lose patience and the governments will step in, possibly turning ICANN's ccTLD role over to the ITU.[108] But the distance that remains between ICANN and the European ccTLDs was clearly shown by the response of CENTR to ICANN's proposed 2004-2005 budget. In a May 2004 letter to ICANN, CENTR accused ICANN of a "lack of financial prudence" and refused to support it "financially or otherwise" in its "unrealistic political and operational targets."[109] Specifically, it said: "ICANN/IANA should focus on doing a few administrative tasks well and not seek to make decisions—decisions are best handled elsewhere."

Alternative B: "Thin" ICANN

Description

Many ccTLDs would favor a much more limited role for ICANN, essentially reducing it to performance of a technical coordination function and eliminating all policy functions. Under this approach, ICANN would continue to run the IANA function, maintaining the database of ccTLDs and the ccTLD entries in the root zone file. However, decisions about the delegation of responsibility for a ccTLD when it is a subject of dispute would not be made by ICANN. Rather, they would be made, in the first instance, by the local Internet community relying on national laws and processes as necessary, and if that failed, by a process established by the ccTLD community. In this model, the ccTLDs would agree to pay the cost incurred by ICANN in maintaining the database of ccTLDs and ccTLD entries in the root zone file through a fee based on the size of each ccTLD's membership.

---

[108]Speech by EC Commissioner Erkki Liikanen quoted by Kieren McCarthy, "EC Tells Europe and ICANN to Make Peace," *The Register,* April 28, 2004, available at <http://www.theregister.co.uk/2004/04/28/ec_icann_warning_shot/>.

[109]Paul M. Kane, letter to Paul Twomey, May 26, 2004, available at <http://www.centr.org/docs/statements/CENTR-Response-2004-Budget.pdf>.

Evaluation

Alternative B would reduce ICANN to performance of a technical/administrative root registry function, eliminating its role in determining who among alternative claimants should have the right to be the registry for a specific ccTLD. In that sense, it is compatible with the approaches to gTLD selection that favor the use of auctions to determine which gTLDs should enter the root zone file. A combination of the two approaches would virtually eliminate ICANN's role as a gatekeeper to the root and leave it primarily as the record keeper and, presumably neutral, validator of the technical qualifications of registries.

Alternative C: International Oversight

Description

In the third model, a major part of the IANA function would be removed from ICANN and turned over to a third-party organization established by the ccTLDs. That organization would be responsible for maintaining an up-to-date ccTLD database and sending the appropriate information to ICANN for entry into the root zone file. Presumably, there would be a corresponding agreement with the DOC (as long as it retained its stewardship role) to accept the information from the third-party organization as authoritative. If that organization had broad international participation in its governance and activities, this might alleviate some of the discontent with the U.S. government's current central role as steward of the DNS. One possibility would be, for example, to turn the ccTLD database and delegation responsibilities over to the ITU. However, the ITU is an intergovernmental organization, responsible primarily to the telecommunication ministries of governments. Yet, as noted earlier, many ccTLDs are either simply independent from their governments or operating in delicate balance with them. They would probably not like a process whose only recourse is to the governments.

Evaluation

This alternative takes alternative B a step further by eliminating even the record-keeping function of ICANN with respect to the ccTLDs. Its role would simply be to pass the appropriate entries to the organization responsible for distributing the root zone file (currently VeriSign). In fact, this amounts to establishing an "ICANN" for the ccTLDs, leaving the present ICANN with responsibility only for the gTLDs. Although alternative C would certainly eliminate any ccTLD discontent with ICANN, it might simply shift the focus of concern to the new organization, depending on how the issue of delegation/redelegation decision making was decided. This possibility suggests that finding a solution to the delegation/redelegation decision process within the existing ICANN that is satisfactory to the ccTLDs and their governments would preclude ccTLD support for alternative C.

Alternative D: Self-governing Root Management Organization

Description

An additional possibility would be an ICANN focused solely on root management responsibilities whose members are limited to those groups, including the ccTLDs, having a direct interest in the root. (See "Alternative C: ICANN as Registry for the Root" in Section 5.2.4.) This model assumes that the ccTLDs would take an active role in ICANN's governance and would, therefore, be more willing to see ICANN play an active, "thick" role in ccTLD oversight. By creating a ccNSO and giving it greater influence on board composition and enabling it to submit recommendations to the board for its unmodified approval or rejection, ICANN has taken a step in this direction.

Evaluation

Alternative D, discussed in greater detail as one of the ICANN alternatives, could achieve the goal of bringing the ccTLDs fully into the management of an organization whose authority would be strictly limited to management of the root. Once again, however, the issue would devolve to the sensitive one of how delegation/redelegation decisions are made. This alternative might be more attractive to the ccTLDs because it would presumably increase the strength of their influence over ICANN's operations and decision-making processes. However, the issue still remains the degree to which they, a highly diverse group, would all be comfortable with the policies and practices that would determine which registry is delegated or redelegated responsibility for a ccTLD.

Comparison of the Four Alternatives

The four alternative models described above for oversight of ccTLDs are compared in Table 5.4 on two dimensions: who maintains the ccTLD database and who recommends redelegations (to DOC). Three models assume that ICANN will continue to manage the ccTLD database. Only one posits an independent manager of the database. Two models foresee the decision/policy responsibility for delegations and redelegations being removed from ICANN.

TABLE 5.4 Alternatives for Oversight of the Country Code Top-Level Domains

	Maintainer of ccTLD Database	
Recommender of Redelegations	ICANN	Third Party
ICANN	A. Thick ICANN D. Self-governing root management organization	
Third Party	B. Thin ICANN	C. International oversight

5.5.3 Conclusions

Conclusion: Resolution of ICANN's role vis-à-vis the ccTLDs is one of the critical steps on the path to establishing an ICANN that is viewed as a legitimate and appropriate steward for the DNS.

The creation of the ccNSO represents progress in that direction whose success will depend on the ccNSO's ability to attract an increasing number of members, both from the large ccTLDs that are needed for financial and other support of ICANN and the smaller ccTLDs that can benefit from the support that ICANN could offer them. Even more critical is the refinement of the principles and processes for delegation and redelegation of ccTLD registries and their acceptance by most of the ccTLDs.

Conclusion: If the creation of the ccNSO does not result in increased participation by the ccTLDs in ICANN policy making, then ICANN may find itself subject to increasing pressures to constrain its role to that of gTLD management and root zone file record keeping.

5.6 RESOLUTION OF CONFLICTS OVER DOMAIN NAMES

Issue: Does the UDRP need to be improved? If so, how should it be improved?

Administrative processes, such as the Uniform Domain Name Dispute Resolution Policy (UDRP), are playing an important role in helping to resolve certain private-party disputes related to the use of domain names, without requiring ISPs, registries, registrars, registrants, or other parties to appear in court to provide evidence or to protect their interests. Such processes contribute to the smooth operation of the economic and legal framework associated with the DNS. At the same time, while the highly simplified rules created by the UDRP and similar dispute resolution procedures (e.g., those adopted by some ccTLDs) and dispute avoidance efforts (e.g., sunrise provisions) make it possible for some actual or potential disputes to be resolved quickly at relatively low cost and without requiring the parties to be represented by legal counsel, they can also undermine the potential for fair outcomes. The UDRP is the primary subject of this section, since most attention has been paid to issues concerning it.

During 2003, the ICANN staff carried out a review of the UDRP. It produced an issues report in August 2003.[110] The report cataloged and identified the pros and cons of proposed solutions to both procedural and substantive issues and concluded that "while there are some areas where improvements may be possible, there does not appear to be an urgent need for revision." Furthermore, it noted that "revision of the UDRP is likely to be contentious; there are not many (if any) areas that are obviously amenable to achieving consensus." (Since the UDRP is a consensus policy, according to provisions of the ICANN registry and registrar agreements it must be revised by consensus.)

To provide an understanding of the issues that have given rise to those proposals, this section begins with an assessment of the UDRP and then examines the major proposals for improvement. It incorporates the committee's conclusions and recommendations. The section concludes with a discussion of the potential consequences of deployed internationalized domain names (IDNs) for dispute resolution.

5.6.1 Assessment of the UDRP

Many observers believe that the UDRP has functioned well to resolve disputes over domain names.[111] However, there are others who believe that the current system is biased toward the interests of trademark holders and away from the interests of individuals.[112] Notwithstanding its perceived disadvantages, numerous decisions have been rendered under

---

[110]ICANN, "Staff Manager's Issues Report on UDRP Review," August 2003, available at <http://www.icann.org/gnso/issue-reports/udrp-issues-report-01aug03.htm>.

[111]One such favorable assessment appears in Colm Brannigan, "The UDRP: How Do You Spell Success?," *Digital Technology Law Journal* 5(1, July), 2004, available at <http://wwwlaw.murdoch.edu.au/dtlj/2004/vol5_1/brannigan.pdf>. A careful assessment of the pros and cons of the UDRP can be found in Laurence Helfer and Graeme Dinwoodie. 2001. "Designing Non-national Systems: The Case of the Uniform Domain Name Dispute Resolution Policy," *William and Mary Law Review* 43(1, October):141-273, 2001, available at <http://www.kentlaw.edu/depts/ipp/intl-courts/docs/dh.pdf>.

[112]See, for example, A. Michael Froomkin, "ICANN's 'Uniform Dispute Resolution Policy'—Causes and (Partial) Cures," *Brooklyn Law Review* 67(3):608-718, 2002, available at

the UDRP, and other domain name dispute policies have been modeled after the UDRP as described in "Resolving Domain Name Conflicts" in Section 3.5.2. Thus, the UDRP has both positive and negative aspects, which differ, however, depending on whether they are being considered from the perspective of the complainants or of the respondents.

- *General benefits.* The UDRP crosses national boundaries and relies on communication technology to bring the parties together It is more informal than litigation in national courts and relies on panelists who are experts in the areas of trademark law and domain name issues. The proceedings are *quasi-in-rem,* meaning that even though both parties are included, the action is focused on resolving which party has rights to the domain name, rather than assessing fault or monetary damages against either party. Although it is international in scope, it raises no jurisdictional issues, which may be present in court litigation in some countries, by requiring all domain name registrants to agree to submit to a mandatory administrative proceeding as part of the registration agreement. The UDRP requires that the proceeding be conducted in the language of the registration agreement, which eliminates language as a potential barrier to participation by domain name registrants.
- *Complainant's benefits.* From the complainant's (generally, trademark holder's) point of view, the UDRP's positive features include that it provides a quick and relatively inexpensive method of resolving a domain name dispute and obtaining the transfer of a domain name to the trademark owner. Domain name disputes brought under the UDRP are generally resolved within 45 to 60 days of the domain name dispute provider's receipt of the complaint. In addition, the UDRP is not limited to registered trademarks identical to the domain name, and it allows trademark owners to file a complaint against a registrant of a domain name that is "confusingly similar" to the owner's mark. Further, owners with common-law rights in trademarks may also take advantage of the UDRP as there are no trademark registration prerequisites to commencing a UDRP action.

The UDRP is a cost-effective dispute resolution mechanism overall because it (1) is based primarily on the pleadings of the parties, (2) only

<http://personal.law.miami.edu/~froomkin/articles/udrp.pdf>. In addition, see Michael Geist, "Fair.com? An Examination of the Allegations of Systemic Unfairness in the ICANN UDRP," University of Ottawa, Faculty of Law, August 2001, available at <http://aix1.uottawa.ca/~geist/guistudrp.pdf>. See also a follow-up piece by the same author in March 2002, "Fundamentally Fair.com? An Update on Bias Allegations and the ICANN UDRP," available at <http://aix1.uottawa.ca/~geist/fairupdate.pdf>.

allows in-person hearings under exceptional circumstances, and (3) only allows additional evidence at the discretion of the panel.[113] Furthermore, the parties are generally not required to travel in order to participate in the proceeding, which is usually conducted by postal mail, e-mail, or facsimile. This last point can be seen as a greater advantage for the complainants, since ordinary court proceedings would occur in the respondents' locales, thus, requiring the complainants to travel.

• *Respondent's benefits.* From the respondent's perspective, the panel can grant the complainant the requested remedy (i.e., transfer or cancellation of the domain name registration) only if the complainant succeeds in showing all three of the UDRP elements (see "Remedies to Conflicts over Names in the DNS" in Section 3.5.2), even if the respondent did not submit a response. Respondents see other advantages to the UDRP as well, since it requires trademark owners to comply with a standard stricter than that of the courts—demonstrating that the respondent had both registered and used the domain name in bad faith (although it has been argued that not all panelists have adhered to this requirement). In addition, the UDRP allows a party against which an adverse decision is rendered to take the decision to the courts.

Moreover, the UDRP provides limited remedies to trademark owners, namely simply transfer or cancellation of the domain name. To receive monetary damages or an injunction, a trademark owner would have to proceed to litigation.

• *Complainant's disadvantages.* From the complainant's perspective, the preparation of a proper complaint and necessary appendices can be time-consuming and costly, and although much less costly than preparing for litigation, it is still viewed by many complainants as excessive.

In addition, the only avenue, at present, for correcting what the complainant views as an improper decision by the panel is to litigate the same matter before a court having *in personam* jurisdiction over the respondent, or in some cases in *in rem* jurisdiction over the domain name in dispute. This is not perceived as an advantage by all complainants, especially if the respondent is not located in the same location as the complainant and the domain name was not registered in the United States, where *in rem* jurisdiction is possible in some cases.

Moreover, complainants see disadvantages in the limitations on remedies (no potential damage recovery no matter how egregious the respondent) and in panels' inconsistent definitions of critical terms, such as "confusing similarity," "use," and "bad faith."

---

[113]ICANN, "Rules for Uniform Domain Name Dispute Resolution Policy," October 24, 1999, Paragraph 12.

• *Respondent's disadvantages.* There are also, however, disadvantages that fall primarily on the respondents. Although the UDRP allows administrative proceedings to be conducted in languages other than English, the UDRP itself is written in English. Many non-native-English speakers who register domain names with registrars that do not provide translated versions of their registration agreements or the UDRP may not be aware that they are subject to the provisions of the UDRP or that they should avoid selecting a domain name that violates the trademark rights of other parties.[114] Additionally, since the complainant selects the dispute resolution service provider, it is possible for complainants to "forum shop" (i.e., to select a provider more likely to favor the complainant, or which has been more sympathetic to similar complaints in the past).[115]

Some critics have also alleged that providers, seeking to increase their chances of being selected by future complainants, purposely choose arbitrators who are more likely to favor complainants, but little concrete evidence supporting this allegation has been provided. Nevertheless, arbitrator selection bias would be a serious issue were it to occur, and service providers should be reviewed on a periodic basis to make sure such bias does not exist.

Once a decision is rendered, the respondent's only recourse for dealing with a decision transferring or canceling the domain name is to proceed to court.

• *General deficiencies.* Critics of the current UDRP[116] have pointed to a number of perceived deficiencies. Among them are that some panelists do not apply the precedents of previous arbitrations appropriately, or in some cases consistently; some panelists (and many respondents) are not well-enough educated in either the operations of the DNS or the policies and rules applicable to domain name disputes; the charges for a UDRP proceeding and the ways in which panelist are compensated can lead to

---

[114]As noted by one reviewer: ". . . many countries have consumer protection laws that require all consumer contracts concluded within the jurisdiction to be in the local language in order to be valid and enforceable. This condition is not satisfied by the UDRP's requirement that the proceedings be conducted in the language of the registration agreement." See Holger P. Hestermeyer, "The Invalidity of ICANN's UDRP Under National Law," *Minnesota Intellectual Property Review* 3(1):1-57, 2002

[115]An early analysis of the UDRP that asserted that "forum shopping" was a source of bias favoring the complainant was in Milton Mueller, "Rough Justice: An Analysis of ICANN's Uniform Dispute Resolution Policy," Convergence Center, Syracuse University School of Information Studies, 2000, available at <http://dcc.syr.edu/miscarticles/roughjustice.pdf>. The INTA study, "UDRP-A Success Story" (2002), is a rebuttal to the Mueller article. Michael Geist's reports, "Fair.com?" (2001) and "Fundamentally Fair.com?" (2002), both provide further data on the asserted complainant-beneficial effects of forum shopping.

[116]See, for example, the Froomkin, Mueller, and Geist articles cited above.

undesired consequences; and there is no appeals process with the UDRP itself—the only appeal is a de novo action before a court.

Each of these perceived deficiencies is described and proposals for remedying them are addressed in the next section.

Conclusion: The UDRP has generally satisfied the need for an effective and cost-efficient means of resolving disputes concerning domain names; however, it has weaknesses for which remedies have been proposed.

5.6.2 Proposed Improvements to the UDRP

In response to the perceived deficiencies of the current UDRP, a number of improvements have been proposed: a better, more consistent application of arbitral precedents; an appeals process; required use of three-member panels; improved training and self-help tools; and revised funding and compensation structures.

- *Better application of precedents.* Some believe that more consistent application of arbitral precedents in UDRP proceedings is needed, so that similar issues can be addressed in a more predictable manner that also supports case-by-case knowledge building. In addition, greater consideration of international legal issues is needed, given that laws vary from country to country. Because the panelists in UDRP proceedings tend to be most knowledgeable about their home country's laws, new issues in disputes tend to be examined through the legal lens of a particular panelist's country. When these decisions are relied on in later cases, panelists unfamiliar with the legal context of the original decision will often assess them—inviting misinterpretation, however well-intentioned a panelist may be. One way to encourage better and more consistent use of arbitral precedents is to have an internal appeals process, whose panelists would be in a better position to require and make use of precedents.
- *Appeals process.* An appeals process could serve the purpose of reversing decisions that were clearly faulty or that covered a situation or issue for which competing bodies of precedent exist.[117] To remain consis-

[117]For a specific proposal, see Patrick Kelley, "Emerging Patterns in Arbitration Under the Uniform Domain-Name Dispute-Resolution Policy," Law and Technology Writing Workshop, Annual Review of Exemplar Papers, School of Law (Boalt Hall), University of California, Berkeley, 2001-2002, available at <http://www.law.berkeley.edu/institutes/bclt/pubs/annrev/exmplrs/final/pkfin.pdf>. Another proposal for an appeals process appears in M. Scott Donahey, "Divergence in the UDRP and the Need for Appellate Review," 2002, available at <http://www.tzmm.com/content/articles/Mil2910.pdf>.

tent with the original purpose of the UDRP, the intent of such a process would be to re-examine only a small percentage of decisions, so as to provide an inexpensive mechanism (as compared to a court case) for resolving relatively straightforward cases. As noted above, an appeals process would have the likely effect of encouraging better and more consistent use of arbitral precedents. But support for an appeals process has been limited, with the emphasis being placed on resolving such issues through a national court proceeding—rather than creating another layer to a relatively quick and inexpensive dispute resolution process. Those who hold that view emphasize that the UDRP, with or without an appeals process, is not intended to serve as a full substitute for national and international law or courts, but simply to provide a quicker and less costly process for the majority of disputes, whose resolution is often obvious. With careful design and restriction to very specific situations, the proposal for a limited appeals process could be consistent with that intent.

- *Three-member panels.* Analyses conducted during 2001 and early 2002 of UDRP proceedings indicated a significant difference in their outcomes, depending on whether they were heard by one-member or three-member panels.[118] (The choice is made by the complainant in the first instance, but the respondent can request a three-member panel.) Three-member panels found for the complainant in a smaller percentage of the cases. Critics have taken this as an indicator of greater bias toward complainants by the one-member panels and have recommended, therefore, that all panels have three members.[119] (In three-member panels, the complainant, the respondent, and the provider each provide lists from which one of the panelists is chosen.) Others have argued that the impression of bias is due to other factors.[120] Both sides agree that three-member panels are more expensive and, therefore, that they erode the benefits of the UDRP as a relatively inexpensive means of resolving domain name disputes. Those who favor them argue that the increase in fairness is worth the cost. In addition, they have suggested the payment of a bond by the complainant that would be used to cover the respondent's costs of the proceeding if the complainant lost and would be refunded if the complainant won.[121]

---

[118]Michael Geist, "Fair.com? An Examination of the Allegations of Systemic Unfairness in the ICANN UDRP," 2001; and Michael Geist, "Fundamentally Fair.com? An Update on Bias Allegations and the ICANN UDRP," 2002.

[119]Michael Geist, "Fair.com?," 2001.

[120]INTA, "The UDRP by All Accounts Works Effectively," 2002.

[121]Milton Mueller, "Success by Default: A New Profile of Domain Name Trademark Disputes Under ICANN's UDRP," Convergence Center, Syracuse University School of Information Studies, June 24, 2002.

• *Improved training and self-help tools.* In many UDRP proceedings the focus is on the use of domain names in Web addresses (URIs). The role of domain names in e-mail addresses and in other applications is often ignored by the panelists, even though the effects can be different from those in Web addresses. One possible reason for this oversight is that some panelists may lack a technical understanding of how the DNS and the Internet operate. Thus, some believe, UDRP proceedings could be improved by enhancing the training requirements for panelists in the technology underlying the DNS, the manner in which domain names can be used, and the application of the policies and rules applicable to domain name disputes. Improvements in the process might be developed to help panelists verify the manner in which domain names are used, either through self-help mechanisms or by changing the rules to request this information from the respondents. Dispute resolution providers could provide training for panelists on a regular basis, with such training being a requirement to maintain panelist status with that provider.

Thorough and detailed self-help tools might also be developed to enable respondents to better understand the UDRP process itself, the timeline involved, and the substance and format of an effective response to better comprehend and respond to a UDRP action.[122]

• *Revised funding and compensation structures.* Under the current funding structure, the revenue for panelists depends on the volume of cases, thereby either creating a disincentive to spend a sufficient amount of time reviewing the facts in a case and writing a well-thought-out opinion, or creating an incentive for marketing strategy and tactics to attract cases by defining lucrative niches, which may or may not correspond to justice in dispute resolution proceedings. Observers assert that such niches exist and that complainants often forum shop—selecting dispute resolution service providers based on their past record of favorable (to the complainant's position) rulings.

Since some parties believe that the $1150 to $1500 fee for filing a complaint regarding a single domain name is already expensive, there is some resistance to any proposed increase. In addition, increasing the fees paid to resolve or avoid a dispute raises the likelihood that, on the one hand, individual domain name holders would be discouraged from employing dispute resolution processes, while, on the other hand, well-financed domain name holders might be discouraged from filing large numbers of not completely justified complaints.

---

[122]Early in 2005 the World Intellectual Property Organization posted on its Web site an "informal overview of panel positions on key procedural and substantive issues," including references to decisions supporting each line of opinion. The "WIPO Overview of WIPO Panel Views on Selected UDRP Questions," which is not binding on the panelists, is available at <http://arbiter.wipo.int/domains/search/overview/index.html>.

On the compensation side, the fee paid to panelists, typically $1000 to $1750, is below the level that highly qualified attorneys and consultants say is needed to attract them to serve or continue to serve as panelists. While it may never be possible to set the level high enough to attract and retain highly paid specialists on the basis of compensation alone, it may be worth examining the fee schedule to see whether a higher level could be established while retaining the low cost of the UDRP.

Recommendation: Arbitral domain name dispute resolution processes, rather than national courts, should continue to be encouraged as the initial and primary vehicle for resolving most disputes associated with the rights to domain names.

Recommendation: The feasibility and desirability of five specific UDRP improvements should be further considered by ICANN: improving consistent use of arbitral precedents, establishing an internal appeals process, using three-member panels, improving panelist knowledge about the technology underlying the DNS, and improving the nature and structure of incentives in the process.

5.6.3 Disputes Concerning Internationalized Domain Names

The widespread deployment of internationalized domain names (IDNs)[123] may well compound the difficulty of resolving disputes over domain names by increasing the possibility that domain names will be created that appear to be the same, but are not.

The introduction of non-ASCII characters introduces a number of opportunities for conflicts, not about domain names themselves, but about characters that look alike. As the most trivial of examples, the upper-case Greek alpha and its Cyrillic equivalent are indistinguishable on the printed page from Roman upper case "A," but the three have different Unicode code points and strings containing them will compare differently. There are several similar combinations involving Roman, Greek, and Cyrillic scripts, but other examples appear in almost all pairings of alphabetic scripts. Another problem occurs because of the overlap between, for example, Simplified and Traditional Chinese, where the characters look different but have the same meanings.

These concerns about similar-appearing, or similarly interpreted, domain names are compounded by the observation that, in some circum-

[123]See Section 4.3 for discussion of internationalized domain names.

stances, a single registered domain name might have dozens, or even hundreds, of such variations. A cybersquatter could turn such conflicts into a potentially lucrative business by offering to sell such variant names to the "legitimate" owner at a fee just below the cost of a UDRP proceeding. Some of the registries and communities that would be most affected have concluded that it is preferable to shift the problem, to the degree possible, from conflict resolution to conflict avoidance by imposing restrictions on the registration of domain names that would conflict or otherwise cause confusion. ICANN has reinforced this approach by creating a guideline that requires that an IDN must be registered only with regard to a specified language, which eliminates some of the difficulties encountered with mixed scripts.[124] This approach is discussed in more detail in Section 4.3.

One view is that the potential for confusion in these cases is not really different from that of existing similar-appearing domain names, for which it has been suggested that UDRP-based name conflict resolution is adequate and appropriate. But variations among similar-looking domain names are such as to generate, potentially, hundreds of possible conflicts with a given character string.

The Joint Engineering Team (JET) guideline model (see Section 4.3.3) addresses this problem by preventing some large fraction of the potential conflicts, rather than devising remedies for them after they occur. The JET guidelines take the position that IDN packages are atomic, and that there should be no mechanism for moving domain names in or out of one once it is created (see Section 4.3 for discussion of IDNs). Under that model, if a domain name conflict arises in the creation of such a package, the conflicting (already-registered or reserved) domain name is simply not placed in the new package. But if the conflicting domain name is later deleted, it does not become part of the later IDN package unless the domain names associated with that package are explicitly deleted and reregistered. That may or may not be the best possible model, but the alternatives, such as having domain names appear as reserved in two or more packages, with a priority order, lead to administrative, policy, or database management nightmares.

But there are constituencies that oppose such systems, some of them on the grounds that dispute resolution is adequate and others, perhaps, on the more cynical grounds that letting things go to dispute resolution permits them to collect registrar and registry fees on the names whether they are valid or not and encourages even more business in defensive registrations.

---

[124]Guidelines are available at <http://www.icann.org/general/idn-guidelines-20jun03.htm>.

Conclusion: The deployment of internationalized domain names introduces new sources of potential conflict over domain name rights. Reduction of such conflicts through guidelines and registration policies should be encouraged.

5.7 PROVISION AND PROTECTION OF WHOIS DATA

Issue: What is the appropriate balance among the various interests in Whois data?

As noted in Chapter 2, the Whois service began as a vehicle for network operators to find and contact those responsible for the operation of an Internet host when, for example, an operational problem arose. However, with the commercialization of the Internet, the Whois service has become an important and valuable tool for intellectual property owners and is often used by trademark owners to determine the identity of suspected infringers and cybersquatters. In addition, it is used by law enforcement agencies, such as the Federal Trade Commission in the United States, to track down the sources of fraudulent or other illegal uses of the Internet. At the same time, there has been concern about its real and potential exploitation by marketers and others who find the information about domain name registrants valuable. These uses have, in turn, given rise to significant and strongly held privacy concerns. Thus, while the ability to search the Whois database has always been limited, because of privacy concerns access and searching of Whois information have become more and more restricted over time.

5.7.1 Assessment of Whois Data Issues

In the early days of the DNS, there were few, if any, concerns about the misuse of Whois data, just as ensuring the integrity of DNS data was deemed to be unnecessary. However, the population of users of Whois data has increased markedly in scale and scope, and assumptions about the good intent of all users have become unfounded. Furthermore, under the UDRP, giving false Whois information and not responding to requests for information have led to a presumption of bad faith by the respondent.

For example, when Whois was used as a Unix command, trademark owners were able to retrieve a wide range of information, including contact information of the domain name registrant and a list of all domain names registered by one particular registrant. Later, and until 2001, Network Solutions, Inc. (NSI) allowed Internet users to retrieve a list of up to 50 domain names registered by a particular registrant, but then changed the maximum number to 10 registrations. Currently, none of the registrars allow Internet users freely to query their Whois databases to determine which domain names a particular registrant has registered. Many registrars charge a fee for each request for a list of domain names registered by one of their registrants. In addition, some of the registrars do not provide a domain name registrant's e-mail address in the contact information, but instead assign each registrant a generic e-mail address[125] that is linked to the e-mail address the registrant provided in registering its domain name.

Data Accuracy

Whois information can be inaccurate, out of date, or false. Indeed, registrants may provide fictitious names and addresses and fail to update any of their contact information promptly, if ever. ICANN's Registrar Accreditation Agreement contractually binds each of its accredited registrars to investigate and correct any reported inaccuracies in contact information for the domain names they maintain.

ICANN established in September 2002 the Whois Data Problem Reports System (WDPRS) to receive public reports of inaccurate or absent Whois data. The sixth amendment to its MoU with the DOC requires that ICANN publish an annual report containing an analysis of the received reports. According to its March 2004 report,[126] over the 18-month period from September 2002 through February 2004, the system received about 24,000 confirmed Whois inaccuracy reports, concerning about 16,000 different domain names. Of these, 82 percent concerned .com; 13 percent, .net; and 5 percent, .org. (An enhanced version of the system that will cover the new gTLDs as well as the legacy ones was launched in 2004.) The complaints received by each registrar were generally proportional to the number of names it registered. On average, each registrar received 4.8 complaints per year per 10,000 names managed. Somewhat more than a third of these complaints resulted in the correction of data or the removal of a domain name.

As a further step to improve Whois data accuracy, ICANN adopted the Whois Data Reminder Policy (WDRP) on March 27, 2003.[127] Since November 2003, all ICANN-accredited registrars must comply with the

[125]This could cause problems in a UDRP proceeding since the generic e-mail address could be interpreted as false and, consequently, a contributor to the presumption of bad faith on the part of the respondent.

[126]ICANN, "Community Experiences with the InterNIC Whois Data Problem Reports System," March 13, 2004, available at <http://www.icann.org/whois/wdprs-report-final-31mar04.htm>.

[127]ICANN, "Whois Data Reminder Policy," June 16, 2003, available at <http://www.icann.org/registrars/wdrp-htm>.

WDRP with respect to registrations they sponsor in all top-level domains for which they are accredited. At least annually, a registrar must present the current Whois information to registrants and remind them that provision of false Whois information can be grounds for cancellation of their domain name registration. Registrants must review their Whois data and make any corrections.

Data Privacy

ICANN posted a staff manager's issues report on privacy issues related to Whois on May 13, 2003,[128] that spelled out a catalog of the issues, the stakeholders, and their apparent positions on the issues. The issues concerned the data collected, including its quality, handling, disclosure, and use; the classification of registrants (i.e., political, commercial, individual); and commercial confidentiality and rights in data.

The various stakeholders were viewed as placing emphasis on different issues. Non-commercial users were viewed as focusing on privacy, whereas commercial users were seen as concerned with accessibility to enforce accountability of uses. The intellectual property interests were understood to stress the importance of ready access to support investigations of intellectual property abuse, while ISPs support it to facilitate resolution of network problems and identification of the sources of spam. Registrars and registries view registrant data as an important business asset that should not be made available to competitors, while at the same time registrars need to access registrant data of competitors to confirm authorization of transfers. Registrars and registries both bear the expense of providing the services and, therefore, have strong incentives to reduce the cost of doing so.

As a consequence of these differences in emphasis among stakeholders, the policy issues surrounding Whois services (as opposed to the Whois protocol) are often framed in adversarial terms. On the one hand, trademark holders and their representatives want comprehensive and free access to all Whois data and would like improvements in Whois services, such as higher quality in the Whois data and the ability to consolidate data across Whois services more easily. They see Whois data as an essential resource in the pursuit of those who compromise their trademarks in

[128]ICANN, "Staff Manager's Issues Report on Privacy Issues Related to Whois," May 13, 2003, available at <http://www.icann.org/gnso/issue-reports/whois-privacy-report-13may03.htm>.

domain names.[129] On the other hand, those who are concerned about individual privacy highlight the problems that could be associated with unconstrained access to Whois data—from junk mailers and marketers to those who may use such data to facilitate more serious, illegal activities such as identity theft.

In recognition of the complexity of the issues and interests involved, the ICANN staff manager's issues report recommended as the next step the formation of a Whois/privacy steering group in the Generic Names Supporting Organization (GNSO) to conduct a fact-finding and issues definition process. Following on the work of that steering group, the Names Council of the GNSO in October 2003 launched three simultaneous task forces on various aspects of Whois privacy. The council intended to align their recommendations for submission to the ICANN board.

Task Force 1 (TF1) was charged with examining what contractual changes (if any) would be required to allow registrars and registries to protect domain name holder data from data mining[130] for marketing purposes. Task Force 2 (TF2) was asked to address issues concerning the data to be collected from registrants, their options to restrict access to the data and be informed of its use, and their ability to remove certain data elements from public access and receive notice if it is accessed. Task Force 3 (TF3) was tasked with looking at verification of the data collected, considering both errors and deliberate falsification. The three task forces presented their preliminary reports at the end of May 2004. They have been posted on the ICANN Web site for comment.[131] Among the significant issues and positions identified were the following.

- *Local law.*[132] In some cases, national privacy laws conflict with the provisions of ICANN's agreement requiring the registrars to collect and

---

[129]In a UDRP proceeding, for example, trademark owners are often required to show a "pattern of conduct" by the respondent of registering domain names incorporating the trademarks of other parties. Unless a trademark owner can guess the domain names registered by the respondent, it can incur considerable costs in obtaining this information, since the respondent may have used several different registrars in registering its domain names or provided slightly different contact details for each registration.

[130]"Data mining" as used here means the use of computerized techniques to extract data about registrants from registrar Whois files in large quantities. Often these techniques are designed to overcome specific limitations imposed by registrars on the number of names that may be requested. The lists are then used for unsolicited mailings (spam) and other possibly illicit (identity theft) purposes.

[131]Links to the preliminary reports are available at <http://gnso.icann.org/issues/whois-privacy/index.shtml>.

[132]For this and the next two items, see the report of TF2 available at <http://gnso.icann.org/issues/whois-privacy/index.shtml>.

make accessible certain data elements about registrants. The ICANN registry/registrar agreement should be modified to exempt registrars who obey local law from the conflicting provisions of the agreement.

- *Data elements.* All of the data elements currently collected are considered by at least some constituencies to be required, although some constituencies dispute the needs for some of them. No consensus exists on whether new elements are needed and whether some existing elements should be made voluntary. The issue is less what should be collected by registries/registrars and more what data should be made available for public access.
- *Publication of data.* Whois data has a wide range of uses (as discussed above.) It is also subject to abuses—telemarketing, identity theft, spamming, stalking, and abuse and harassment have been reported, though not quantified. There is a need to achieve a balance between accessibility and privacy. Possible approaches include tiered access, in which different types of users would have access to different subsets of the data; proxy registration services that would substitute third-party for registrant data and control access to the latter; and the ability of registrants to opt out of publication of certain data on a case-by-case basis. The latter approach has been adopted by some ccTLDs.
- *Data mining and marketing.*[133] If only non-sensitive data (generally, technical information) were to be available via Whois, it would have little value, be unlikely to be data mined, and have little impact on privacy. However, to the extent that sensitive data (generally, personal contact information) is publicly available through registry/registrar Whois services, TF1 members agreed that at a minimum the requestor of Whois information should be required to identify (and authenticate) itself to the Whois provider together with its reasons for seeking the data. They left open the issue, however, of whether notice to the registrant of such a request should be required. They also left open the question of whether and under what conditions automated access to Whois data could be allowed and to whom. Among the possibilities would be enabling a restricted license that would provide data to approved requestors for recognized purposes in human-readable format only. Requestors could be approved generally and centrally (a white list) or locally and specifically (an individual use list).

---

[133]See the report of TF1 available at <http://gnso.icann.org/issues/whois-privacy/index.shtml>.

5.7.2 Whois and Internationalized Domain Names[134]

Just as it does for the UDRP, the introduction of internationalized domain names (IDNs) raises technical and institutional issues for the Whois service. For the most part, these are issues about the languages in which Whois queries will be posed and responded to.

At the basic query level, the current Whois service expects to receive ASCII characters only; it cannot receive queries in Unicode (which is used to encode the many different character sets of contemporary human languages), and its responses are similarly in ASCII. But in an internationalized environment, domain names will not all be written in ASCII (although, as explained in Section 4.3, they will all be mapped into ASCII strings). This raises the first question: What character sets should be acceptable in a query? The choices include not only Unicode, but also IDNA puny code (see Section 4.3) and local character sets, or some combination of them.

Similarly, responses to Whois queries are currently provided in ASCII. This raises the second question: What language should be acceptable in a response, and how should it be encoded? The choices of language include the language of the nation in which the registrar or the registrant is located or English. Or one might permit some "international languages," such as English, Chinese, French, Spanish, Russian, Arabic, and so on. If the response is to be useful to most questioners on the international Internet, then would it be reasonable to expect them to have to hire translators? Or should the Whois registrant be required to list its information in some commonly accepted language? If the language is other than English, then issues about coding arise that are similar to the question regarding queries. For example, should Unicode be required and, if so, which encoding form of Unicode? Or should local character encodings, which might be in much more general use with the particular relevant language or script, but less easily accessible internationally, be permitted?

A third question arises since IDN practices for complex languages actually create packages of reserved names (see Section 4.3). In such cases, how much information should Whois provide about other names in the package in response to a query about one of them?

None of these issues had been resolved by September 2004. However, as IDNs are more widely adopted, the lack of their early resolution will increase the likelihood of problems arising and the difficulty of introducing the necessary changes.

---

[134]This section draws on material in John C. Klensin, "'Whois' Internationalization Issues," presentation at the ICANN meeting in Carthage, Tunisia, October 2003, available at <http://www.icann.org/presentations/klensin-whois-carthage-29oct03.ppt>.

On the other hand, the work on a new protocol to replace Whois (see Section 5.7.3) has explicitly addressed some internationalization issues. Although that work does not address all of the issues raised above, it at least makes it possible to transmit and receive Unicode characters without somehow encoding them into ASCII form and, if it is desired to support local character encodings, to construct a framework for identifying and using them.

Recommendation: The IETF and ICANN should address Whois data internationalization issues with high priority in order to enable their resolution and implementation of the results together with the widespread introduction of IDNs.

5.7.3 Conclusion and Recommendation

The issues concerning the accuracy of and access to Whois data engage the interests of many stakeholders with legitimate but sometimes conflicting interests. They entail actual and potential conflicts with differing national privacy laws. Furthermore, the ICANN agreements with registrars and registries obligate them to accept only consensus policies. Consequently, the best way to achieve improvements in the Whois policies and practices appears to be through the consensus policy development process in which ICANN is engaged. Attempts by individual governments to impose specific requirements on Whois, such as recent legislative initiatives in the U.S. Congress,[135] can interfere with these efforts and have counterproductive consequences by inducing registrants to find ways to hide their identities.

Conclusion: Legislative or technical initiatives that construe Whois narrowly will not be productive in the long run and serve only to energize those constituencies that perceive their interests as being compromised.

The committee agrees that access to Whois data should be viewed as a tiered decision, and not as a binary decision. Gradations should exist, as they do in local telephone directories where entries are included by default, but where unlisted numbers can be obtained. Moreover, under certain conditions, law enforcement officials can obtain an individual's information, even if the individual has opted not to be included in the public directory. Alternatively, individuals can sometimes embellish their ge-

[135]H.R. 3754, 108th Congress, Fraudulent Online Identities Sanctions Act (FOISA).

neric entry (for a fee). Thus, changes to the Whois process need to be conceived in a systematic way that accounts for the varying legitimate perspectives. The example of local telephone directories is offered for illustrative purposes only. The committee is not recommending this specific model per se, although the analogy can also be helpful since personal data (name, address, and phone number) are made publicly available through printed (and now online) directories, just as they are through Whois services.

Recommendation: Future systems that support Whois data management and access should be designed to allow for gradations in access while maintaining some degree of free access to Whois information. The Whois protocol will have to be replaced to accommodate the desired gradations in access.[136]

[136]The IETF had, by October 2004, approved as "standards-track" documents (see Box 3.3) several elements of a proposed replacement protocol, which is called IRIS and defined by the CRISP Working Group, that will implement this capability. The protocol also addresses most or all of the other perceived deficiencies of the Whois protocol, including its inability to deal with non-ASCII characters. More detail on those deficiencies is available in the statement of requirements for the new protocol in A. Newton, "Cross Registry Internet Service Protocol (CRISP) Requirements," RFC 3707, February 2004, available at <http://www.rfc-editor.org>. However, in May 2005 it was still unclear how long it would take for all the elements to be approved, published, and implemented.

6

Internet Navigation: Emergence and Evolution

As the previous chapters show, the Domain Name System has been a foundation for the rapid development of the Internet. Domain names appear on the signposts designating origins and destinations linked by the Internet and in the addresses used by the principal applications traversing the Internet—e-mail and the World Wide Web. And they have been useful for navigating across the Internet: given a domain name, many Web browsers will automatically expand it into the Uniform Resource Locator (URL) of a Web site; from a domain name, many e-mail users can guess the e-mail address of an addressee. For these reasons, memorable domain names may often acquire high value. Their registrants believe that searchers can more readily find and navigate to their offerings.

However, as the Internet developed in size, scope, and complexity, the Domain Name System (DNS) was unable to satisfy many Internet users' needs for navigational assistance. How, for example, can a single Web page be found from among billions when only its subject and not the domain name in its URL is known? To meet such needs, a number of new types of aids and services for Internet navigation were developed.[1] While, in the end, these generally rely on the Domain Name System to find specific Internet Protocol (IP) addresses, they greatly expand the range of ways in which searchers can identify the Internet location of the resource they seek.

[1]The difference between a navigation aid and a navigation service is one of degree. A navigation service, such as the offerings of a search engine service provider, are more elaborate and extensive than those offered by a navigation aid, such as the bookmark feature of a Web browser.

These navigational aids and services have, in return, relieved some of the pressure on the Domain Name System to serve as a de facto directory of the Internet and have somewhat reduced the importance of the registration of memorable domain names. Because of these tight linkages between the DNS and Internet navigation, this chapter and the next ones address—at a high level—the development of the major types of Internet navigational aids and services. This chapter is concerned with their past development. The next chapter deals with their current state. And the final chapter on Internet navigation, Chapter 8, considers the technological prospects and the institutional issues facing them.

After describing the distinctive nature of Internet navigation, this chapter traces the evolution of a variety of aids and services for Internet navigation. While its primary focus is on navigating the World Wide Web, it does not cover techniques for navigation within Web sites, which is the subject of specialized attention by Web site designers, operators, and researchers.[2]

6.1 THE NATURE OF INTERNET NAVIGATION

Navigation across the Internet is sometimes compared to the well-studied problem of readers navigating through collections of printed material and other physical artifacts in search of specific documents or specific artifacts. (See the Addendum to this chapter: "Searching the Web Versus Searching Libraries.") That comparison illustrates the differences in the technical and institutional contexts for Internet navigation. Internet navigation for some purposes is similar to searches in library environments and relies on the same tools, whereas navigation for other purposes may be performed quite differently via the Internet. The multiple purposes and diverse characteristics listed below combine to make navigating to a resource across the Internet a much more varied and complex activity than those previously encountered. The library examples provide a point of reference and a point of departure for discussion in subsequent chapters.

6.1.1 Vast and Varied Resources for Multiple Purposes

First, the Internet connects its users to a vast collection of heterogeneous resources that are used for many purposes, including the dissemination of information; the marketing of products and services; communication with others; and the delivery of art, entertainment, and a wide range of commercial and public services. The kinds of resources connected to the Internet include:

---

[2]See, for example, Merlyn Holmes, *Web Usability & Navigation: A Beginner's Guide*, McGraw-Hill/Osborne, Berkeley, Calif., 2002; and Louis Rosenfeld and Peter Morville, *Information Architecture for the World Wide Web: Designing Large Scale Sites*, 2nd edition, O'Reilly & Associates, Sebastopol, Calif., 2002.

• Documents that differ in language (human and programming), vocabulary (including words, product numbers, zip codes, latitudes and longitudes, links, symbols, and images), formats (such as the Hypertext Markup Language (HTML), Portable Document Format (PDF), or Joint Photographic Experts Group (JPEG) format), character sets, and source (human or machine generated).

• Non-textual information, such as audio and video files, and interactive games. The volume of online content (in terms of the number of bytes) in image, sound, and video formats is much greater than that of most library collections and is expanding rapidly.

• Transaction services, such as sales of products or services, auctions, tax return preparation, matchmaking, and travel reservations.

• Dynamic information, such as weather forecasts, stock market information, and news, which can be constantly changing to incorporate the latest developments.

• Scientific data generated by instruments such as sensor networks and satellites are contributing to a "data deluge."[3] Many of these data are stored in repositories on the Internet and are available for research and educational purposes.

• Custom information constructed from data in a database (such as product descriptions and pricing) in response to a specific query (e.g., price comparisons of a product listed for sale on multiple Web sites).

Consequently, aids or services that support Internet navigation face the daunting problem of finding and assigning descriptive terms to each of these types of resource so that it can be reliably located. Searchers face the complementary problem of selecting the aids or services that will best enable them to locate the information, entertainment, communication link, or service that they are seeking.

6.1.2 Two-sided Process

Second, Internet navigation is two-sided: it must serve the needs both of the searchers who want to reach resources and of the providers that want their resources to be found by potential users.

From the searcher's perspective, navigating the Internet resembles to some extent the use of the information retrieval systems that were developed

---

[3]See Tony Hey and Anne Trefethen, "The Data Deluge: An e-Science Perspective," *Grid Computing: Making the Global Infrastructure a Reality*, Fran Berman, Geoffrey Fox, and Anthony J.G. Hey, editors, Wiley, 2003.

over the last several decades within the library and information science[4] and computer science communities.[5] However, library-oriented retrieval systems, reflecting the well-developed norms of librarians, were designed to describe and organize information so that users could readily find exactly what they were looking for. In many cases, the same people and organizations were responsible both for the design of the retrieval systems and for the processes of indexing, abstracting, and cataloging the information to be retrieved. In this information services world, the provider's goal was to make description and search as neutral as possible, so that every document relevant to a topic would have an equal chance of being retrieved.[6] While this goal of retrieval neutrality has carried over to some Internet navigation services and resource providers, it is by no means universal. Indeed, from the perspective of many resource providers, particularly commercial providers, attracting users via the Internet requires the application to Internet navigation of non-neutral marketing approaches deriving from advertising and public relations as developed for newspapers, magazines, radio, television, and yellow-pages directories.[7] Research on neutral, community-based technology for describing Internet resources is an active area in information and computer science and is a key element of the Semantic Web (see Box 7.1).[8]

---

[4]For an overview, see Elaine Svenonius, *The Intellectual Foundation of Information Organization*, MIT Press, Cambridge, Mass., 2000; and Christine L. Borgman, *From Gutenberg to the Global Information Infrastructure: Access to Information in the Networked World*, MIT Press, Cambridge, Mass., 2000.

[5]For an overview, see Ricardo Baeza-Yates and Berthier Ribiero-Neto, *Modern Information Retrieval*, Addison-Wesley, Boston, 1999; and Karen Sparck Jones and Peter Willett, editors, *Readings in Information Retrieval*, Morgan Kaufmann, San Francisco, 1997. For typical examples of early work on information retrieval systems, see, for example, George Schecter, editor, *Information Retrieval—A Critical View*, Thompson Book Company, Washington, D.C., 1967. For work on retrieval from large databases, see the proceedings of the annual text retrieval conference (TREC), currently sponsored by the National Institute of Standards and Technology and the Advanced Research and Development Activity, available at <http://trec.nist.gov>.

[6]See Svenonius, *The Intellectual Foundation of Information Organization*, 2000.

[7]See, for example, John Caples and Fred E. Hahn, *Tested Advertising Methods*, 5th edition, Prentice-Hall, New York, 1998.

[8]E. Bradley, N. Collins, and W.P. Kegelmeyer, "Feature Characterization in Scientific Datasets," pp. 1-12 in *Proceedings of the 4th International Conference on Advances in Intelligent Data Analysis* (*Lecture Notes in Computer Science*, Vol. 2189), Springer-Verlag, 2001; V. Brilhante, "Using Formal Metadata Descriptions for Automated Ecological Modeling," pp. 90-95 in *Environmental Decision Support Systems and Artificial Intelligence*, AAAI Press, Menlo Park, Calif., 1999; E. Hovy, "Using an Ontology to Simplify Data Access," *Communications of the ACM* 46(1):47-49, 2003; OWL Web Ontology Language Guide, "W3C Recommendation (10 February 2004)," November 24, 2004, available at <http://www.w3.org/TR/owl-guide>; and P. Wariyapola, S.L. Abrams, A.R. Robinson, K. Streitlien, N.M. Patrikalakis, P. Elisseeff, and H. Schmidt, "Ontology and Metadata Creation for the Poseidon Distributed Coastal Zone Management System," *Proceedings of the IEEE Forum on Research and Technology Advances in Digital Libraries*, IEEE Computer Society, Los Alamitos, Calif., 1999, pp. 180-189.

For commercial providers, therefore, the challenge is how to identify and reach—in the complex, diverse, and global audience accessible via the Internet—potential users who are likely to be interested (or can be made interested) in the provider's materials. That is done in traditional marketing and public relations through the identification of media and places (television or radio programs, magazines, newspapers in specific locations) that an audience with the desired common characteristics (for example, 18- to 24-year-old males) frequents. Similar approaches can be applied on the Internet (see Section 7.2.2), but unlike the traditional media, the Internet also offers providers the distinctive and extremely valuable opportunity to capture their specific audience during the navigation process itself, just when they are searching for what the provider offers—for example, by paying to be listed or featured in a navigation service's response to specific words or phrases. (See "Monetized Search" in Section 7.1.7.) Marketers have found ways to use the specific characteristics of the Internet,[9] just as they have developed methods appropriate for each new medium.[10] This has led, for example, to the establishment of companies that are devoted to finding ways to manipulate Internet navigation services to increase the ranking of a client's Web site and, in response, to the development of countermeasures by the services. (See "Search Engine Marketing and Optimization" in Section 7.1.7.)

For non-commercial resources, the situation is somewhat different, since the providers generally have fewer resources and may have less incentive to actively seek users, at least to the extent of paying for Web advertising or search engine marketing. At the same time, the existence of a specific non-commercial resource may be well known to the community of its potential users. For example, the members of a scholarly community or a non-profit organization are likely to be aware of the Internet resources relevant to their concerns. Those new to a community or outside it are dependent on Internet navigation tools to locate these resources.

Internet navigation is a complex interplay of the interests of both the searchers for and the providers of resources. On the Internet, the

---

[9]See, for example, Joe Cappo, *The Future of Advertising: New Media, New Clients, New Consumers in the Post-Television Age*, McGraw-Hill, New York, 2003; and Barbara Cox and William Koelzer, *Internet Marketing*, Prentice-Hall, New York, 2004.

[10]It should be noted that the Internet, by making the marginal cost of an e-mail message extremely low, has also enabled providers to conduct a non-discriminating search for potential users by broadcasting spam e-mail. Although this might be considered a variant of Internet navigation, where the provider actively advertises its location to a vast audience whose members may or may not be interested, its one-sided benefits and frequent use for dishonest or illegal purposes disqualify it for inclusion in this report, which focuses on searcher-beneficial navigation aids and services.

librarian's ideal of neutral information retrieval often confronts the reality of self-interested marketing.

6.1.3 Complexity and Diversity of Uses, Users, and Providers

Third, the complexity and diversity of uses of resources on the Internet, of their users, and of their providers significantly complicate Internet navigation. It becomes a multidimensional activity that incorporates behaviors ranging from random browsing to highly organized searching and from discovering a new resource to accessing a previously located resource.[11]

Studies in information science show that navigation in an information system is simplest and most effective when the content is homogeneous, the purposes of searching are consistent and clearly defined, and the searchers have common purposes and similar levels of skills.[12] Yet, Internet resources per se often represent the opposite case in all of these respects. Their content is often highly heterogeneous; their diverse users' purposes are often greatly varied; the resources the users are seeking are often poorly described; and the users often have widely varying degrees of skills and knowledge. Thus, as the resources accessible via the Internet expand in quantity and diversity of content, number and diversity of users, and variety of applications, the challenges facing Internet navigation become even more complex.

Indeed, prior to the use of the Internet as a means to access information, many collections of information resources, whether in a library or an online information system, were accessed by a more homogenous collection of users. It was generally known when compiling the collection whether the content should be organized for specialists or lay people, and whether skill in the use of the resource could be assumed. Thus, navigation aids, such as indexes or catalogs, were readily optimized for their specific content and for the goals of the people searching them. Health information in a database intended for searching by physicians could be indexed or cataloged using specific and highly detailed terminology that assumed expert knowledge. Similarly, databases of case law and statute law assumed a significant amount of knowledge of the law. In fields such as medicine and law, learning the navigation tools and the vocabularies of the field is an essential part of professional education. Many such databases are now accessible by specialists via the Internet and continue to assume a skillful and knowledgeable set of users, even though in some

---

[11]See Shan-ju Chang and Ronald E. Rice, "Browsing: A Multidimensional Framework," *Annual Review of Information Science and Technology* 28:231-276, 1993.

[12]See Borgman, *From Gutenberg to the Global Information Infrastructure*, 2000.

cases they are also accessible by the general public. With the growth in Internet use, however, many more non-specialist users have ready access to the Web and are using it to seek medical, legal, or other specialized information. The user community for such resources is no longer well defined. Few assumptions of purpose, skill level, or prior knowledge can be made about the users of a Web information resource. Consequently, it is general-purpose navigation aids and services and less specialized (and possibly lower-quality) information resources that must serve their needs.

6.1.4 Lack of Human Intermediaries

Fourth, the human intermediaries who traditionally linked searchers with specific bodies of knowledge or services—such as librarians, travel agents, and real estate agents—are often not available to users as they seek information on the Internet. Instead, users generally navigate to the places they seek and assess what they find on their own, relying on the aid of digital intermediaries—the Internet's general navigation aids and services, as well as the specialized sites for shopping, travel, job hunting, and so on. Human intermediaries' insights and assistance are generally absent during the navigation process.

Human search intermediaries help by selecting, collecting, organizing, conserving, and prioritizing information resources so that they are available for access.[13] They combine their knowledge of a subject area and of information-seeking behavior with their skills in searching databases to assist people in articulating their needs. For example, travelers have relied on travel agents to find them the best prices, best routes, and best hotels, and to provide services such as negotiating with hotels, airlines, and tour companies when things go wrong. Intermediaries often ask their clients about the purposes for which they want information (e.g., what kind of trip the seekers desire and how they expect to spend their time; what they value in a home or neighborhood; or what research questions their term paper is trying to address), and elicit additional details concerning the problem. These intermediaries also may help in evaluating content retrieved from databases and other sources by offering counsel on what to trust, what is current, and what is important to consider in the content retrieved.

With the growth of the Internet and the World Wide Web, a profound change in the nature of professional control over information is taking place. Travel agents and real estate agents previously maintained tight control over access to fares and schedules and to listings of homes for

---

[13]See Chapter 7, "Whither, or Wither, Libraries?," in Borgman, *From Gutenberg to the Global Information Infrastructure*, 2000.

sale. Until recently, many of these resources were considered proprietary, especially in travel and real estate, and consumers were denied direct access to their content. Information seekers had little choice but to delegate their searches to an expert—a medical professional, librarian, paralegal, records analyst, travel agent, real estate agent, and so on. Today, travel reservation and real estate information services are posting their information on the Internet and actively seeking users. Specialized travel sites, such as Expedia.com and travelocity.com, help the user to search through and evaluate travel options. Similar sites serve the real estate market. Travel agents that remain in business must get their revenue from other value-added services, such as planning customized itineraries and tours and negotiating with brokers. Although house hunters now can do most of their shopping online, in most jurisdictions they still need real estate agents with access to house keys to show them properties and to guide them in executing the legal transactions. Libraries have responded to the Web by providing "virtual reference services" in addition to traditional on-site reference services.[14] Other entities, including the U.S. Department of Education, have supported the creation of non-library-based reference services that use the Internet to connect users with "people who can answer questions and support the development of skills" without going through a library intermediary.[15]

6.1.5 Democratization of Information Access and Provision

Fifth, the Internet has hugely democratized and extended both the offering of and access to information and services. Barriers to entry, whether cost or credentials, have been substantially reduced. Anyone with modest skill and not much money can provide almost anything online, and anyone can access it from almost anywhere. Rarely are credentials required for gaining access to content or services that are connected to the public Internet, although paid or free registration may be necessary to gain access to some potentially relevant material. Not only commercial and technical information are openly accessible, but also the full range of political speech, of artistic expression, and of personal opinion are readily available on the public Internet—even though efforts are continually be-

---

[14]See, for example, the more than 600 references about such services in Bernie Sloan, "Digital Reference Services Bibliography," Graduate School of Library and Information Science, University of Illinois at Urbana-Champaign, November 18, 2003, available at <http://www.lis.uiuc.edu/~b-sloan/digiref.html>.

[15]For example, the Virtual Reference Desk is "a project dedicated to the advancement of digital reference." See <http://www.vrd.org/about.shtml>. This service is sponsored by the U.S. Department of Education.

ing made to impose restrictions on access to some materials by various populations in a number of countries.[16]

In a great many countries, anyone can set up a Web site—and many people do. The freedom of the press does not belong just to those who own one; now nearly anyone can have the opportunity to publish via a virtual press—the World Wide Web.[17] Whether or not what they publish will be read is another matter. That depends on whether they will be found, and, once found, whether they can provide content worthy of perusal—at least by someone.

For the most part, in many places, provision of or access to content or services is uncensored and uncontrolled. On the positive side, the Internet enables access to a global information resource of unprecedented scope and reach. Its potential impact on all aspects of human activity is profound.[18] But the institutions that select, edit, and endorse traditionally published information have no role in determining much of what is published via the Internet. The large majority of material reachable via the Internet has never gone through the customary editing or selection processes of professional journals or of newspapers, magazines, and books.[19] So in this respect as well, there has been significant disintermediation, leaving Internet users with relatively few solid reference points as they navigate through a vast collection of information of varying accuracy and quality. In response to this widely acknowledged problem, some groups have offered evaluations of materials on the World Wide Web.[20] One

---

[16]These range from the efforts of parents to prevent their children from accessing age-inappropriate sites to those made by governments to prevent their citizens from accessing politically sensitive sites. The current regulations placed on libraries in the United States to filter content are available at <http://hraunfoss.fcc.gov/edocs_public/attachmatch/FCC-03-188A1.pdf>. See also, information on the increasing sophistication of filtering efforts in China in David Lee, "When the Net Goes Dark and Silent," *South China Morning Post*, October 2, 2002, available at <http://cyber.law.harvard.edu/people/edelman/pubs/scmp-100102-2.pdf>. For additional information, see Jonathan Zittrain and Benjamin Edelman, *Empirical Analysis of Internet Filtering in China*, Beckman Center for Internet & Society, Harvard University, 2002, available at <http://cyber.law.harvard.edu/filtering/china/>.

[17]The rapid growth in the number of blogs (short for Web logs) illustrates this. According to "How Much Information?," there were 2.9 million active Web logs in 2003. See Peter Lyman and Hal R. Varian, "How Much Information?," 2003, retrieved from <http://www.sims.berkeley.edu/research/projects/how-much-info-2003> on April 27, 2005.

[18]See Borgman, *From Gutenberg to the Global Information Infrastructure*, 2000; and Thomas Friedman, "Is Google God?", *New York Times*, June 29, 2003.

[19]However, it must be acknowledged that many "traditional" dissemination outlets (e.g., well-known media companies) operate Web sites that provide material with editorial review.

[20]See, for example, *The Information Quality WWW Virtual Library* at <http://www.ciolek.com/WWWVL-InfoQuality.html> and *Evaluating Web Sites: Criteria and Tools* at <http://www.library.cornell.edu/okuref/research/webeval.html>.

example is the Librarians' Index to the Internet,[21] whose motto is "Information You Can Trust."

6.1.6 Lack of Context or Lack of Skill

Sixth, most general-purpose Internet navigation services can assume nothing about the context of a search beyond what is in the query itself. The circumstances of the person searching the Internet—who could be anyone, searching for almost any purpose, from almost any place—are generally not known or, if known, not used.[22] While an unskilled user planning a European trip who types "Paris" into a navigation service may expect to receive back only information on the city of Paris, France, or if studying the *Iliad* may expect to find out about the Greek hero, the navigation service has no knowledge of that context. If it relies on the text alone, it may return information about both, as well as information about sources for plaster of paris, the small town in Texas, movies set in Paris, and people with the first or family name of Paris.

While any general-purpose navigation service would be unable to ascertain which of those specific answers was desired, the person initiating an Internet request always knows its context, and if experienced or trained, should be able to incorporate some of that information in the query. An experienced searcher could incorporate context by expanding the query to "Paris France," "Paris and Iliad," "Paris Texas," or "plaster of paris." So the lack of context in many navigation requests is closely related to the user's level of training or experience in the use of navigation services.[23]

---

[21]"Librarians' Index to the Internet (LII) is a searchable, annotated subject directory of more than 12,000 Internet resources selected and evaluated by librarians for their usefulness to users of public libraries. LII is used by both librarians and the general public as a reliable and efficient guide to Internet resources." Quoted from <http://lii.org/search/file/about>, accessed on May 2, 2004.

[22]An online advertising company, DoubleClick, launched a service in 2000 to track people's Internet usage in order to serve ads based on personal taste. After considerable controversy, especially from federal regulators and privacy advocates, and an inability to develop an adequate market, the profiling service was terminated at the end of 2001. See Stefanie Olsen, "DoubleClick Turns Away from Ad Profiles," *c/net news.com*, January 8, 2002, available at <http://news.com.com/2100-1023-803593.html>. However, Yahoo! indicates in its privacy policy that it does use information provided by those who register at its site "to customize the advertising and content you see, fulfill your requests for products and services . . . ."

[23]See, for example, Steven Johnson, "Digging for Googleholes," *Slate.com*, July 16, 2003, available at <http://slate.msn.com/id/2085668/>; Donald O. Case, *Looking for Information: A Survey of Research on Information Seeking, Needs, and Behavior*, Academic Press, San Diego, Calif., 2002; and Paul Solomon, "Discovering Information in Context," *Annual Review of Information Science and Technology*, Blaise Cronin, editor, Information Today, Inc., Medford, N.J., 2002, pp. 229-264.

The incorporation of context is also related to the degree to which the navigation service is itself specialized. When people searched in traditional information sources, the selection of the source usually carried information about the context for a search (e.g., seeking a telephone number in the White Pages for Manhattan in particular, or looking for a home in the multiple listing service for Boston specifically). Furthermore, there were often intermediaries who could obtain contextual information from the information seeker and use that to choose the right source and refine the information request. Although the former approach is also available on the Internet through Internet white pages and Internet real estate search sites, the latter is just developing through the virtual reference services mentioned earlier.

General-purpose navigation services are exploring a variety of mechanisms for incorporating context into search. For example, both Yahoo! and Google now allow local searches, specified by adding a location to the search terms. The site-flavored Google Search customizes searches originating at a Web site to return search results based on a profile of the site's content. Other recent search engines such as Vivisimo (www.vivisimo.com) return search results in clusters that correspond to different contexts—for example, a search on the keyword "network" returns one cluster of results describing cable networks, another on network games, and so on.[24]

Still, issues of context complicate Internet navigation because the most widely used navigation services are general purpose—searching the vast array of objects on the Internet with equal attention—and because many users are not experienced or trained and have no access to intermediaries to assist them.

6.1.7 Lack of Persistence

Seventh, there is no guarantee of persistence for material at a particular location on the Internet. While there is no reason to believe that everything made accessible through the Internet should persist indefinitely, there are a great many materials whose value is such that many users would want to access them at the same Internet address at indefinite times in the future. For example, throughout this report there are two kinds of references: those to printed materials—books, journals, newspapers—and those to digital resources that are located via Web pages. There is a very high probability that whenever this report is read, even years after its publication, that every one of the referenced printed materials will be ac-

---

[24]See Chris Gaither, "Google Offers Sites Its Services," *Los Angeles Times*, June 19, 2004, p. c2. Also see <http://www.google.com/services/siteflavored.html>, accessed on June 18, 2004.

cessible in unchanged form through (though not necessarily in) any good library (at least in the United States). There is an equal certainty that whenever this report is read, even in the year of its publication, some of the referenced Web pages either will no longer be accessible or will no longer contain the precise material that was referenced. The proportion of missing or changed references will increase over time. To the extent that it would be valuable to locate the referenced Web material, there is a problem of persistence (see Box 6.1) of resources on the Internet.[25]

The problem of persistence arises because material connected to the Internet is not generally governed by the conventions, standards, and practices of preservation that evolved with regard to printed material. The material may change in many ways and for many reasons. It may remain the same, but the location may change because of a change of computers, or a redesign of a Web site, or a reorganization of files to save space, or a change in Internet service providers (ISPs).[26] Or it may be replaced at the same location by an improved version or by something entirely different but with the same title. It may disappear completely because the provider stops operating or decides not to provide it any more or it may be replaced by an adequate substitute, but at a different location. Thus, navigation to an item is often a one-time event. Incorporating a reference or a link to that item in another document is no guarantee that a future seeker will find the same item at the same location. Nor is there any guarantee that something once navigated to will be there when the recorded path is followed once more or that it will be the same as it was when first found.

The problem is exacerbated for material on the World Wide Web by its structure—a hyperlinked web of pages. Even if a specific Web page persists indefinitely, it is unlikely that the many pages to which it links will also persist for the same period of time, and so on along the path of linked pages. So to the extent that the persistent page relies on those to which it links, its persistence is tenuous.

---

[25]One example of the lack of persistence of important information is U.S. Government documents published only on the Web. The U.S. Government Printing Office has begun an effort to find and archive such electronic documents. See Florence Olsen, "A Crisis for Web Preservation," *Federal Computer Week*, June 21, 2004, available at <http://www.fcw.com/fcw/articles/2004/0621/pol-crisis-06-21-04.asp>.

[26]Thomas Phelps and Robert Wilensky of the University of California at Berkeley have suggested a way to overcome the difficulties caused by shifting locations. They add a small number of words carefully selected from the page to its URL. If the URL is no longer valid, the words can be used in a search engine to find the page's new location. See Thomas Phelps and Robert Wilensky, "Robust Hyperlinks: Cheap, Everywhere, Now," *Proceedings of the 8th International Conference on Digital Documents and Electronic Publishing* (*Lecture Notes in Computer Science*, Vol. 2023), Springer-Verlag, 2004.

BOX 6.1 Discovery, Retrieval, and Persistence

Navigation is a two-step process: discovery and then retrieval. The discovery process involves identifying the location of the desired material on a Web site. The retrieval process involves obtaining the located material at the identified URL. (See Box 6.2.) Discovery may find dynamically generated pages for which only a transient URL exists, such as driving directions between two locations or an online order, or a constant URL that has ever changing information, such as a weather service. It may not be possible or even feasible (last year's weather forecast) to retrieve the same pages again. Thus, not even a hyperlink to that material can be embedded in other pages, nor can the page be bookmarked for future reference.

Even if the resource is itself static, such as the text of a research report, it may be moved, invalidating the URL. More problematically, it may be necessary to decide whether what is retrieved a second time (even if it is in the same place) is the same as what was retrieved previously. Unless the original object and the (possibly) new one are identical bit-by-bit, the question of whether the two are "the same," or identical, raises long-standing questions that are typically very subjective and/or contextual: Is a translation into another language the same as the original? If a document is reformatted, but all of the words are the same, is it identical to the original? If a document is compressed, or transposed into a different character code, or adapted to a different version of a viewer program, is it still the same document? Is a second edition an acceptable match to a request for the first edition? And so on. For each of these questions, the correct answer is probably "sometimes," but "sometimes" is rarely a satisfactory answer, especially if it is to be evaluated by a computer system.

If things are abstracted further so that, instead of discovering a URL directly, the user utilizes an updatable bookmark that incorporates a reference to the discovery processes, the meaning of persistence becomes even more ambiguous. Such a bookmark, intended to reference a list of restaurants in a particular city, might upon being used not only discover a newer version of the same list, but also find a newer, more comprehensive, list from a different source and at an entirely different location on the network. So what is persistent in this case is not the answer, but the question.

These are arguably not new conundrums—analogies occur with editions of books and bibliographies, but the opportunities on the Internet for faster turnover and for changes of finer granularity, as well as the ability to update search indexes at very high frequency, make the meaning and achievement of Internet persistence more complex and ambiguous and difficult to understand for the casual user.

6.1.8 Scale

Eighth, the Internet—in particular, the World Wide Web—vastly exceeds even the largest traditional libraries in the amount of material that it makes accessible.[27] In 2003, the World Wide Web was estimated to contain 170 terabytes of content in its surface, readily accessible—public—sites. This compares with an estimated 10 terabytes of printed documents in the Library of Congress (which also contains many terabytes of material in other media). In addition, the "dark" Web is estimated to contain 400 to 450 times as much content in its databases and in other forms inaccessible to search engines,[28] a ratio that may be increasing. (See in Section 7.1.7 the discussion titled "The Deep, Dark, and Invisible Web.")

6.1.9 The Sum of the Differences

For all the reasons described above, navigation on the Internet is different from navigating through traditional collections of documents; finding information or services through the use of knowledgeable intermediaries; locating the television audience for a commercial or political message; or reaching the readers for an essay. Navigating the Internet is even more than the sum of all those differences over a much larger extent and variety of resources and a much greater number and diversity of users and providers.

Conclusion: Finding and accessing a desired resource via the Internet poses challenges that are substantially different from the challenges faced in navigating to resources in non-digital, non-networked environments because of differences in content, purpose, description, user community, institutional framework, context, skill, persistence, and scale.

Fortunately, the Internet has also served as the infrastructure for the development of new means for responding to these challenges. As the following section and the next chapter show, a wide range of navigation aids and services now permit large segments of the Internet to be traversed rapidly and efficiently in ways previously unimaginable, providing ready access to a vast world of human knowledge and experience to users across the globe and opening an international audience to purveyors of content and services no matter where they may be located.

---

[27]Because the Web contains a large amount of "format overhead" and non-reliable information, this comparison was disputed for the Web of 2000 (25-50 terabytes estimated) by researchers from OCLC. See Edward T. O'Neill et al., "Trends in the Evolution of the Public Web 1998-2002," *D-Lib Magazine* 9(4), 2003, at <http://www.dlib.org/dlib/april03/lavoie/04lavoie.html>.

[28]These data are taken from Lyman and Varian, "How Much Information?," 2003.

6.2 INTERNET NAVIGATION AIDS AND SERVICES—HISTORY

Aids and services to assist Internet navigation have had to evolve steadily to keep pace with the growth in the scale, scope, and complexity of material on the Internet.[29]

In the first years of the Internet,[30] the 1970s and 1980s, information was accessed through a two-step process: first, the host on which a desired resource resided was found,[31] and then the desired file was found.[32] A good example of this host-oriented navigation is the File Transfer Protocol (FTP). Retrieving a file using FTP required that the user (using FTP client software) already know the name of the host (which would be using FTP server software) on which the file was stored,[33] have a login name and password for that host (unless anonymous login was permitted), know a file name, and sometimes have other information such as an account name for computer time billing.[34] The File Transfer Protocol made it possible to retrieve data from any FTP server to which one was connected by a network. File names and server locations could be obtained in various ways—from friends, from newsgroups and mailing lists, from files that identified particular resources, or from a few archive servers that contained very large collections of files with locally created indexing. However, such ad hoc and labor-intensive processes do not scale well. More automated processes were needed as the number of Internet users and topics of interest increased substantially.

---

[29]The early period of rapid development of Internet navigation aids was not well documented, nor are there many good references. Many of the critical developments are included in this brief history, but it is not intended to be comprehensive.

[30]In this section, the "Internet" also includes the ARPANET. See Chapter 2.

[31]While a few protocols did not explicitly name a host, in most cases that meant that the host name was implicit in the service being requested (e.g., running a program that queried a central database that resides only on the Network Information Center (NIC) computer implies the host name of interest).

[32]At a technical level, this still occurs, but is less visible to the user. For example, a URL contains a domain (host) name, and the client (browser in the case of the Web) uses some protocol (usually the Hypertext Transfer Protocol (HTTP) in the case of the Web) to open a connection to a specified host. The rest of the URL is then transmitted to that host, which returns data or takes other action.

[33]Once the desired FTP server was located, FTP eventually included capabilities to travel down directory hierarchies to find the desired files. (At the time FTP was designed, the protocol did not contain any provision for dealing with hierarchical files—that was added somewhat later.) User names and the account command were, on many systems, the primary mechanism for providing context for the file names. That is, "user" and "acct" were navigational commands as much as they were authentication and authorization commands.

[34]Frequently, some documentation about the content of directories was provided in files with the file name of "readme.txt" or some variation thereof, such as AAREAD.ME, to take advantage of alphabetic sorting when the directory was retrieved.

6.2.1 Aiding Navigation via the Internet

The first response to the need for automated processes was Archie,[35] a selective index of those files thought to be "interesting" by those who submitted them to the index and of the FTP servers on which they were located. When Archie was first released in 1989, many people were skeptical of the idea of having an index of such large size on one computer, but Archie was a success. It consisted of three components: the data gatherer, the index merger, and the query protocol. The gathering of data was not done by brute force. The company that took over operation of the Archie service (Bunyip Information Systems) relied on licensed Archie server operators all over the world (who knew which FTP archives were reliable) to run a data gatherer that indexed local files by searching each local site.[36] Each local gatherer passed the partial index upstream, and eventually the partial indexes were merged into a full index having fairly simple functionality, primarily limited to single-level alphabetic sorting. This process of collaborative gathering saved time and minimized the bandwidth required. A special protocol allowed clients to query the full index, which was replicated on servers around the world, to identify the FTP server that contained the requested file.

Archie still required users to employ FTP to download the files of interest for viewing on their local computers. The next aid, Gopher, was developed as a protocol for viewing remote files, which were in a specified format, on a user's local computer. It became the first navigation aid on the Internet that was easily accessible by non-computer-science specialists.[37] The Gopher "browser" provided users with the capability to look at the content of a file on the computer that stored it, and if the file included a reference to another file, to "click" directly on the link to see the contents of the second file. Gopher included some metadata[38] so that, for example, when a user clicked on a link, the user's client software would

---

[35] "Archie" is not an acronym but is a shortening of the word "archive" to satisfy software constraints. Peter Deutsch, Alan Emtage, Bill Heelan, and Mike Parker at McGill University in Montréal created Archie.

[36] The burden this imposed on the FTP servers led the operators of many of them to create and keep up to date an Archie-usable listing of the server in its root directory and to keep those listings up to date, obviating the need for Archie to search the server.

[37] Gopher, created in 1991 by Marc McCahill and his technical team at the University of Minnesota, is not an acronym but is named after the mascot at the University of Minnesota. See Chris Sherman, "SearchDay," Number 198, February 6, 2002, available at <http://searchenginewatch.com/searchday/02/sd0206-gopher.html>.

[38] Metadata are data that describe the characteristics or organization of other data. See Murtha Baca, *Introduction to Metadata: Pathways to Digital Information*, Getty Information Institute, Los Angeles, 1998.

automatically check the metadata, choose the desired document format, and start the appropriate program to deal with the data format.

To overcome Gopher's limitation to files on a single computer, a central search aid for Gopher files—Veronica—was created in 1992.[39] It did for Gopher what Archie did for FTP. Veronica was the first service that used brute-force software robots (software that automatically searched the Internet) to collect and index information and, therefore, could be seen as the forerunner of Web search engines. In 1993, Jughead added keywords and Boolean search capabilities to Veronica.[40]

The next step in the evolution of Internet navigation aids was the wide area information server (WAIS) that enabled search using word indices of specified files available on the Internet.[41] The WAIS search engine received a query, sought documents relevant to the question in its database by searching the word indices, and returned a list of documents ordered by estimated relevance to the user. Each document was scored from 1 to 1000 based on criteria such as its match to the user's question as determined by how many of the query words it contained and their importance in the document. WAIS did not index the entire Internet, but rather only specific files and servers on it. At its peak, WAIS linked up to 600 databases, worldwide.[42] It was used, for example, by Dow Jones to create a fully indexed online file of its publications. WAIS was an important step beyond FTP, Gopher, and Archie (and friends) because it built on known information-retrieval methods[43] and standards, including the Z39.50 "search and retrieve" standard as its key data representation model.[44]

---

[39]Veronica (Very Easy, Rodent-Oriented, Net-Wide Index to Computerized Archives) was created in November 1992 by Fred Barrie and Stephen Foster of the University of Nevada System Computing Services group.

[40]Jughead (Jonzy's Universal Gopher Hierarchy Excavation And Display) was created by Rhett "Jonzy" Jones at the University of Utah computer center. The names of these two protocols were derived from characters in Archie comics. See <http://www.archiecomics.com/>.

[41]WAIS was developed between 1989 and 1992 at Thinking Machines Corporation under the leadership of Brewster Kahle. Unlike Archie (and friends), Gopher, and the Web, WAIS was firmly rooted in information sciences approaches and technology.

[42]Richard T. Griffiths, "Chapter Four: Search Engines," *History of the Internet*, Leiden University, The Netherlands, 2002, available at <http://web.let.leidenuniv.nl/history/ivh/chap4.htm>.

[43]Many of the navigation aids and services described in this history drew inspiration and methodology from the long line of research in information science, as well as computer science. It has not been possible to give full credit to those antecedents in this brief history.

[44]For information about the Z39.50 protocol, see National Information Standards Organization, Z39.50 resource page, available at <http://www.niso.org/z39.50/z3950.html#other>; and Mark Needleman, "Z39.50–A Review, Analysis and Some Thoughts on the Future," *Library HiTech* 18(2):158-65, 2000, available at <http://www.biblio-tech.com/html/z39.50.html>, accessed on June 23, 2004.

FTP with Archie, Gopher with Veronica and Jughead, and WAIS demonstrated three ways to index and find information on the Internet.[45] They laid the foundation for the subsequent development of aids for navigating the World Wide Web.

6.2.2 Aiding Navigation Through the World Wide Web

While those early navigation aids were being developed, a new way of structuring information on the Internet[46] —the World Wide Web—was under development at the European Organization for Nuclear Research (CERN) in Geneva.[47] Many of the concepts underlying the Web existed in Gopher, but the Web incorporated more advanced interface features, was designed explicitly for linking information across sites, and employed a common language, called Hypertext Markup Language (HTML), to describe Web content. With the deployment of the Mosaic browser[48] and its widely adopted commercial successors—Netscape's Navigator and Microsoft's Internet Explorer—it became easy to view HTML formatted documents and images located on the Web, making it much more appealing to most users than Gopher's text-oriented system.

Indeed, the use of browsers on the Web eventually replaced the use of WAIS, FTP/Archie and Gopher/Veronica. At the same time, the Web unintentionally made domain names valuable as identifiers, thereby raising their profile and importance. While FTP and Gopher sites used do-

---

[45]See Michael F. Schwartz, Alan Emtage, Brewster Kahle, and B. Clifford Neuman, "A Comparison of Internet Discovery Approaches," *Computing Systems* 5(4):461-493, 1992.

[46]The Web's structure is hypertext, which was anticipated in the form of "associative indexing" by Vannevar Bush in a famous article, "As We May Think," published in the *Atlantic Monthly* in July 1945. The term "hypertext" was coined by Theodor (Ted) Nelson in the early 1960s. Nelson spent many years publicizing the concept and attempting early implementations. Douglas C. Engelbart's NLS/Augment project at the Stanford Research Institute (which in 1977 became known as SRI International) first demonstrated a hypertext system in 1968. Apple Computer introduced HyperCard, a commercial implementation of hypertext for the Macintosh, in 1987. The practical implementation of a hypertext data structure on the Internet at a time when computer capacity and network speed were finally sufficient to make it practical was CERN's contribution.

[47]Tim Berners-Lee and his team developed the Web in 1990. It was first released to the physics community in 1991 and spread quickly to universities and research organizations thereafter. See <http://public.web.cern.ch/public/about/achievements/www/history/history.html>.

[48]Mosaic, which was released in 1993 by the National Center for Supercomputing Applications (NCSA) at the University of Illinois, Urbana-Champaign, was the first Web browser with a graphical user interface for the PC and Apple environments. It had an immediate effect on the widespread adoption of the Web by non-research users. Marc Andreessen, one of the developers of Mosaic, became a co-founder of Netscape. See <http://www.ncsa.uiuc.edu/Divisions/Communications/MosaicHistory/>.

main names, these names attracted little attention per se. However, the development of the Web and its meteoric growth linked domain names and the Web very closely through their prominent inclusion in browser addresses as a key part of Uniform Resource Locators (URLs). (See Box 6.2.) As noted in Chapter 2, it was commonplace to navigate across the World Wide Web just by typing domain names into the address bar, since browsers automatically expanded them into URLs. Often, at that time, the domain names were simply guessed on the assumption that trying a brand name followed by .com had a high probability of success.

The Web, whose underlying structure is hypertext—resources connected by links—also introduced a new and convenient means of navigation: "clicking" on hyperlinks on a page displayed in a browser. Hyperlinks generally have text, called anchor text, which many browsers display by underlining and color change. When the user moves the pointer to the anchor text of a hyperlink and clicks the mouse button, the browser finds the associated URL in the code for that page and accesses the corresponding page.[49] Thus, navigation across the Web from an initial site can consist of nothing more than a series of clicks on the anchor text of hyperlinks.

The World Wide Web has experienced rapid and continual growth[50] since the introduction of browsers. In 1993, when the National Center for Supercomputing Applications' (NCSA) Mosaic browser was made publicly available, there were just 200 sites on the Web. The growth rate of Web traffic in 1993 in transmitted bytes was 340,000 percent, as compared with 997 percent for Gopher traffic.[51] By March 1994, Web traffic exceeded Gopher traffic in absolute terms.[52] Based on one estimate of the number of Internet hosts,[53] the exponential growth of Web sites continued from

---

[49]Since there is no required association between the hyperlink and its anchor text, there is an opportunity for malicious or criminal misdirection to deliberately bogus sites, which has been exploited recently as a vehicle for identity theft and is referred to as "phishing" or "brand spoofing."

[50]There is difficulty in measuring the rate of growth of and the volume of information on the Web because of the lack of consistent and comprehensive data sources. The lack of consistent measurements over time is also attributable to the very factors that continue to enable the Web's growth—as the technology and architecture supporting the Web have evolved, so have the methods of characterizing its growth.

[51]See Robert H. Zakon, "Hobbes' Internet Timeline," RFC 2235, November 1997, available at <http://www.rfc-editor.org>.

[52]See Susan Calcari, "A Snapshot of the Internet," *Internet World* 5(1, September):54-58, 1994. Also, Merit Network, Inc., Internet statistics, 1995, available at <ftp://nic.merit.edu/nsfnet/statistics>. Graphics and tables of NSFNET backbone statistics are available at <http://www.cc.gatech.edu/gvu/stats/NSF/merit.html>.

[53]Internet Systems Consortium provides host data, which are available at <http://www.isc.org/>.

BOX 6.2 Uniform Resource Identifiers (URIs)

The Uniform Resource Identifier (URI)[1] is a general name for resource identifiers on the Internet. Several distinct types of URIs have been defined: Uniform Resource Locators (URLs), Uniform Resource Names (URNs), and Uniform Resource Characteristics (URCs), each of which identifies a resource differently. URLs are, by far, the most commonly used of the three.

URLs are URIs that identify resources by their location. Although URLs can be used to locate many different types of resources on the Internet, the most common URLs are those used to identify locations on the World Wide Web.[2] Web URLs, such as <http://www.nas.edu>, include "http" to designate the Hypertext Transfer Protocol (HTTP) and "www.nas.edu" to designate the Web location of interest. The example below shows the URL for the committee's charter document in HTML format located in the directory[3] /cstb/committees/indns, located on the www.nas.edu HTTP server.

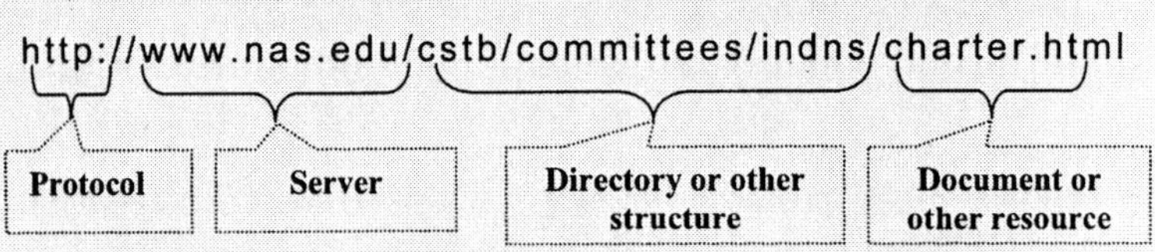

A URL cannot separate the location from the name of a resource. Therefore, a URL is outdated when a resource is moved to a new location, yet it remains unchanged even when the resource at that location is changed.

The URN type of URI was defined to meet the need for a more persistent identifier. A URN identifies a resource by assigning it a permanent and globally unique name drawn from a specified name space that is not tied to a location.[4] However, there needs to be a continually updated table linking each URN to the current location of the resource it names.

A third class of URI, the URC, was proposed to incorporate metadata about resources and their corresponding URNs. URCs have not achieved widespread acceptance or use.

1993 to 1998, with the number of hosts approximately doubling each year. After 1998, the rate of growth in hosts slowed to a doubling every 2 years. Web server data[54] provides the number of active Web sites located via the DNS as a measure of the growth in the volume of information on the Web. Although data are discontinuous, from June 1993 to December 1995, the number of Web sites doubled every 3 months; from December 1997 to December 2000, the number doubled approximately every 10 months.

[54]Matthew Gray of the Massachusetts Institute of Technology compiled data on the growth of Web sites from June 1993 to June 1995, which is available at <http://www.mit.edu/people/mkgray/net/web-growth-summary.html>; the Netcraft Web Server Survey began in August 1995 and is available at <http://www.netcraft.com/Survey/Reports/>.

An approach different from URIs for naming resources on the Internet motivates the Handle System.[5] A handle consists of two parts separated by a forward slash. The first part is a naming authority—a unique, arbitrary number assigned within the Handle System, which identifies the administrative unit that is the creator of the handle, but not necessarily the continuing administrator of the associated handles. The part after the slash is a local name that identifies the specific object. It must be unique to the given naming authority. The Handle System allows a handle to map to more than one version or attribute of a resource and resolve more than one piece of data. The multiple resolution capabilities of handles support extended services such as reverse lookup, multi-versioning, and digital rights management.

[1]For a formal definition, see T. Berners-Lee, R. Fielding, and L. Masinter, "Uniform Resource Identifiers (URI): Generic Syntax," RFC 2396, August 1998, available at <http://www.rfc-editor.org>. For further information, see M. Mealling and R. Denenberg, editors, "Report from the Joint W3C/IETF URI Planning Interest Group: Uniform Resource Identifiers (URIs), URLs, and Uniform Resource Names (URNs): Clarifications and Recommendations," RFC 3305, August 2002, available at <http://www.rfc-editor.org>.

[2]The Internet Assigned Numbers Authority maintains a register the types of resources and access methods supported by URIs. See <http://www.iana.org/assignments/uri-schemes>.

[3]More generally, this string is passed to a server and then interpreted. Frequently, this string is interpreted as a (partial) directory path and file name.

[4]IANA maintains a register of name spaces at <http://www.iana.org/assignments/urn-namespaces>.

[5]The Handle System was developed in 1994 by Robert E. Kahn, founder and president of the Corporation for National Research Initiatives (CNRI). For the foundational paper describing the components of this system, see Robert E. Kahn and Robert Wilensky, "A Framework for Distributed Digital Object Services," May 13, 1995, Corporation for National Research Initiatives, Reston, Va., available at <http://www.cnri.reston.va.us/k-w.html>. Current status and available software can be found at <http://www.handle.net/>.

As the volume of material on the Web grew exponentially, simple guessing and hypertext linking no longer served to find the sites users wanted. Nor was the almost daily un-indexed list of new sites that NCSA published (as "NCSA What's New") from June 1993 to June 1996[55] sufficient. New methods for navigating to Web resources were badly needed and the need unleashed a flurry of innovation, much of it based in universities and often the product of graduate students and faculty, who recognized the opportunity and had the freedom to pursue it. The new naviga-

[55]An archive of those listings is available at <http://archive.ncsa.uiuc.edu/SDG/Software/Mosaic/Docs/whats-new.html>.

tion services took two primary forms: directories and search engines. Directories organized Web resources by popular categories. Search engines indexed Web resources by the words found within them.

The sequence of key developments from 1993 through 2004 in both forms of Web navigation system is shown in detail in Box 6.3. A broad overview of the development follows.

Web navigation service development began in 1993, the year the Mosaic browser became available, first to universities and research laboratories, and then more generally on the Internet. The first directory and the first search engines were created in that year. But it was 1994 when the first of the widely used directories—Yahoo!—and the first full-text search engine—WebCrawler—were launched. Over the next few years, technological innovation occurred at a rapid pace, with search engines adding new features and increasing their speed of operation and their coverage of the Web as computing and communication technology and system design advanced. Lycos, launched in 1994, was the first Web search engine to achieve widespread adoption as it indexed millions of Web pages. It was followed in 1995 by Excite and Alta Vista. Alta Vista in particular offered speed improvements and innovative search features. With the launch of Google in beta in 1998 and as a full commercial offering in 1999, the general nature of the technology of search engines appeared to reach a plateau, although there is continual innovation in search algorithms and approaches to facilitate ease of use. The commercial evolution of search services continued rapidly both through additional entries into the market and an increasingly rapid pace of consolidation of existing entries. The evolution of directory technology has been less visible and probably less rapid. The focus of that evolution appears, rather, to have been on the means of creating and maintaining directories and on the addition of offerings, including search engines, to the basic directory structure.

By the first years of this century, the two worlds of search engines and directories had merged, at least commercially. In 2004, Google offered Google directory (supplied by Open Directory) and Yahoo! offered Yahoo search (provided by its acquisition—Inktomi) with paid ads (provided by its acquisition—Overture). By 2004 most commercial navigation services offered advertisements associated with specific responses. These paid ads are the principal source of funding and profit for commercial navigation services. (Commercial Internet navigation is discussed in further detail in Section 7.2.) Associated with this latter development has been the rapid rise of the business of search engine marketing, which helps commercial Web sites to decide in which search engines and directories they should pay for ads; and search engine optimization, which helps to design Web sites so search engines will easily find and index them. (Organizations that provide these services generally also provide assistance with bidding strategies and assistance in advertising design.) Finally, by 2004, many search services had established themselves as portals—sites whose front pages offer access to search; news, weather, stock prices, entertainment listings, and other information; and links to travel, job search, and other services.

The development of Internet navigation aids and services, especially those focused primarily on the Web, stands in interesting contrast to the development of the Domain Name System as described in Chapter 2.

Conclusion: A wide range of reasonably effective, usable, and readily available Internet navigation aids and services have been developed and have evolved rapidly in the years since the World Wide Web came into widespread use in 1993.

Large investments in research and development are currently being made in commercial search and directory services. Still, many of the unexpected innovations in Internet navigation occurred in academic institutions. These are places with strong traditions of information sharing and open inquiry. Research and education are "problem-rich" arenas in which students and faculty nurture innovation.

Conclusion: Computer science and information science graduate students and faculty played a prominent role in the initial development of a great many innovative Internet navigation aids and services, most of which are now run as commercial enterprises. Two of those services have become the industry leaders and have achieved great commercial success—Yahoo! and Google.

Conclusion: Because of the vast scale, broad scope, and ready accessibility of resources on the Internet, the development of navigation aids and services opens access to a much wider array of resources than has heretofore been available to non-specialist searchers. At the same time, the development of successful Internet navigation aids and services opens access to a much broader potential audience than has heretofore been available to most resource providers.

One cannot know if the past is prelude, but it is clear that the number and the variety of resources available on the Internet continue to grow, that uses for it continue to evolve, and that many challenges of Internet navigation remain. Some of the likely directions of technological development are described in Section 8.1

BOX 6.3 Key Events in the Development of Navigation Aids and Services for the World Wide Web

1989

Work started on the InQuery engine at the University of Massachusetts that eventually led to the Infoseek engine.

1993

First Web robot or spider.[1] The World Wide Web Wanderer was created by MIT student Matthew Gray. It was used to count Web servers and create a database—Wandex—of their URLs.

Work on the Architext search engine using statistical clustering was started by six Stanford University undergraduates, which was the basis for Excite search engine launched in 1995.

First directory. WWW Virtual Library was created by Tim Berners-Lee.

ALIWEB, an Archie-like index of the Web based on automatic gathering of information provided by webmasters, was created by Martijn Kosters at Nexor Co., United Kingdom.

First robot-based search engines launched. The World Wide Web Worm, JumpStation, and Repository-Based Software Engineering (RBSE) were launched. None indexed the full text of Web pages.

1994

The World Wide Web Worm indexed 110,000 Web pages and Web-accessible documents; it received an average of 1500 queries a day (in March and April).

First searchable directory of the Web. Galaxy, created at the MCC Research Consortium, provided a directory service to support electronic commerce.

First widely used Web directory. Yahoo! was created by two Stanford graduate students, David Filo and Jerry Yang, as a directory of their favorite Web sites. Usage expanded with the growth in entries and addition of categories. Yahoo! became a public company in 1995.

First robot-based search engine to index full text of Web pages. Web Crawler was created by Brian Pinkerton, a student at the University of Washington.

Lycos was created by Michael Mauldin, a research scientist at Carnegie Mellon University. It quickly became the largest robot-based search engine. By January 1995 it had indexed 1.5 million documents and by November 1996, over 60 million—more than any other search engine at the time.

Harvest was created by the Internet Research Task Force Research Group on Resource Discovery at the University of Colorado. It featured a scalable, highly customizable architecture and tools for gathering, indexing, caching, replicating, and accessing Internet information.

Infoseek Guide, launched by Infoseek Corporation as a Web directory, was initially fee based, and then free.

The OpenText 4 search engine was launched by Open Text Corporation based on work on full-text indexing and string search for the *Oxford English Dictionary*. (In 1996 it launched "Preferred Listings," enabling sites to pay for listing in top-10 search results. Resultant controversy may have hastened its demise in 1997.)

1995

The Infoseek search engine was launched in February and in December became Netscape's default search service, displacing Yahoo!

First metasearch service. SearchSavvy, created by Daniel Dreilinger, a graduate student at Colorado State University, queried multiple search engines and combined their results.

First commercial metasearch service. MetaCrawler, developed by graduate student Erik Selberg and faculty member Oren Etzioni at the University of Washington, was licensed to go2net.

The Excite commercial search engine, based on the Stanford Architext engine, was launched.

The Magellan directory was launched by the McKinley Group. It was complemented by a book, *The McKinley Internet Yellow Pages,* that categorized, indexed, and described 15,000 Internet resources and that accepted advertising.

Search engine achieved record speed: 3 million pages indexed per day. AltaVista, launched by Digital Equipment Corporation, combined computing power with innovative search features—including Boolean operators, newsgroup search, and users' addition and removal of their own URLs—to become the most popular search engine.

1996

First search engine to employ parallel computing for indexing: 10 million pages indexed per day. Inktomi Corporation launched the HotBot search engine based on work of faculty member Eric Brewer and graduate student Paul Gauthier of the University of California, Berkeley. HotBot used clusters of inexpensive workstations to achieve supercomputer speeds. It adopted the OEM search model—providing search services through others—and was licensed to *Wired* magazine's Web site, HotWired.

Continued

BOX 6.3 Continued

First paid listings in an online directory. LookSmart was launched as a directory of Web site listings. Containing both paid commercial listings and non-commercial listings submitted by volunteer editors, it also adopted the OEM model.

First Internet archive. Archive.org was launched by Brewster Kahle as an Internet repository with the goal of archiving snapshots of the Web's content on a regular basis.

Consolidation begins: Excite acquired WebCrawler and Magellan.

1997

First search engine to incorporate automatic classification and creation of taxonomies of responses and to use multidimensional relevance ranking. The Northern Light search engine also indexed proprietary document collections.

AOL launched AOL NetFind, its own branded version of Excite. The Mining Company directory service, started by Scott Kurnitt and others, used a network of "guides" to prepare directory articles.

First "question-answer" style search engine. Ask Jeeves was launched. The company was founded in 1996 by a software engineer, David Warthen, and a venture capitalist, Garrett Gruener. The service emphasized ease of use, relevance, precision, and ability to learn.

Alexa.com was launched by Brewster Kahle. It assisted search users by providing additional information—site ownership, related links, and a link to *Encyclopedia Britannica*—and also provided a copy of all indexed pages to Archive.org.

Alta Vista, the largest search engine, indexed 100 million pages total and received 20 million queries per day.

Open Text Corporation ceased operation.

1998

First search engine with paid placement ("pay-per-click") in responses. Idealab! launched the GoTo search engine. Web sites were listed in an order determined by what they paid to be included in responses to a query term.

First open source Web directory. Open Directory Project was launched (initially with the name GNUhoo and then NewHoo) with the goal of becoming the Web's most comprehensive directory through the use of the open source model—contributions by thousands of volunteer editors.

First search engine to use "page rank," based on number of links to a page, in prioritizing results of Web keyword searches. Stanford graduate students Larry Page and Sergey Brin announced Google, which was designed to support research on Web search technology. Google became available as a "beta version" on the Web.

Microsoft launched MSN Search using the Inktomi search engine.

The Direct Hit search engine was introduced. It ranked responses by the popularity of sites among previous searchers using similar keywords.

Yahoo! Web search was powered by Inktomi.

Consolidation heats up: GoTo acquired WWW Worm; Lycos acquired Wired/HotBot; Netscape acquired the Open Directory; Disney acquired a large stake in Infoseek.

1999

Google, Inc. (formed in 1998) opened a fully operational search service. AOL/Netscape adopted it for search on its portal sites.

The Norwegian company Fast Search & Transfer (FAST) launched the AllTheWeb search engine.

The Mining Company was renamed About.com.

Northern Light became the first engine to index 200 million pages.

The FindWhat pay-for-placement search engine was launched to provide paid listings to other search engines.

Consolidation continued: CMGI acquired AltaVista; At Home acquired Excite.

2000

Yahoo! adopted Google as the default search results provider on its portal site.

Google launched an advertising program to complement its search services, added Netscape Open Directory to augment its search results, and began 10 non-English-language search services.

Consolidation continued: Ask Jeeves acquired Direct Hit; Terra Networks S.A. acquired Lycos.

By year's end, Google had become the largest search engine on the Web with an index of over 1.3 billion pages, answering 60 million searches per day.

2001

Google acquired the Deja.com Usenet archive dating back to 1995.

Continued

BOX 6.3 Continued

Overture, the new name for GoTo, became the leading pay-for-placement search engine.
The Teoma search engine, launched in April, was bought by Ask Jeeves in September.
The Wisenut search engine was launched.
Magellan ceased operation.
By the end of the year, Google had indexed over 3 billion Web documents (including a Usenet archive dating back to 1981).

2002

Consolidation continued: LookSmart acquired Wisenut.
The Gigablast search engine was launched.

2003

Consolidation heated up:
Yahoo acquired Inktomi and Overture, which had acquired AltaVista and AllTheWeb.
FindWhat acquired Espotting.
Google acquired Applied Semantics and Sprinks.
Google indexed over 3 billion Web documents and answered over 200 million searches daily.

2004

Competition became more intense:
Yahoo! switched its search from Google to its own Inktomi and Overture services.

6.3 ADDENDUM—SEARCHING THE WEB VERSUS SEARCHING LIBRARIES

Searching on the public Web has no direct analog with searching libraries, which is both an advantage and a disadvantage. Library models provide a familiar and useful comparison for explaining the options and difficulties of categorizing Web resources.

First, locating an item by its URL has no direct equivalent in library models. The URL usually combines the name of a resource with its precise machine location. The URL approach assumes a unique resource at a unique location. Library models assume that documents exist in multiple

Amazon.com entered the market with A9.com, which added Search Inside the Book™ and other user features to the results of a Google search.

Google included (in February) 6 billion items: 4.28 billion Web pages, 880 million images, 845 million Usenet messages, and a test collection of book-related information pages.

Google went public in an initial public offering in August. Ask Jeeves acquired Interactive Search Holdings, Inc., which owned Excite and iWon.

In November, Google reported that its index included over 8 billion Web pages.[2]

In December, Google, four university libraries, and the New York Public Library announced an agreement to scan books from the library collections and make them available for online search.[3]

SOURCES: Search Engine Optimization Consultants, "History of Search Engines and Directories," June 2003, available at <http://www/seoconsultants.com/search-engines/history.asp>; iProspect, "A Brief History of Search Engine Marketing and Search Engines," 2003, available at <http://www.iprospect.com/search_engine_placement/seo_history.htm>; Danny Sullivan, "Search Engine Timeline," *SearchEngineWatch.com,* available at <http://www.searchenginewatch.com/subscribers/factfiles/article.php/2152951>; and Wes Sonnenreich, "A History of Search Engines," *Wiley.com*, available at <http://www.wiley.com/legacy/compbooks/sonnenreich/history.html>.

---

[1]A spider is a program that collects Web pages by traversing the Web, following links from site to site in a systematic way. See Box 7.2.

[2]See David A. Vise, "Search Swagger," *Washington Post,* November 11, 2004, p. E1.

[3]John Markoff and Edward Wyatt. 2004. "Google Is Adding Major Libraries to Its Database," *New York Times*, December 14, 2004, available at <http://www.nytimes.com/2004/12/14/technology/14google.html>.

locations, and separate the name of the document (its bibliographic description, usually a catalog record or index entry) from its physical location within a given library. Classification systems (e.g., Dewey decimal or Library of Congress) are used for shelf location only in open-stack libraries, which are prevalent in the United States. Even then, further coding is needed to achieve unique numbering within individual libraries.[56] In

---

[56]The shelf location ZA3225.B67 2000 for Borgman, *From Gutenberg to the Global Information Infrastructure*, 2000, at the University of California at Berkeley library consists of the Library of Congress Call Number (ZA3225) plus a local number to order the author name (B67 for Borgman) and the date (2000) to create a unique shelf placement in this library.

closed-stack libraries where users cannot browse the shelves, such as the Library of Congress, books usually are stored by size and date of acquisition. The uniqueness of name and location of resources that is assumed in a URL leads to multiple problems of description and persistence, as explained in this chapter.

Second, resources on the Web may be located by terms in their pages because search engines attempt to index documents in all the sites they select for indexing, regardless of type of content (e.g., text, images, sound; personal, popular, scholarly, technical), type of hosting organization (e.g., commercial, personal, community, academic, political), country, or language. By comparison, no single index of the contents of the world's libraries exists. Describing such a vast array of content in a consistent manner is an impossible task, and libraries do not attempt to do so. The resource that comes closest to being a common index is WorldCat,[57] which "is a worldwide union catalog created and maintained collectively by more than 9,000 member institutions" of the Online Computer Library Center (OCLC) and in 2004 contained about 54 million items.[58] The contents of WorldCat consist of bibliographic descriptions (cataloging records) of books, journals, movies, and other types of documents; the full content of these documents is not indexed. Despite the scope of this database, it represents only a fraction of the world's libraries (albeit most of the largest and most prestigious ones), and only a fraction of the collections within these libraries (individual articles in journals are not indexed, nor are most maps, archival materials, and other types of documents). The total number of documents in WorldCat (54 million) is small compared with those indexed by Google, InfoSeek, AltaVista, or other Internet search engines.

Rather than create a common index to all the world's libraries, consistent and effective access to documents is achieved by dividing them into manageable collections according to their subject content or audience. Library catalogs generally represent the collections of only one library, or at most a group of libraries participating in a consortium (e.g., the campuses of the University of California[59]). These catalogs describe books, journals (but not individual journal articles), and other types of documents. Many materials are described only as collections. For example, just one catalog record describes all the maps of Los Angeles made by the U.S. Geological Survey from 1924 to 1963. It has been estimated that individual records in the library catalog represent only about 2 percent of the separate items in a typical academic library collection.[60] Thus, library catalogs are far less

[57]See <http://www.oclc.org/worldcat/default.htm>.

[58]Accessed May 7, 2004.

[59]See <http://melvyl.cdlib.org/>.

[60]See David A. Tyckoson, "The 98% Solution: The Failure of the Catalog and the Role of Electronic Databases," *Technicalities* 9(2):8-12, 1989.

comprehensive than most library users realize. However, online library catalogs are moving away from the narrower model of card catalogs. Many online catalogs are merging their catalog files with records from journal article databases. Mixing resources from different sources creates a more comprehensive database but introduces the Web searching problem of inconsistent description.

Nor do libraries attempt the international, multilingual indexing that search engines do. The catalogs of libraries may be organized consistently on a country-by-country basis, at best. The descriptive aspects of cataloging (e.g., author, title, date, publisher) are fairly consistent internationally, as most countries use some variation of the Machine Readable Cataloging (MARC) metadata structure. (Metadata are data about data or, more generally, about resources.) However, many variations of the MARC format exist, each tied to a national or multinational set of cataloging rules. The United States and United Kingdom share the Anglo-American Cataloging Rules but store their data in USMARC and UKMARC formats, respectively. These formats are finally being merged, after nearly 40 years of use. In 2004, the national libraries of the United States and the United Kingdom implemented a common format, MARC 21, and other countries are following suit.[61] Other MARC formats include UNIMARC, HUMARC (Hungary), and FINNMARC (Finland). The OCLC WorldCat database merges these into an OCLC MARC format. Each catalog describes its holdings in its local language and may also include descriptions in the language of the document content. For example, OCLC WorldCat contains records describing resources in about 400 languages; each record has some descriptive entries in English. Thus, libraries achieve interoperability through highly decentralized cataloging activities. The cataloging enterprise is economically feasible in the United States because most published resources are described by the publishers and the Library of Congress and contributed to OCLC WorldCat and other shared databases. Despite the relative national and international success in establishing cataloging rules and formats among libraries, incompatibilities continue to exist within these communities, and the archives and museum communities employ yet other metadata formats. Given the difficulty of achieving agreement on basic descriptive models among these established institutions run by information management professionals, the likelihood of getting universal agreement on

---

[61]See British Library, *MARC 21 and UKMARC*, British Library, London, November 24, 2004, available at <http://www.bl.uk/services/bibliographic/nbsils.html>; and *MARC 21 Concise Format for Bibliographic Data*, Concise Edition, Library of Congress, Washington, D.C., November 24, 2003, available at <http://www.loc.gov/marc/bibliographic/ecbdhome.html>.

descriptive standards for Web documents is low. Decentralized models for data creation, combined with mapping between similar formats, are the most feasible way to achieve interoperability.

Third, while a rich subject index to the Web would certainly be extremely useful, universal subject access is almost impossible to achieve. American libraries attempt general subject access via the Library of Congress Subject Headings (LCSH), but these apply only two or three headings per book. Few other countries appear to use the LCSH, as many of the concepts are specific to U.S. culture. Unified access via classification systems such as the Dewey Decimal Classification (DDC) and Library of Congress Classification (LCC) are more common. These are also country- and culture-specific. DDC and LCC are little used outside the United States; the Universal Decimal Classification (UDC) system has broader international adoption. Many other country-specific classifications exist.

Consistent subject access in any depth is feasible only within topical areas due to a number of well-understood linguistic problems.[62] These include synonymy (multiple terms or phrases may have the same meaning), polysemy (the same terms and phrases may have multiple meanings), morphological relationships (structure of words, such as variant endings—e.g., acid and acidic; dog and dogs; mouse and mice, and semantic relationships (conceptual relationships (e.g., two words may have the same meaning in one context and different meanings in other contexts). Both automatic and manual methods to provide consistent retrieval by controlling the meaning of words work best when the subject area is constrained. Controlled sets of terms (e.g., thesauri, ontologies) can be constrained to their meaning within one field, such as computer science, economics, arts, or psychology. Libraries construct or purchase indexes specific to each field within the scope of their collections.

Fourth, Web directories are more analogous to topic-specific library indexes than to library catalogs. However, Web directories cover only a small portion of the content of the Web, and their descriptions of each item are often less complete and can be less reliable than those created by professional librarians. Consequently, structured and formal characterizations of material can be accomplished most effectively in a library catalog or bookstore database, rather than in a general Web directory.

Selecting the proper resource to search remains an important starting point in seeking information, whether online or offline.

---

[62]See Richard K. Belew, *Finding Out About: A Cognitive Perspective on Search Engine Technology and the WWW*, Cambridge University Press, Cambridge, U.K., 2000; Peter Brusilovsky and Carlo Tasso, "Preface to Special Issue on User Modeling for Web Information Retrieval," *User Modeling and User-Adapted Interaction: The Journal of Personalization Research* 14(2-3):147-157, 2004; and William A. Woods, "Searching vs. Finding," *ACM Queue* 2(4), 2004, available at <http://www.acmqueue.com/modules.php?name=Content&pa=showpage&pid=137>.

7

Internet Navigation: Current State

At this point in the development of Internet navigation, there are at least seven basic ways for a user to navigate to a desired Web resource, which is generally located on a page within a Web site. Five of them are direct—users' actions take them immediately to the desired resource. Two are indirect—users must first employ a navigation service, either a directory or a search engine, to find the address of a desired resource and then, using that information, go to the desired resource. These basic ways can be and often are used in combination with one another. Table 7.1 summarizes and characterizes the various Internet navigation aids and services.

This discussion is concerned with navigation across the Internet and not specifically with navigation within sites, although the tools deployed in both cases are usually similar. Most Web sites—except those with only a few pages—now incorporate one or more means of navigation within the site itself. These include hyperlinks, directories (menus), site maps, and search engines. Because they are usually limited to the contents of the site, the problems of general-purpose Web navigation aids are diminished. For example, the context is delimited, the users are relatively homogeneous, the scale is relatively small, and material that is difficult to automatically index (such as multimedia and images) can usually be manually indexed.

TABLE 7.1 Principal Internet Navigation Aids and Services

Method	Steps	Indexing Process	File Structure	Match
1. Domain Name—known or guessed	1 or 2	Human	Hierarchical	Exact
2. Hyperlink	1	Human	Network	Exact
3. Bookmark	1	Human	Flat or hierarchical	Exact
4. KEYWORD[a]	1	Human	Flat or hierarchical	Exact
5. Metadata	1	Human	Flat or hierarchical	Exact
6. Directory	2	Human/computer	Hierarchical or multi-hierarchical	Fuzzy
7. Search engine	2	Computer	Inverted	Ranked

[a]"KEYWORD" is capitalized to distinguish it from the use of keywords in traditional information retrieval or in Internet search engines (see Sections 7.1.4 and 7.1.7). In this use, each KEYWORD is part of a controlled vocabulary for which the match to a specific Internet resource is one to one.

7.1 NAVIGATION AIDS AND SERVICES

7.1.1 Direct Access via a Uniform Resource Locator or Domain Name

One of the major factors in the success of the Web was the development of Uniform Resource Locators (URLs) for Web sites. Because those identifiers offered a standardized way to identify resources on the Web, resource providers and resource seekers had a common way to refer to their locations. But the URLs were intended as codes hidden behind meaningful objects—the anchor text—in a document, not directly typed by the user. The designers of the Web may have been surprised when URLs began appearing on the sides of buses and on billboards.

URLs are typically not managed to be permanent and can be difficult to remember, especially when they require many elements to describe a resource deep within a Web site. (Examples of such URLs abound in the footnoted references throughout this report.) Despite their flaws, however, they have thrived as a robust means of navigation.

In some browsers, users can also navigate through the Web by typing only a domain name because the browsers will automatically expand it into a URL that may identify a Web site. This use of domain names for navigation is effective to the degree that the searcher knows or is able to guess the domain name exactly and is satisfied with being taken to the home page of a Web site. If the name entered is incorrect, then the browser, e-mail server, or other Internet service consumes resources (in the local computer and in the Internet) trying to find a DNS match. Mistaken guesses can create extra traffic and burden the DNS, as discussed in Chapter 3. However, most browsers now treat invalid domain names as search terms and return a list of possible matches.[1]

Furthermore, as Web sites have grown more complex, discovering the site has often had to be followed by a second navigation process to find relevant information or pages within the site. But some users would prefer to go directly to the page that contains the specific information being sought. Remembering or guessing does not suffice for such navigation because the URLs of inner pages comprise more than the domain name.

In addition, as network services proliferate and as additional top-level domains are added, users will have many more sites of interest to which to navigate, but at the probable cost of domain names that are more difficult to remember or guess. Furthermore, not only information, entertainment, and service resources, but also many personal electronic devices and home appliances may well be connected to the Internet. For convenience, users will probably want to assign easy-to-remember domain names to such devices. But because of competition for the easiest and shortest names, they may have to settle for less-readily remembered ones. In either event, they can use bookmarks (see Section 7.1.3) to simplify access.

For these reasons, remembering or guessing correct domain names is likely to become less dependable and, therefore, a less important aid to navigation as the number of locations on the Internet continues to expand.

7.1.2 Direct Access via Hyperlinks

Because the Web is a network of sites through which users can navigate by following links between documents on the sites, once the first site has been found, one can move across sub-networks of related and relevant information and services. The address of the linked-to information may be visible or, more typically, hidden behind anchor text. A human being defines the linkages within and from a site during site design.

There is no publicly available Internet-wide file of links; they are maintained locally. However, linkage information is collected and used by all major search engines as an important part of the ranking of responses. For example, Google maintains an extensive file of linkages, and it is possible to use Google to find all the pages that link to a given page (within the scope of what is indexed by Google; see "The Deep, Dark, or Invisible Web" in Section 7.1.7).

---

[1]As discussed in Chapter 4, VeriSign tried to offer a service to users who enter an incorrect .com or .net domain name that directed them to possible matches, raising technical and policy issues.

Navigation by following hyperlinks is an effective tool for moving between related sites once the first relevant site has been found. However, since Web site operators establish the linkages, they may or may not lead to the specific sites of interest to the user. Thus, navigation by hyperlinks is both a valuable and a limited aid. It generally must be supplemented by other means of finding starting sites and of identifying sites of interest that may not be on the radiating set of paths from the initial point.

7.1.3 Direct Access via Bookmarks

The URLs for sites of continuing interest that have been found after a search and those of frequently accessed sites can be stored locally—"bookmarked" or placed on a "favorites" list—and managed in most browsers. By doing so, the user can return directly to a location, perhaps deep within a site, with a single click. However, these local files can become difficult to manage over time, due both to scaling problems (as the list of bookmarks grows, it may require its own database) and to the likelihood of broken links or changed content as URLs age. For these reasons, bookmarks may become less useful with the scaling and maturing of the Internet, leading users to rely on search engines to find even familiar sites and Web pages.

The bookmark/favorite mechanism as implemented in current browsers and described above is fairly weak, providing a simple association between a name (provided by either the user or the Web page) and a URL. Richer methods are possible. For example, prior experience in both information retrieval and software engineering suggests that it would be useful to store, in some form, both the query that produced the reference and information about how long the reference was likely to remain current. With this information available, it would become easier to repeat the discovery process when a link went bad, perhaps even automatically. Some work is now underway to recast bookmarks as a type of local cache with this information included and some reference updating and recovery capabilities. That work also expects to unify the results of multiple types of navigation, from search engine output, to Uniform Resource Identifiers (URIs) obtained from colleagues, to links obtained from pages being traversed, into a single framework. (In information retrieval and library practice since the early 1960s, queries have been stored and then periodically executed to support Current Awareness or Selective Dissemination of Information services.[2] However, unlike the bookmark case, the queries are run by a service on a regular schedule and not by users only when they need to update their bookmarks.)

[2]See Robert R. Korfhage, *Information Storage and Retrieval*, Wiley, New York, 1997; and C.B. Hensley, R.R. Savage, A.J. Sowarby, and A. Resnick, "Selective Dissemination of Information—A New Approach to Effective Communication," *IRE Transactions of the Professional Group on Engineering Management* EM-9:2, 1962.

7.1.4 Direct Access via KEYWORDS

The term "keyword" is used in several contexts, with slightly different meanings, in Internet navigation.

Its most common current use is to denote the terms entered into the search window of a search engine for matching against the search engine's index of words appearing on Web pages.[3] In this meaning, a "keyword" can be any phrase and can be treated in a variety of ways by individual search mechanisms. It is also used in this sense in search engine marketing to refer to the search terms for which a particular marketer is willing to pay.[4]

However, "keyword" has also been used to denote terms in a controlled vocabulary linked to specific Internet locations by a specific Internet (generally, Web) service. To distinguish this meaning, it is written here in capitals. Typically, KEYWORDS are associated with a particular organization or service and that organization or service has paid to have them linked uniquely to its location. Usually, just a single KEYWORD (or phrase) is entered and only one site appears in the response. They apply, however, only within a specific Web service and are not generally interpretable in the same way by others. One of the best-known uses of KEYWORDS is that of America Online (AOL) in which KEYWORDS can be typed into the AOL address bar.[5] AOL KEYWORDS link uniquely to a network resource—"NYTIMES" links to www.nytimes.com, or to an AOL feature or service—"STOCK MARKET" links to the AOL Market News Center. (The latest versions of AOL now offer a choice between: "Go to AOL keyword: 'NY Times'" or "Search the Web for 'NY Times'".) Typing the AOL KEYWORDS into MSN or into Internet Explorer will not necessarily lead to the same location. Indeed, both "NYTIMES" and "STOCK MARKET" when typed into Internet Explorer and Netscape Navigator[6] are treated as search terms (keywords in the more general sense), and the response is a ranked list of possibly matching sites.

---

[3]This is similar to the sense in which "keyword" has conventionally been used in information retrieval, where a "keyword" is "one of a set of individual words chosen to represent the content of a document." See Korfhage, *Information Storage and Retrieval*, 1997, p. 325.

[4]The marketer's site or advertisement will appear as one of the responses to any query that includes those keywords. In this context, there generally are several keywords entered in the query and many responses in the list produced by the search engine. This use of "keyword" is treated in detail in Section 7.2.2.

[5]See Danny Sullivan, "AOL Search Big Improvement for Members," *SearchEngineWatch.com*, 1999, available at <http://searchenginewatch.com/sereport/article.php/2167581>. See also Dominic Gates, "Web Navigation for Sale," *The Industry Standard*, May 15, 2000, available at <http://www.thestandard.com/article/0,1902,14735,00.html?body_page=1>.

[6]Test carried out in March 2005.

Several years ago, there were a number of attempts to offer more widely applicable KEYWORDS on the public Internet. A service offered by RealNames, Inc. was available for several years. It was adopted, for example, by MSN, which, however, terminated its use in June 2002.[7] RealNames closed shortly thereafter. KEYWORDS have been replaced in most cases—except for services catering to non-English language users[8] and AOL—by search engines, which provide a wider-ranging response to keyword terms, and by the sale of search engine keywords to multiple bidders.

KEYWORDS have many of the same strengths and weaknesses as domain names for navigation. If known, they lead exactly to the location to which the purchaser of the KEYWORD wishes to lead the searcher (which may not be the same as the searcher's intent). If guessed, they either succeed, lead to the wrong site, or fail. However, since many browsers and services now treat non-URL entries in their address lines as search terms, "failure" now generally produces a ranked list of possible matches. Thus, KEYWORD systems—including AOL's—now default to search systems, just as domain name guesses generally do.[9]

Unlike the DNS, a variety of KEYWORD systems applicable to specific topic areas and with or without hierarchical structure are conceptually possible. Implementation of a KEYWORD system on the Web requires an application or a service, such as a browser or Netpia, that recognizes the KEYWORD terms when entered into its address line or when they reach the service's name server. And, whereas in the early days of the Web such an innovation might have been relatively easy, the general implementation of standardized browser software in various versions makes the widespread introduction of a new feature much more difficult

[7]See Danny Sullivan, "RealNames to Close After Losing Microsoft," *SearchEngineWatch.com*, June 3, 2002, available at <http://www.searchenginewatch.com/sereport/article.php/2164841>. The committee heard testimony from Keith Teare, then chief executive officer of RealNames, at its July 2001 meeting.

[8]Two prominent native language KEYWORD systems are the following: (1) Netpia, a Korean Internet service, offers Native Language Internet Address (NLIA) for 95 countries (as of May 2, 2005). NLIA enables substitution of a native language word or phrase (a KEYWORD) for a unique URL. See <http://e.netpia.com>. (2) Beijing 3721 Technology Co., Ltd., has offered Chinese language keywords since 1999. See <http://www.3721.com/english/about.htm>.

[9]In July 2004, Google added a "Browse by Name" feature to its search, enabling a user to enter a single name in the tool bar and returning a single site if the term is specific or well known; if not, it defaults to a traditional search. It is not clear how the single response names are selected and whether or not they are paid for. See Scarlett Pruitt, "Google Goes Browsing by Name," *PC World*, July 15, 2004, available at <http://www.pcworld.com/news/article/0,aid,116910,00.asp>.

(although specific services, such as AOL or Netpia, can still implement them for their users).

Moreover, within any specific database, digital library, or community repository (such as the large databases of primary scientific data being assembled around the world), terms can take on local meanings. Generally speaking, meanings are constrained by the use of a controlled vocabulary, which defines each term as applied in this system. Well-known examples of controlled vocabularies include the Library of Congress Subject Headings, the Medical Subject Headings (MeSH), Subject Headings for Engineering (SHE), and the Association for Computing Machinery (ACM) Classification System.

KEYWORD systems also face the problems that arise from scale. The larger the number of locations to which they seek to assign simple and unique names, the greater the pressure to become complex and structured. The system must either remain manageably small or develop an institutional framework that allows decentralization, while centrally determining who can use which names to designate which locations. AOL and Netpia both centrally determine the assignment of names. However, Netpia implements KEYWORDS through decentralized name servers located at collaborating ISPs, while AOL implements its smaller list of KEYWORDS through its own service system.

7.1.5 Direct Access via Metadata

Since the early days of the Web, there has been a desire—especially, but not only, by those in the library and information science community—to establish a more consistent and more controlled way to categorize and describe Web resources based on the use of "data about data," or metadata.[10]

However, differences between the Web[11] and conventional libraries and data collections complicate fulfillment of that desire. First, the number, scope of content, and diversity of form of resources on the public Web exceed that in any library. Second, the quality of the, often self-provided, metadata is highly variable. And third, there is no organization or group of organizations that is able and willing to assume responsibility

---

[10]For an overview, see Tony Gill, *Introduction to Metadata: Metadata and the World Wide Web*, Getty Research Institute, July 2000, available at <http://www.getty.edu/research/conducting_research/standards/intrometadata/2_articles/gill/index.html>.

[11]Hypertext Markup Language (HTML)—the programming language of Web site construction—specifies the expression of metadata in the form of "metatags" that are visible to search engines (as they collect data from the Web—see Box 7.2) but are not typically displayed to humans by browsers. To see metatags, if they are present on a Web page, go to View/Source in Internet Explorer or View/Page Source in Netscape Navigator.

for assigning metadata tags to a significant portion of the resources accessible on the Web, as the Library of Congress does for books.

Efforts to adapt metadata for the description and categorization of sufficiently valuable Web resources began in the mid-1990s, when standard ways to express metadata—metadata schemes—were proposed as the answer to interoperability and scaling of the expanding Web.[12] But a reexamination in 2002 of the mid-1990s' recommendations forced their proponents to consider why metadata had not been successfully used.[13] The error was in their assumptions: They had expected to find high-quality—clean and honest—information, not the large amount of misrepresented and deliberately incorrect metadata that was provided for resources on the Web.

It seems that any feasible attempt to develop metadata schemes and apply them broadly to the Web would have to be decentralized and based on the efforts of a large number of autonomous organizations with specific knowledge of the content and quality of the resources they describe. Yet decentralization raises the question of coordination among the many potentially inconsistent and non-interoperable metadata schemes that the autonomous organizations might otherwise develop. Through coordination, their separate efforts could cover a significant portion of the Web and open access to their resources to a wider audience beyond the organizations themselves. Two approaches have been taken to the coordination of metadata schemes produced by autonomous organizations.

The first approach to coordination is for organizations to collaborate in defining common metadata elements that will be used by all of them as a core for their metadata schemes. The best known and best developed of these is the Dublin Metadata Core Element Set, known as the Dublin Core,[14] so named because it originated at a meeting in Dublin, Ohio, that was sponsored by the Online Computer Library Center (OCLC). It comprises fifteen metadata elements, which were thought to be the minimum number required to enable discovery of document-like resources on the Internet. Thus, Dublin Core can be used to discover an item, to determine

---

[12]See Clifford A. Lynch and Hector Garcia-Molina, *Interoperability, Scaling, and the Digital Libraries Research Agenda*, 1995, available at <http://www-diglib.stanford.edu/diglib/pub/reports/iita-dlw/main.html>, accessed July 9, 2004.

[13]Christine L. Borgman, "Challenges in Building Digital Libraries for the 21st Century," *Proceedings of the 5th International Conference on Asian Digital Libraries* (ICADL 2002), Ee-Peng Lim, Schubert Foo, Christopher S.G. Khoo, H. Chen, E. Fox, U. Shalini, and C. Thanos, editors (*Lecture Notes in Computer Science*, Vol. 2555), Springer-Verlag, 2002, available at <http://www.springer.de/comp/lncs/index.html>.

[14]The Dublin Core Web site is at <http://www.purl.org/dc/>. Official reference definitions of the metadata elements can be found there.

where fuller descriptions can be found, and to identify its detailed format (e.g., MARC for books or the Environmental Markup Language for biocomplexity data). Dublin Core works best when a professional cataloger creates descriptions. To achieve wide adoption, some believe that it needs to be made more suitable to machine-generated descriptions.[15]

The second approach to coordination is to provide a higher-level structure that can incorporate multiple metadata schemes, enabling them to be deployed in combination to describe a resource with the assurance that the resultant description will be correctly interpreted by any computer program that is compatible with the higher-level structure. The best known and best developed of these higher-level structures is the Resource Description Framework (RDF) developed by the World Wide Web Consortium (W3C).[16] It extends another W3C standard, Extensible Markup Language (XML),[17] which is used to describe data where interchange and interoperability are important, to describe resources. Any Web resource—that is, any object with a URI—can be described in a machine-understandable way in the RDF, although for some objects the description might contain little information. The resource—Web object—is described by a collection of properties—its RDF description. These properties can come from any metadata scheme since the RDF description incorporates reference information about the metadata scheme and the definition for each property. The advantage of the RDF is that it provides a widely applicable framework within which specialized metadata sets can be combined. For example, to describe geographic resources on the Web, an RDF description might incorporate the Dublin Core to describe the bibliographic provenance and a geographic metadata scheme to describe the geographic coverage of each resource. The developers of the RDF believe that its existence will encourage the development of a large number of metadata schemes for different resource domains and that where there is overlap in their coverage, they will, in effect, compete for adoption by those who describe resources. See Box 7.1.

While the RDF may provide a useful framework within which various metadata schemes may be developed and combined, it does not resolve the more difficult problem of actually using these metadata schemes to describe resources on the Web. That problem has three components: determining

---

[15]See Carl Lagoze, "Keeping Dublin Core Simple: Cross-Domain Discovery or Resource Description," *D-Lib Magazine* 7(1), 2001, available at <http://www.dlib.org/dlib/january01/lagoze/01lagoze.html>. Lagoze provides a useful discussion of the tradeoffs in simple and complex metadata descriptions and the relationship between Dublin Core, RDF, and other schema.

[16]See *Resource Description Framework (RDF)/W3C Semantic Web Activity*, available at <http://www.w3c.org/rdf>, and *RDF Primer Primer* [correct as written], available at <http://notabug.com/2002/rdfprimer/>.

[17]See *Extensible Markup Language (XML)*, available at <http://www.w3c.org/xml>.

BOX 7.1 The Semantic Web

Despite the problems of characterizing most resources on the public Web with RDF metadata, there are islands of application and, over the long term, they may extend to cover ever more terrain. With that prospect in mind, Tim Berners-Lee and his colleagues at the W3C have proposed a way of linking these islands into a formalized network of knowledge that they call the "Semantic Web."[1] They do so by introducing "ontologies" that consist of relational statements (propositions) and inference rules for specific domains of knowledge and are used to define terms used on the Web. In their vision, the Semantic Web would enable Web agents to draw upon that network of machine-accessible knowledge to carry out complex functions with less explicit direction than is currently required. While its area of application is far broader than navigation, its developers foresee, for example, that software agents will "use this information to search, filter, and prepare information in new and exciting ways to assist the Web user."[2] Like metadata and RDF, the applicability and feasibility of the Semantic Web remains the subject of dispute between its advocates and the skeptics.[3]

The practical implementation and use of the Semantic Web is highly dependent on the broad adoption of RDF and the ontologies it requires. That work has proceeded slowly thus far.

---

[1]See Tim Berners-Lee, James Hendler, and Ora Lassila, "The Semantic Web," *Scientific American*, May 2001, available at <http://www.sciam.com/article.cfm?articleID=00048144-10D2-1C70-84A9809EC588EF21&catID=2>.

[2]See James Hendler, Tim Berners-Lee, and Eric Miller, "Integrating Applications on the Semantic Web," *Journal of the Institute of Electrical Engineers of Japan* 122(10):676-680, 2002, available at <http://www.w3c.org/2002/07/swint>. For an imaginative exploration of the possibilities, see Paul Ford, "August 2009: How Google Beat Amazon and Ebay to the Semantic Web," July 26, 2002, available at <http://www.ftrain.com/google_takes_all.html>.

[3]See, for example, Clay Shirky, "The Semantic Web, Syllogism, and Worldview," November 7, 2003, available at <http://www.shirky.com/writings/semantic_syllogism.html>. Also see Paul Ford, "A Response to Clay Shirky's 'The Semantic Web, Syllogism, and Worldview'," November 13, 2003, available at <http://www.ftrain.com/ContraShirky.html>.

who will assign the metadata to each resource; finding incentives for metadata use; and determining how the metadata will be used.

The resolution of that three-component problem is easiest within communities, whether organized by topic, geographic region, or some other shared subject area.[18] Individual communities in several academic disciplines are creating their own repositories with their own metadata frameworks. Among the repositories that have been established are IRIS for

---

[18]See Chris Sherman, "Search Day—Metadata or Metagarbage," *SearchEngineWatch.com*, March 4, 2002, available at <http://www.searchenginewatch.com/searchday/article.php/2159381>.

seismology, KNB for biocomplexity, and NCAR—among others—for environmental data.[19] Other communities have established portals to gather resources and links to other resources on their topic of interest. Communities build these metadata-based repositories and portals out of self-interest—with accurate metadata they can provide better access to community resources. As both the creators and the users of the metadata, the self-interest of cohesive communities leads them to want trustworthy metadata and to provide the resources needed to create and keep them current and accurate.[20]

Solving that three-component problem is more difficult for the general Web user "community." Metadata would either have to be supplied by independent editors (as it is now for use in directory services) or applied by the resource providers and collected automatically by search engines. Although search engines look at the metatags—a type of information about a Web page that can be placed in the code describing the page but not made visible to users—on Web sites, it is not always clear whether and how they make use of the metadata they find there. And the fundamental difficulty of unreliable self-assigned metadata is difficult to overcome through automatic means.

However, one important current use of metadata is to characterize images and audio and video files on the general Web so that they can be indexed and found by search engines. The metadata tags are generally either extracted from text accompanying the images or supplied manually by editors or the resource provider and appear, generally, to be reliable. (See Section 8.1.3.)

Thus, it is highly unlikely that general metadata schemes, even if they were designed, could be reasonably implemented for the Web generally. However, metadata schemes may be practical and useful for specific sets of resources with interested user communities, such as professional organizations, museums, archives, libraries, businesses, and government agencies and for non-textual resources, such as images, audio, and video files. Moreover, even in specialized resources, establishing the framework and assigning the metadata terms to a large number of items are very different matters, since the latter is far more labor intensive. Thus, the widespread use of metadata would become easier with the improvement of automatic

---

[19]IRIS (Incorporated Research Institutions for Seismology) is at <http://www.iris.edu/>; KNB (The Knowledge Network for Biocomplexity) is at <http://knb.ecoinformatics.org/home.html>; and NCAR (National Center for Atmospheric Research) is at <http://www.ncar.ucar.edu/ncar/>.

[20]See, for example, work done by the Education Network Australia, including EdNA Online, *The EdNA Metadata Standard*, 2003, available at <http://www.edna.edu.au/edna/go/pid/385>, and the listing of activities at <http://www.ukoln.ac.uk/metadata>.

indexing (automatic metadata tagging), a topic that has long been pursued in information retrieval.[21]

7.1.6 Navigation via Directory Systems

In general, the term "directory" refers to a structured collection of objects organized by subject, much like a library card catalog or yellow pages telephone listing. Structuring a directory—usually using a taxonomy of some form—and placing objects under specific subject headings are done by humans. They may assign the same subject heading to more than one object and the same object may be assigned to more than one subject—that is, it may appear under more than one heading. In the case of Internet directories, the objects are Internet locations—Web sites or Web pages, typically.

Only the Web sites that have been submitted to or found by an Internet directory service and whose content has been classified and described, either by the editors of the directory or by the creators of the Web site, will be available in the directory. As a result of the heavy requirements for skilled labor, Internet directories can include only a small selection of all the sites connected by the Web. However, in contrast to search engines, they have the advantage of being able to incorporate listings of many Web sites in the "dark" Web (see "The Deep, Dark, or Invisible Web" in Section 7.1.7) because the sites themselves solicit a listing or because they become known to the directory editors through other means.

The listings, categorized under subject hierarchies, can be browsed by narrowing down subject categories or can be searched by matching search terms against summary descriptions of the Web site content.[22] For example, the Yahoo! directory of the Internet classifies Web sites by 14 topics. Under the "computers and Internet" topic, there are two commercial (sponsored) categories and 48 additional categories. The latter grouping includes topics such as "communications and networking" with 1108 entries grouped into 40 subtopics; "supercomputing and parallel computing" with 9 subtopics and 11 sites; and "software" with 50 subtopics.[23]

Users search a typical, hierarchically organized directory by starting at the top of the tree and moving deeper along branches labeled (by the directory editors) with terms that seem to match their interests.[24] Thus, a

---

[21]See, for example, Gerard Salton, editor, *The SMART Retrieval System: Experiments in Automatic Document Processing*, Prentice Hall, Englewood Cliffs, N.J., 1971.

[22]Three of the largest directories include the Open Directory, Yahoo!, and LookSmart.

[23]Directory accessed on March 5, 2005.

[24]Many directories have added the ability for users to jump directly to a subtopic within a directory.

user interested in administration tools for the DNS could trace the following path in Yahoo!:

> Directory→Computers and Internet→Communications and Networking→Protocols→DNS→Administration Tools[25]

The success of the user's navigation depends on the user's skill in identifying appropriate paths (but backing up and trying another path is relatively easy), on the editors' skill in describing and placing the site in the directory, and on the site's accuracy in describing itself to the editors (unless they visit and characterize each site themselves).

Directories present the user with a taxonomic view of some of the Web sites on the Internet, which can enable users to reach their goals through successive refinement. However, if the taxonomy is poorly implemented or does not roughly match the view of the user, it can be very difficult to use. There are hundreds of directories, general and specific, available on the Web and listed in various directories of directories.[26]

Work is now underway by several groups (a majority with at least loose links to each other)[27] to reexamine analogies to the time-tested "yellow pages" model for the Internet. Whereas search engines are modeled on a "search through the visible Web and see where appropriate material can be found" model (augmented, as discussed below, by paid placements), a yellow pages system is one in which all of the entries are there because their owners want them there, there is considerable content-owner control over presentation, and although a classification system is used to organize the information, the categories in which a listing is placed are generally chosen by the listing (content) owner, not the site operator or an automated process. In its paper form, that type of system has been thoroughly demonstrated over the years and is useful precisely because the information content is high and the amount of extraneous material low. Since the combination of several of the factors discussed in this section has resulted in most searches for products leading to merchants that sell those products, and to a good deal of extraneous information as well, a directory that is organized the way the merchants want (and pay for) may be more efficient technically and economically. Of course, these models can apply to many types of listings, goals, and content other than commercial ones.

---

[25]Directory accessed on March 5, 2005.

[26]See, for example, the directory of directories at Galileo (Georgia's Virtual Library) <http://www.usg.edu/galileo/internet/netinfo/director.html>.

[27]For example, the work by Beijing 3721 Technology Co., Ltd. (also known as "3721"), which was recently acquired by Yahoo!

One of the major differences between a traditional yellow pages and some of these systems is that the yellow pages (and even their online versions that support broader geographical scope[28]) are organized around a single hierarchical category system. That is necessitated by the organization of the material for publication on paper. But a computer-based system can take advantage of a multi-hierarchical environment in which, for example, the location of an entity (at various degrees of precision) is specified in a hierarchy different from that for content descriptors (such as category of store), rather than having to be a superior category in the hierarchy.

Because directories are typically built and maintained by humans, they can cover only a small portion of the Web, have difficulty keeping up with changes in locations, and are labor intensive. (However, as noted above, specialized directories that are supported by those who want to be found, such as commercial yellow pages listings, can overcome the latter two problems.) One way to address all of these problems is to decentralize responsibility for maintaining the directory, just as the DNS name files are decentralized. For example, 475 "guides" who are selected and trained to cover a specific subject area maintain the About.com directory.[29] Its 475 "guides" are responsible for "more than 50,000 topics with over 1 million pieces of original content, which are grouped into 23 channels."[30] Another way, which is becoming common, is to combine directories with search engines, which index a much larger portion of the Web using automated processes. Netscape began an ambitious directory project using volunteers and called Open Directory, which continues to this day and is incorporated into Google.

7.1.7 Navigation via Search Engines

Search engines rely on indices generated from Web pages collected by software robots, called crawlers or spiders.[31] These programs traverse the Web in a systematic way, depositing all collected information in a central repository where it is automatically indexed.[32] The selection and ranking of Web pages to include in the response to a query are done by programs that search through the indices, return results, and sort them according to a generally proprietary ranking algorithm. Consequently, basic search by search engines is often referred to as algorithmic search. (See Box 7.2 for an expanded description of how search engines work.)

---

[28]See <http://www.superpages.com>.

[29]See <http://www.about.com>.

[30]About.com Web site, March 5, 2005. For more information see <http://ourstory.about.com/>.

[31]See <http://www.searchenginewatch.com> for a wealth of information about search engines and directories.

[32]Many search algorithms do not depend on the script or language used, so almost all the Internet's visible Web pages can be included—regardless of their language.

When Web site operators pay to have their sites listed in response to queries, the search is referred to as monetized search. The desire of Web sites to obtain advantageous positions in the listing of responses to queries relevant to their offerings has led to the development of specialized strategies and tactics that are called search engine marketing and optimization. Despite their best efforts, search engines cannot, for a variety of reasons, reach all sites on the World Wide Web. The untouched part of the Web is called, variously, the "deep," the "dark," or the "invisible" Web. Finally, the searcher can obtain more comprehensive results to a query by looking at the results of searches conducted by several search engines combined by a "metasearch" engine. The following sections examine these search engine topics in more detail.

Algorithmic Search

Because they are automated, search engines are the only currently available navigation aids capable of finding and identifying even a moderate fraction of the billions of Web pages on the public Internet. To index and retrieve that much information from the Web, search engine developers must overcome unique challenges in each of the three main parts that make up a search engine: the crawler, the indexer, and the query engine. (See Box 7.2.)

The principal challenges facing the crawler (robot or spider) are determining which Web sites to visit and how frequently to do so. Search engines vary substantially in the number of Web sites visited, the depth of their search, and the intervals at which they return. In general, increasing the size of the computing facility can increase the number, the depth, and the frequency of visits and, consequently, it is a business judgment by the search engine operators that determines these parameters.

The principal challenge facing the indexer is in determining when two terms are equivalent, bearing in mind singular versus plural versions, misspellings, differing translations or transliterations, synonyms, and so on. Moreover, these challenges are language-specific. These problems can be addressed to some extent during the creation of an index, but are often left to the search engine. A search engine typically allows for partial matching to the query and returns many results. Searching for "cook rutabaga" may return pointers to results with those words, but also to results containing "cooked rutabaga" or "cooking rutabaga."

The major challenges facing the query engine are matching the query words appropriately and calculating the relevance[33] of each response.

[33]Research on relevance in traditional information retrieval has identified dozens of factors, such as degree of topical match, authority of the source, how current the material is, familiarity of the terminology, ease and cost of acquiring the content, and so on. See, for example, Linda Schamber, "Relevance and Information Behavior," Chapter 1 in Martha E. Williams, editor, *Annual Review of Information Science and Technology*, Vol. 29, pp. 3-48, 1994.

BOX 7.2 How Search Engines Work

Search engines are technical systems comprising computer programs that perform three interrelated functions: searching the Web to collect Web pages, indexing the Web pages found, and using the index to respond to queries.

The Web search programs, called crawlers or spiders, collect Web pages by traversing the Web, following links from site to site in a systematic way. By beginning with Web sites that are densely populated with links, a crawler is able to spread across the most frequently accessed parts of the Web, and then increase speed as it travels to other less frequently visited sites. Search engines use different algorithms to determine the coverage and depth of the pages that are visited. Some may focus more on breadth, covering only pages linked from the home page of a Web site, rather than depth, visiting pages deeper within the Web site's hierarchical structure. Because of the constant changes of Web site content and the addition of new Web sites, Web crawling by search engines is never completed. The frequency with which Web pages are re-crawled directly affects the freshness of the results returned from a search engine query.

Once the Web pages are retrieved, indexing programs create a word index of the Web by extracting the words encountered on each Web page and recording the Uniform Resource Locator (URL) and possibly additional information for each one. Indexes are then created that list the URLs of all pages on the Web for a given word. They may also record additional information about the word such as whether it appeared in a title, anchor text, heading, or plain text; the relative size of its type; and its distance from other words.

In response to queries, query engines will search the index for the query words to find the pages where they appear. For example, if the query is for "CSTB committees," the search engine will retrieve a list of all the pages on which both the strings "CSTB" and "committees" appear. A search may return tens or thousands or even millions of responses, which users will typically not examine in full. Therefore, the critical question is the order in which the retrieved list of pages is returned. The goal is to return the pages

Determining the relevance of a response to a query is a complex problem, since relevance depends on the user's specific needs, which may not be clear from the words chosen for the query. (See the example of a search for "Paris" in Section 6.1.6.) Different search engines use different criteria to calculate relevance, with examples being the location and frequency of words matching the query terms on a Web page and the patterns and quality of links among Web pages.

Relevant results, once retrieved, can be sequenced by other factors that the system or the user considers appropriate. Few people will view dozens, much less thousands, of matches to a query; typically, only the first one or a few pages of results are viewed. Among the 1400 or so re-in decreasing order of relevance. The determination of relevance is both critical to the quality of response and very difficult to assess, because of the large number of indexed pages and the short queries that search engines typically receive. Each distinct search engine has developed its own proprietary algorithms for determining relevance.

Google, currently the general-purpose search engine with the largest database, is noted for its algorithm, PageRank™, which uses the link structure of the Web as a key part of the relevance calculation. It assumes that a link from page A to page B is a vote by page A for the quality of content on page B. A's vote is given higher weight if the Web site of page A is also highly linked. The relevance ranking assigned to a page by PageRank™ is based on the intrinsic value of the page plus the endorsements from the other pages linked to it. The qualitative performance of the PageRank™ algorithm is better than keyword algorithms alone, since it makes use of more information than just the content on the pages.[1]

The retrieved Web pages used to create the index may also be stored, or cached, beyond the time needed to create the index. Caching of results enables them to be returned more quickly in response to a request but also adds to the enormous storage capacity needed to create indexes required for large-scale search engines. Estimates of the computing resources used by one search engine to index the Web and handle 200 million queries per day—approximately one-third of the total daily Web searches—is 54,000 servers, over 100,000 processors, and 261,000 disks.[2]

Currently operating search engines include AlltheWeb, Alta Vista, Google, Inktomi, MSN Search, and Teoma.

[1]See Arvind Arasu, Junghoo Cho, Hector Garcia-Molina, Andreas Paepcke, and Sriram Raghavan, "Searching the Web," *ACM Transactions on Internet Technology* 1(1, August): 2-43, 2001.

[2]See John Markoff and G. Pascal Zachary, "In Search of the Web, Google Finds Riches," *New York Times*, Sec. 3, p. 1, April 13, 2003; and John Markoff, "The Coming Search Wars," *New York Times*, February 1, 2004.

spondents to a survey of search engine users in the spring of 2002, only 23 percent went beyond the second page and only about 9 percent read more than three pages.[34] Thus, the matching and ranking criteria of search engines strongly influence the material that people actually view and use.

No single set of matching and ranking criteria is likely to suit all users' purposes. Consequently, it is in general users' interest that multiple

[34]See "iProspect Search Engine Branding Survey," reported in "iProspect Survey Confirms Internet Users Ignore Web Sites Without Top Search Engine Rankings," iProspect press release, November 14, 2002, available at <http://www.iprospect.com/media/press2002_11_14.htm>.

search engines employing different relevance criteria be available. The more options, the more likely it is that users will find a search engine that consistently ranks highly the content or services they seek. Very skilled and experienced users might even want to know the criteria by which a search engine ranks its results, enabling them to choose the search engine whose criteria best meets their needs. However, commercial search services treat the details of their ranking algorithms as proprietary since they are a primary means of the services differentiating themselves from their competitors and of minimizing the capacity of Web site operators to "game" the system to achieve higher ranks.

Search engines are able to return a high proportion of all the relevant Web pages that are available for indexing—though often in such a large number that they exceed the searcher's ability to review most of them—and to give a reasonable probability of retrieving less-well-known Web pages related to particular topics, though not necessarily in the first few pages of results. Furthermore, since information on the Web is dynamically changing, heterogeneous, and redundant, no manual system can list and remain current with more than a small fraction of all sites. Only search engines have the capacity to keep their indices relatively current by continually revisiting accessible sites, although (as noted above) the frequency with which sites are visited varies among search engines and, probably also, depends on specific site characteristics. As the Web expands, so may the number of responses that search engines return for a query, although the relationship is not generally proportional. Because it is likely that they will receive large numbers of responses to a query, searchers naturally favor search engines whose ranking of responses reliably provides close to the top of the listing the pages that best meet their needs.

Monetized Search

The growing use of search engines offers the opportunity for information and service providers to affect the presentation of search results to users through a variety of direct and indirect means. When viewed from the traditional information retrieval perspective, this appears to contradict a user's "right" or expectation of neutrality in his or her information sources (except when seeking information from sources with an obvious viewpoint, such as political or commercial sources.) However, when seen from the marketing perspective, it is an especially efficient way for providers to reach prospective users just at the time when the users have expressed interest in what they have to offer.

The search engine companies have responded to the providers' interest through a variety of advertising, "pay for placement" and "pay for inclusion" opportunities. These practices as a group are often called monetized search. Payment can result in having an advertisement placed ahead or alongside of the search results for specified search terms, having a site visited more frequently or more deeply by the crawler, having a page assured a place in the results, or having a link placed at the top of the list of results. (However, concerns about the latter two practices—paid inclusion and paid ranking—have led some search engines that offer them either to phase them out or to consider doing so.[35])

The consequence of these opportunities is that the first page of results of a search engine query for, say, "Florida holidays" generally now includes not only the neutral results ranked according to the relevance algorithm used by the engine, but also sponsored listings along the top or the sides from advertisers that paid to have their listings presented whenever the keywords "Florida" or "holiday" or "Florida holidays" appeared in the query.

Providers' payments have become the major source of revenue for most search engines, which searchers use for free. (See Section 7.2.2 for a further discussion of advertising and the search engine market.)

Search Engine Marketing and Optimization

The opportunity to pay for listings in response to certain key words on specified search engines has led to the development of search engine marketing. Its practitioners help operators of Web sites to decide which key words to pay for on which search engines to attract the greatest number of prospective customers to their sites. This is very similar to the role that advertising agencies play in helping advertisers to decide what ads to run in which media. However, advertising on search engines has the distinct advantage that the message is presented only to prospective customers who have expressed an interest in a topic that may be related to the advertisers' wares at the time of their interest. In many cases, the advertiser pays only if prospective customers actually click on the link that takes them to the advertiser's site.

Web site operators have also responded to their perceived business need to be ranked higher in the non-paid results of searches (e.g., florists in the search for "flowers") by adopting means to improve their rankings.[36] This has led to the development of search engine optimization in which the site design is optimized to include simple, common

---

[35]See Stefanie Olsen, "Search Engines Rethink Paid Inclusion," *c/net news.com*, June 23, 2004, available at <http://news.com.com/2100-1024-5245825.html>.

[36]See Mylene Mangalindan, "Playing the Search-Engine Game," *Wall Street Journal*, June 16, 2003, p. R1.

terms likely to turn up in searches and to include metatags (metadata) that are invisible to users but are picked up by some search engines. Specialized firms have grown up to help companies both in marketing and optimizing their Web sites.

Other approaches are less savory. For example, "pagejackers" falsify information in the meta tags on their site to emulate the appearance of another Web site that would rank higher; "spamdexers" seek placement under search terms that are unrelated to the content of their pages by placing many repetitions of the unrelated terms on their site in invisible form (e.g., white text on white background, which can nevertheless be read by the search engine). In response to providers' tactics, search engines eliminate from their databases those companies that they believe are using unscrupulous methods to improve rankings.[37] Not surprisingly, this has led to a continuing battle between Web site operators trying new ways to improve their ranking and search engines introducing countermeasures as each new tactic is discovered.

The Deep, Dark, or Invisible Web

Although they are far more comprehensive than directories, general search engines still index and retrieve only a portion of the content available on the Internet. First, they do not reach every page that is visible to them because of limits on how often they will crawl the Web, on the capabilities of their crawlers, and on how much of each visited site they will crawl. Second, a large majority of the information potentially reachable on the Web is not visible to them. The parts that they cannot see are called the "deep," the "dark," or the "invisible" Web.[38] Various estimates place the size of the invisible Web at hundreds of times larger than the visible or public World Wide Web.[39] Web pages can be invisible to search engines for a variety of reasons.[40]

A primary reason is the increasing use of databases to deliver content

---

[37]See, for example, Google's guidelines at <www.google.com/webmasters/guidelines.html>.

[38]See Chris Sherman and Gary Price, *The Invisible Web*, Information Today, Inc., Medford, N.J., 2001.

[39]See Michael K. Bergman, "The Deep Web: Surfacing Hidden Value,"August, *Journal of Electronic Publishing* 7(1, August), 2001, available at <http://www.press.umich.edu/jep/o7-01/bergman.html>.

[40]See Genie Tyburski and Gayle O'Connor, "The Invisible Web; Hidden Online Search Tool," presentation to ABA Techshow, April 3, 2003, Chicago, available at <http://www.virtualchase.com/iweb>.

dynamically. If material is available only in response to queries and actually does not exist until a question is asked, there is no practical way for a general search engine's crawler to "see" it since those systems cannot synthesize the queries that will generate the relevant material. Thus, engines[41] cannot crawl inside searchable databases such as library catalogs, the Thomas register of manufacturing information, or indexes of journal literature. A search engine query on "Shakespeare" may retrieve sites that specialize in Shakespearean memorabilia (as described in their Web pages), sites of theaters that are currently performing Shakespearean plays, and Shakespeare fan clubs, but usually will not retrieve catalog records for books in libraries or for records in archives. There are Web sites that serve as directories to many "invisible" resources, such as library catalogs and databases, on the Internet.[42] Moreover, specialized search engines, such as those used by shopping comparison[43] or travel reservation sites,[44] are designed to synthesize the appropriate queries and submit them to multiple databases in order to obtain the comparison information requested by the user. Furthermore, as noted earlier, directories can be useful in this situation since they can manually identify or seek submission of database sites, enabling the searcher to find a relevant database and then submit a specific query to it.

Content virtualization[45] produces a considerable amount of dynamic information that is unavailable to Web crawlers. Google has made an attempt to overcome some of the challenges of rapidly changing content and the increasing use of "virtual" content, particularly among large news Web sites, by creating special arrangements with news organizations to continually update, retrieve, and index content from a preselected list of news Web sites.[46]

---

[41]See Clifford A. Lynch, "Metadata Harvesting and the Open Archives Initiative," *ARL Bimonthly Report* 217:1-9, 2001.

[42]One such directory is "Those Dark Hiding Places: The Invisible Web Revealed," which can be found at <http://library.rider.edu/scholarly/rlackie/Invisible/Inv_Web.html>.

[43]Such as, for example, epinions (www.epinions.com) and bizrate (www.bizrate.com).

[44]For example, Travelocity (www.travelocity.com) and Expedia (www.expedia.com), or metasites, such as SideStep (www.sidestep.com) and Mobissimo (www.mobissimo.com).

[45]"Content virtualization—or content integration as some know it—leaves data in its originating system and pulls it together in real time when requested by the user." Quoted from Lowell Rapaport, "Manage Content Virtually," *Transform Magazine*, April 2003, available at <http://transformmag.com/shared/cp/print_article_flat.jhtml?article=/db_area/archs/2003/04/tfm0304tp_1.shtml>.

[46]For more information about news aggregation services by Google, see <http://news.google.com/>. For other approaches to news aggregation services, see Blogdex at <http://blogdex.net/>.

The dark Web also encompasses the vast intranets of many corporations, governments, and other organizations. Resources are not indexed if they are behind firewalls, require payment, or are otherwise coded "off limits" to search engines.

Progress on the dark Web problem is being made via efforts such as the Open Archives Initiative (OAI), which enables information providers to offer their metadata for harvesting.[47] Additionally, new kinds of Web pages for which indexing is probably infeasible are emerging. Personalized content such as the "My Yahoo personal news page" is an example of this type of content, since it is created only when the user requests it and is not available to others on the Web. However, it comprises a selection of materials from public Web pages, so indexing it would add little other than information about an individual's selections—and that would probably be constrained by considerations of privacy. Some ephemeral content, such as "instant messaging" and "chat," is not indexed because it is dynamic and not readily accessible to search engines unless it is archived. Google indexes the complete Usenet archives and the archives of many important Internet mailing lists.

Another source of new and rapidly changing information on the Web is the profusion of journals in the form of Web logs, called blogs. Software that has made it very easy for individuals to construct and modify Web sites and the availability of services to house them have made Web publishing common. The ease of creating and changing blogs has lowered the barriers to entry for publishing to large audiences. This has led to their increasing number, types, and ranges of quality. They often incorporate a large number of links to other blogs and Web sites, making them a distinctive medium that contains not only the authors' contributions, but also the authors' identification of "communities of interest" whose ideas are germane to theirs.

These new forms of content pose further requirements for search engines to retrieve information more frequently and also to return the wide variety of information posted to Web logs in a useful way. Some of these challenges are being met by specialty search engines, which go beyond the features presented by Google. One of these is Daypop,[48] which uses its own kind of link analysis to identify Web logs that are pointed to other Web log sites from their front pages, rather than from archived or back

---

[47]Scholarly Publishing and Academic Resources Coalition, "The Case for Institutional Repositories: A SPARC Position Paper," available at <http://www.arl.org/sparc/IR/ir.html>.

[48]See Greg Notess, "The Blog Realm: News Source, Searching with Daypop, and Content Management," *Online* 26(5), 2002. For more information about Daypop, see <http://www.daypop.com/>; see also Technorati for another search engine approach to Weblogging, at <http://www.technorati.com/>.

pages, and allows popular commentary, or responses to original posts on a Web log, to be comparatively searched across a number of Web logs.

Finally, multimedia materials are increasingly populating the Internet. They range from still photographs to full-length videos and films. These can readily be indexed by their descriptions, but unless a human indexer provides descriptive terms—metadata—a photo or song cannot yet be automatically searched and indexed by its content at a commercially viable scale.

The inability to search everything accessible via the Internet is not necessarily a problem, since much of it may not be useful and there is necessarily a cost associated with sorting through ever larger amounts of material. However, while some of the unsearchable material may be of little value, it is likely that some of it (say, major library catalogs or government databases) would be of great value, if it could be readily searched.

Metasearch Engines

"Metasearch" engines take the keywords entered by the user and submit them to a number of independent search engines. They present the combined results to the user. This would appear to offer the advantage of time saving and the possibility of getting the best results from the sum of the engines searched. However, whether those advantages are realized depends on how the metasearch engine combines and orders the results from several search engines, each using different relevance and ranking criteria. Among the metasearch engines available in 2004[49] were Dogpile, Vivisimo, Kartoo, and Mamma.

7.1.8 Use of Navigation Aids

How much use is made of these aids to navigation? Complete data are unavailable, but use of search engines (and their associated directory services) is being measured. According to the Pew Internet & American Life Project:[50]

- In total, Americans conducted 3.9 billion searches in June 2004.
- The average search engine user conducted 33 searches in June 2004.

---

[49]For a listing of metasearch engines, see Chris Sherman, "Metacrawlers and Metasearch Engines," *SearchEngineWatch.com*, March 15, 2004, available at <http://searchenginewatch.com/links/article.php/2156241>.

[50]See Deborah Fallows, Lee Rainie, and Graham Mudd, "The Popularity and Importance of Search Engines," data memo, Pew Internet & American Life Project, August 2004, available at <http://www.pewinternet.org/pdfs/PIP_Data_Memo_Searchengines.pdf>. The results came both from a telephone survey of 1399 Internet users and from tracking of Internet use by comScore Media Metrix.

- Eighty-four percent of Americans who use the Internet have used search engines—more than 107 million people.
- On an average day, about 38 million of the 64 million Americans who are online use a search engine. Two-thirds of Americans who are online say they use search engines at least twice a week.
- Using search engines is second only to using e-mail as the most popular Internet activity, except when major news stories are breaking, when getting the news online surpasses using search engines.
- "There is a substantial payoff as search engines improve and people become more adept at using them. Some 87% of search engine users say they find the information they want most of the time when they use search engines."
- "More than two-thirds of search engine users say they consider search engines a fair and unbiased source of information."
- ". . . 92% of searchers express confidence in their skills as searchers—over half of them say they are 'very confident' they can accomplish what they want when they perform an online search."
- ". . . 44% of searchers say that all or most of the searches they conduct are for information they absolutely need to find."
- "A third of searchers say they couldn't live without Internet search engines." However, about a half say that, while they like using search engines, they could go back to other ways of finding information.

How do Internet users deploy the available aids to navigation? Do they generally go to the Web sites they seek by entry of a domain name or keyword or through bookmarks? Do they follow hyperlinks from Web page to Web page? Or do they commonly make use of search engines and directories? There is little publicly available research that addresses these specific questions. One analysis, based on survey data from March 2003 and 1 year earlier, provides some insights.[51] According to that analysis, search engines produced 13.4 percent of site referrals on the day measured, which was an increase from 7.1 percent 1 year earlier. Navigation through entry of a known or guessed URL or use of a bookmark also increased from 50.1 percent to 65.5 percent over the year. The decline occurred in the flow along hyperlinks, which decreased from 42.6 percent to 21 percent. This survey indicates that Internet users tend to use certain sites and services consistently, visiting them repeatedly, using their book-

[51]The data were collected on March 6, 2003, by WebSideStory's StatMarket from about 12 million visitors to 125,000 sites using its proprietary analytical platform and were compared with figures from the previous year. Reported in Brian Morrissey, "Search Guiding More Web Activity," *CyberAtlas*, March 13, 2003, available at <http://cyberatlas.internet.com/big_picture/traffic_patterns/article/0,1323,5931_2109221,00.html>.

marks or remembered URLs. This suggests that much of their Web use is routine: checking e-mail, visiting a few standard sites, and exchanging instant messages with some Internet buddies. The need for search engines or directories arises primarily when a user needs a specific piece of information or wants a new or a replacement source of information, entertainment, or other material.

When a search is required, a survey of 1403 Internet users in spring 2002[52] showed a strong user allegiance to one or a small number of navigation services. More than half (52 percent) generally relied on the same search engine or directory and close to 35 percent used several interchangeably. Only 13 percent used different services for different kinds of searches. With respect to the usefulness of search engines, at that time almost half (45.9 percent) believed their searches were successful almost always. When they were not successful, 27 percent of the users switched to another search engine, rather than refining the search with more terms—only 7.5 percent did that. One third of the users felt that their searches were successful three-quarters of the time and 13 percent reported successful searches only half the time. (Though presented differently, these figures are not inconsistent with the results of the Pew study reported above.)

Users of diverse skills and interests, located across the world, have a range of information and services literally "at their fingertips," whether at work, at home, or on the road, that far exceeds that available even to information specialists before 1993. This is true especially for those seeking commercial products and services. Comparable navigation tools for scholarly and public interest materials are generally less well developed.

Conclusion: The further development of Internet navigation services, such as subject-specific directories, that enable discovery of specialized databases and similar resources not readily indexed by search engines, is desirable. They can be of particular value to non-commercial groups, whose information resources may not be able to support active marketing.

Conclusion: As the material accessible through the Internet continues its rapid increase in volume and variety and as its societal importance grows, Internet navigation aids and services are likely to be challenged to deliver more precise responses, in more convenient forms, to more diverse questions, from more users with widely varying skills.

---

[52]See "iProspect Search Engine Branding Survey," reported in "iProspect Survey Confirms Internet Users Ignore Web Sites Without Top Search Engine Rankings," iProspect press release, November 14 2002, available at <http://www.iprospect.com/media/press2002_11_14.htm>.

Prospective improvements in Internet navigation technology and processes are discussed in Section 8.1.

7.2 INTERNET NAVIGATION—INSTITUTIONAL FRAMEWORK

In contrast to the provision of domain name services, Internet navigation is not the function of a single integrated technical system. While there is just one Domain Name System, there are many ways of navigating the Internet, only three of which currently involve distinct technical systems dedicated to navigation—KEYWORDS,[53] search engines, and directories. Moreover, the institutional framework of the technical systems supporting Internet navigation is an open market, with many independent and competing providers offering their services. While some providers are non-profit or governmental institutions, such as national libraries or professional societies, the most frequently used navigation systems are provided by commercial organizations. This section concentrates on the commercial market for directory and search engine services.

7.2.1 The Commercial Providers of Navigation Services

As noted in Section 6.2.2, the early distinctions between providers of directories and providers of search engines—when each Web search site featured either algorithmic search engine results or human-powered directory listings[54]—have increasingly become blurred. Technology has helped to automate some of the classification processes for the Yahoo! directory,[55] and most general-purpose Web search sites now feature search results from both human-based directories and crawler-based search engines, with one type providing the majority of search results. See Table 7.2 for a listing of navigation services and the sources of the results they provide.

The navigation services market is dynamic. The relationships shown in Table 7.2, which applied in July 2004, are continually changing. For

---

[53]In June 2004, the commercial market for KEYWORDS comprised primarily AOL, Netpia, and Beijing 3721. Yahoo! purchased Beijing 3721 in 2004.

[54]See Danny Sullivan, *How Search Engines Work,* October 14, 2002, available at <http://searchenginewatch.com/webmasters/article.php/2168031>.

[55]In "A History of Search Engines," Wes Sonnenreich explains that "as the number of links grew and their pages began to receive thousands of hits a day, the team created ways to better organize the data. In order to aid in data retrieval, Yahoo! became a searchable directory. The search feature was a simple database search engine. Because Yahoo! entries were entered and categorized manually, Yahoo! was not really classified as a search engine. Instead, it was generally considered to be a searchable directory. Yahoo! has since automated some aspects of the gathering and classification process, blurring the distinction between engine and directory." See "A History of Search Engines," available at <http://www.wiley.com/legacy/compbooks/sonnenreich/history.html>.

TABLE 7.2 Navigation Services and the Providers of Their Results

Navigation Service	Process Used to Obtain Main Results	Provider of Main Results	Provider of Paid Results	Provider of Directory and/or Backup Results
AllTheWeb (Overture-owned; Yahoo!-acquired)	Search	AllTheWeb	Overture	n/a
Alta Vista (Overture-owned; Yahoo!-acquired)	Search	Alta Vista	Overture	LookSmart
AOL Search	Search	Google	Google	Open Directory
Ask Jeeves	Search	Teoma	Google	Open Directory
Google	Search	Google	Google	Open Directory
HotBot	Search	Choice of: Inktomi (Yahoo!-owned) Google, Ask Jeeves	Overture	n/a
LookSmart	Directory	LookSmart	LookSmart	Zeal
Lycos	Search	AllTheWeb	Overture	Open Directory
MSN Search	Search	MSN/Search	Overture	n/a
Netscape	Search	Google	Google	Open Directory
Overture (Yahoo!-owned)	Paid	Overture	Overture	Backup from Inktomi
Open Directory	Directory	Open Directory	n/a	n/a
Teoma (Ask Jeeves-owned)	Search	Teoma	Google	n/a
Yahoo!	Search/Directory	Inktomi (Yahoo!-owned)	Overture	Yahoo!

SOURCE: Based on SearchEngineWatch.com, 2003, available at <http://www.searchenginewatch.com/webmasters/article.php/2167981#chart> and updated in March 2005.

instance, the early search engine Lycos, which began in 1994, ceased providing its own search listings in April 1999 and has since used AllTheWeb to power its Web search site. Google, which generates it own Web search results, also provides algorithmic search services to others such as AOL and, until March 2004, Yahoo!, which paid Google $7.2 million in 2002 for the search queries it handled.[56]

Over the past 4 years from 2000 to 2004 in the United States, Google rose from eleventh position among navigation sites with a 5.8 percent market share in December 2000, as measured by "audience reach,"[57] to first position with an estimated share of 34.7 percent in February 2004, as measured by "share of search."[58] (See Figure 7.1.) The previous leading Web navigation site, Yahoo!, fell from a 48 percent share to second position with 30 percent during that time. Two of the other high-ranking Web navigation sites were MSN with 15.4 percent and AOL with 15 percent of searches in February 2004. However, note that during that period Inktomi provided search services for MSN, while Google provided search services for AOL. For international Internet users (English-language using populations), Google had an even larger lead in February 2004, capturing more than 43 percent of searches to Yahoo!'s 31 percent, MSN's 14 percent, and AOL's 7 pecent. (Since Google still provided search results to both Yahoo! and AOL in February 2004, its actual share of searches was closer to 80 percent, both internationally and in the United States After March 2004, without Yahoo!, its share dropped to 50 percent.)

7.2.2 The Business of Internet Navigation

The primary source of income for commercial Internet navigation services, which provide access to material on the public Internet, has become

---

[56]See Yahoo proxy statement filed March 2002, p. 30, available at <http://www.sec.gov/Archives/edgar/data/1011006/000091205702010171/a2073396zdef14a.htm>.

[57]Nielsen NetRatings reported in Danny Sullivan, "Nielsen NetRatings Search Engine Ratings," February 2003, available at <http://www.searchenginewatch.com/reports/print.php/34701_2156451>. "Audience reach" is the percentage of U.S. home and work Internet users estimated to have searched on each site at least once during the month through a Web browser or some other "online" means.

[58]The new metric generated monthly by comScore Media Metrix, beginning in January 2003, provides a better measure of market share by focusing on the number of *searches* that a search engine handles per month rather than the number of *searchers* that perform at least one query on the Web search site. The Web search site queries are based on a panel of 1.5 million Web users located within the United States and in non-U.S. locations. The February 2004 results are from a comScore Media Metrix press release on April 29, 2004, available at <http://www.comscore.com/press/default.asp>.

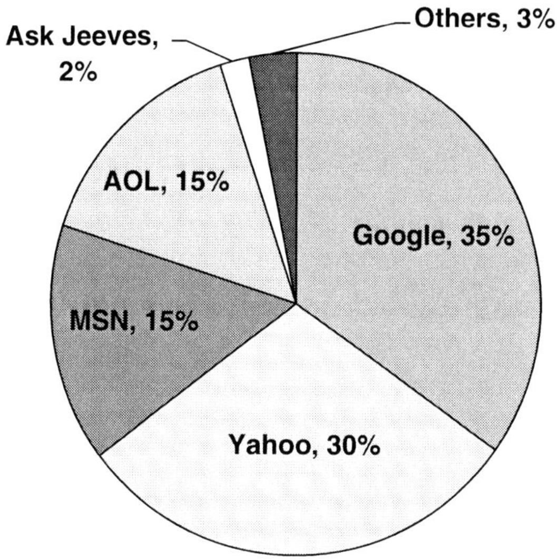

FIGURE 7.1 Company share of U.S. Web searches by home and work users, February 2004. SOURCE: comScore Media Metrix qSearch press release, April 28, 2004, available at <http://www.comscore.com/press/default.asp>.

selling advertising and placement on their sites.[59] Consequently, as in many broadcast media, it is the content and service providers that are subsidizing users' access to navigation services in order to present advertisements to them at the time of their expressed interest in a topic. This contrasts sharply with traditional commercial information search services, such as Lexis, Westlaw, and Dialog, which have obtained their income directly from their users, who pay to access the services' proprietary (but free of marketing influence) information. Typically, those pay-for-access companies also provide other services, such as training, documentation, and extensive customer support, to their users.

[59]Commercial search engine companies are exploring possibilities beyond their own search sites. For example, publishers such as the *Washington Post* have turned to Google or Overture to sell advertisements associated with the content that a visitor selects. See Bob Tedeschi, "If You Liked the Web Page, You'll Love the Ad," *New York Times*, August 4, 2003, available at <http://www.nytimes.com/2003/08/04/technology/04ECOM.html>. In addition, Google and others license their search engine technology for use by other Web sites and by corporate intranets.

The advertising that supports search services can take several forms: banner advertisements, popup advertisements, or search-linked ads. Banners are typically displayed at the top or side of a Web page and are generally priced on a per-impression (view) basis, which means that the advertiser pays based on how many people see its advertisement, with prices quoted in CPMs (cost per thousand impressions), as is traditional in the advertising industry. A typical rate for a generic banner advertisement is 2 cents per impression, or $20 CPM. Banner sizes are standardized so that sellers and buyers of advertising space can find it easy to negotiate pricing and other contract terms.[60] So-called "skyscrapers" are vertically oriented banner ads. Popup advertisements are similar to banners, except that they pop up as separate windows. Their shape is also standardized. (The intrusive nature of popup advertisements has led to a variety of software products—separate programs or browser features—that automatically prevent them from appearing.[61])

Search-linked advertisements appear as the result of a search. For example, the searcher mentioned above who enters the keyword search term "Florida vacation" might see advertisements for Florida hotels, condo rentals, theme parks, towns and cities, and the like. These may be displayed as banners, popups, sidebars, or—as noted earlier—presented with the search results themselves. Sophisticated algorithms are used by the search services to select which advertisements will appear. These algorithms take into account, among other things, the amount the advertiser is willing to pay if the user clicks on the advertisement, the relevance of the advertisement, and the historic success of the advertisement in generating clicks. All services place limits on the number of advertisements they will display.

Not surprisingly, search-linked advertisements are much more valuable than generic banners. They are priced both by impression and by click-through. Practices differ among search services, but Google displays up to two advertisements at the top of the page (which it calls "Premium Sponsorships" and up to eight advertisements on the right side of the

---

[60]Further information regarding these standards may be found at <http://www.iab.net/standards/guidelines.asp>.

[61]Additionally, software known as "adware" or "spyware" has been developed that is installed on a user's computer and covertly gathers information about a user during navigation of the Internet and transmits such information to an individual or company. In turn, the individual or company transmits information back to the user's computer to display specific banner advertisements based on the user's navigation of the Internet. Such activity has resulted in state legislatures considering or enacting spyware regulation laws; see, for example, *Utah Spyware Control Act* (H.B. 323 2004), California law (A.B. 2787 April 13, 2004; S.B. 1436 March 23, 2004), and Iowa law (S.F. 2200 March 1, 2004), and litigation to undo such laws; see, for example, *WhenU.com, Inc. v. Utah*, No. 040907578 (Utah Dist. Ct. 3d Dist. April 23, 2004).

page (which it calls "Adwords Select"). Typically, these ads can appear on every page of results.

At one time Google priced the top ads on a CPM basis and the side ads on a CPC (cost per click) basis. In the latter case, the advertiser pays only when the user actually clicks on an advertisement. However, Google has eliminated the CPM pricing, and now all its ads are priced on a CPC basis. The ads placed at the top of the page are chosen from the side ads on the basis of price and performance. Prices for a click-through are over 10 times as much as the price of a generic impression.[62] However, some search engines will drop a click-through advertiser that does not produce a sufficient number of hits.

The two leading providers of search-linked advertisements (or monetized search) are Overture (now owned by Yahoo!) and Google, which also distribute search-linked advertisements to other search sites. The paid listings provided by Overture to its affiliated network of Web search sites, including Yahoo!, MSN, Infospace, and Alta Vista, have been estimated to have handled 46.8 percent of all U.S.-based paid searches; and the paid listings provided by Google, appearing on the search results pages of Google, AOL, Infospace and Ask Jeeves, accounted for 46.6 percent of all U.S. paid searches in January 2003.[63] Google provides search services to several hundred other partners, in the United States and abroad, although AOL and Ask Jeeves are the biggest U.S. customers.

Search-linked advertisements have been very successful. According to its initial public offering (IPO) prospectus, Google had revenues of $961.9 million in 2003 and profits of $105.6 million, but without some unusual provisions, its operating profit margin is 62 percent. Before its acquisition by Yahoo!, Overture reported revenues of $103 million in 2000, $288 million in 2001, and $668 million in 2002. In 2003 it claimed over 95,000 advertisers, who received over 646 million clicks in the second quarter of 2003 for which they paid an average of 40 cents per click.[64] These figures dramatically illustrate that Internet navigation services—unlike many other Internet services that were tested in the 1990s—have apparently found a financial model that is capable of supporting them and enabling their continued development. At the same time, the struggle to capture advertising dollars has been one of the forces driving the continuing consolidation of the industry, as some of the most successful search services have acquired their competitors in order to increase their share of the market.

---

[62]From Overture, "Annual Report," January 2003.

[63]See <http://www.imediaconnection.com/content/news/050503c.asp>.

[64]Data collected on August 16, 2002, and December 4, 2003, from <http://www.overture.com/d/USm/about/news/glance.jhtml>.

Spending on paid listings (guaranteed separate listings on the search engine results pages) and paid inclusion (guaranteed inclusion in the regular search engine results, but ranking not assured)[65]—two of the three forms of search-related marketing—grew by 40 times in 4 years since 2000.[66] Globally such spending is expected to grow 5-fold to $7 billion a year by 2007, from $1.4 billion in 2002. Outside the United States, 10-fold growth to $2 billion in 2007 from about $200 million in 2003 is expected.[67]

The revenues from monetized search are often shared between the site and the search service that provides the advertisements. For example, Google currently provides algorithmic search and monetized search for AOL and they split the revenues from the monetization. Overture provided monetized search for Yahoo! on a shared-revenue basis until its acquisition, while Google provided algorithmic search service to Yahoo! until March 2004 for a flat fee. Google and Overture both use an auction model to price their search-linked advertisements: Users can specify a price that they are willing to pay for various positions, and the highest bidder gets the highest position in response to a specific query. For example, a rental car agency could bid to be listed first in any search for "rental cars." Minimum bids vary, but generally the range of bidding starts at 5 cents a click and goes up to $100 for some mortgage-related items, although Google caps bids at $50. The model is sufficiently popular that, as noted earlier, a secondary market of search engine marketers/optimizers has arisen to advise Web sites on how to optimize their bidding for queries.[68] The details of the auction systems differ, but the advantage of auctions is that hundreds of thousands of prices can be set by actual demand rather than having to be preset and posted.

Since these auctions are subject to gaming, navigation services actively watch for potential fraud by advertisers and monitor the content of advertisers with editorial spot-checking. If they suspect cheating, the advertiser will be removed from bidding. To become qualified bidders, advertisers

---

[65]Ask Jeeves announced in June 2004 that it was phasing out its paid inclusion program because its algorithmic search had become sophisticated enough to find all necessary Web sites and refresh them as required, making paying for inclusion unnecessary. See Stefanie Olsen "Search Engines Rethink Paid Inclusion," *c/net news.com*, June 23, 2004, available at <http://news.com.com/2102-1024_3-5245825.html>.

[66]See Wall Street Journal On-line, accessed May 5, 2004. Data from InterActive Advertising Bureau, PriceWaterhouseCoopers LLP, eMarketer.

[67]According to U.S. Bancorp's Piper Jaffray as reported by Mylene Mangalindan, "Playing the Search-Engine Game," *Wall Street Journal*, June 16, 2003, available at <http://www.morevisibility.com/news/wsj-playing_the_searchengine_game.html>.

[68]See sites such as Wordtracker, at <http://www.wordtracker.com/>, and <http://www.paid-search-engine-tools.com/> for a description of their Keyword Bid Optimizer (KBO); and Traffick at <http://www.traffick.com/>.

provide information about themselves, their business, their interests, the keywords on which they wish to bid, and how much they wish to bid.

These advertiser-driven business models for navigation services contrast with the non-commercial model of neutral information searching and navigation of public and academic libraries, although they more closely resemble the business models for newspapers and other media where advertising and editorial matter are expected to be rigorously separated. Nevertheless, users need to be cautious about how they treat the results of Internet searches, especially those about subjects with commercial significance. As noted above, the major search services currently identify the sponsored results (sponsored links or sponsored search listings) and set them off from the direct results of the algorithmic search, following the newspaper model. As long as the distinction is clear and users are aware of it, sponsored search should present few problems while providing the great benefit of "free" search services to the user. However, the potential for abuse exists. It would be possible, for example, for a search service to accept payment for assured placement in the "top 10" of what would appear to be a neutral listing. (None have been accused of doing so, but some will accept payment to ensure inclusion, but not ranking, in the otherwise neutral listing.) Or the distinct placement and typography of the sponsored listing could be weakened to the point that a casual user would not be aware of its difference from the algorithmic search results. Thus far, competition among sites and third-party evaluations have served as important countervailing forces. Should abuses grow, however, search services could find themselves under increased public pressure for government scrutiny or facing more disputes and criticism concerning such activities from other commercial entities. (See the discussion in Section 8.2.1.)

7.2.3 The Navigation Services Market

As seen above, a large number of navigation services have entered the market, attempting to achieve profitability by selling advertising. Although it can be very profitable, this has turned out to be a difficult and expensive venture. Furthermore, competition among search engines has forced them to invest in improved software and extensive computer and storage facilities with substantial communications capacity to increase the breadth, depth, and frequency of their coverage of the Web.

Consolidation

Over the past 4 years, there has been considerable consolidation in the search services market.[69] Several large search engine service provid-

---

[69]See, for example, <http://www.imediaconnection.com/content/news/050503c.asp>.

ers have left the market, and others have been combined into a single firm. At the same time, there has been increased vertical integration as operators of Web sites have acquired operators of search engines. In 2003, Overture, with a primary focus on providing paid search listings, acquired Alta Vista for $140 million and AlltheWeb, the Fast Search and Transfer (FAST) Web search unit, for $70 million. Overture aimed to strengthen its core business of paid search listings by eventually integrating it with its algorithmic search and paid inclusion services.[70] Also in 2003, however, the directory-based Yahoo! purchased the search engine Inktomi for $235 million, and then in July 2003, acquired Overture for $1.62 billion.[71] Google, while not an aggressive acquirer, went public with an IPO in 2004 that raised $1.67 billion,[72] which provided it with a war chest that can be used for acquisitions. The one new player that has entered the search services market is Microsoft, which built the staff and technology to launch its own search service, which it is very likely to integrate into its next-generation operating system. In February 2005, Microsoft unveiled a revised MSN search that bore strong visual similarities to Google's search interface.[73]

Yahoo! has apparently decided to vertically integrate by buying both a paid-listing provider and a search engine. It is now able to produce by itself the paid listings previously supplied by an independent Overture and the algorithmic search services previously provided by Google. The net result of this latest phase of consolidation is that there are only a few major independent navigation services left—Google and Yahoo! are the largest.

In 2004, Google, which then provided search services to both Yahoo! and AOL, actually had 80 percent share of searches. This dropped when Yahoo! replaced Google with its own algorithmic search engine. However, whether the acquisitions result in sustained shifts in search shares will depend on whether, for example, users of the Yahoo! search site continue to search there or instead switch to another site that uses Google. These changes in the search services industry are likely to influence other

---

[70]See Brian Morrissey, "Overture to Buy FAST," *Australia Internet.com*, February 26, 2003, available at <http://www.breakfastforums.com.au/r/article/jsp/sid/12837>.

[71]See "Yahoo! to Acquire Overture," press release, July 14, 2003, available at <http://www.corporate-ir.net/ireye/ir_site.zhtml?ticker=OVER&script=410&layout=0&item_id=430830>; and Mylene Mangalindan, Nick Wingfield, and Robert Guth, "Rising Clout of Google Prompts Rush by Internet Rivals to Adapt," *The Wall Street Journal*, July 16, 2003.

[72]See Dawn Kawamoto and Stefanie Olsen, "Google Gets to Wall Street—and Lives," *c/net news.com*, August 19, 2004, available at <http://news.com.com/Google+gets+to+Wall+Street—and+lives/2100-1038_3-5317091.html>.

[73]See Juan Carlos Perez, "Microsoft Turns Spotlight on Its Search Engine," *Computerworld*, February 1, 2005, available at <http://www.computerworld.com/softwaretopics/software/story/0,10801,99416,00.html>.

Web search sites, primarily AOL, which currently outsource both Web search results and paid listings, to consider creating or acquiring their own in-house services. Now that Microsoft has entered the search engine competition, it is possible that AOL will feel compelled to do the same.

Innovation

In the past, as described in Section 6.2, there has been a cycle of innovation, adoption, and displacement of navigation services. It began when some new search engine or directory emerged with new technology, or a better user interface, or both than the incumbent-favored service. The new service attracted attention and gained market share. Then as it and the Internet grew, its searches returned a larger number of irrelevant answers, even though its precision may not have changed. Then yet another new service with better technology or a better interface or both appeared. The market tipped to the new leader and the cycle repeated. If this innovative cycle were to continue into the future, or if more specialized navigation services were developed and succeeded, then the current consolidation might be only temporary, a pause until a significant new and better technology or services arose.

Rapid changing of the leader is unlikely to happen under current conditions in the navigation services industry (though the entry of Microsoft may represent an exception). The current consolidation reflects the increasing importance of economies of scale—the fact that the considerable hardware and software costs of developing and operating a search engine are independent of the number of users, whereas revenues from advertising are directly dependent on them. This makes it difficult for innovative services to start small and build volume over time unless they have a very large amount of patient investment capital. So in the future, competition among navigation services is more likely to take the form of rivalry among a small number of established large players rather than competition with a large number of small newcomers.

Conclusion: The Internet navigation services industry has successfully financed the development and evolution of services that meet many of the needs of a wide range of searchers at little or no cost to them, especially when they are seeking commercial material. At the same time, it has provided advertisers with an efficient, cost-effective means to gain access to potential customers at the time that they are most interested in the advertiser's product or service.

Conclusion: The consolidation of the Internet navigation services industry could reduce the opportunity for innovative new services to enter the market for general Internet-wide navigation in competition with existing services. However, the new services or their technology could alternatively be acquired by an incumbent, thus making it available to users, or could focus on a niche that is not well served by the more general services.

So long as no single service becomes dominant, each competitor will have continuing pressure to improve its offerings. The net effect of these factors on innovation cannot be predicted.

Conclusion: The importance of the Internet as the infrastructure linking a growing worldwide audience with an expanding array of resources means that improving Internet navigation will remain a profitable goal for commercial developers and a challenging and socially valuable objective for academic researchers.

Conclusion: Since competition in the market for Internet navigation services promotes innovation, supports consumer choice, and prevents undue control over the location of and access to the diverse resources available via the Internet, public policies should support the competitive marketplace that has emerged and avoid actions that damage it.

8

Internet Navigation: Selected Prospects and Issues

In this chapter, the committee explores a number of factors that are likely to shape the future of Internet navigation. The exposition that follows should not be construed as a comprehensive or representative treatment of these issues. Internet navigation encompasses a number of the established subdisciplines of computer and information science such as information retrieval, database management, human-computer interface, computer algorithms, information economics, and intellectual property law, to name only some of them. The brief discussion that follows only touches on a selected number of these subdisciplines—and only for those issues that came to the attention of the committee during its deliberations.

8.1 TECHNOLOGICAL PROSPECTS

Despite the relative success of the current array of Internet navigation services in satisfying their diverse and numerous users and providers, in the future they will be faced both with pressures to improve further and with technology-driven opportunities to do so.

Those pressures and opportunities have motivated a wide range of research and development activity. Part of this activity is devoted to advancing key technologies, three of which are navigation service algorithms and operations, navigation interfaces, and navigation to audio and visual materials. Another part is dedicated to improving navigation performance by addressing some of the distinctive features of Internet navigation (as noted in Section 6.1)—making use of contextual information, improving persistence, and understanding user behavior.

8.1.1 Navigation Service Algorithms and Operations

Efforts to improve Internet navigation services[1] are being undertaken in several areas that include:

- *Increasing the amount of material indexed and the frequency of indexing.*[2] This is a topic of competitive research and development among commercial search services and is dependent primarily on the available computing and storage capacities. Most of the effort goes into increasing the computing capabilities and storage facilities deployed. There is also a trade-off between the size of the computational resources and the depth to which sites are searched.
- *Improving algorithms for matching requests with results.*[3] Commercial search services devote substantial effort to improving these algorithms, and there is a large and vibrant community studying them in academic and other research institutions.[4]
- *Delimiting and describing specific regions of search.* In many cases, users wish to limit the scope of their search. For example, searches may be limited to a particular site or Uniform Resource Locator (URL), to definitions, to telephone numbers, to a range of dates, to specific locations, and to a number of other special regions. Many other categories could be used to limit or filter results (e.g., a person, a book, an article).
- *Autonomous collection of information by search agents.* Software agents[5] to automate access to information have long been predicted. Research efforts continue to look for ways to use agents automatically to aggregate news and information based on a person's interests. Some of

---

[1]For an overview of research on information retrieval that underlies much of Internet navigation technology, see Ricardo Baeza-Yates and Berthier Ribeiro-Neto, *Modern Information Retrieval*, Addison-Wesley, Wokingham, U.K., 1999.

[2]See, for example, Baeza-Yates and Ribeiro-Neto, Chapter 8, "Indexing and Searching," written with Gonzalo Navarro, in *Modern Information Retrieval*, 1999.

[3]See, for example, Baeza-Yates and Ribeiro-Neto, Chapter 5, in *Modern Information Retrieval*, 1999.

[4]For example, see Michael Kanellos, "Next Generation Search Tools to Refine Results," *Techrepublic.com*, August 9, 2004, available at <http://techrepublic.com.com/5100-22_11-5302095.html>. In addition, the considerable worldwide research activity is reported in conferences and publications sponsored by TREC (Text Retrieval Conference), which is supported by the National Institute of Standards and Technology and the Department of Defense, and the Special Interest Group on Information Retrieval (SIGIR) of the Association for Computing Machinery (ACM). Information on TREC can be found at <http://trec.nist.gov>. Information on SIGIR can be found at <http://www.acm.org/sigir>.

[5]According to the Dublin Core Metadata Glossary, "A computer program that carries out tasks on behalf of another entity. Frequently used to reference a program that searches the Internet for information meeting the specified requirements of an individual user." The Dublin Core Web site is at <fttp://www.purl.org/dc/>.

the more interesting recent examples look for "deals"—on, for example, auction sites and travel sites.[6]

- *Search specialized for non-Roman scripts and various cultures.* There has been a considerable amount of work on commercial navigation tools, much of it government supported, in Asia, especially Korea and China. Although it is inspired by the need to work with distinctly different Asian language/culture/character sets, the techniques developed may prove to be applicable globally. The work has focused on intentionally populated directory systems and especially KEYWORD (see Section 7.1.4) systems.[7]

Efforts to improve the algorithms and operations of Internet navigation services will continue, and are likely to increase, because of competitive pressures, evolving user requirements, and technological advances. Unlike the early days, when almost all research and even development was done within academic settings, commercial organizations now devote substantial resources to development and even research. However, research at universities and research organizations continues to be active, often with federal government support, and can be a source of distinctly new approaches. Furthermore, many academics are working collaboratively with commercial technologists, facilitating the transfer of ideas between academia and industry.

8.1.2 Navigation Interfaces

Interfaces play a key role both in the creation of a query and in the display of the results of that query.[8] One of Google's most attractive features, which has been adopted by other search services, for many of its general users is the simplicity of its single-line basic query interface. For those so inclined and skilled, queries can be further specified through the additional capabilities in "Advanced Search." The clarity of the structure of Google's display of results, with a clear separation between algorith-

---

[6]For flights, hotels, and rental cars, SideStep (<http://www.sidestep.com>) claims to search the Web for travel values, presenting them to the user side by side with Expedia or Travelocity results, allowing for comparisons. For extensive information on software agents, see the University of Maryland, Baltimore County's Agent Web, accessible at <http://agents.umbc.edu/about.shtml>.

[7]Two examples are (1) Netpia, a Korean Internet service that enables substitution of a native language word or phrase (a KEYWORD) for a unique URL (see <http://e.netpia.com>) and (2) Beijing 3721 Technology Co., Ltd., which has offered Chinese language keywords since 1999 (see <http://www.3721.com/english/about.htm>).

[8]For background on this subject, see, for example, Marti Hearst, "User Interfaces and Visualization," Chapter 10 in Baeza-Yates and Ribeiro-Neto, *Modern Information Retrieval*, 1999.

mic search results and those that are sponsored, has also contributed to its success with many users.

Further improvements in the query interface that would enable relatively unsophisticated users to characterize their queries more precisely would be desirable, although to succeed they will have to remain very easy to use.

There is, as well, room for improvement in the display of query results. For example, the relevance-ranked listing that most search engines produce or the alphabetical listing that many directories provide might be improved by displaying the relationships among the listed responses in a more-readily grasped visual form.

A substantial body of research on the display of information exists. In the late 1980s and early 1990s, the Xerox Palo Alto Research Center (PARC),[9] in particular, developed several novel display representations including cones, fish-eye views, and hyperbolic trees.[10] Researchers at Apple, the Massachusetts Institute of Technology, and elsewhere have experimented with arranging webs of information (including search results) as three-dimensional spaces; see, for example, the (now discontinued) Apple Hot Sauce project.[11] Others have experimented with mapping results on to two-dimensional spaces. See, for example, Kartoo, a metasearch engine that displays the search term (keyword) in a map with links to a range of related terms,[12] and Grokker2 that groups and maps the results of a metasearch of the Web (and some sites, including Amazon.com) by subtopics.[13] The display of query results is a subset of the larger field of information visualization, which incorporates the visual display of data of all kinds.[14] Research in that field may very well lead to new methods for visualizing query results.

Still other experiments have been directed at simplifying the management of the search. Built-in search boxes, add-in tool bars, frames (in Web pages), sidebars, and tabs are a few of the browser additions that help users manage searches (among other things). At times, a number of companies offered browser add-ons or browser companions to aid Web navigation and searching by collecting and displaying commentary on the

---

[9]Xerox PARC was founded in 1970. In 2002, it became incorporated as PARC, a subsidiary of the Xerox Corporation. See <http://www.parc.com/about/factsheet.html>.

[10]See <http://www2.parc.com/istl/projects/uir> for a description of the Palo Alto Research Center's user interface research projects.

[11]See <http://www.eclectica-systems.co.uk/complex/hotsauce.php>.

[12]See <http://www.kartoo.com/>.

[13]See <http://www.groxis.com/>.

[14]The annual IEEE Symposium on Information Visualization is a good source of information on current research on the subject. For information about the 2004 conference, see <http://infovis.org/infovis2004/>.

pages being viewed. Most of these applications failed as commercial products, even though their interface ideas appeared to have merit.

Microsoft is expected to incorporate an Internet search interface in its next-generation operating system, code-named "Longhorn." It is anticipated that the search interface will be the same for searching the Internet, the local network's files, and the local computer files.[15] This feature will encourage users to consider search an integral function of the operating system, rather than a separate application available only through a browser.

Future interface designers will also continue to be faced with designing interfaces to fit within form factors[16] ranging from small (e.g., cell phones[17] and personal digital assistants) to expansive (multiscreen wall-size displays) and with employing one or more of a variety of sensory systems (auditory, visual, tactile) to communicate under diverse circumstances.

8.1.3 Navigation to Audio and Visual Materials

The increase of multimedia materials—containing digital images, audio, or video—available via the Internet has complicated the process of navigation by search engines whose crawlers are challenged to extract index terms from still or moving images or from sounds. Tools to index audio well enough to support search services exist, but generally only for a particular input domain such as television news broadcasts or application-specific telephone conversations. Commercial video often has closed-captioning, obviating the need for recognition. Some technologies exist for searching images based on colors and shapes, but they are still in a relatively early stage of development.[18] Resources that incorporate mul-

---

[15]See Michael Kanellos, "Microsoft Aims for Search on Its Own Terms," c/netnews.com, November 24, 2003, available at <http://news.com.com/Microsoft+aims+for+search+on+its+own+terms/2100-1008_3-5110910.html?tag=nl>. "Microsoft has set a firmer date for the release of its desktop search software, after Google launched a test version of its rival program for scouring a PC's hard drive,"reported in Ina Fried, "Microsoft Fixes Date for Desktop Search Tool," *c/net news.com*, October 22, 2004, available at <http://news.zdnet.com/2100-3513_22-5423080.html>.

[16]The "form factor" of a device is its physical size and shape. The form factors of cell phones, personal digital assistants, and laptop computers differ substantially, resulting in different size displays that generally require different interface designs.

[17]In October 2004, both Yahoo! and Google began offering search services from cell phones. Yahoo!'s service is called Yahoo! Mobile, and Google's is Google SMS.

[18]For background on this subject, see, for example, Christos Faloutsos, "Multimedia IR: Indexing and Searching," Chapter 12 in Baeza-Yates and Ribeiro-Neto, *Modern Information Retrieval*, 1999.

tiple media, such as electronic literature that contains text, images, animation, and voice, are a particularly challenging search problem.[19]

Full accessibility for most multimedia materials, comparable to that for textual materials, will require development of technologies for their automatic indexing by search engines, which is a very difficult technology problem. For the foreseeable future, most effective multimedia search will depend on the use of metadata and associated text (see Section 7.1.5). This can be done manually; can be picked up by Web crawlers from page metatags; or can be extracted from text associated with still image, video, or audio files. A number of navigation services using these techniques are available on the Web to find multimedia materials.[20] Among them are Google Images, Yahoo! Search Images, Alta Vista Photo Finder, FAST Multimedia Search, and Lycos Pictures and Sounds.

A navigation challenge common to all forms of multimedia search is standardization and automatic capture of the metadata to be used for indexing, which would improve the availability and accessibility of such materials.[21] Considerable research progress is being made in the searching of music by text, sound, and music notation,[22] which is an active area of academic research.[23] Video metadata is being pushed by industry forces, so it is reasonably far along. The MPEG-7 standard[24] for describing multimedia content in a form that can be used by a device or a program is highly developed, and deployment is likely to begin soon.

---

[19]For background on this subject, see, for example, Elisa Bertino, Barbara Catania, and Elena Ferrari, "Multimedia IR: Models and Languages," Chapter 11 in Baeza-Yates and Ribeiro-Neto, *Modern Information Retrieval*, 1999. Current research activities are reported, for example, in the Conferences on Image and Video Retrieval (CIVR), a series held since 1998. Links to the conferences can be found at <http://www.informatik.uni-trier.de/~ley/db/conf/civr/>.

[20]See Danny Sullivan, "Multimedia Search Engines," *SearchEngineWatch*, January 25, 2002, available at <http://www.searchenginewatch.com/links/article.php/2156251>.

[21]See <http://www.chin.gc.ca/English/Standards/metadata_multimedia.html> for an overview of the topic. Research on computer-assisted extraction of metadata from scholarly material associated with images is underway in the CLiMB project at Columbia University. See <http://www.columbia.edu/cu/cria/climb/>.

[22]For example, look at the work presented at the 5th International Conference on Music Information Retrieval, available at <http://ismir2004.ismir.net/>.

[23]One example is the work underway at Carnegie Mellon University in the infomedia project on "digital video understanding," which aims "to achieve machine understanding of video and film media, including all aspects of search, retrieval, visualization and summarization in both contemporaneous and archival content collections." See <http://www.informedia.cs.cmu.edu/>.

[24]See <http://www.chiariglione.org/mpeg/index.htm> and also Rob Koenen, "From MPEG-1 to MPEG-21: Creating an Interoperable Multimedia Infrastructure," 2001, available at <http://www.chiariglione.org/mpeg/from_mpeg-1_to_mpeg-21.htm>.

Query by example[25] is another promising approach to multimedia search. Given an image, it is possible in experimental systems (and in some commercial image-processing software) to find others with similar shapes and colors.[26] However, given an image of horses, such techniques can only find other images with the general shapes, colors, and textures in the sample image, while missing images that have to do with horses, but differ in those respects.

Conclusion: Indexing and retrieving multimedia materials on the Internet is an extremely difficult technical problem in its full generality, when there are few textual clues. However, for specific purposes or contexts, where textual descriptions are associated with the media, or where relatively low precision can be tolerated, the existing systems can suffice. Research prototypes and commercial offerings can be expected to continue to make slow but useful progress by focusing on specific subcases.

8.1.4 Making Greater Use of Contextual Information

As noted in Section 6.1.6, most current general Internet navigation services do not remember users' recent searches. In most cases, each query is treated the same; the service collects no information about its users' interests or search goals. While this protects the searcher's privacy, it can also reduce the responsiveness of the search. In contrast, some site-specific navigation services make considerable use of previous search history to create user models and provide context for specifying searches. Amazon.com, for example, gathers and displays a running history of what has been seen within the current session and retains considerable information about what has been searched for or purchased previously that it uses to make user-specific recommendations. Theoretically, general Internet search engines could offer similar services to improve the ranking or filtering of results or to suggest additional searches.

Another approach, which is less likely to raise privacy concerns, would be to have a navigation aid that captures contextual information on the user's computer and uses that information to formulate context-aware requests to an Internet navigation service.

For many searches, knowing the geographical location of the users can help in providing the desired information. But should navigation services assume that users are seeking local or global information? At present, the default assumption of a general Internet navigation service is

[25]Query by example for textual queries is used in several conventional database systems. The concept was developed by IBM in 1975.

[26]See <http://elib.cs.berkeley.edu/vision.html>.

that users are seeking global information. However, in theory, navigation services could sort multiple matches by geographic location (for objects with geographic data, such as stores, restaurants, and libraries), listing the nearest matches first, as specialized travel reservation services already can do for hotels around a specific place. In response to this perceived need, both Google and Yahoo! now allow searches to be localized through the entry of an address, a zip code, or a city name together with the subject keyword (e.g., "San Francisco Italian restaurants").[27] The result is a listing of locally relevant Web sites, maps, and listings from businesses in the area. Both services also offer local businesses the opportunity to advertise in response to localized keyword queries. In addition, Google can obtain general information about the location of a query from the Internet Protocol (IP) address of the user, while Yahoo! could make use of its users' addresses, which they provide when registering for e-mail, photo exchange, or other Yahoo! services.

The demand for geographically localized context information is likely to grow rapidly as information appliances become smaller and more portable. A New Yorker searching the Web from his or her cell phone while in Chicago is likely to want to find a restaurant in Chicago.[28] A navigation tool that made that assumption might, in that situation, be appreciated. However, although with today's Internet there is no fully reliable way to determine the location of a searcher, technical tools do exist that offer good enough guesses to allow search engines to tune results to specific geographic areas (through, for example, the IP address). For example, such tools are currently being used to implement certain nationally required censorship practices on Yahoo! and e-Bay, such as the prohibition of the sale of Nazi memorabilia in France or of *Mein Kampf*[29] in Germany. Google will recognize Canada as the source of a search dialed in from there.[30] Of course, when the user enters geographic information voluntarily, or the device enters it automatically—as cell phones may soon be able to do—

---

[27]See Stefanie Olsen, "Google Goes Local," *cNet news.com*, March 17, 2004, available at <http://news.com.com/2100-1038-5173685.html>; and Jefferson Graham, "Websites Test Local Search Marketing," *USA Today*, February 6, 2004, available at <http://www.usatoday.com/tech/news/2004-02-04-localsearch_x.htm>.

[28]However, it is worth noting that while geographic context can increase the likelihood of obtaining more relevant information, it is not a perfect process. In the example given, the New Yorker might be searching for the name and phone number of a New York restaurant to provide to a Chicagoan in response to a query about recommendations for good restaurants in New York.

[29]There are a number of versions of Adolf Hitler's *Mein Kampf*. One version is a translation to English by Ralph Manheim, Houghton-Mifflin, Boston, 1971.

[30]Examples provided by an anonymous reviewer.

such geographic searches can be made easily. However, the automatic reporting of a user's location to a search engine or other Internet service would raise significant privacy concerns.[31]

Conclusion: The collection of some contextual information about users by navigation services can be used to improve Internet navigation, but as the data become more detailed, difficult conceptual and implementation issues should be resolved and the associated privacy concerns addressed.

The increased use of contextual information is likely to include some combination of improvements in the collection and use of such information by the navigation services, extension of the option for users to enter specific contextual information (e.g., location), development of context-sensitive local aids directly under the user's control, and improvements in the training and experience of users. The incorporation into queries of information about the location of users, either automatically or voluntarily, and the addition of location filters into navigation services' ranking algorithms is already underway and is likely to expand rapidly under the impetus of local advertising revenue.[32]

User modeling—the collection, retention, and use of information about specific users to assist in responding to their queries—is an active research area.[33] Creation of user models generates privacy concerns, and this is another area of active research.[34] Those user models where the user's identity is known to the organization creating the model (such as

---

[31]Such systems are likely to work effectively only if the user wants to be located. The user will have the option to disguise her location or to disable the system.

[32]In the latter part of 2004, several major Internet navigation service providers took steps to increase the level of personalization in their services. See Chris Sherman, "Yahoo Introduces Personal Search," *SearchEngineWatch*, October 5, 2004, available at <http://searchenginewatch.com/searchday/article.php/3417111>; Gary Price, "Ask Jeeves Serves It Your Way," *SearchEngineWatch*, September 21, 2004, available at <http://searchenginewatch.com/searchday/article.php/3410441>; and Leslie Walker and David A. Vise, "Google's New Tool Brings Search Home," *Washington Post*, October 15, 2004, p. E1, available at <http://www.washingtonpost.com/wp-dyn/articles/A34099-2004Oct14.html>.

[33]See Peter Brusilovsky and Carlo Tasso, "Preface to Special Issue, User Modeling for Web Information Retrieval," *User Modeling and User-Adapted Interaction: The Journal of Personalization Research* 14(2):147-157, 2004.

[34]See Alfred Kobsa, "Personalized Hypermedia and International Privacy," *Communications of the ACM* 45(5):64-67, 2002; Alfred Kobsa, "Tailoring Privacy to Users' Needs," *8th International Conference on User Modeling*, Springer-Verlag, Sonthofen, Germany, 2001, available at <http://www.ics.uci.edu/~kobsa/papers/2001-UM01-kobsa.pdf>; and Alfred Kobsa and Jörg Schreck, "Privacy Through Pseudonymity in User-adaptive Systems," *ACM Transactions on Internet Technology*, 2003, available at <http://www.ics.uci.edu/~kobsa/papers/2003-TOIT-kobsa.pdf>.

Amazon.com) raise the greatest privacy concerns, as discussed further in Section 8.2.2. User models that are maintained on the client-side and where the user can maintain control over what is known about him or her raise relatively fewer privacy concerns.

8.1.5 Improving Persistence

Section 6.1.7 characterizes the many reasons that resources once discovered at a particular location on the Internet may not be there when subsequently sought. While this transience is not a problem for many resources, it can be a difficulty for many others. For example, the references to Web resources throughout this report provide examples of materials that the report's authors and readers would like to see persist—but cannot control.

The notion of "persistence" of materials on the Internet is related to, but not identical with, the more traditional notion of "preservation." Generally speaking, the goal of persistence is to maintain the same material at the same address for an indefinite period, so that once discovered there it can always be retrieved from that location in the identical form. Preservation, however, has the goal of saving the material for future reference, but not necessarily at the same address. In other words, to find something that has been preserved will require at least one additional discovery step—finding the location (e.g., in an archive) at which it has been preserved.

Persistence is most likely to be achieved through the adoption of practices by Web site managers and designers that leave unchanged the URLs of material judged valuable enough to persist and locate modified versions of those materials at new URLs. Consequently, unless there were to be widespread adoption by Web site managers and designers of common persistence practices, the problem of transient persistence will persist.

However, there are services that provide a degree of persistence for some materials on the World Wide Web. Google offers access to the cached version, which is the version of a resource available at the time it was most recently added to the index. However, there is no attempt to provide access to earlier versions, and so persistence is very short.

That leaves preservation as the most viable alternative. Web preservation initiatives comprise three approaches: harvesting, selection, and deposit.[35]

---

[35]Michael Day, "Preserving the Fabric of Our Lives: A Survey of Web Preservation Initiatives," *Research and Advanced Technology for Digital Libraries, 7th European Conference, EDCL, Trondheim, Norway*, Springer, Berlin, Germany, 2003.

The most far-reaching approach to preservation has been taken by the Internet Archive,[36] a non-profit corporation founded and run by Brewster Kahle, which is supported by contributions from individuals, foundations, and corporations. Rather than being concerned with the persistence of specific material on the Internet, the Internet Archive is devoted to capturing (and preserving) a sequence of snapshots of what is publicly accessible on the Internet. Its goal is preserving the history both of the Internet and of the vast range of human activities reflected in the constantly evolving materials on it. The Internet Archive, also called the "Wayback Machine," has taken and stored snapshots of materials on the Internet since 1996. In December 2003 it comprised over 11 billion Web pages and over 300 terabytes of data storage, increasing at 12 terabytes per month.[37] It is often the only way to locate digital documents that were moved to other sites or taken offline and, therefore, is of great value to users and scholars—and to copyright holders, who can track the use of their content.

At present, the Internet Archive is the only active effort in the United States to preserve and provide access to the history of a significant portion of Internet materials.[38] In other countries, however, the national libraries are undertaking similar efforts.[39] The International Internet Preservation Consortium (IIPC) was formally chartered at the Bibliothèque Nationale de France with 12 participating institutions, all national libraries (including the Library of Congress) and the Internet Archive.[40] Its goals are as follows:

- To achieve the collection of a rich body of Internet content from around the world to be preserved in a way that it can be archived, secured and accessed over time.
- To foster the development and use of common tools, techniques and standards that enable creation of international archives.
- To encourage and support national libraries everywhere to address Internet archiving and preservation.

During the 3 years of IIPC's initial agreement, membership is limited to the charter institutions. It will open to other national libraries in 2006.

---

[36]For information on the Internet Archive, see <http://www.archive.org>.

[37]Paul Marks, "Way Back When," *New Scientist* (date unknown), available at <http://www.newscientist.com/opinion/opinterview.jsp?id=ns23701>; latest information at <http://www.waybackmachine.org>.

[38]The Internet Archive is mirrored at the New Library of Alexandria, Egypt, and at the time of writing it is in the process of establishing a European Internet Archive in Amsterdam, The Netherlands.

[39]For example, the Australian National Library's PANDORA project, which has been archiving Australian online publications since 1996, is described at <http://www.nla.gov.au/initiatives/digarch.html>.

[40]See <www.netpreserve.org> for full information on the IIPC.

However, the IIPC will not serve as an operational archive. Rather, it will provide a forum for sharing knowledge; develop and recommend standards; develop tools and techniques to acquire, archive, and provide access to Web sites; and raise awareness of preservation issues through meetings and publications.[41]

In a similar vein, the Library of Congress has been leading since 2001 a cooperative national digital-strategy effort, called the National Digital Information Infrastructure and Preservation Program.[42] The Library, working with government and private partners, is to "develop a national strategy to collect, archive and preserve the burgeoning amounts of digital content, especially materials that are created only in digital formats, for current and future generations." There is currently no commonly accepted way to decide which material on the Internet should be retained or to ensure the availability of the resources or incentives needed to achieve that goal. These are among the issues that the Library of Congress effort is addressing.

8.1.6 Understanding User Behavior

User behavior in navigating through traditional information resources has been a subject of considerable research, but less is known about the Internet case. If such information were available, it is likely that more effective Internet navigation aids and services could be designed.

Research on information seeking in print environments dates back to early in the 20th century, and research on information seeking in electronic environments dates to the 1960s. Although a large body of empirical data exists, it is not clear how much of it is relevant to Internet navigation. Much of the prior research is in library (or comparable) contexts and assumes more homogeneous content, more constrained searching goals, and non-commercial environments. Although relatively little is known about how people navigate the Internet generally, there is a small but growing body of empirical research on the use of the World Wide Web. However, research on the Web is severely restricted because search companies have been unwilling to share samples of the enormous amount of data they collect every day with researchers in academic environments.

Conclusion: Basic research aimed at a better understanding of user behavior in a variety of Internet navigation tasks using a variety of methods and services is highly desirable.

---

[41]Information obtained from the IIPC Web site on September 3, 2004.

[42]See the program's Web site at <http://www.digitalpreservation.gov/>.

However, standard methods to evaluate searching performance on the Internet are lacking. The most advanced evaluation methods are constrained to text searching in bounded databases. A broader set of metrics, measures, and test beds is needed for the Internet and digital libraries, and their development would also be desirable.[43] An array of new National Science Foundation initiatives in cyberinfrastructure may contribute to these efforts.[44]

8.2 INSTITUTIONAL ISSUES

Most of the institutional issues affecting Internet navigation arise with respect to the commercially supported navigation services, and especially with respect to services whose results are influenced by advertiser payments. The expectation by users that they will be able to understand and trust the results presented by navigation systems leads to efforts by governments to impose disclosure requirements on navigation system operators, similar to the way other advertising practices are regulated in many countries. The desire by information providers to protect their ownership of trademarked and copyrighted material must be balanced with the needs of other providers to incorporate some of that material in descriptions of their own material. These issues are examined in this section.

8.2.1 Regulation

It is generally assumed by researchers and other observers of the industry that users want access to navigation services that are neutral, or at least services whose biases match their own.[45] In either event, they are assumed to want to know enough about the criteria by which results are returned so that they can judge if those results are trustworthy. Yet these

---

[43]See Christine L. Borgman, *Evaluation of Digital Libraries: Testbeds, Measurements, and Metrics*, final report to the National Science Foundation, Fourth DELOS Workshop, Hungarian Academy of Sciences, Computer and Automation Research Institute (MTA SZTAKI), Budapest, Hungary, June 6-7, 2002, available at <http://www.sztaki.hu/conferences/deval/presentations/final_report.html>.

[44]See Daniel Atkins, *Revolutionizing Science and Engineering Through Cyberinfrastructure: Report of the National Science Foundation Blue-Ribbon Panel on Cyberinfrastructure*, January 2003, available at <http://www.cise.nsf.gov/sci/reports/toc.cfm/>. See also the new NSF Division on Shared Cyberinfrastructure, whose Web site is available at <http://www.cise.nsf.gov/div/index.cfm?div=sci>, and similar programs in other directorates.

[45]See Deborah Fallows, Lee Rainie, and Graham Mudd, "The Popularity and Importance of Search Engines," data memo, Pew Internet & American Life Project, August 2004, available at <http://www.pewinternet.org/pdfs/PIP_Data_Memo_Searchengines.pdf>; 68 percent of respondents to the Pew/Internet survey thought that Internet search engines are a fair and unbiased source of information, while 19 percent thought they were not.

assumptions are not proven; more complete understanding is needed of the value that users place on the explicit disclosure of search and results ranking criteria and on having a choice among navigation systems employing a range of different criteria. In addition, there is a presumed social benefit in having an information infrastructure that can be trusted.

A searcher's need to understand the criteria for ranking the results of a search has risen in importance now that advertising has become the primary source of revenue for search engine companies. That need conflicts with the objectives of some advertisers, who would like their listings to appear as much as possible like the high-ranking results of a neutral search. Consequently, it is not surprising that U.S. Federal Trade Commission (FTC) regulators concluded in June 2002 that some Internet search engines[46] were not adequately informing consumers when advertisers paid for prominent placement in search results. The FTC Division of Advertising Practices sent a letter[47] to major search services recommending that they

> review their Web sites and make any changes necessary to ensure that:
>
> - any paid ranking search results are distinguished from non-paid results with clear and conspicuous disclosures;
> - the use of paid inclusion is clearly and conspicuously explained and disclosed; and
> - no affirmative statement is made that might mislead consumers as to the basis on which a search result is generated.

In addition, "to the extent that search engine companies provide search results to third-party Web sites, including other search engines or guides, [the FTC is] encouraging the companies to discuss with the third-party Web sites whether the above criteria are being met with respect to any supplied search results that involve a payment of any kind for ranking, insertion of paid results into unpaid results, or any pay-for-inclusion program." Furthermore, the FTC staff recognized "that search engine companies' business models vary and that there is a need for flexibility in the manner in which paid placement and paid inclusion are clearly and conspicuously disclosed."

The FTC letter went on to say that the few studies of consumer views on paid inclusion and paid placement that have been done indicate that many consumers are not aware of the practice. It referred explicitly to two studies:

---

[46]Other search engines, such as Google and AltaVista, clearly designate or segregate the sponsored listings. See section 5.4.2.

[47]Letter from FTC to Gary Ruskin, executive director of Commercial Alert, June 27, 2002, available at <http://www3.ftc.gov/os/closings/staff/commercialalertletter.htm>.

> A Consumers Union national survey found that 60% of U.S. Internet users had not heard or read that certain search engines were paid fees to list some sites more prominently than others in their search results. After being told that some search engines take these fees, 80% said it is important (including 44% who said it is very important) for a search engine to disclose, in its search results or in an easy-to-find page on its site, that it is being paid to list certain sites more prominently. If clearly told in the search results that some sites are displayed prominently because they paid, 30% said they would be less likely to use that search engine, 10% said more likely, and 4% said don't know/refused. Consumers Union also reported that "given the complicated situation, 56% say it would make no difference to them." It stated that the "combination of users' low level of knowledge of search engine practices and their strong demand that search engines should come clean leaves users splintered about how to react."[48] A recent BBC-commissioned survey found that 71% of U.K. users were unaware that some search engines let advertisers pay to get more prominent positions in search results.[49]

Against this background, the FTC also issued, in September 2002, a consumer alert, "Being Frank About Search Engine Rank," which advises users to be aware that the results of their searches may be affected by various pay-for-placement programs of Internet search engines.[50]

Although neither of these actions constitutes an enforcement action with the force of law, they do alert the navigation services operators to the interest of the FTC and the possibility that in the absence of change it might consider more formal action.

In addition, Internet advertising, whether search engine linked or not, is subject to the same types of national regulation as other advertising with respect to fraudulent or misleading claims and so on. In the United States, the FTC has pursued various cases on those grounds. Furthermore, search engines typically have guidelines for the content they will provide. In 2003, Yahoo! and Google announced that they would restrict advertisements from unlicensed pharmacies in response to consumer concerns about illegal online drug sales.[51]

The way in which search engines provide rankings has also been the subject of a U.S. District Court case. SearchKing, an online advertising network, sued Google because it asserted that Google reduced the

---

[48]See "A Matter of Trust: What Users Want from Web Sites," April 16, 2002, available at <www.consumerwebwatch.com/news/report1.pdf>.

[49]See, for example, "BBC Launches Its Non-Commercial Search Engine in Response to 'Tainted' Results," May 2, 2002, available at <http://www.VentureReporter.net> (subscription required).

[50]Available at <http://www3.ftc.gov/bcp/conline/pubs/alerts/searchalrt.htm>.

[51]Saul Hansell, "Search Engines Limit Ads for Drugs but Ease Rules on Sex," *New York Times*, December 3, 2003.

PageRank™ of its site after SearchKing created a network of sites that had the effect of boosting all the members' PageRanks™. By reducing SearchKing's PageRank™, Google also had the countervailing effect of reducing the PageRank™ of the network members. SearchKing asserted that Google's action harmed its business. The court, however, found that Google had the right to adjust PageRank™ value since it constituted an opinion and was covered by First Amendment protections.[52]

These two examples illustrate the nascent engagement of national regulatory agencies and legal systems with issues arising in navigation services. As Internet navigation continues its growth as a major source of contacts for information and service providers and as a major advertising medium, it may be expected that the scrutiny and activity of regulatory agencies and legal systems—and legislatures—will increase as well.

Conclusion: The behavior of commercial navigation services can have a substantial influence on the kind, quality, and appropriateness of the information that Internet users receive. Although there is no evidence that abuse has yet occurred, the potential for abuse is inherent in the navigation services' ability to affect users' access to information for commercial or other reasons.

Recommendation: Although competition and the desire to be seen as useful by searchers are incentives for fair and open behavior, appropriate regulatory agencies of the U.S. federal government and of other governments should pay careful and continuing attention to the result ranking and display practices of Internet navigation services and their advertisers to ensure that information can flow freely and that those critical practices are fully disclosed.

Recommendation: Since competition in the market for Internet navigation services promotes innovation, supports consumer choice, and prevents undue control over the location of and access to the diverse resources available via the Internet, public policies should support the competitive marketplace that has emerged and avoid actions that damage it.

8.2.2 Privacy

Privacy issues affect Internet navigation, in both overt and subtle ways. The crux of the privacy concerns rests on the ability of Web sites and other online resources to track their visitors and to capture data about

---

[52]See "Google Wins Over SearchKing in PageRank Case," *Pandia Search Engine News*, June 2, 2003, available at <http://www.pandia.com/sw-2003/21-searchking.html>.

what is being viewed, read, downloaded, or otherwise used without the consent of users.[53] As noted in the discussion of context (Section 6.1.6), the more that a system knows about a person's goals, intentions, and prior activities, the greater the context that can be provided and the more tailored the searching can be. The negative sides of tracking are equally significant, however.

Tracking what people read or view could violate long-established liberties in the United States and in many other free societies if that information were made available, freely or under subpoena, to government agencies. Lack of privacy also has a potential "chilling effect." People are less likely to act on their freedom of speech if they feel that their queries are being recorded and may be disclosed without their permission.

Yet the Internet is the site of illegal activities, such as identity theft, illegal transactions, and non-protected speech, such as child pornography. Law enforcement has always had means to target illegal activities without undermining basic democratic principles and needs them on the Internet as well. The designers of future navigation services and of the laws that affect them will, of necessity, be trying to find a workable balance among the services' desire to use individual information to improve service, the individual's right to privacy, and the government's legitimate needs to know.[54]

Issues of privacy are both important and complex and relate to the Internet and information technology more broadly, not only to navigation. This study could not do them justice, but there are a number of reports and ongoing studies on Internet privacy.[55]

8.2.3 Trademarks and Copyright

Intellectual property rights is an issue whose link to Internet navigation may not be obvious. However, a number of court cases have arisen in which the use of trademarked material in the navigation process has been in dispute.[56] Moreover, the extent to which search engines may make use

---

[53]See Fallows, Rainie, and Mudd, "The Popularity and Importance of Search Engines," 2004. According to the Pew/Internet survey, 85 percent of search engine users rate "knowing that personal information will not be shared without permission" as an important attribute of search engines, but only 55 percent believe that they deliver.

[54]Google's privacy policy is available at <http://www.google.com/privacy.html>; Yahoo!'s, at <http://privacy.yahoo.com/>.

[55]For example, the Computer Science and Telecommunications Board of the National Research Council has an ongoing study, whose report is forthcoming in 2006, on privacy in the information age. For further details, see <http://www.cstb-privacy.org/>.

[56]See Cindy Sherman, "Search Engines and Legal Issues—October 23, 2002," *SearchEngineWatch*, 2002, available at <http://www.searchenginewatch.com/searchday/article.php/2161041>.

of copyrighted material has been and is certain to continue to be a significant issue.

Trademark

As in the DNS, the use of trademarked names is a source of contention in Internet navigation. Whereas for the DNS the issue is the use of trademarks in domain names, in navigation the issue is their use in metatags and keywords. Unlike the DNS, for which the non-judicial Uniform Domain Name Dispute Resolution Process (UDRP) has been established, most disputes in Internet navigation that are not resolved through navigation services' own policies have found their way to the courts. However, thus far, there have been far fewer trademark cases concerning navigation than concerning domain names.

One trademark dispute that reached the courts concerned the right to use such terms in metatags, the invisible markers of a Web site selected by the site creator and sometimes used by search engines as keywords. Playboy Enterprises sued a former playmate for incorporating some of its trademarked terms in the metatags at her site. The court, however, decided in her favor on the grounds that she had a legitimate right to use those terms in describing herself and had not done so with the intent of attracting users seeking the Playboy site.[57]

Another trademark dispute concerned allowing non-trademark holders to bid for a trademarked term. Mark Nutritionals filed suit against Overture (then GoTo) and other paid placement providers for auctioning its trademarked phrase "Body Solutions" to their competitors. As a result, those competitors were showing up higher in searches for "body solutions" than was Mark Nutritionals, which claimed that this constituted trademark infringement as well as unfair competition.[58]

In a third dispute, J.K. Harris & Co. sued Taxes.com because the Taxes.com site was higher ranked in search engine results than the J.K. Harris site for the search term "J.K. Harris." The suit was for trademark infringement, unfair competition, false and misleading advertising, and defamation. The reason for the higher ranking was that the phrase "J.K. Harris" appeared frequently (75 times) on the Web page entitled "Complaints about J.K. Harris," which contained e-mails detailing the site owner's conversations with investigators about J.K. Harris. The judge

---

[57]The court decision is available at <http://caselaw.lp.findlaw.com/data2/circs/9th/0055009p.pdf>.

[58]See Christopher Saunders, "Weight Loss Company Sues Search Engines," *Internetnews.com*, February 1, 2002, available at <http://www.internetnews.com/IAR/article.php/12_966901>.

ruled that the site had the right to use the "J.K. Harris" term, but did not like the number of times that it was used. A preliminary injunction against Taxes.com was issued by the court but was due for reconsideration as a result of a brief filed by the Electronic Frontier Foundation.[59] Note that this case was against the Web site owner, not the search engine company.

Presumably to avoid becoming the subject of frequent suits, Google has established a complaint procedure to enable companies to claim "reasonable" rights to their trademarked terms.[60] In a prominent use of that procedure, eBay asked Google in August 2003 to refuse to sell ads that use eBay's trademarked name, either alone or in phrases and variations, "so that third-party advertisers do not abuse the intellectual property of the company." eBay submitted a 13-page list of terms, such as "eBay selling" and "eBay power seller," that it wanted Google to bar. eBay says that Google has complied with its requests.[61] eBay's trademarks can still be referenced under fair-use provisions, which allow an advertiser to use some one else's trademarked term for description or comparison of its product—for example, to sell the book *eBay for Dummies*.[62]

However, in France, Google has been sued by three companies and in three significant cases has been ordered by regional French courts to stop selling a company's trademarked terms as keywords to other companies and to pay damages. In the first case, a regional court ordered Google to pay 75,000 euros to two travel companies whose trademarked terms were sold as keywords to rival companies. The court said that Google should "find the means to block advertisements by third parties who have no right to [the] trademarks." In the second case, a Nanterre court told Google to stop selling trademarked terms of the Le Meridien hotel chain as keywords to its competitors or pay a daily fine of 150 euros.[63] In the third case, a Paris district court ordered Google not to sell keywords incorporating trademarks of the luxury goods firm Louis Vuitton Malletier and to pay a fine of 200,000 euros.[64]

In an effort to block a similar case in the United States, Google has

---

[59]See Cindy Sherman, "Search Engines and Legal Issues—October 23, 2002," 2002, available at <http://searchenginewatch.com/searchday/article.php/2161051>.

[60]See <http://www.google.com/tm_complaint.html>.

[61]See Brian Morrisey, "eBay Invokes Trademark on Google Keywords," *Internetnews*, August 11, 2003, available at <http://www.internetnews.com/IAR/print.php/2447071>.

[62]Marsha Collier and Roland Woerner, *eBay for Dummies*, 2nd edition, Hungry Mind Press, St. Paul, Minn., 2000.

[63]See Stefanie Olsen, "Google Loses Trademark Dispute in France," *c/net news.com*, January 20, 2005, available at <http://news.com.com/Google+loses+trademark+dispute+in+France/2100-1030_3-5543827.html?tag=nl>.

[64]See Stefanie Olsen, "Google Loses Trademark Case in France," *c/net news.com*, February 4, 2005, available at <http://news.com.com/Google+loses+trademark+case+in+France/2100-1030_3-5564118.html>.

asked a U.S. district court judge for a declaratory judgment on trademark issues raised by American Blind, which sells wallpaper and window coverings. The company complained that Google was selling AdWords infringing its trademarks, listing over 30 terms ranging from the obvious to more generic terms, such as "American wallpaper discount." Google agreed to block the trademarks, but not variant terms because they were descriptive terms that other advertisers had the right to use. In January 2004, American Blind filed a lawsuit.[65] Shortly before, Google had made a request for a judgment that AdWords do not infringe American Blind's trademarks and demanded a jury trial. The outcome can be quite significant for Google, and other advertising-dependent search engines, since it could affect the degree of scrutiny that they would have to apply to each keyword sale, potentially increasing costs and reducing the number of available words.

In December 2004, Google won a U.S. victory when a judge of the U.S. District Court granted Google's request to dismiss a trademark-infringement complaint from the insurance company, Geico. The judge ruled that it is not trademark infringement to use trademarks as keywords to trigger advertising.[66]

Copyright

Only a few contentious issues have arisen regarding copyright and navigation services. One such issue involves the so-called "notice and take down" provisions of the Digital Millennium Copyright Act (DMCA),[67] which requires any Internet service provider (ISP) (which would include any search engine operator) to remove or disable access to any third-party content that has been identified in a statutorily compliant notice provided to the ISP by the owner, or its agent, of the copyright in such content. In order to be statutorily compliant, a DMCA notice must (1) be signed by someone authorized to act on behalf of the owner of the exclusive right that is allegedly infringed; (2) identify the copyrighted work allegedly infringed; (3) identify the allegedly infringing content or activity and provide enough information to enable the ISP to find the content; (4) provide information that is reasonably sufficient to permit the ISP to contact the complaining party, such as a mailing address, telephone number, or

[65]See Stefanie Olsen, "Google Faces Trademark Suit Over Keyword Ads," *c/net news.com,* January 28, 2004, available at <http://news.com.com/Google+faces+trademark+suit+over+keyword+ads/2100-1024_3-5149780.html?tag=nl>.

[66]See Stefanie Olsen, "Google Wins in Trademark Suit with Geico," *c/net news.com,* December 15, 2004, available at <http://news.com.com/Google+wins+in+trademark+suit+with+Geico/2100-1024_3-5491704.html?tag=nl>.

[67]Public Law 105-304.

e-mail address; and (5) include a statement that the complaining party has a good-faith belief that use of the allegedly infringing content is not authorized by the copyright owner, its agent, or the law. Back in 1996 and 1997, when the DMCA was being negotiated, hyperlinks to third-party content were thought to be outside the scope of the notice and take down (NTD) provisions of the DMCA, and in fact a few courts have refused to enforce the DMCA when asserted in this context. However, the nature of providing links, at least within the context of search engines, has changed over the years, in that many search engines now include excerpts of the information as part of the link, and so the applicability of the NTD provisions is less clear. Accordingly, some search engine operators have taken to complying with DMCA notices, even though they may not be technically required to do so. For example, in 2002, Google removed some 126 pages that the Church of Scientology claimed infringed its copyright. One of the pages was the home page of an anti-Scientology site that had gained a high ranking in searches on the term "scientology" through the efforts of anti-Scientology activists to build links to it. After protest, Google restored that page, saying that it was "inadvertently removed."[68] The case shows the potential danger from use of the DMCA to unfairly shut down access to Web sites. However, according to Google, the case was unusual. It generally gets one or two DMCA complaints per week that it describes as "open and shut."

Although the DMCA requires only that the complaining party attest to its good-faith belief that the content in question is infringing, the DMCA also provides a counternotice provision that enables the provider of the questionable content to challenge the complaining party's notice and have the information restored until the complaining party avails itself of the federal courts and obtains injunctive relief. One of the primary purposes of the DMCA, other than to extend the protections of the copyright laws to digital works published over the Internet, was to remove ISPs from being caught in between third-party providers of content and the owners of copyrights when a fight broke out over who owned the rights to that content. By filing a counternotice, the provider of the content is effectively accepting the jurisdiction of a U.S. court should the original complainant want to pursue its complaint, and so many content providers may choose not to avail themselves of this protection. It should also be noted, however, that the DMCA does not obligate search engines to inform content providers when their content has been removed or blocked. According to the statement of DMCA policy on its Web site,[69] however, Google will

[68]See David F. Gallagher, "New Economy; a Copyright Dispute with the Church of Scientology Is Forcing Google to Do Some Creative Linking," *New York Times*, April 22, 2002, p. C4.

[69]Available at <http://www.google.com/dmca.html>.

make a "good-faith attempt to contact the owner or administrator of each affected site so that they may make a counter notification."

Conclusion: As with the Domain Name System, the most contentious intellectual property issues affecting navigation services concern trademarks. Since there is no arbitral process, such as the UDRP, by which such disputes could be resolved outside the courts and with worldwide effect, it seems likely that conflicting court decisions in different jurisdictions, worldwide, will establish the potentially conflicting rules by which navigation services will have to abide. Potential rulings in some jurisdictions could substantially reduce the ability of search engines to sell keywords using the current automated methods with restriction of specifically trademarked terms only.

9

The Domain Name System and Internet Navigation

As the preceding chapters show, the relationship between Internet navigation and the Domain Name System is complex and multi-dimensional.

The Domain Name System (DNS) was defined centrally under the leadership of a relatively small group of Internet engineers in response to an operational need. Although its effective implementation occurred over several years, during which relatively small changes were made as required, the basic design of the system has remained the same for two decades. As described in Chapter 3, the Internet Engineering Task Force (IETF) and the Internet Architecture Board (IAB) provide technical leadership and coordination for developing changes to the protocols and other standards affecting the DNS. Changes in the root zone file are controlled by the Internet Corporation for Assigned Names and Numbers (ICANN) and the U.S. Department of Commerce. But a mix of academic, governmental, commercial, and non-profit organizations with distributed responsibilities operates and manages the domains. The DNS stands, therefore, as an example of a technical system that was designed centrally but is operated by a distributed set of organizations.

In contrast, Internet navigation aids and services have evolved through a sequence of innovations by separate and independent individuals and organizations, initially primarily by academics, and more recently, by commercial entities. Their evolution has been shaped by the response to the cumulative knowledge obtained through publication, the responses of the market to successive offerings, and the close study of competitive offerings. Innovation continues, although perhaps at a slower pace than in the first few years. No central organization has affected the design or evolution of navigation aids and services, except to the extent that widely accepted Web protocols specify the structure of Web sites to be searched by search robots. Internet navigation aids and services are good examples of technologies that have developed and operated in a decentralized environment with investors, users, and advertisers—that is, market forces—determining which designs are successful.

Despite the differences in the way in which they developed, the relationship between the DNS technical system and Internet navigation aids and services is strong and fundamental—the DNS has served as the stable core on which the incremental evolution of the different navigation aids and services has depended. Domain names are a key part of the Uniform Resource Locators (URLs) that identify the Web resources found by all Internet navigation aids and services, and when the user navigates to an identified resource, it is the DNS that retrieves its Internet Protocol (IP) address. However, since search engines and directories actually identify the IP address of a server resource directly, they could simply display it as the link to the resource without displaying its URL. That, of course, would deprive the user of the additional information that the descriptive elements of the URL, specifically the domain name, provide about the resource. But it suggests that, in the absence of a functioning DNS, search engines and directories could still allow users to navigate to many (if not all) desired locations on the public Internet.

In sum, it is the DNS and Internet navigation aids and services working together that enables searchers to have successful and convenient access to the vast realm of Web resources.

The institutional frameworks of the DNS and navigation services provide illuminating contrasts. The DNS is a single hierarchical technical system whose implementation is decentralized, but which adheres to open technical standards promulgated by an international technical community. It is guided by the general oversight of a non-profit organization and the stewardship of the U.S. government, and is operated by a diverse, global collection of organizations and individuals. Except for the leasing of domain names, its services are made available at no direct charge to users. In contrast, Internet navigation services are provided by a large number of autonomous organizations, both commercial and non-commercial, operating proprietary or licensed technical systems, without any general oversight of either their technology or their operations. However, Internet navigation services are also offered at no direct charge to the users; advertisers cover much of the costs through the purchase of advertising insertions associated with search terms.

The rapid development of navigation technology in the past decade appears to have had a significant effect on the unintended uses of the DNS and the commercial pressures on it. In the early days of the Web, guessing of domain names played an important role in navigation to Web sites. As noted in Chapter 2, that led to a rapid increase in the economic and social value of "good" domain names, especially those in the .com domain, and to a correspondingly "hot" market in their sale and resale. While such domain names remain valuable for their identifier function (in a URL or on the side of a bus), their role in navigation has been replaced to a significant degree by the use of search terms in search engines. Correspondingly, much of the commercial concern about registering notable domain names appears to have been transferred to the commercial business of purchasing effective search terms on the various navigation services. To some extent, this also appears to be shifting some of the concern with protecting trademark rights on the Internet from domain names to search terms.

Conclusion: Both the Domain Name System and Internet navigation services will be significant elements of the Internet for the foreseeable future. Both will continue to evolve, as will the interrelationships between them.

Conclusion: The governance and administration of the DNS should not become a vehicle for addressing political, legal, or economic issues beyond those of the DNS itself.

Conclusion: The development of Internet navigation services is likely to continue to relieve some of the commercial pressures on the DNS as users become increasingly comfortable with using these services as their primary means to navigate the Internet.

Conclusion: The preservation of a stable, reliable, and effective Domain Name System will remain crucial both to effective Internet navigation and to the operation of the Internet and most of the applications that it supports.

Recommendation: The demonstrated success of the DNS and navigation aids and services in meeting the basic needs of Internet users should not be jeopardized by efforts to constrain or direct their evolution outside of the open architecture of the Internet, or to use them to enable control of the free flow of information across the Internet.

Appendixes

A

Biographies of Committee Members and Staff

ROGER LEVIEN, *Chair*, is the principal and founder of Strategy & Innovation Consulting, a personal consultancy established to provide strategy and innovation consulting services to the senior managers of public and private organizations. His career has focused on the integrative use of information from social, environmental, and physical science research and technology to analyze and inform the choices faced by public and private institutions. Previously, he was corporate vice president for strategy and innovation at Xerox Corporation; director of the International Institute for Applied Systems Analysis in Austria; and department head and deputy vice president with responsibility for system sciences and nonmilitary policy research at the RAND Corporation in Santa Monica, California, and Washington, D.C. He is the author of three books: *The Emerging Technology* (McGraw-Hill, 1972), *R&D Management* (Lexington, 1975), and *Taking Technology to Market* (Crisp, 1997). He has also written chapters in *Systems, Experts and Computers* (MIT Press, 2000) and *Technology 2001* (MIT Press, 1991). He was awarded the Ehrenkreuz, First Class, in Science and Arts by the Austrian government and is a member of the Connecticut Academy of Science and Engineering, Phi Beta Kappa, Sigma Xi, and Tau Beta Pi. Dr. Levien received his Ph.D. (1962) and M.S. (1958) degrees in applied mathematics (computer science) from Harvard University. He also received his B.S. degree in engineering (highest honors) from Swarthmore College in 1956.

S. ROBERT AUSTEIN is a software engineer at the Internet Systems Consortium, focused primarily on development and deployment of standards-based Internet protocols. Prior to this, he was vice president of Engineering at InterNetShare, Incorporated, architect for the Epilogue Embedded Products Group at Integrated Systems, Inc., vice president of Engineering at Epilogue Technology Corporation, and a member of the research staff at MIT's Laboratory for Computer Science. At various times he has served as a member of the Internet Architecture Board (IAB), a member of the gTLD-MoU Policy Oversight Committee, as chair of the Internet Engineering Task Force's (IETF's) Domain Name System, DNS Operations, IPsec Key, and Intellectual Property Rights working groups, and has helped both to specify extensions to the DNS protocol within the IETF and to implement various portions of the DNS on everything from mainframes to embedded systems since 1985. He holds a B.A. in mathematics from Wesleyan University.

STANLEY M. BESEN is a vice president at Charles River Associates, Washington, D.C. Besen has served as a Brookings Economic Policy fellow, Office of Telecommunications Policy, Executive Office of the President (1971-1972); co-director, Network Inquiry Special Staff, Federal Communications Commission (1978-1980); co-editor, *RAND Journal of Economics* (1985-1988); senior economist, RAND Corporation (1980-1992); and a member of Office of Technology Assessment Advisory Panels on Communications Systems for an Information Age (1986-1988) and Intellectual Property Rights in an Age of Electronics and Information (1984-1985) and on the National Research Council's Committee on Licensing Geographic Data and Services (2002-2004). He currently serves as a member of the editorial board of *Economics of Innovation and New Technology*. Dr. Besen has taught at Rice University (1965-1980) where he was the Allyn M. and Gladys R. Cline Professor of Economics and Finance, Columbia University (1988-1989) where he was the visiting Henley Professor of Law and Business, and the Georgetown University Law Center (1990-1991) where he was a visiting professor of law and economics. He holds a Ph.D. in economics from Yale University (1964). Dr. Besen has published widely on telecommunications economics and policy, intellectual property, and the economics of standards and has consulted with many companies in the telecommunications and information industries. He is the author of "The Economics of Telecommunications Standards" in R.W. Crandall and K. Flamm (eds.), *Changing the Rules: Technological Change, International Competition, and Regulation in Communications* (with G. Saloner); "Choosing How to Compete: Strategy and Tactics in Standardization," *Journal of Economic Perspectives*, 1994 (with J. Farrell); "Intellectual Property," in *The New Palgrave Dictionary of Economics and the Law*, Macmillan Press, 1998; "Advances in Routing Technologies and Internet Peering Agreements," *American Economic Association Papers and Proceed-*

ings," 2001 (with P. Milgrom, B. Mitchell, and P. Srinagesh); and "Vertical and Horizontal Ownership in Cable TV: Time Warner-Turner (1996)," in J.E. Kwoka and L.J. White, *The Antitrust Revolution*, Scott, Foresman, 1998 (with E.J. Murdoch, D.P. O'Brien, S.C. Salop, and J.R. Woodbury).

CHRISTINE L. BORGMAN holds the Presidential Chair in Information Studies at the University of California, Los Angeles (UCLA), where she has been a faculty member since 1983. She spent a sabbatical year (2004-2005) at the Oxford Internet Institute, University of Oxford, U.K. Dr. Borgman's teaching and research interests include digital libraries, information infrastructure, scholarly communication, social studies of science, and information technology policy. Dr. Borgman has published more than 150 articles, conference papers, reports, and books in the fields of information studies, computer science, and communication; she has lectured or conducted research in more than 20 countries. She is currently a co-principal investigator for the Center for Embedded Networked Systems (CENS) and for the Alexandria Digital Earth Prototype (ADEPT) project, both funded by the National Science Foundation. She currently chairs Section T (Information, Computing, and Communication) of the American Association for the Advancement of Science (AAAS) and is a fellow of the AAAS. Her professional responsibilities include current membership on the advisory board to the Electronic Privacy Information Center and on the Association for Computing Machinery Public Policy Committee, and prior membership on the Advisory Committee to the Computer, Information Sciences, and Engineering Directorate of the National Science Foundation (1998-2001), the Board of Directors of the Council on Library and Information Resources (1992-2000), and the International Advisory Board to the Soros Foundation Open Society Institute Regional Library Program (1994-1997). She was program chair for the First Joint Conference on Digital Libraries (ACM and IEEE) in 2001 and continues to serve on program committees for the International Conference on Asian Digital Libraries, the Joint Conferences on Digital Libraries, and the European Conference on Digital Libraries. Other international activities include service as a visiting professor at Loughborough University, U.K. (1996-2002), a scholar-in-residence at the Rockefeller Foundation Study and Conference Center in Bellagio, Italy (1994), and as a Fulbright visiting professor in Budapest, Hungary (1993). Her most recent book, *From Gutenberg to the Global Information Infrastructure: Access to Information in a Networked World* (MIT Press, 2000), won the Best Information Science Book of the Year award from the American Society for Information Science and Technology. She holds the Ph.D. in communication from Stanford University, an M.L.S. from the University of Pittsburgh, and a B.A. in mathematics from Michigan State University.

TIMOTHY CASEY is the executive director of the Institute for Innovation and Informatics at the University of Nevada, Reno as of July 1, 2005. Casey was a partner in Fried, Frank, Harris, Shriver, and Jacobson's Washington, D.C., and New York offices, where he was chair of the firm's Intellectual Property and Technology Law Department. Casey has also been an adjunct professor of law at American University, Washington College of Law, since 2003, where he has taught advanced patent law. Casey joined Fried Frank in 2000 after serving as chief technology counsel, senior vice president, and assistant secretary for MCI since 1995. In addition to managing the worldwide technology law and intellectual property operations of MCI's predecessors WorldCom and MCI Communications Corporation, Casey played a pivotal role in the development of the U.S. Digital Millennium Copyright Act (DMCA) and the European Union's E-Commerce Directive. Casey was also an invited, but unpaid, advisor to WIPO leading up to the first WIPO process and an informal mediator between the parties negotiating the terms of the Uniform Domain Name Dispute Resolution Policy (UDRP). He has been a UDRP panelist and has rendered over 28 decisions. Casey was director of intellectual property for Silicon Graphics from 1992 to 1995, divisional patent counsel for Apple Computer from 1989 to 1992, and in private practice in California from 1986 to 1989. Casey received his J.D. from Santa Clara University School of Law, where he was editor-in-chief of the *Computer & High Technology Law Journal* and where he was also an adjunct professor of law. He received his B.S. in electrical engineering from the University of Nevada, Reno. He is admitted to the bar in California and the District of Columbia and is registered to practice before the U.S. Patent and Trademark Office.

HUGH DUBBERLY is a principal in Dubberly Design Office (DDO), a San Francisco-based consultancy that focuses on making software easier to use through interaction design and information design. At Apple Computer in the late 1980s and early 1990s, Dubberly managed cross-functional design teams and later managed creative services for the entire company. While at Apple, he co-created a technology-forecast film called "Knowledge Navigator" that presaged the appearance of the Internet in a portable digital device. Intrigued by what the publishing industry would look like on the Internet, he next became director of interface design for Times Mirror. This led him to Netscape, where he became vice president of design and managed groups responsible for the design, engineering, and production of Netscape's Web portal. In 2000, he co-founded DDO. In addition to his practice, Dubberly also teaches. While at Apple, he also served at Art Center College of Design in Pasadena as the first and founding chair of the computer graphics department. He has also taught classes in the Graphic Design Department at San Jose State University, at the Institute of Design at IIT, and in the Computer Science Department at Stanford University. He graduated from Rhode Island School of Design with a B.F.A. in graphic design and earned an M.F.A. in graphic design from Yale University.

PATRIK FÄLTSTRÖM is a consulting engineer in the Corporate Development section of Cisco Systems. At Cisco, Fältström is involved with many things touching applications, especially the Domain Name System, electronic mail, and Internet telephony. Previously, Fältström was a technical specialist in the Internet Strategies and Coordination group at Tele2, systems manager at the Royal Institute of Technology in Stockholm, and a programmer in the Swedish Royal Navy as well as at Bunyip Information Systems in Montréal, Canada. He has been working with Unix since 1985 and has been involved in Internet-related standardization since 1989, both in Sweden and worldwide. Fältström also works with the Internet Engineering Task Force (IETF), was one of two area directors of the applications area between 1998 and 2003, and is the author of several RFCs. Among those are RFCs on how to send Apple Macintosh files with e-mail, on the Whois++ directory service, on global indexing of textual data, on ENUM (the Telephone Number Mapping protocol) on Uniform Resource Names, and on Internationalized Domain Names. Since 2003 he has been a member of the Internet Architecture Board and from September 2003 also an appointed advisor to the IT Minister of Sweden as a member of the Swedish Government IT Policy and Strategy Group. Fältström holds an M.Sc. degree in mathematics from the University of Stockholm.

PER-KRISTIAN (KRIS) HALVORSEN is vice president and director of the Solutions and Services Research Center (SSRC) at Hewlett-Packard (HP). The center creates and transfers technology for HP's services and solutions businesses and it houses HP's research initiatives for developing markets. There are six research laboratories in the United States, the United Kingdom, and India. SSRC's research focus is on software and systems that enable secure, inter- and intra-enterprise collaboration, with a particular emphasis on trust, security, and content management. This is complemented by a new and growing activity aimed at bringing the benefits of information technology to large groups of people and enterprises in developing countries through the discovery of new functionalities and design. Prior to joining HP in 2000, Halvorsen was the founding director of the Information Sciences and Technologies Laboratory at Xerox PARC. Under his direction, the lab became a leading center for research on the fundamental forces driving the evolution of the Web and the Internet. Dr. Halvorsen is an inventor on more than 10 patents, and he has published widely in the areas of linguistics, natural language processing, and knowledge management and information access. He holds a Ph.D. in theoretical linguistics and he received his education at the University of Oslo, the University Texas at Austin, and the Massachusetts Institute of Technology. He has been a professor at the University of Texas at Austin and the University of Oslo, and a consulting professor at Stanford University, as well as a principal at the Center for Study of Language and Information at Stanford. Dr. Halvorsen has been a member of the board of directors of several technology companies (Symantec, Autodesk, Finn and FinnTech), and a member of the National Advisory Board of the College of Computer Sciences at the University of Arkansas.

MARYLEE JENKINS is a partner at the law firm of Arent Fox, PLLC and heads the firm's New York Intellectual Property Group. Ms. Jenkins specializes in intellectual property matters involving computers and the Internet and counsels an array of international companies on domain name disputes and domain name strategy and enforcement and management issues. She is the American Bar Association (ABA) Section of Intellectual Property Law's representative to the Intellectual Property Constituency of the Internet Corporation for Assigned Names and Numbers (ICANN) and is also the Section's Division Chair on Information Technology. Ms. Jenkins has previously been a member of the Section's Council and is a former chairperson of the Section's Special Committee on Trademarks and the Internet. Ms. Jenkins is a member of the ABA Standing Committee on Technology and Information Systems (SCOTIS) and is a domain name panelist to the World Intellectual Property Organization Arbitration and Mediation Center. She is also a member of Columbia University School of Engineering and Applied Science's Engineering Council and a member of John Marshall Law School's Intellectual Property Law Advisory Board. She writes and lectures frequently on computer- and Internet-related intellectual property issues to legal, business, and governmental groups at conferences worldwide. She holds a B.S. in mechanical engineering from Columbia University School of Engineering and Applied Science, a B.S. in physics from Centre College of Kentucky, and a J.D. from New York Law School.

JOHN C. KLENSIN is an independent consultant, focusing primarily on Internet standards, application protocols, and their implementations and deployment. Formerly, he was Internet Architecture vice president at AT&T Labs. He served as a member of the Internet Architecture Board from 1996 to 2002 and as its chair for the last 2 of those years and, before that, as area director for Applications of the Internet Engineering Task Force (IETF), chair of its working group on electronic mail transport extensions, and in several other capacities. Since 2004 he has served as liaison from the IETF to the ICANN board, a position that gives him some insight into ICANN internal processes but no obligations to, or benefits from, ICANN itself. Prior to joining AT&T, he was distinguished engineering fellow at MCI and then MCI WorldCom. Outside his corporate commitments, he has had significant responsibility for the present generation of Internet applications standards, as well as standards work in other areas. He served as a member of ANSI's Information Systems Standards Board from 1986 to 2000 and was its vice chair for 2 years. His involvement with what is now the Internet began in 1969 and 1970, when he participated in the working group that created the File Transfer Protocol (FTP) and that made the decision to include electronic mail capability in the network's design. Dr. Klensin was on the permanent research staff at Massachusetts Institute of Technology (MIT) for about 25 years, participating in or directing a wide variety of projects, many of them involving the application or development of computer networking or related technologies to applied problems including measurement of mass media use and impact, taxation policy, automatic indexing of politically oriented natural language texts, management of statistical databases, statistical computing, and urban development planning. Dr. Klensin has also been involved with international development work with a United Nations University project on food composition data, archives of images in Islamic architecture, and the Network Startup Resource Center. Dr. Klensin served on the CSTB committee that produced the report *The Internet's Coming of Age*. He holds a Ph.D. from MIT in computer applications and use in the social and policy sciences.

MILTON L. MUELLER is professor and director of the graduate program in telecommunications and network management, Syracuse University School of Information Studies. Since 1982 he has conducted research on the political economy of telecommunications and information, including topics such as monopoly and competition in communication industries, Internet trademarks and domain names, DNS economics, radio-frequency allocation, and telecommunication industry reform in New Zealand, China, and Hong Kong. Two recent publications of import include the book *Ruling the Root: Internet Governance and the Taming of Cyberspace* (MIT Press, 2002) and *Universal Service: Competition, Interconnection, and Monopoly in the Making of the American Telephone Syste*m (MIT Press, 1997). His current research focuses on Internet governance, civil society advocacy, and the impact of digital convergence on market structure. Dr. Mueller founded and directs the Convergence Center at Syracuse University. He is a founder of the Internet Governance Project, a multi-university consortium for research and policy analysis. He participates in the WSIS-Civil Society's Internet Governance Caucus. He is on the editorial boards of the scholarly journals *The Information Society*, *Telecommunications Policy*, and *Info: the Journal of Policy, Regulation and Strategy for Telecommunications, Information and Media*. Dr. Mueller received the Ph.D. from the University of Pennsylvania, Annenberg School of Communication, in 1989. Dr. Mueller was a founder of, and currently chairs, ICANN's Noncommercial Users Constituency, a part of the policy-making structure in ICANN's Generic Names Supporting Organization. As a member of NCUC, he has shaped policy on the .org reassignment, Whois and privacy, and other issues. He served as a Uniform Domain Name Dispute Resolution Policy panelist for WIPO from 2000 to 2003.

SHARON L. NELSON is the senior assistant attorney general serving as chief of the Consumer Protection Division of the Washington State Attorney General's office. From 2000 to 2003 she served as director of the Shidler Center for Law, Commerce, and Technology at the University of Washington School of Law. Previously, Ms. Nelson served two terms as chair of the Washington Utilities and Transportation Commission (WUTC), from February 1985 to August 1997. Prior to joining the WUTC, she taught history and anthropology in secondary schools (1969-1973), served as staff counsel to the U.S. Senate Commerce Committee (1976-1978), and served as legislative counsel to Consumers Union of the United States (1978-1981). She has also been a lawyer in private practice (1982-1983) and served as staff coordinator for the Washington State Legislature's Joint Select Committee on Telecommunications (1983-1985). Ms. Nelson received her B.A. from Carleton College, an M.A.T. from the University of Chicago, and a J.D. from the University of Washington. She is the past president of the National Association of Regulatory Utility Commissioners (1989-1990). She currently serves as chair of the Board of Directors for Consumers Union and sits on the Board of Trustees for the North American Electric Reliability Council (NERC) and the Board of Directors of the Itron Corporation, and serves as a commissioner on the National Energy Policy Commission (funded by the William and Flora Hewlett Foundation).

CRAIG PARTRIDGE is a chief scientist at BBN Technologies (an independent high-tech research company), where he has led a variety of Internet-related research projects. Recent major projects involved building and developing a method for tracing packet attacks across the Internet and designing a high-performance encrypter. In the 1980s, Dr. Partridge developed the rules for how systems use the DNS to route email. Dr. Partridge is the past-chair of the Association for Computing Machinery's Special Interest Group in Data Communication (one of the two major professional societies in data communications). He is the former editor-in-chief of both *ACM Computer Communication Review* and *IEEE Network Magazine* and a consulting editor for Addison-Wesley's Professional Computing Series. From 1992 to 2001, he was a consulting professor of computer science at Stanford University and in 1991 was a research fellow at the Swedish Institute of Computer Science. Partridge holds A.B., M.Sc., and Ph.D. degrees from Harvard University. He is a fellow of the IEEE and ACM.

WILLIAM J. RADUCHEL is the chair and CEO of Ruckus Network, a digital entertainment network for students at colleges and universities over the university network. He is a director of Chordiant Software and In2Books and serves as chair of PanelLink Cinema Partners PLC and as adviser to its parent company, Silicon Image. Dr. Raduchel is also an adviser to Myriad International Holdings, Hyperspace Communications, and Wild Tangent. Through 2002 he was executive vice president and chief technology officer of AOL Time Warner, Inc., after earlier being senior vice president and chief technology officer of AOL, where he also served as a strategic adviser after leaving AOL Time Warner. In 2001 he was named CTO of the year by *Infoworld*. Dr. Raduchel joined AOL in September 1999 from Sun Microsystems, Inc., where he was chief strategy officer and a member of its executive committee. In his 11 years at Sun, he also served as chief information officer, chief financial officer, acting vice president of human resources, and vice president of corporate planning and development and oversaw relationships with the major Japanese partners. He was recognized separately as CIO of the year and as best CFO in the computer industry. In addition, Dr. Raduchel has held senior executive roles at Xerox Corporation and McGraw-Hill, Inc. He is a member of the National Advisory Board for the Salvation Army (and chair of its committee on business administration), the Conference of Business Economists, and the Board on Science, Technology, and Economic Policy of the National Research Council. He has several issued and pending patents. Raduchel received his undergraduate degree in economics from Michigan State University and earned his A.M. and Ph.D. degrees in economics at Harvard University. In both the fall and spring of 2003 he was the Castle Lecturer on computer science at the U.S. Military Academy at West Point.

HAL R. VARIAN is a professor in the School of Information Management and Systems at the University of California, Berkeley. He is also a professor in the Haas School of Business and in the Department of Economics, and he holds the Class of 1944 Professorship. From 1995 to 2004, Dr. Varian served as dean of the School of Information Management and Systems. He has taught at the Massachusetts Institute of Technology (MIT), Stanford University, Oxford University, the University of Michigan and other universities around the world. Dr. Varian is a fellow of the

Guggenheim Foundation, the Econometric Society, and the American Academy of Arts and Sciences. He has served as co-editor of the *American Economic Review* and is on the editorial boards of several journals. Dr. Varian has published numerous papers in economic theory, industrial organization, financial economics, and econometrics and information economics. He is the author of two major economics textbooks, which have been translated into 11 languages. His recent work has been concerned with the economics of information technology and the information economy. He has been a consultant and advisor to several technology companies, including IBM and Google. He is the co-author of a best-selling book on business strategy, *Information Rules: A Strategic Guide to the Network Economy*, and writes a monthly column on economics for *The New York Times*. He received his S.B. degree from MIT in 1969 and his M.A. (mathematics) and Ph.D. (economics) from the University of California, Berkeley in 1973.

STAFF

ALAN S. INOUYE, *Study Director* (through December 2004), is the Coordinator of the President's Information Technology Advisory Committee (PITAC), a federal advisory committee that provides advice to the President through the National Science and Technology Council. From 1997 through 2004, Dr. Inouye served as a study director at the National Research Council's Computer Science and Telecommunications Board (CSTB). His completed CSTB studies include *Beyond Productivity: Information Technology, Innovation, and Creativity*; *LC21: A Digital Strategy for the Library of Congress*; *The Digital Dilemma: Intellectual Property in the Information Age*; and *Trust in Cyberspace*. In addition, Dr. Inouye served as the staff liaison on projects in other units of the National Academies, resulting in the completion of four reports: *National Automated Highway System Research Program: A Review*; *Advanced Engineering Environments: Achieving the Vision, Phase 1*; *Advanced Engineering Environments: Design in the New Millennium*; and *Review of the U.S. Department of Defense Air, Space, and Supporting Information Systems Science and Technology Program*. Prior to joining CSTB, Inouye completed a Ph.D. from the School of Information Management and Systems at the University of California, Berkeley. In a previous life, Dr. Inouye worked in Silicon Valley as a programmer (Atari Corporation), statistician and programmer/analyst (Verbatim Corporation), and manager of information systems (Amdahl Corporation). Dr. Inouye also completed other degrees—in information systems (M.S.), systems management (M.S.), business administration/finance (M.B.A.), liberal studies (B.S.), and mathematics (B.A.).

CHARLES N. BROWNSTEIN is the director of the Computer Science and Telecommunications Board (CSTB) of the National Research Council. He is also the study director for the project on improving cybersecurity research in the United States. He joined CSTB in 2004 from the Corporation for National Research Initiatives (CNRI), where since 1994 he directed the Cross Industry Working Team and did independent research with support from the National Science Foundation (NSF) and DARPA. His interests are in innovation, applications, and impacts of information technology, Internet performance, and the technology-policy interface. Dr. Brownstein joined CNRI in 1994 after a 20-year career at NSF. There he served in positions including program director for Telecommunications Policy and IT Applications, division director for Information Science and Technology, deputy assistant director and assistant director of NSF for Computer and Information Science and Engineering (CISE), and director of the Office of Planning and Assessment. At NSF, he led in the creation of CISE, nurtured the development of NSFnet, and set strategic directions for federal information infrastructure. He was a principal in organizing the interagency High Performance Computing and Communications initiative, and he was executive director of the National Science Board Special Committee on the Future of NSF. He presided over information technology and policy working groups at the Organization for Economic Cooperation and Development, was founding chair of the Federal Networking Council, and participated on the Board of Regents of the National Library of Medicine. He organized and co-chaired the White House National Performance Review Working Group for Reinventing Government through Information Technology. He was a founding trustee of the Internet Society, chaired the Association for Computing Machinery public policy activity, USACM, and is currently a director of Fortec, which provides the IETF Secretariat. From 1971 to 1975, Dr. Brownstein taught at Lehigh University and was a founder of the Institute of Social and Behavioral Research. There he was a principal investigator on NSF and industry-supported research awards on telecommunications policy, information industry innovation, two-way cable field experimentation, and interactive learning technologies. He also taught research design at the University of Michigan Inter-university Consortium for Social and Political Research. His Ph.D. is in political science, from Florida State University, 1971.

MARGARET MARSH HUYNH, senior program assistant, has been with the Computer Science and Telecommunications Board since January 1999 supporting several projects. She is currently supporting studies on wireless technology prospects and policy options, and biometrics. She previously worked on the studies that produced the reports *Getting Up to Speed: The Future of Supercomputing; Beyond Productivity: Information Technology, Innovation, and Creativity; IT Roadmap to a Geospatial Future; Building a Workforce for the Information Economy;* and *The Digital Dilemma: Intellectual Property in the Information Age*. Ms. Huynh also assisted with the project on exploring information technology issues for the behavioral and social sciences (Digital Divide and Digital Democracy). She assists on other projects as needed. Prior to coming to CSTB, Ms. Huynh worked as a meeting assistant at Management for Meetings (April 1998 through August 1998) and as a meeting assistant at the American Society for Civil Engineers (September 1996 through April 1998). Ms. Huynh has a B.A. (1990) in liberal studies with minors in sociology and psychology from Salisbury University, Salisbury, Maryland.

KRISTEN BATCH is a research associate with the Computer Science and Telecommunications Board of the National Research Council. She is currently involved with projects focusing on wireless communication technologies, biometrics, and privacy in the information age. While pursuing an M.A. in international communications from American University, she interned at the National Telecommunications and Information Administration, in the Office of International Affairs, and at the Center for Strategic and International Studies, in the Technology and Public Policy Program. She also earned a B.A. from Carnegie Mellon University in literary and cultural studies and Spanish, and received two travel grants to conduct independent research in Spain.

B

Speakers at Meetings and Participants at Site Visits

COMMITTEE MEETING
APRIL 9-10, 2001
NATIONAL RESEARCH COUNCIL
WASHINGTON, D.C.

J. Beckwith Burr, Wilmer, Cutler and Pickering
Aubrey Bush, National Science Foundation
Alan Davidson, Center for Democracy and Technology
Michael Froomkin, University of Miami
M. Stuart Lynn, Internet Corporation for Assigned Names and Numbers
Steven Metalitz, Copyright Coalition on Domain Names
Amy Page, U.S. Department of Commerce, Patent and Trademark Office
David Post, Temple University
Michael Roberts, formerly of the Internet Corporation for Assigned Names and Numbers
Karen Rose, U.S. Department of Commerce, National Telecommunications and Information Administration
Shari Steele, Electronic Frontier Foundation
Robert Stoll, U.S. Department of Commerce, Patent and Trademark Office
George Strawn, National Science Foundation
Emerson Tiller, University of Texas, Austin

COMMITTEE MEETING
JULY 11-13, 2001
UNIVERSITY OF CALIFORNIA
SCHOOL OF INFORMATION MANAGEMENT AND SYSTEMS
BERKELEY, CALIFORNIA

Yves Arrouye, RealNames
Karl Auerbach, Internet Corporation for Assigned Names and Numbers
Eric Brewer, University of California, Berkeley and Inktomi
kc claffy, Cooperative Association for Internet Data Analysis, San Diego Supercomputer Center, University of California, San Diego
Leslie Daigle, VeriSign, Inc. (by telephone)
Mark Handley, AT&T Center for Internet Research, International Computer Science Institute, University of California, Berkeley
Marti Hearst, University of California, Berkeley
Joe Hellerstein, University of California, Berkeley
Paul Hoffman, Internet Mail Consortium
David Lawrence, Nominum
Clifford Lynch, Coalition for Networked Information
Carl Malamud, NetTopBox, Inc.
Eric Schmidt, Novell and Google, Inc.
Keith Teare, RealNames
Tan Tin Wee, National University of Singapore

COMMITTEE MEETING
NOVEMBER 5-6, 2001
NATIONAL RESEARCH COUNCIL
WASHINGTON, D.C.

Ari Balogh, VeriSign Global Registry
Elana Broitman, Register.com
Brian Kahin, University of Maryland
Elliot Noss, Tucows

SITE VISIT
NOVEMBER 7, 2001
VERISIGN AND AOL TIME WARNER
DULLES, VIRGINIA

Michael Aisenberg, VeriSign, Inc.
Ari Balogh, VeriSign, Inc.
Joe Barrett, AOL Time Warner, Inc.
Leslie Daigle, VeriSign, Inc.

Matt Korn, AOL Time Warner, Inc.
Mark Kosters, VeriSign, Inc.
Geraldine MacDonald, AOL Time Warner, Inc.
Michael Mealing, VeriSign, Inc.
Mark Rippe, VeriSign, Inc.
Ken Silva, VeriSign, Inc.

SITE VISIT
NOVEMBER 12-15, 2001
ICANN MEETING
MARINA DEL REY, CALIFORNIA

Carl Bildt, AG Global Solutions and ICANN At-large Study Committee
Paul Twomey, ICANN Government Advisory Committee

COMMITTEE MEETING
JANUARY 7-8, 2002
BECKMAN CENTER
IRVINE, CALIFORNIA

M. Stuart Lynn, Internet Corporation for Assigned Names and Numbers

COMMITTEE MEETING
FEBRUARY 27-MARCH 2, 2002
HARVARD UNIVERSITY
JOHN F. KENNEDY SCHOOL OF GOVERNMENT
CAMBRIDGE, MASSACHUSETTS

Tim Berners-Lee, Massachusetts Institute of Technology and World Wide Web Consortium (W3C)
David D. Clark, Massachusetts Institute of Technology
Francis Gurry, World Intellectual Property Organization
Richard Hill, International Telecommunication Union